W9-BJB-323

Premenstrual Syndrome: A Clinician's Guide

DIAGNOSIS AND TREATMENT OF
MENTAL DISORDERS
Allen Frances, M.D., *Series Editor*

PREMENSTRUAL SYNDROME: A CLINICIAN'S GUIDE
Sally K. Severino and Margaret L. Moline

PREMENSTRUAL SYNDROME
A Clinician's Guide

Sally K. Severino, M.D.
Margaret L. Moline, Ph.D.
Cornell University Medical College

Foreword by Allen Frances, M.D.

The Guilford Press
New York   London

To our mothers and our grandmothers,
who encouraged us to strive for excellence.

© 1989 The Guilford Press
A Division of Guilford Publications, Inc.
72 Spring Street, New York, NY 10012

All rights reserved.

No part of this book may be reproduced, stored in a retrieval system,
or transmitted, in any form or by any means, electronic, mechanical,
photocopying, microfilming, recording, or otherwise, without written
permission from the Publisher.

Printed in the United States of America

This book is printed on acid-free paper.

Last digit is print number: 9 8 7 6 5 4 3 2 1

Library of Congress Cataloging-in-Publication Data
Severino, Sally K.
    Premenstrual syndrome : a clinician's guide / Sally
K. Severino and Margaret L. Moline.
        p.   cm.
    Bibliography: p.
    ISBN 0-89862-181-X
    1. Premenstrual syndrome.   I. Moline, Margaret L.   II. Title.
    [DNLM: 1. Premenstrual Syndrome.   WP 560 S498p]
RG165.S48   1989
618.1'72—dc19
DNLM/DLC   89-2054
for Library of Congress   CIP

Foreword

This is an important book on a very difficult and controversial problem. Premenstrual symptoms have been described in the medical literature for thousands of years but only relatively recently have empirical data been gathered. There remains considerable disagreement among clinicians and researchers not only whether there is a definable syndrome related to the menstrual cycle, but whether this syndrome should be conceived of as a mental disorder, what causes it, and how best to treat it. Despite the obvious clinical and research utility of defining a menstrually related mental disorder, questions have been raised about its possible misuse. Would the presence of such a diagnosis in an official nomenclature lead to the prejudicial stereotyping of women?

These concerns coalesced during the revision of the American Psychiatric Association's Diagnostic and Statistical Manual III. Suggestions to include premenstrual disorder were met by vociferous objections that too little research data supported the value of such a diagnosis and that it would promote more stigma than it was worth. During these discussions, Dr. Severino provided balance in what was often a very heated and polarized debate.

The decision for DSM-III-R was to include a category with the cumbersome name Late Luteal Phase Dysphoric Disorder within the appendix of the manual, but not to give it official status in the nomenclature. This was meant to promote research on the disorder, while minimizing possible misuse of the diagnosis. The validity of the diagnostic category is currently being reviewed once again by the DSM-IV work group on Late Luteal Phase Dysphoric Disorder, of which Dr. Severino is a member and Dr. Moline is an advisor.

Whatever the fate of a menstrually related disorder in DSM-IV, it is clear that many women present with emotional problems associated with the menstrual phase. Most of us have received grossly inadequate training in the assessment, diagnosis, and treatment of such problems, in part because major advances in the understanding of how best to do this have occurred in recent years. This book provides a practical clinical approach that will be of great value to psychiatrists and other mental health workers, as well as to other physicians and health care providers.

The strength of this book derives from the different and complementary backgrounds of the two authors. Sally Severino, M.D., is a psychiatrist with extensive clinical and research experience in the diagnosis and treatment of women with premenstrual complaints. The coauthor of the book, Margaret Moline, Ph.D., is a physiologist who has studied the effects of hormones on circadian rhythms. Dr. Moline is also an expert on experimental method and provides a critical review of the special design issues encountered by investigators of premenstrual problems. The authors are skilled writers who present the issues comprehensively, clearly, and fairly. I have learned a great deal from them.

Allen Frances, M.D.

Preface

Premenstrual Syndrome (PMS)! For many, the term calls to mind women incapacitated by the influence of raging hormones. Cartoons and calendars depict women gorging on food to satisfy premenstrual cravings or caricature them as so bloated they resemble balloons or elephants. Yet behind this facetiousness and frivolity lies a legitimate medical condition that affects a significant percentage of women, some of them quite seriously.

Although some progress has been made toward reaching a consensus on the definition of the syndrome, some clinicians still doubt the existence of PMS as an entity separate from other medical conditions (Sutherland & Stewart, 1965). Some believe that PMS is simply a more symptomatic occurrence of menstrual molimina (Prior, 1984). Others believe that PMS has a validity independent of other medical conditions, especially affective disorders (Roy-Byrne et al., 1986b). Why are there such controversies? The answers are inherent in several ongoing issues with PMS.

First, *its cause remains unknown*. While numerous etiologies have been proposed, none has been conclusively identified (Chapter 5). Multiple contributors to symptom formation, including biological, psychological, and social factors, vie for attention and need to be understood.

Second, the *symptoms of PMS are heterogeneous*. Not only do symptoms differ among women given the same diagnosis of PMS, but they often vary from month to month in the same woman. Further, nearly every symptom ever attributed to any illness has been reported to be a symptom of PMS (Chapter 3).

Third, *there is disagreement regarding appropriate diagnostic techniques*. It is generally believed that a diagnosis of PMS must be confirmed by prospective daily symptom ratings and that retrospective histories will overreport PMS (Rapkin et al., 1988). It should be noted that one major research group believes not only that a retrospective history is sufficient but also that retrospective reporting has been given bad press (Magos &

Studd, 1986). These researchers believe that if studies carefully exclude symptom-free women, then retrospective reports of PMS will accurately identify women with the syndrome. This issue will be discussed more fully in Chapter 6.

Fourth, *more than 50 treatments have been suggested, and each one "works."* Obviously, this cannot be the case (see Chapter 7). PMS treatment studies often contain serious methodological flaws, including inadequate study design, subject selection, and study duration. The placebo response rate is very high, often between 50% and 90%.

It is no wonder, then, that clinicians who see women for PMS complaints are in a quandry. Lack of information and guidelines may lead to poor clinical care. Some recent reports in the literature highlight the need for more information. In the first such study, a survey was sent to 110 family practice, general practice, and obstetric/gynecological specialists living within a 50-mile radius of Hattisburg, Mississippi (Hailey et al., 1988). Of the 51 who responded, all rated themselves as very familiar with PMS but expressed a need to know more about etiological, diagnostic, and treatment issues. Another study (Atkinson & Kozitza, 1988) reported that even though 40 psychotherapists were able to distinguish between PMS and non-PMS symptoms based on their cyclical nature, 22% misdiagnosed PMS and 17% prescribed inappropriate treatments. Still a third article, a review of reported cases of menstrually related mood disorders in adolescents, suggested that PMS may be overlooked and underdiagnosed in some symptomatic groups, such as developmentally disabled young women (Kaminer et al., 1988).

Our main objective in this book is clinician education. We have reviewed the literature extensively and present chapters on historical views of PMS (Chapter 2) and women's issues (Chapter 9) in addition to more traditional chapters on background (the normal menstrual cycle and definitions, Chapter 1), symptoms (Chapter 3), proposed etiologies (Chapter 5), diagnosis (Chapter 6), and management (Chapter 8). Since so many treatments have been reported, we have provided a separate chapter on treatment options (Chapter 7), so that the interested reader can assess the rationale behind a particular proposed treatment before reading our recommendations in the management chapter. In addition we have included a chapter on psychological factors and the menstrual cycle (Chapter 4), reflecting both the background of the authors and the realization that the relationship between PMS and psychological illness is a knotty one.

We hope this book will enable our readers to assume a responsible and informed role in critically evaluating the literature, in planning future research, in educating the public about PMS and, above all, in recognizing and creatively managing the symptoms of patients who suffer from the disorder.

Acknowledgments

We would like to thank the many individuals who have helped us prepare this manuscript. The comments of Allen Frances, M.D., Series Editor, Elissa Benedek, M.D., and Judith Gold, M.D., were particularly helpful to us. The encouragement of our research colleagues, Daniel Wagner, M.D., Stephen Hurt, Ph.D., and Charles Pollak, M.D., was invaluable. We are also grateful to Sheldon W. Moline, Ph.D., for his advice regarding nutrition and treatment issues.

The librarians at the New York Hospital–Cornell Medical Center, Westchester Division—Marsha Miller, Marilyn Bottjer, and Lillian Wahrow—worked diligently to collect what we hope is an exhaustive bibliography.

We were fortunate to have excellent typing and graphic art support from Suellen Brown, Arlene Estberg, Brenda Miles, Petra Perkins, and Robin Shindler.

Special thanks are due to our husbands, Lawrence Severino, M.D. (OB/GYN), and Neil McDonell, Esq., for their support and help on the manuscript.

Contents

Diuretics and Antihypertensives, *195*;
Prostaglandin-Related Treatments, *203*;
Histamine-Related Treatments, *206*; Nutritional
Supplements, *207*; Psychotherapy, *224*; Psychoactive
Agents, *226*; Miscellaneous Treatments, *238*.

CHAPTER 1

Background and Definitions

This chapter is designed to review the normal menstrual cycle and to define those terms that will be used throughout the book. The review of the menstrual cycle is condensed primarily from the third edition of *Clinical Gynecologic Endocrinology and Infertility,* an excellent text by Speroff and colleagues (1984). In most cases, the definitions will be consistent with those that have appeared in the literature (Halbreich et al., 1985).

THE NORMAL MENSTRUAL CYCLE

The human menstrual cycle typically is 26 to 32 days long and occurs throughout the reproductive lifespan of a woman from puberty to menopause unless interrupted by pregnancy, lactation, or illness. The cycle can be divided into three phases: the follicular phase, ovulation, and the luteal phase. It is a complex, dynamic biological process involving hypothalamic, pituitary, and ovarian hormone secretion as well as morphological changes in the ovary and uterus. This review covers these events as follows: those occurring at the hypothalamus and pituitary, at the ovary, and at the uterus.

Events at the Hypothalamus and Pituitary

The two most important anterior pituitary hormones that are responsible for the menstrual cycle, luteinizing hormone (LH) and follicle stimulating hormone (FSH), are both released in response to the neurohormone, gonadotropin releasing hormone (GnRH). GnRH is produced in the medial basal hypothalamus, mostly in the arcuate nucleus.

GnRH, like most (if not all) hormones, is released in pulses. For normal gonadotropin secretion to occur, the pulse frequency (rate) and concentration of GnRH must remain within a critical range. Excessive

1

GnRH secretion actually shuts down reproductive function in women (and men) and has been proposed as a specific treatment for PMS (see Chapter 7, p. 188). Release of GnRH is also sensitive to both positive and negative feedback effects from a variety of factors, including other neurohormones (norepinephrine, dopamine, endorphins), gonadotropins, and ovarian steroids as well as itself (see Figure 1.1). "Feedback" refers to modulation of hormone secretion by other factors. Positive, facilitory feedback means that the presence of the factor increases the release of the hormone. Negative or inhibitory feedback indicates that release of the hormone decreases as the concentration of the other factor increases. "Long" feedback loops occur between endocrine organs, and in this case involve the gonads, hypothalamus, and pituitary. The long loops may be facilitory or inhibitory, as indicated by Figure 1.1. "Short" loops (more local within the brain) occur negatively between pituitary and hypothalamus, such that LH and FSH secretion decrease the release of GnRH.

GnRH pulsatile release is mediated by catecholamines, with gonadal steroids and endorphins (endogenous opiates) modifying the pattern as well. Norepinephrine is thought to promote GnRH secretion, while dopamine inhibits it. Dopamine also inhibits prolactin release from the anterior pituitary. Endogenous opiates, other products of the anterior pituitary, decrease FSH and LH by inhibiting GnRH neurons in the arcuate nucleus. More frequent and higher amplitude GnRH pulses result when opiate receptors are blocked (as with naltrexone, another proposed treatment for PMS; see Chapter 7, p. 237).

Catecholestrogens, so called since they have a catechol (biological amine) side and an estrogen side, can interact with both systems. The effects of gonadal steroids may mediate GnRH release through their catechol forms (see Figure 1.1).

While LH and FSH cannot be secreted without GnRH, the feedback interactions that control the ovulatory surge of gonadotropins occur not at the hypothalamus but at the level of the anterior pituitary. The roles of GnRH in the ovulatory process are to ensure (1) that gonadotropins are synthesized and stored by the anterior pituitary, leading to a reserve pool, (2) that LH and FSH can move from the reserve pool to a pool ready for secretion, and (3) that they can be secreted immediately upon the appropriate signal.

During the follicular phase of the cycle, estradiol concentrations begin to rise, leading to synthesis and storage of LH but not much secretion, since the steroid inhibits the response of the pituitary to GnRH (negative feedback). As ovulation approaches, the pituitary can respond more to GnRH, indicating that the storage pool of gonadotropins is being mobilized. Finally, estradiol concentrations are high

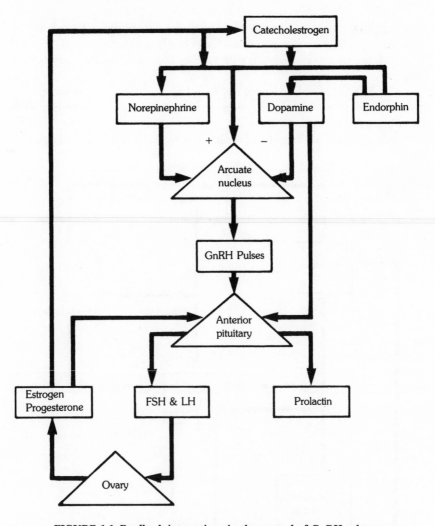

FIGURE 1.1 Feedback interactions in the control of GnRH release.
Adapted with permission from Speroff L, Glass RH, Kase NG (Eds): *Clinical Gynecologic Endocrinology & Fertility*. Baltimore, Williams & Wilkins, 1984, p. 56.

enough for long enough to change from inhibiting LH release to stimulating its surge (positive feedback). Thus the timing of the LH surge depends on the amount of estradiol produced by the very follicle that will be ovulated.

An FSH surge also occurs midcycle, as a response to progesterone (see next section). The interactions leading to the LH and FSH surges are depicted in Figure 1.2.

After ovulation, negative feedback of steroids again inhibits gonad-

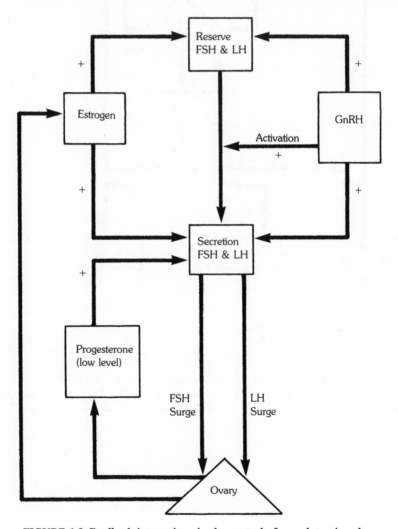

FIGURE 1.2 Feedback interactions in the control of gonadotropin release.
Adapted with permission from Speroff L, Glass RH, Kase NG (Eds): *Clinical Gynecologic Endocrinology & Fertility*. Baltimore, Williams & Wilkins, 1984, p. 64.

otropin release (see Figure 1.3). The high progesterone and estrogen concentrations produced by the corpus luteum decrease GnRH. At the pituitary, progesterone may deplete estrogen receptors, thus interfering with estrogen's effects on pituitary responses to GnRH. At the end of the cycle, progesterone (and estrogen) concentrations fall. The next cycle begins with the secretion of estrogen from the new follicle.

Events at the Ovary

During the follicular phase, the follicle(s) destined to ovulate matures. In 10 to 14 days, a primordial follicle develops into a preantral, then antral,

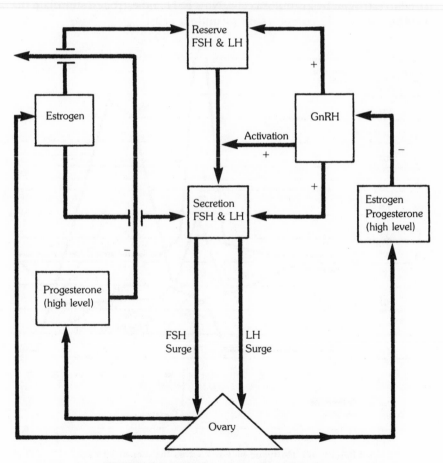

FIGURE 1.3 Inhibition of gonadotropin release.
Adapted with permission from Speroff L, Glass RH, Kase NG (Eds): *Clinical Gynecologic Endocrinology & Fertility.* Baltimore, Williams & Wilkins, 1984, p. 65.

and finally preovulatory follicle. While initial follicular growth is independent of hormones, further development to the preantral stage requires the pituitary gonadotropin FSH, whose secretion begins to rise at the end of the preceding menstrual cycle (see Figure 1.4). FSH induces the synthesis of estrogen in granulosa cells through the aromatization of androgens. Together, estrogen and FSH increase the number of FSH receptors on the preantral follicle.

As estrogen production increases, pituitary secretion of FSH is inhibited. Only the dominant follicle has enough FSH contained within to continue the maturation process to this, the antral, stage. Meanwhile, rising estradiol concentrations exert positive feedback on LH release. LH stimulates thecal cells to produce androgen, which is then aromatized to estrogen by granulosa cells. Now FSH and estrogen stimulate the production of LH receptors on granulosa cells.

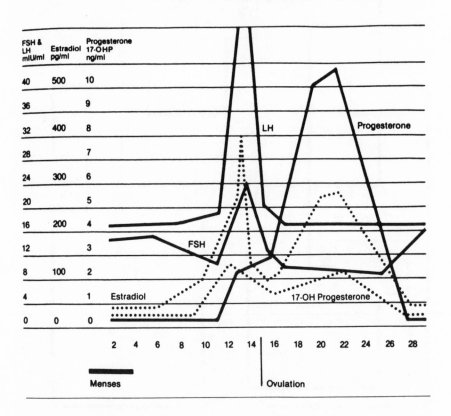

FIGURE 1.4 Hormone patterns across the menstrual cycle.
Reprinted with permission from Speroff L, Glass RH, Kase NG (Eds): *Clinical Gynecologic Endocrinology & Fertility.* Baltimore, Williams & Wilkins, 1984, p. 81.

As the antral follicle matures to the preovulatory follicle, estradiol concentrations rise enough to induce the LH surge. With the increase in estrogens, FSH decreases toward its minimum while LH steadily increases. Some luteinization and progesterone production occurs in the granulosa cells, stimulated by LH. The preovulatory progesterone facilitates the positive feedback of estrogen and induces the FSH surge that accompanies the LH surge. Estradiol peaks 24 to 36 hours prior to ovulation.

The LH surge preceeds ovulation by about 10 to 12 hours. The surge has many functions: It stimulates meiosis, luteinizes the granulosa cells, and promotes the synthesis of progesterone and prostaglandins within the follicle. The prostaglandins and enzymes activated by progesterone lead to the rupture of the follicular wall. Finally, the FSH surge leads to the detachment of the oocyte, so that it free-floats within the follicle. FSH also ensures that adequate LH receptors are available for a normal luteal phase.

After the follicle ruptures and the ovum is released, the granulosa cells enlarge, become vacuolated and vascularized, and accumulate yellow lutein. Progesterone production increases, peaking 8 days after the LH surge. Estrogen and androgens are also produced by the new corpus luteum.

About 9 to 11 days following ovulation, the corpus luteum declines rapidly due to an unknown mechanism. (It may be estrogen, however, via prostaglandins.) Thus, in the normal menstrual cycle, the luteal phase is close to 14 days long. Differences in cycle length, then, are due more to the time it takes for a follicle to mature than to the duration of the relatively fixed luteal phase.

Events at the Uterus

During an ovulatory menstrual cycle, five phases of endometrial change have been described: (1) menstrual endometrium, (2) proliferative phase, (3) secretory phase, (4) preparation for implantation, (5) endometrial breakdown.

The menstrual endometrium is dense but thin, comprised of some residual stratum spongiosum and nonfunctional basalis tissue. It is a transitional state between the previous menstrual breakdown and the proliferative stage that comes next.

The proliferative stage accompanies increased estrogen secretion by the ovarian follicle and continues until ovulation. Glands grow and become linked. The stroma swells and becomes increasingly vascular. Tissue components are restored under the influence of estrogen, and cells now incorporate ions, water, and amino acids.

For the 7 days following ovulation, the secretory phase occurs under the influence of both progesterone and estrogen. The glands become tortuous, and spiral vessels coil extensively. The stroma appears edematous. At the end of this phase, implantation will either have occurred, and the implantation phase continues, or endometrial breakdown will ultimately ensue.

When implantation does not occur, which is what happens in women with PMS, the breakdown phase begins. As the brief life of the corpus luteum draws to a close, progesterone and estrogen concentrations decline as well. At the endometrium, three events occur: vasomotor reactions, tissue loss, and menstruation. The endometrium shrinks in height, accompanied by cycles of vasoconstriction and relaxation of spiral arterioles that cause ischemia of the endometrium. As the ischemia continues, blood from interstitial hemorrhaging enters the uterine cavity. Thrombin–platelet plugs form on blood vessels to limit blood loss. The endometrium shrinks further, and parts of necrotic cells and vessels contribute to the menstrual flow. In the end, only the dense, thin menstrual endometrium remains. The process begins again with the resumption of estrogen secretion by the next follicle.

DEFINITIONS

Follicular phase—Defined from Day 1 of the cycle (onset of menses) to ovulation. The duration of the follicular phase is variable.

Luteal phase—The time from ovulation to the onset of menses, during which time the corpus luteum is functional. It is usually about 14 days long.

Premenstrual phase or *late luteal phase* or *premenstruum*—Refers to the days immediately preceding menses, usually 5 to 7 days before.

Premenstrual symptoms—Refer to those physical, behavioral, or mood changes that appear to change in severity during the late luteal phase of the cycle, do not exist in the same form or severity during the mid or late follicular phase, and disappear or return to their usual level of severity during the full flow of menses.

Premenstrual Syndrome (PMS)—Refers to the cyclic covariance of several premenstrual symptoms in the way described above. In Chapter 3 we will describe several attempts to delineate symptom clusters: Moos's factor analysis method (Moos, 1968); Steiner and colleagues' categorical diagnostic method (1980), Hargrove and Abraham's (1982) link of symptom clusters to putative pathophysiological mechanisms, and Halbreich and Endicott's (1982) dimensional method. Specific criteria for this disorder can be found in Chapter 6.

Premenstrual Tension (PMT) or *Premenstrual Tension Syndrome (PMTS)*— Names used by other authors as synonyms for PMS.

Late Luteal Phase Dysphoric Disorder (LLPDD)—A newly defined diagnosis for a subgroup of women with PMS whose symptoms are primarily affective (depression, mood swings, anger, anxiety) but restricted to the late luteal phase of the menstrual cycle. Symptoms must be so severe that they seriously impair the woman's functioning. Specific criteria for this diagnosis can be found in Chapter 2 and are discussed in Chapter 6.

Premenstrual exacerbation—Refers to the cyclic worsening of chronic conditions at the premenstrual phase of the cycle. For example, a woman with a major depression may become more depressed during the premenstruum, with a return to her usual symptom intensity once menses begins.

Molimen (pl., *molimina*)—Refers to the laborious performance of a normal function.

Menstrual molimina—Unpleasant symptoms—such as a feeling of weight in the pelvis, circulatory or nervous disturbances, among others—that occur during the menstrual period. Menstrual molimina is often confused with PMS, leading to overstating the number of women with PMS. An example of this is Kinch's (1978) statement that "premenstrual tension attacks almost all women."

Dysmenorrhea—Painful or difficult menstruation, not equivalent to PMS.

Menorrhagia—Excessive menstrual bleeding.

Mastodynia or *Mastalgia*—Pain in the breasts.

CHAPTER 2

History of Premenstrual Syndrome

ANTIQUITY TO 1931

While premenstrual syndrome has received increasing amounts of attention lately in both the scientific and lay press, it is not a diagnosis that has been discovered only within the past 50 years. In the annals of medicine there are descriptions of the relationships among menstrual cycle phase and mood and behavioral disorders dating to the time of Hippocrates. In a treatise titled "The Sickness of Virgins," written by Hippocrates' disciples and believed to represent his doctrines, a variety of behavioral disturbances were attributed to retained menstrual blood: delusions, hallucinations, suicidal ideation, and suicidal acts (in Adams, trans., 1939).

Pliny, the first century historian, wrote:

> It would indeed be a difficult matter to find anything which is productive of more marvelous effects than the menstrual discharge. On the approach of a woman in this state, milk will become sour, seeds which are touched by her become sterile, grafts wither away, garden plants are parched up, and the fruit will fall from the tree beneath which she sits. Her very look, even, will dim the brightness of mirrors, blunt the edge of steel, and take away the polish from ivory. A swarm of bees, if looked upon by her, will die immediately; brass and iron will instantly become rusty, and emit an offensive odour; while dogs which may have tasted of the matter so discharged are seized with madness, and their bite is venomous and incurable. (in Bostock & Riley, trans., 1856–1893, pp. 151–152)

In the 18th and 19th centuries, a number of phenomenologists described a variety of mood disorders, primarily mania, confined to the menses or occasionally occurring in the premenstrual phase. Prichard

10

described what would be considered by some to be a premenstrual syndrome:

> States of the constitution connected with irregularities of the uterine functions are well known to coexist or to display themselves in connection with various disorders of the brain. Among these madness is one. . . . Some females at the period of the catamenia undergo a considerable degree of nervous excitement: morbid dispositions of mind are displayed by them at these times, a wayward and capricious temper, excitability in the feelings, moroseness in disposition, a proneness to quarrel with their dearest relatives, and sometimes a dejection of mind approaching to melancholia. (Prichard, 1837, pp. 156–157)

In the United States, childbirth attendance was originally in the hands of women. In 1762, William Shipper created a school for the instruction of men as well as women in midwifery. This was the forerunner of formal medical education in the specialty of obstetrics and gynecology (Barker-Benfield, 1976).

Female anatomy, menstrual cycle physiology, and mental functioning had always been intimately associated. By the 19th century, women were viewed as "sick" simply because they were women; indeed, a nervous hypochondriasis seemed epidemic, especially among middle- and upper-class women (Ehrenreich & English, 1978; Connors, 1985). Women's problems were defined as rooted in their biology. This is typified by the following quote from one of the first medical specialty journals, the *American Journal of Insanity,* published quarterly by the State Lunatic Asylum in Utica, New York. In this journal, the 19th-century view of women is described:

> With women it is but a step from extreme nervous susceptibility to downright hysteria, and from that to overt insanity. In the sexual evolution, in pregnancy, in the parturient period, in lactation, strange thoughts, extraordinary feelings, unreasonable appetites, criminal impulses, may haunt a mind at other times innocent and pure. (Ray, 1866, p. 267)

Women in the middle and upper socioeconomic classes were expected to be genteel. It was not only stylish to retire to bed with unmentionable female troubles; it was considered a mark of intellect and sensitivity. The requirements of fashion reinforced this: Tight-laced corsets produced short-term symptoms of shortness of breath, constipation, weakness, and indigestion, as well as such long-term results as bent or fractured ribs, displacement of the liver, and uterine prolapse (Ehrenreich & English, 1978).

Because women were considered innately frail, they were counseled against higher education. Studies were used to confirm the belief that higher education could cause women's uteri to atrophy and/or drive them crazy (Ehrenreich & English, 1978). For example, a 1902 study showed that 42% of the women admitted to insane asylums were well educated, compared to 16% of the men.

Women's sickness came to be viewed as related to their reproductive organs. The underlying rationale is unclear. We can suppose that because women were considered "sicker" than men and because women differed from men anatomically with respect to their sexual organs, the erroneous conclusion was drawn that women's reproductive organs were the source of their "sickness." As a result, women's symptoms were treated by ministering to their female organs, either medically or surgically. The first hysterectomy was performed in 1853 by Dr. L. P. Burnham of Lowell, Massachusetts (Barker-Benfield, 1976).

Primary responsibility for treating the female psyche shifted from gynecologists to psychiatrists in the early 1900s as the interest of psychiatrists in the treatment of hysteria grew (Ehrenreich & English, 1978). The perceived connection between psychiatric disease and female anatomy is reflected in the etymology of the word *hysteria*, which derives from the Greek word for uterus. Psychiatrists opened the door to discussing such female functions as menstruation. This new candor paralleled changes in society, which allowed, for example, the marketing of sanitary napkins: Kotex in 1921 and Tampax in the early 1930s (Toth et al., 1981; Patterson & Hale, 1985).

Freud, whose opinions on the matter influenced psychiatrists in the early 1900s, viewed disturbances of menstruation as a model for determining the effect of a physical disturbance on ego functioning. He believed that a weak ego was the decisive factor in the genesis of a neurosis. He also believed that a physical illness could weaken the ego and produce a neurosis. Thus a disturbance of menstruation could theoretically result in a condition in which a woman's instincts were too strong for the enfeebled ego to cope with them (Freud, 1926). Modern psychoanalysts view women's menstrual cycle experience as much more complex and multidetermined than that set forth in Freud's formula.

Interest in the menstrual cycle effect on psyche and soma continued to be shared by those interested in mental and physiological phenomena. In 1925, Okey and Robb tried to correlate the human menstrual cycle with variations in blood sugar or in sugar tolerance. Their most interesting finding occurred during menses, not during the premenses. During menstruation, they observed that normal women had a tendency toward low blood sugar values 1 to 2 hours after ingesting a test amount of glucose. However, they also found a greater number of high blood glucose values during menstruation. Although these observations have not been confirmed, and most data rule out a blood glucose problem as the etiology of PMS, even today a hypoglycemic diet is often prescribed as treatment.

In this same period, a fascinating set of experiments were conducted by Macht and colleagues (Macht & Lubin, 1923, 1924; Macht, 1943) demonstrating the presence of a toxic substance, "menotoxin," in the blood of menstruating women:

> Thus it was found that menstrual blood serum and saliva, unlike normal blood serum and saliva from the same women, definitely retarded root growth and stem growth and effected pathologic changes in protoplasmic streaming, respiration, transpiration and other physiologic functions of higher plants and also profoundly depressed the reproductive capacity of yeasts, fungi and various bacteria. (Macht, 1943, p. 282)

They identified "menotoxin" as a substance closely related to oxy-cholesterol. When they injected menstrual serum into rats, large doses killed the rats and small doses depressed the neuromuscular system, disturbing rats' performance in mazes. They believed that "menotoxin" provided a physical explanation of the myths and superstitions associated with the menstrual cycle.

THE 1930s AND 1940s

In the 1930s, those observing menstrual cycle effects on the psyche emphasized psychoanalytic views. Lewin (1930) and Chadwick (1932) postulated that women unconsciously experience their first menstruation as castration. It followed, then, that a woman who experienced premenstrual symptoms was discharging feelings of tension and rage "that she is not the man she wishes to be, the disappointment over her sex reaching a climax each month at the same time, a few days before, during or after the actual period of the flow" (Chadwick, 1932, p. 39). Horney (1931) was convinced that premenstrual tension reflected intense wishes for a child in a woman with strong fears about having a child. Benedek and Rubenstein (1939a, 1939b), on the other hand, correlated the effect of hormones on women's libidos, noting that high estrogen levels were associated with heterosexual desires while high progesterone levels were linked with homosexual or passive receptive desires.

Yet another approach was to try to correlate menstrual disturbances with other psychiatric disorders. Allen and Henry (1933) studied 100 women for periods of 3 months to 5 years, according to length of psychiatric hospitalization. They described 34 women with manic–depressive psychoses. Seventeen acutely manic patients demonstrated little interruption of menses, whereas 17 out of 26 depressed women were amenorrheic. Women with schizophrenia showed irregularities in duration, amount of flow, and interval between periods according to the acuteness of the illness. The more acute the schizophrenic episode, the more irregular the periods. Indeed, hormones (ovarian extracts, pituitary extracts, and thyroid) were used to treat schizophrenia before the discovery of insulin treatment (Hoskins & Sleeper, 1929; Allen & Henry, 1933; Fischer, 1939).

With the description by Robert Frank in 1929 and 1931 of premenstrual tension, researchers focused on premenstrual tension as a syndrome. Thereafter, each investigator in the field wanted to be the one to find the cause, the treatment, or a novel description of the symptoms. The current notion that the menstrual cycle might serve as a *Zeitgeber* (time cue) or as a director of autonomous mood disturbances was not the focus of attention.

Those viewing premenstrual symptoms from a physiological perspective focused primarily on the effects of gonadal steroids. Frank (1931), in his classic paper based on biopsy data, concluded that premenstrual tension was caused by an excess of circulating estrogen.

> The group of women to whom I refer especially complain of a feeling of indescribable tension from ten to seven days preceding menstruation which, in most instances, continues until the time that the menstrual flow occurs. These patients complain of unrest, irritability, "like jumping out of their skin" and a desire to find relief by foolish and ill considered actions. Their personal suffering is intense and manifests itself in many reckless and sometimes reprehensible actions. Not only do they realize their own suffering, but they feel conscience-stricken toward their husbands and families, knowing well that they are unbearable in their attitude and reactions. Within an hour or two after the onset of the menstrual flow complete relief from both physical and mental tension occurs. [In these women] an excess accumulation of hormone caused the symptom complex complained of, and could be temporarily relieved by venisection and permanently improved by reduction in the amount of female sex hormone in the circulation. (Frank, 1931, pp. 1054–1055)

Frank suggested several different treatments based on purging the system of excess estrogen, including stimulating urine or fecal routes of elimination by diuretics or cathartics.

Israel (1938), in turn, attributed premenstrual tension to faulty luteinization with consequent progestin deficiency and a relative hyperestrogenemia. His description of premenstrual tension deserves to be quoted:

> When well marked, premenstrual tension is readily recognized. It occurs in women between the ages of 20 and 40 years and is characterized by a cyclic alteration of personality. This alteration appears abruptly from ten to fourteen days prior to the expected menstruation and terminates dramatically with the onset of the flow. The monotonous periodicity of the syndrome and its precursive relationship to the menses are striking phenomena. The illness regularly begins as a dire and foreboding sensation of indescribable tension. The patient often inadequately describes this sensation by saying that she "would like to jump out of her skin," and her feeling is manifest to observers by her unusual behavior. When the tension periodically reaches its maximum height, the manic activity of the patient beggars description. There are marked physical unrest and constant irritability. The illness may mimic an oncoming mental disease when the more exhausting episodes of motor activity are followed by brief periods of depression and hebetude. The forbearance of the patient's family is taxed beyond endurance by her unnatural and extreme annoyance with trifles. Unreasonable emotional outbursts and causeless crying spells, similar to those which characterize the menopausal syndrome, are frequent. Persistent insomnia, vertigo, painful turgidity of the breasts and constant headache are frequent accompaniments of the syndrome. Nymphomania, when present, is an arresting symptom and commands the deepest sympathy. (p. 1721)

Israel also tried several treatment modalities, but when progesterone injections proved inconvenient, he used roentgen therapy on his patients (see Chapter 7). Of course in his day, X-rays were viewed as a safe treatment.

Thorn and colleagues (1938) focused attention on water retention across the normal menstrual cycle. In a study of 50 women, 24 women gained 2.2 lbs or more during the premenstrual period, 9 gained weight but lost it once menses began, 2 lost weight premenstrually, and 15 showed no weight change in the 7 to 10 days preceding menses. Thirty-eight women, however, had a marked, temporary weight gain at ovulation. Thorn and colleagues (1938) attributed the premenstrual weight gain to an observed increase in appetite and thirst thought to be secondary to increased secretion of sex hormones. This concept of water retention brought with it various labels for premenstrual symptoms: premenstrual intoxication (Stieglitz & Kimble, 1949), water toxemia, or abnormal water storage (Bickers & Woods, 1951). Diuretics, then, became one treatment approach for women with premenstrual symptoms. Ammonium chloride (Greenhill & Freed, 1941) and ammonium nitrate (Stieglitz & Kimble, 1949), two common diuretics of the time, were used in doses of 1 gram, three times daily, starting 10 to 12 days before menses. Other diuretics are still prescribed for patients with PMS today (see Chapter 7, pp. 195–203).

It was then hypothesized that estrogen levels could be elevated not only because of increased secretion but also because of decreased inactivation in the liver. This putative failure of the liver to deactivate estrogen was thought to be due to a deficiency of Vitamin B complex. The B-vitamin theory ushered in the use of B vitamins (especially Vitamin B_6) for the treatment of premenstrual tension (Biskind et al., 1944), a practice that continues today without compelling etiological or research support.

McCance and colleagues (1937) reminded readers that women normally experience physical and emotional cycles. They obtained daily symptom ratings from 167 normal women for 6 months (780 menstrual cycles). The symptoms they studied were fatigue, digestive disturbances, bowel action, pain, illnesses, breast changes, depression, elation, anxiety and worry, irritability, tension, mood swings, tendency to cry, social relations, capacity for intellectual work, sexual feelings, and sexual intercourse. They found the premenstrual phase in these normal women to be associated with four symptoms: increased fatigue, increased abdominal pain, breast swelling, and increased effort needed to do intellectual work.

The 1940s saw a focus of attention on low progesterone levels as the cause of premenstrual tension (Gillman, 1942; Rees, 1953a), with progesterone replacement being the treatment of choice (Blumberg & Billig, 1942; Schmidt, 1943).

An interesting historical digression has to do with an alternative meaning to the acronym PMS—pregnant mares' serum. Cole and Hart (1930) discovered that pregnant mares' serum contained a hormone that could be measured in the blood stream between the 37th and 142nd days of gestation (in the horse), reached a maximum concentration about the 70th day, and decreased and disappeared between the 130th and 180th days. This hormone, it was believed, produced an effect similar to that of normal gonadotropic secretion of the anterior pituitary (Goss & Cole, 1931). It is now well established that pregnant mares' serum gonadotropin (PMSG) acts on the reproductive system like a combination of follicle stimulating hormone (FSH) and luteinizing hormone (LH).

A look at the annual volumes of the *Index Medicus* from 1930 through 1945 uncovered seven references to PMSG. The first was written in 1937 by R. T. Frank, the physician who is credited with coining the term *premenstrual tension*. PMSG was used to treat amenorrhea, oligomenorrhea, menorrhagia, sterility, endometrial hyperplasia, and metrorrhagia. In two of the seven articles, both authored by Frank, pregnant mares' serum proved an ineffective treatment (Frank et al., 1937, 1940). In all other studies, favorable results were obtained in some women by restoring normal ovarian function (Kennedy & Shelton, 1939; Gray, 1940; Huber & Davis, 1940; Siegler, 1940; Vogt & Sexton, 1941). However, "estrogenic substances" prepared from pregnant mares' urine were given to a patient who suffered from a postpartum psychotic depression without relief of her symptoms (Blumberg & Billig, 1942).

THE 1950s TO 1970s

Beginning in the 1950s, and continuing through the next three decades, Katherina Dalton's work in England has been crucial in establishing PMS as a bona fide condition of women. She wrote prolifically, describing the symptoms of the syndrome (Dalton & Greene, 1953; Dalton, 1954, 1955, 1959b), its appearance in teenagers (Dalton, 1960a, 1960c, 1968, 1974), the effects of a mother's PMS on her children (Dalton, 1966, 1970), the relationship of PMS to accidents (Dalton, 1960b) and crime (Dalton, 1961, 1980), the relationship of PMS to other disorders (Dalton, 1959a, 1967, 1971), and the treatment of PMS (Dalton 1959c, 1973, 1976, 1977a, 1977b, 1985). Dalton herself has PMS and was one of the first treated successfully with progestins (Dalton, 1984). Dalton is still working and contributing to the field (Dalton 1987a, 1987b, 1988).

Evidence in support of the hypothesis that unantagonized estrogen due to faulty luteinization would be the primary cause of premenstrual tension was presented by Morton (1950). He based his conclusions on data from 29 women from whom he obtained endometrial biopsies, vaginal smears, basal body temperatures, and urinary hormone assays. The "unopposed estrogen" accounted for increased epithelial proliferation in the breast and pelvic organs (engorgement), altered electrolyte and water metabolism (edema), and altered carbohydrate metabolism (subclinical hypoglycemia).

In the 1950s, antihistamines were being recommended for the treatment of dysmenorrhea (Bickers, 1953). It was also noted that in some women, antihistamines released tension associated with the menstrual cycle (Geiringer, 1951; Bickers, 1953). A problem in that decade, however, was that women with tension and irritability associated with premenstrual exacerbations of allergies were not differentiated from women with PMS (see Chapter 5). Nevertheless, the conclusion that premenstrual tension responded to antihistamine treatment led to the development of tablets containing a combination of antihistamine, diuretic, and Vitamin B complex, such as Pre-mens of Babylon Pharmaceutical Co., Inc. (Morton et al., 1953). Even today, several similarly formulated over-the-counter preparations (Midol PMS, Pamprin, Prem-syn) claim to relieve premenstrual tension (see Chapter 7, p. 238–242).

Attention to the psychological aspects of PMS was not lost, however (Morton, 1953). Rees (1953b) studied 145 women (61 without psychiatric illness and 84 with psychiatric illness) and found that premenstrual tension could exist in women who had no psychiatric diagnosis; conversely, many women with psychiatric illness were free from PMS. He perhaps should be given credit for the first conceptualization of a bio-psychosocial model for viewing PMS (see Figure 2.1): "The syndrome should always be regarded and treated as a manifestation of the patient's total personality functioning as a psychosomatic unity" (Rees, 1953b, p. 73).

CONTEMPORARY

This biopsychosocial integration has followed from significant advances made in biological approaches to understanding the correlations between biological and mental phenomena. Mason (1968) has pointed out that the discovery in the 1930s of highly purified hormone preparations furthered progress in the study of hormone metabolism and the effects of hormones on body tissues. Some 20 years later, advances in hormone assay methodology allowed the study of endocrine regulation. Furthermore, during the course of the last 20 years, we have come to realize that estrogen and progesterone directly effect nerve cell functions and, thus, have profound influences on behavior, mood, and the processing of sensory information—all of which are known to fluctuate during the normal menstrual cycle (Davis & McEwen, 1982). In addition, these hormones modulate central neurotransmitters and protein synthesis.

Together with advances in biological approaches, many studies have examined the interface of PMS with psychiatric illness. These findings are described in Chapter 4. Approaching the subject from a contemporary anthropological perspective, Johnson (1987) conceptualizes PMS as a culture-bound syndrome. He defines such a syndrome as one wherein a group of symptoms is considered by a culture to be a disease. The etiology of the disease symbolizes core social realities, and treatment is specific to the cultural ideology. More specifically, he describes PMS as the result of a cultural role conflict Western women experience, needing to be both productive (have a career) and reproductive (have a family). By developing PMS symptoms, a woman

> simultaneously and symbolically [denies] the possibility of each: in menstruating, one is potentially fertile but obviously nonpregnant; in hav-

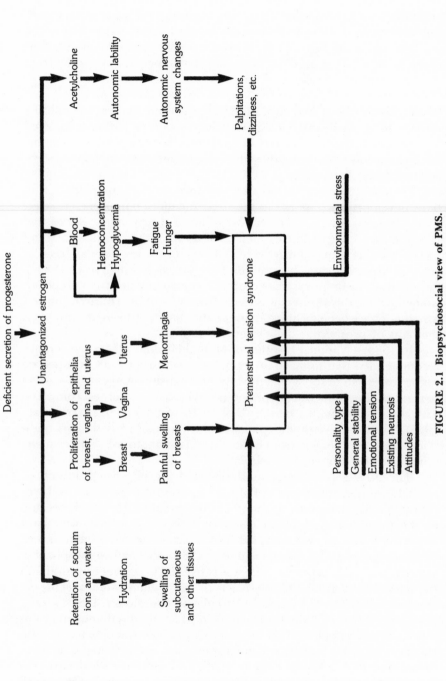

FIGURE 2.1 Biopsychosocial view of PMS.

Adapted with permission from Rees L: Psychosomatic aspects of the premenstrual tension syndrome. *J Ment Sci* 99:62–73, 1953.

ing incapacitating symptomatology one is exempted from normal work role expectations. With PMS, women can be seen as "victims" who did not "choose" to be sick. . . . [PMS] is a symbolic cultural "safety valve" which recognizes the need for women to simultaneously turn away from *either* alternative role demand. (p. 349)

While this causation may indeed apply to certain women, it would be difficult to reconcile this etiology with survey studies that have reported fewer premenstrual complaints in mothers who work outside the home and with cross-cultural studies that document PMS in non-Western cultures (see Chapter 3).

Considerable progress has also been made in defining PMS. Definitions developed in response to the need for more homogeneous selection of women for research on PMS. One of the primary reasons that research on etiology and treatment of PMS has been contradictory and inconclusive is that women were selected for study on the basis of retrospective reporting of symptoms (Rubinow & Roy-Byrne, 1984a). Since diagnosis by retrospective history greatly inflates the number of women with the syndrome, it is clear that many of the research subjects would not have been included in the studies had they been diagnosed on the basis of prospective daily symptom ratings.

In 1983, a National Institute of Mental Health (NIMH) conference recommended that to make or receive a diagnosis of PMS, prospective rating scales had to show "mean symptom intensity changes of at least 30 percent in the premenstrual period (six days before menses) compared with the intermenstrual period (Days 5–10 of the cycle)" (Parry et al., 1985). However, even these guidelines have not addressed many questions: (1) A 30% change from what? (2) What symptoms? (3) How many symptoms? (4) How many cycles?

The NIMH conference itself reflected the increasing interest of mental health professionals in PMS. The reason that premenstrual syndrome has attracted such attention in the mental health field is because of the prominence of mood disturbance in most women who have menstrually related symptoms sufficiently severe to cause them to seek clinical attention. Therefore, in June of 1985 (as described by Spitzer et al., 1989), an advisory committee was convened to consider including in the revised third edition of the *Diagnostic and Statistical Manual of Mental Disorders* (DSM-III-R) (American Psychiatric Association, 1987), a category for a subset of PMS disturbances in which the predominant symptoms are psychological. The Advisory Committee was selected in consultation with the NIMH, which co-sponsored the meeting. The committee consisted of Robert L. Spitzer, M.D., Chair of the Work Group to Revise DSM-III; Janet B. W. Williams, D.S.W., a member of the Work

Group; Harrison Pope, M.D., a psychiatrist who has actively participated in revising several of the DSM-III categories; and 11 investigators with special expertise in the area: Judith Abplanalp, Ph.D., Susan Blumenthal, M.D., Jean Endicott, Ph.D., Ira Glick, M.D., Jean Hamilton, M.D., Wilma Harrison, M.D., Roger Haskett, M.D., Howard Osofsky, M.D., Ph.D., Barbara Parry, M.D., David Rubinow, M.D., and Sally Severino, M.D. (Drs. Spitzer, Williams, Pope, Haskett, Parry, and Severino constituted a subcommittee that worked on revisions of the text and criteria for the category.)

The Advisory Committee first reviewed previous attempts to define PMS. It postponed a discussion of the relative merits of including or not including some version of PMS until it had first drafted an initial set of criteria for cases of PMS in which mood disturbance was an essential feature. This draft definition served as the basis for the discussion about whether to include it in the manual.

In developing diagnostic criteria, an attempt was made to clarify ambiguities in the definition of PMS that have been obstacles to communication between researchers and clinicians. Table 2.1 presents the final criteria that appear in the appendix in DSM-III-R.

While developing the diagnostic criteria, the committee also considered names for the disorder. The first name used by the committee was Premenstrual Dysphoric Disorder, chosen to emphasize that the essential symptoms were unpleasant (dysphoric) mood states. Next, with recognition that the disorder can occur in women who do not menstruate (e.g., hysterectomized women with intact ovaries), the name was changed to Periluteal Phase Dysphoric Disorder. The name was changed once again when it was recognized that, strictly speaking, the symptoms did not occur *around* (peri) the luteal phase but actually occurred *during* the late luteal phase. Thus, the final name, for better or for worse, is Late Luteal Phase Dysphoric Disorder. (Recognizing the advantage of a shorthand way to refer to the disorder, in the rest of the book we will refer to the disorder as LLPDD.)

The Advisory Committee then discussed the advantages and disadvantages of including this category in DSM-III-R. Participating in the discussion was Dr. Teresa Bernardez, a nonvoting representative of the American Psychiatric Association's Committee on Women. Dr. Bernardez presented her committee's many objections to the inclusion of LLPDD in the manual. With the exception of two members of the Advisory Committee, Drs. Abplanalp and Hamilton, the committee strongly supported the inclusion of the category in the new classification. The issues bearing on the possible inclusion of LLPDD in DSM-III-R that were considered at this meeting and subsequently, are discussed in detail in Chapter 9.

TABLE 2.1 Late Luteal Phase Dysphoric Disorder

Diagnostic Criteria

A. In most menstrual cycles during the past year, symptoms in B occurred during the last week of the luteal phase and remitted within a few days after the onset of the follicular phase. In menstruating females, these phases correspond to the week before, and a few days after, the onset of menses. (In nonmenstruating females who have had a hysterectomy, the timing of luteal and follicular phases may require measurement of circulating reproductive hormones.)

B. At least five of the following symptoms have been present for most of the time during each symptomatic late luteal phase, at least one of the symptoms being either (1), (2), (3) or (4):
   1. marked affective lability, e.g., suddenly sad, tearful, irritable or angry
   2. persistent and marked anger or irritability
   3. marked anxiety, tension, feelings of being "keyed up," or "on edge"
   4. markedly depressed mood, feelings of hopelessness, or self-deprecating thoughts
   5. decreased interest in usual activities, e.g. work, friends, hobbies
   6. easy fatigability or marked lack of energy
   7. subjective sense of difficulty concentrating
   8. marked change in appetite, overeating, or specific food cravings
   9. hypersomnia or insomnia
   10. other physical symptoms, such as breast tenderness or swelling, headaches, joint or muscle pain, sensation of "bloating," weight gain

C. The disturbance seriously interferes with work or with usual social activities or relationships with others.

D. The disturbance is not merely an exacerbation of the symptoms of another disorder, such as Major Depression, Panic Disorder, Dysthymic Disorder or a Personality Disorder (although it may be superimposed on any of these disorders).

E. Criteria A, B, C and D are confirmed by prospective daily self-ratings during at least two symptomatic cycles. (The diagnosis may be made provisionally prior to this confirmation.)

Reprinted with permission from the *Diagnostic and Statistical Manual of Mental Disorders, Third Edition, Revised*, Copyright 1987 American Psychiatric Association, p. 369.

Over the ensuing months, members of the Advisory Committee attempted to convince the Ad Hoc Committee to Review DSM-III-R of the Board of Trustees and Assembly of District Branches of the American Psychiatric Association of the wisdom of including the category in DSM-III-R. At the same time, opponents of the category, representing many professional groups, mounted a vigorous campaign against its inclusion that included letters, petitions, and use of the mass media. In the end, after careful deliberation, the Board of Trustees of the American Psychiatric Association decided to include the category (with two other controversial categories) in an appendix of DSM-III-R. To date, opponents of the LLPDD category continue to campaign against the diagnosis based on their view that it is damaging to women (Braude, 1988; Guinan, 1988). We do not believe that it is.

Yet the debate about including LLPDD in DSM-III-R had many benefits. The interest in the category assured that the diagnostic criteria were developed with care and attention to the problems of differential diagnosis. The issue of whether the condition should be classified as a mental or a physical disorder demonstrated the common mis-understanding that many people have regarding the concept of "mental disorder." To many, a "mental disorder" implies only psychological causation and psychological treatment. Finally, the concern with the stigmatizing effect on women of the category demonstrates a pervasive fear in our culture that the gains women have made toward equality in recent years can be easily undermined by recognizing women's special health care needs.

Even though the DSM-III-R criteria are more specific in clinically defining a subset of women with PMS who meet criteria for a mental disorder, more stringent research methods are still needed to discover the answers to the following questions:

1. Looking across days, which symptoms show significant changes in relation to the menstrual cycle?
2. Looking across cycles, are there any regular covariations in symptomatology associated with the menstrual cycle? If yes, which group of symptoms covary?
3. Looking across women, what other factors have an impact on menstrual cycle symptoms? For example, what is the effect on PMS of having a psychiatric disorder?

SUMMARY

It is always useful to review the history behind a syndrome. In the case of PMS, the concern that people will discriminate against a woman because she has a "woman's disease" remains today, even with increasing aware-ness of the prevalence, symptoms, and treatment options for PMS.

Many contemporary proponents of various treatments (pro-gesterone, Vitamin B_6, diet) base their rationales on work published 50 years earlier in some cases, research that has never been substantiated in the intervening time.

We are still at a relatively naive period in our understanding of this disorder. Only with an open mind toward new ideas, but with a critical eye on the past, can we expect to make progress.

CHAPTER 3

Symptoms

Premenstrual symptoms have been defined as physical, behavioral, and mood changes (1) that appear or change in severity during the luteal phase of the menstrual cycle, (2) that do not exist in the same form or severity during the mid- or late follicular phase, and (3) that disappear or return to their usual level of severity during the full flow of menses (Halbreich et al., 1985).

More than 100 symptoms have been attributed to PMS. Since each menstrual cycle is distinct, any individual woman's symptoms may differ from month to month in both type and severity. Seasonal variations in symptom appearance have also been reported (Hallman, 1986; Parry et al., 1987).

Most of the studies described in this chapter used what are now considered to be inadequate techniques of subject selection. We cannot directly dispute a diagnosis, but we can highlight when an investigator used more than retrospective histories to confirm the diagnosis of PMS. Thus whenever we have written "women with PMS," usually only retrospective histories were used. Exceptions will be noted otherwise.

EPIDEMIOLOGY

A clinician can be helped in his or her clinical assessment of a patient by understanding such factors as the influence of family history and cultural characteristics on the prevalence of PMS. Not much research has been conducted on the topic, but several approaches have been taken. Some studies have attempted to describe the development of premenstrual tension from menarche through adolescence to adulthood. In considering these studies it should be kept in mind that a report of premenstrual symptoms does not mean that a woman has PMS. The literature often uses the two concepts interchangeably, as illustrated in the paper by Dor-Shav (1976).

Other studies have looked strictly at prevalence, often cross-culturally. This work is important for the clinician who treats women from different cultures, since the tendency to complain or not complain about specific symptoms may, in part, be a cultural reaction.

Developmental Studies

One set of developmental studies was done by Finnish investigators (Widholm et al., 1967; Kantero & Widholm, 1971a; Widholm & Kantero, 1971; Widholm, 1979) on more than 5,000 adolescent girls who were 10–20 years old. Both the adolescent girls and their biological mothers answered a questionnaire that was analyzed both by chronological age and by number of years after menarche. The incidence of fatigue and/or irritability during the premenstruum was in the 50% to 60% range for both the adolescent group and their mothers. The incidence of edema differed by age. It was relatively low in the younger girls (3–4%), but increased with time, reaching 16.5% after 5 years of menstruation. Mothers reported a 20.7% incidence. In another article, Kantero and Widholm (1971b) reported a high familial incidence of premenstrual tension. They observed that 70% of daughters of mothers who suffered from nervous symptoms were themselves symptomatic, whereas only 37% of daughters of unaffected mothers were symptomatic.

Other developmental studies were done in New Jersey (Clarke & Ruble 1978; Brooks-Gunn & Ruble, 1979a, 1979b, 1980, 1982). Over 600 fifth-grade (10–11 years old) to twelfth-grade (17–18 years old) public school girls were measured by two scales of the Moos Menstrual Distress Questionnaire (MDQ) (Moos, 1968b): water retention and negative affect. The older postmenarcheal girls reported more severe water retention and negative affect than did the younger girls. This is similar to the pattern described above for edema in the Finnish studies.

Two longitudinal studies have been reported. One study selected 158 girls at an urban parochial school, aged 15 to 16 (Golub & Harrington, 1981). The girls were given the Moos MDQ. Three weeks later, they completed the State–Trait Anxiety Inventory (STAI) (Spielberger et al., 1970) and the Depression Adjective Check List, Form A (Lubin, 1967). Two weeks after that, the students again took the STAI and the Depression Adjective Check List, Form D. Twenty-nine adolescents were tested within 4 days preceding menses, and 23 adolescents were tested during the first 4 days of menses. When these girls were compared for magnitude of anxiety and depression experienced, no significant differences in mood were attributable to cycle phase.

The second longitudinal study followed 140 Swiss girls for the first 6 years postmenarche (Flug et al., 1985). At half-yearly intervals, a questionnaire measured the occurrence and the intensity of three symptoms on a scale of none–mild–severe. This study reported the presence of premenstrual abdominal pain in 9% to 28% of the subjects, premenstrual headache in 0% to 5%, and premenstrual vaginal discharge in 10% to 22%, depending on postmenarcheal age. Premenstrual pain and frequency of vaginal discharge increased with age, whereas headaches decreased.

Prevalence Studies

In both adolescent and adult populations, the prevalence of common premenstrual symptoms has varied, depending not only on which population was studied but also on which symptom(s) was examined (Kessel & Coppan, 1963; Andersch et al., 1986; Tippy et al., 1986; Boyle et al., 1987; Brown et al., 1988; Johnson et al., 1988) and what criteria were used for diagnosing PMS (Anderson et al., 1988). It is generally agreed that 20% to 40% of all women experience some symptoms, whereas only 5% report some degree of significant impact on work or lifestyle (American College of Obstetricians and Gynecologists Committee Statement, Number 66, January 1989).

Andersch and colleagues (1986) studied the prevalence of premenstrual discomfort in 1,083 Swedish women and found that premenstrual anxiety increased with age. In addition, sadness and swelling of fingers, legs, and breasts were more common in the oldest age group (39–46 years old) compared to the youngest age group (18–25 years old). Boyle and colleagues (1987) also found that breast pain appeared to increase with age, whereas weight gain or bloating tended to decrease with age in a group of 520 Connecticut women.

A cross-cultural study found that premenstrual symptoms were present in a number of diverse cultural groups, including Turks, Nigerians, Americans, Apaches, Greeks, and Japanese (Janinger et al., 1972). A few specific symptoms showed marked variation. For example, breast complaints were significantly lower in the Japanese women, and headaches were significantly higher in the Nigerian women.

A more recent study of 120 Nigerian women reported that breast swelling and tenderness were the most frequent premenstrual symptoms reported (Adenaike & Abidoye, 1987). Irritability, diarrhea, tension, depression, and headaches were also frequent complaints. Unfortunately, data analysis was based on retrospective reports, and the age range of the women spanned 16 to 49 years. Symptoms were not analyzed in relation to age.

A prospective study of premenstrual tension symptoms in 30 healthy Australian women asked them to complete the Eysenck Per-

sonality Inventory, Form A; the Cattell 16 Personality Factors Questionnaire, Form A; and the Layton Obsessional Inventory on one occasion
(Beaumont et al., 1978). The women then completed three questionnaires daily for 35 days: (1) a questionnaire regarding intercurrent
illnesses or events causing emotional upset, (2) a questionnaire rating 22
physical symptoms, and (3) a questionnaire containing 18 items related
to mood. The mean scores for the women on the psychological inventories were similar to those of normal populations reported in the literature. Furthermore, the maximal incidence of minor physical and psychological symptoms was observed in the first few days of menstruation.
The authors used their data to argue that the term *premenstrual tension*
should be discarded. We suggest, instead, that their 30 women did not
have PMS.

A more recent study of 152 women living in Australia compared
premenstrual symptom complaints among women who were Australian
born to women originally from Italy, Greece, Turkey, or Vietnam
(Masin et al., 1988). For each ethnic group, a different premenstrual
symptom was commonly reported. Australian-born reported irritability;
Italian-born reported tension; Greek-born reported headache; Turkish-
born reported breast pain; and Vietnamese-born reported abdominal
pain. This was a retrospective study, however, in women where the
diagnosis of PMS was not obtained.

A group of 384 women with a wide variety of lifestyles (including
nuns, prison inmates, and lesbians) completed a 147-item questionnaire
designed to evaluate cognitive, affective, behavioral, and physical symptoms (Friedman & Jaffe, 1985). The survey found that housewives and
women with less formal education had more fluid retention and autonomic nervous system symptoms and that they scored higher on
negative affect scales during the premenstruum. No relationship was
found with age, race, sexual preference, pronounced athletic activity
(an unexpected finding; see Chapter 7, pp. 164–165), marital status, or
income.

Of particular interest is one report of the incidence of PMS in twins
(Dalton et al., 1987). The investigators studied 15 pairs of monozygous
twins, 16 pairs of dizygous female/female twins, and siblings of 77
control women. All but one of the monozygous twins of the probands
with PMS were also symptomatic. In that one set, the index twin suffered
from PMS dating from the birth of her first child. Her twin sister was
nulliparous at the time of the study.

In the dizygous twins, only 7 of the 16 twin siblings of the probands
with PMS also had a diagnosis of PMS. The control subjects with PMS
had 121 female siblings. Thirty-eight had PMS. Thus the concordance
rate of PMS was significantly higher in monozygous twins (94%) compared to 44% in the dizygous twins and 31% in the controls. There was

no significant difference between dizygous twins and controls. The trend was, however, in the familial direction.

In support of this report, Van den Akker and colleagues (1987) obtained information by questionnaire from 462 female twin pairs who were either members of the Institute of Psychiatry Volunteer Twin Register or of the Birmingham Population Register. Their data, like Dalton's, suggested that premenstrual symptoms were hereditary.

In summary, premenstrual symptoms are not culture-specific, although particular symptoms may be reported more frequently in one culture compared to another. Some evidence from developmental studies shows that daughters of mothers with premenstrual tension are more likely to complain of premenstrual tension than daughters of mothers who are symptom free. In addition, if one monozygotic twin girl develops PMS, the other twin is extremely likely to be symptomatic as well.

STUDIES OF SPECIFIC SYMPTOMS

A variety of different approaches has been used to catalog symptoms related to the menstrual cycle. Some studies of symptoms are surveys from random samples of women in general, while others have specifically surveyed women with PMS. Still others have described individual premenstrual symptoms or have tried to delineate clusters of symptoms that regularly covary. We will review all of these approaches in order.

Symptoms in Random Samples of Women

This section is relevant only to the extent that the clinician wants to understand how women in general compare to women with PMS in their reporting of premenstrual symptoms. A summary of findings appears at the end of this section. It should also be noted that many of the large-scale survey studies examined the data with respect to differences between users and nonusers of oral contraceptives. These studies are relevant to the discussion of oral contraceptives as a treatment for PMS, which can be found in Chapter 7, pp. 181–184).

In 1974, 3,298 women students registered at Edinburgh University answered a questionnaire about menstrual cycle symptoms (Sheldrake & Cormack, 1976). Of these women, 756 were taking oral contraceptives; the other 2,542 were not. In general, women taking a contraceptive pill reported symptoms less often. The most common premenstrual symptoms in both groups were irritability, depression, headache, and stomachache. These findings (frequency and type of symptoms) were consistent with data from two other studies reported in the Sheldrake and Cormack article, one by Short (1974b) and another by Kessel and Coppen (1963).

Sheldrake and Cormack's (1976) survey also examined other factors related to the reporting of menstrual cycle symptoms. Art students reported more "emotional" premenstrual symptoms than did students from the sciences. Birth order did not affect the reporting of premenstrual symptoms. Cycle length was important. Very long cycles (> 40 days) and regular cycles, in general, were less symptomatic and reflected primarily physical symptoms: stomachache, backache, and lethargy. Those women with cycles from 31 to 40 days in length were the most symptomatic premenstrually, and they reported both physical and emotional symptoms. Women with short, irregular cycles complained primarily of premenstrual emotional symptoms: depression, tension, and irritability.

Woods and colleagues (1982c), in a survey of 179 women living in five southeastern city neighborhoods, found the most prevalent premenstrual symptoms to be mood swings, irritability, weight gain, swelling, tension, skin disorders, depression, fatigue, painful breasts, headache, anxiety, and cramps. Parity, age, education, income, and oral contraceptive use were negatively associated with some premenstrual symptoms. Consistent with the Sheldrake and Cormack study (1976), long menstrual cycles and regular cycles were positively associated with premenstrual swelling, stomachache, backache, and lethargy.

Slade (1984) obtained daily symptom reports from 118 nursing students over an 8-week period. Seventy of these women were not taking oral contraceptives; 48 were. Pain and water retention increased significantly premenstrually in both groups. Emotional symptoms occurred randomly throughout the cycle.

Van den Akker and Steptoe (1985) analyzed daily symptom ratings from 100 women volunteers for 35 days. Menstrual symptoms were reported more frequently than premenstrual ones. As expected, menstrual complaints tended to be physical in nature, whereas premenstrual symptoms were more emotional. These authors studied 33 women, none of whom had sought PMS treatment, in more detail. They compared changes in heart rate, skin conductance, muscle tension, respiration volume, and respiration rate in three groups: women with paramenstrual symptoms (12 women), women with menstrual symptoms (12 women), and asymptomatic women (9 women). They found no association between menstrual cycle symptoms and marked changes in autonomic activity (Van den Akker & Steptoe, 1987).

Graham and Sherwin (1987) assessed retrospective symptoms reported by 101 oral contraceptive users and 149 nonusers. Like Slade's (1984) findings, but unlike those of Sheldrake and Cormack (1976) and Woods and colleagues (1982c), women using oral contraceptives did not complain of fewer or less severe premenstrual symptoms overall. On certain subscales, however, their severity scores were lower. Those premenstrual subscales were anxiety, fatigue, depression, water retention, and impaired social functioning.

Johnson and colleagues (1988) surveyed 996 female nurses who graduated from the University of Iowa College of Nursing in 1963, 1964, 1965, 1969, 1974, and 1979 as well as all of the female sophomore and senior nursing students enrolled in that school in the fall of 1984. Each subject received a 46-item questionnaire eliciting information on menstrual, gynecologic, obstetric, and sociodemographic variables. Information about psychiatric illness was not collected. Seven hundred and thirty women responded. These women were first categorized as "ever" or "never" having premenstrual symptoms. Those with symptoms were classified as mild (never taken medication, no work effect), moderate (had used coping techniques but no prescription drugs, work mildly affected), moderately severe (took prescription drugs or had poor work records), or severe (frequent inability to work). The women were then categorized for menstrual states: 494 were spontaneously menstruating, 109 were using oral contraceptives, 32 were pregnant, 28 were postmenopausal, and 59 were amenorrheic for a number of other reasons. Eight women were not accounted for in the report.

This group of researchers found no differences between women with or without symptoms on any demographic variable (age, education, full-time work, marital status). Eighty-seven percent of the total 730 women had an overall lifetime prevalence of premenstrual symptoms, but only 3.2% rated their symptoms as severe. Importantly, only a few women were (subjectively) impaired in the workplace. The symptoms most frequently reported were breast tenderness, feeling of bloatedness, temper outbursts, mood swings, "tendency to nag," and food cravings.

Lalinec-Michaud and Kovess (1988) surveyed 1,744 households in Quebec Province, Canada. Eight hundred and fifty women (15–45 years old) reported their actual symptoms and phase of the menstrual cycle at the time they answered the questionnaire. The investigators found no significant differences between women in the premenstrual phase and women in other menstrual cycle phases regarding cognitive or autonomic reactions. Women in the premenstrual phase did report more negative affect (irritability and tension), more pain, and decreased appetite than did women in other phases of their menstrual cycles.

Busch and colleagues (1988) studied nursing students using the Moos (1968b) questionnaire, but without adding the scores to yield a composite value. They reported that the level of severity of symptoms could not be predicted from the number of symptoms reported. Further, 46% of the 308 women reported severe symptoms (5 or 6 on a 6-point scale). Severe premenstrual symptoms were not associated with absenteeism. The investigators concluded that "the prevalence of severe perimenstrual symptoms has been underestimated" (p. 70).

In summary, women will generally report premenstrual symptoms when asked to fill out a retrospective survey (McFarlane et al., 1988). The reported frequency and intensity of symptoms may be affected (1) by the use of oral contraceptives, (2) by the cycle phase during which a questionnaire is completed, and (3) by the length of the menstrual cycle. In large random studies such as these, conclusions drawn by the investigators have varied. Nevertheless, the clinician should be alert to these major influences. As always, one must be cautious about making a diagnosis of PMS in a patient solely on the basis of retrospective history.

Symptoms in Women with PMS

This section reviews studies comparing symptom reporting by (1) women who have PMS, (2) women who think they have PMS but do not, and (3) women who do not have PMS.

One of the most definitive studies of symptoms in women with PMS was conducted by Haskett and colleagues (1980). Forty-two women with severe PMS were scheduled for clinic visits on Day 9 of their menstrual cycle and on or around Day 26 of the same menstrual cycle. On each occasion, subjects completed a Visual Analogue Scale (Aitken, 1969; Maxwell, 1978), Menstrual Distress Questionnaire (Moos, 1968b), Multiple Affective Adjective Checklist, State–Trait Anxiety Inventory (Spielberger et al., 1970), Hamilton Depression Scale (Hamilton, 1960), and Carroll Depression Scale (Feinberg et al., 1979). Results from all rating instruments showed an off–on phenomenon between follicular and premenstrual evaluations. The scales for depression and anxiety demonstrated that neither of these affects alone indicated PMS. Item analysis of the MDQ revealed that irritability, depression, tension, and mood swings were the most highly ranked PMS symptoms. The researchers were uncertain whether the physical symptoms were an essential component of PMS or whether they were simply a common accompaniment of PMS.

Two additional studies deserve mention. Each compared symptoms in women with PMS to symptoms in women without PMS. Keye and colleagues (1986) studied 68 women seeking treatment for PMS and 34 gynecology patients without PMS. They discovered a greater frequency of previously undetected medical problems (hypertension, systemic lupus erythematosis, breast masses, meningioma, etc.), psychological problems (suicidality), and marital problems in women with PMS than in the control women. The second study (Hart & Russell, 1986) compared 31 women with PMS with 21 women without PMS, based on eight symptoms rated daily for 1 month. Ratings were made of irritability, depression, tension, anxiety, breast tenderness, abdominal swelling, sleep disturbance, and headache. Symptom severity scores for irritability, depression, tension, and anxiety were significantly higher in the PMS women at baseline. Also, the PMS women demonstrated a significant premenstrual increase in all symptom severity scores except for headache, which increased, but not significantly. The women without PMS demonstrated significant premenstrual increases in only two symptoms: abdominal swelling and irritability. The authors concluded that the physical symptoms seemed to be less important in discriminating between the two groups of women than were the psychological ones. The study also reminds us that women can have significant symptoms but not complain of them.

Schnurr (1988) looked at correlates of prospectively defined premenstrual syndrome in 50 women who came to a PMS clinic for evaluations. Only 12 women met her diagnostic criteria for PMS (a sufficient difference in mood ratings between the post- and premenstrual phases divided by the standard deviation of the entire cycle). Of these women, younger age and working outside the home were positively correlated with the probability of having PMS. The results of this carefully designed study contradict the findings of one large retrospective survey (Johnson et al., 1988), which found no correlation of PMS symptoms with age or full-time work. The PMS women also had a higher mean score on the Hopkins Symptom Checklist depression scale (Lipman et al., 1979).

In summary, it is important for a clinician to rule out previously undiagnosed medical and psychological problems as the source of symptoms in women who seek help for PMS. The question of the relevance of physical versus emotional symptoms to the diagnosis has not been satisfactorily answered yet (York et al., 1989). The clinician is therefore encouraged to read the next section, which reviews the studies of individual symptoms.

Individual Symptoms

Several of the symptoms of PMS have received more attention in the literature than others. This is quite true for psychological symptoms.

Psychological Symptoms

Many psychological symptoms (see Table 3.1) have been associated with the premenstruum (Dennerstein & Burrows, 1979). The major ones are depression, anxiety, irritability, and marked affective lability (mood swings). These will be discussed here under two categories as they appear in the literature: mood changes and depression.

Mood Changes

CLINICAL VIGNETTE: Abby is a 32-year-old woman whose chief complaint was, "I am on a roller coaster for 7 days before my period. I either feel on top of the world and everything is solved or I feel so despondent that it seems like the end of the world." Her symptoms began after the birth of her son 3 years ago and have gotten progressively more severe over the past 6 months. Six months ago her mother died of breast cancer.

While most women without PMS, with or without a psychiatric disorder, do not experience significant or disruptive fluctuations in mood across the menstrual cycle (O'Neil et al., 1984), women with PMS do (Dennerstein et al., 1984b). Abby's history is typical. She describes mood swings during the premenstrual week. Her symptoms began in her late 20s after an event, pregnancy, which interrupted her menstrual periods. In addition, the stress of her mother's death has made her symptoms seem more severe.

Moos and colleagues (1969) studied 15 women with PMS diagnosed by retrospective history. These women then completed symptom ratings and mood measures on Days 2, 7, 14, 19, and 24–28 for two consecutive menstrual cycles. Their findings regarding psychological variables are listed in the quote below:

Anxiety was high during the menstrual phase, decreased rapidly, began to show a slight rise around mid-cycle, and continued to rise quite consistently until the 26th day. Anxiety then showed a slight but not significant decrease on the 28th day; however, it still remained at a much higher level than it was during the 6th–16th day. Aggression was also high during the menstrual phase, and showed a decrease until mid-cycle; however, it then showed a rapid increase at day 18 and a subsequent slow but steady fall until the end of the cycle. Thus, self-rated aggression was highest during the menstrual and post-ovulatory phases; however, premenstrual aggression was reliably higher than aggression at mid-cycle . . . [Pleasantness and activation] were low in the menstrual phase, showed a relatively sharp rise until around mid-cycle, and then showed a fairly steady decrease during the remainder of the cycle. Both variables were lowest in the menstrual and pre-menstrual phases. . . . As expected, sexual arousal was low during the menstrual phase,

TABLE 3.1 Affective Fluctuations During Menstrual Cycle

Study and year	n	Time (months)	Cycle marker	Method	Results	P	M	F	MC	L
McCance et al. (1937)	167	6	Standardized	Ordinal mood	Elation	↑				
					Irritability	↑		↑		
					Fatigue		←			
					Headache		←			
					Tension	NCC				
					Depression	NCC				
					Intellectual efficiency	→	→			
Benedek & Rubenstein (1939a)	9	4–15	Vaginal cytology	Psychoanalysis of dreams	Well-being			↑	↑	
					Passive dependent					↑
					Neurotic conflicts	↑				
Benedek & Rubenstein (1939b)	15	?	Vaginal cytology	Psychoanalysis of dreams	Tension	←				
					Depression	←				
Gottschalk et al. (1962)	5	1–3	Basal temperature	Gottschalk Verbal Anxiety Scale (VAS)	Anxiety	NC				
Pierson & Lockhart (1963)	25	1	Menses	Movement and reaction times (on Days 2, 8, 18, 26)	Reaction and movement times	NC				
Ivey & Bardwick (1968)	26	2	Menses	VAS (on Days 14, 26)	Anxiety	↑				

(continued)

Study	N	Cycles	Method	Tests	Measure			
Kopell et al. (1969)	8	2	Standardized	Nowlis Mood Check List Galvanic skin potential, flash threshold and time (on Days 3, 14, 24, 26, 28)	Time estimation	↑		↑
					Other tests	NC		
Moos et al. (1969)	15	6	Standardized	Moos Mental [sic] Distress Questionnaire (MDQ) Nowlis Mood Check List Plasma progesterone, corticosteroid (on Days 2, 7, 14, 19, 24, 25–28)	Pleasantness			↑
					Anxiety	↑	↑	
					Aggression		↑	↑
					Activation			↑
					Depression	NC		
Morris & Udry (1970)	34	1–3	Reverse cycle day Standardized	Pedometer	Activity	NC		↑
Paige (1971)	38	2	Menses and basal temperature	VAS (Days 4, 10, 16, 26)	Activity	↑	↑	
					Anxiety	↑		
					Hostility	↑		
Somerville (1972)	6	2	Plasma estradiol and progesterone	Migraine	Migraine	↑	↑	
Sommer (1972a)	11 40	1 1	Menses Menses	Watson-Glazer Critical Thinking Test (weekly)	Intellectual performance	NC		
Janowsky et al. (1973)	11	1–2	Reverse cycle day	Mood Scale Weight 24-hour urinary K+/Na+	Negative affect	↑		
					Weight	↑		
					K+/Na+	↑		

TABLE 3.1 (Continued)

Study and year	n	Time (months)	Cycle marker	Method	Results	P	M	F	MC	L
									Presumed menstrual cycle phase	
Udry et al. (1973)	15	1–3	Standardized	General feelings	Worse than usual	↑				
					Better than usual		↑			
Zimmerman & Parlee (1973)	14		Menses and basal temperature	Arm–hand steadiness	Arm–hand steadiness			↑		↑
				Galvanic skin response reaction time	All other tests	NSC				
				Time estimation						
				Digit-symbol substitution						
				Self-rating mood						
Patkai et al. (1974)	6	2	Basal temperature and reverse cycle	Mood-analogue scale	Restlessness	↑				
				Urinary catecholamines	Sleep length	↑				
					Sleep disturbances	↑				
					Urinary Ad, NAD	NC				
Little & Zahn (1974)	12	1	Basal temperature and reverse cycle	Nowlis Mood Check List	Depression	NC				
					Elation				←←	
					Vigor				←	
					Skin conductance				↑	
					"Automatic responsitivity"					→

Study	n		Physiological measures	Measures	Outcome measures	Result				
Persky (1974)	21	1	Menses and basal temperature	MMPI-anxiety MMPI-depression MMPI-lie Hostility Inventory MDQ Beck Depression Affect Check List Plasma estradiol; progesterone; testosterone (on days of menses, mid-cycle, and premenstruum)	State and trait tests	NC				↑
Wuttke et al. (1975)	16	1	Plasma FSH, LH, prolactin, progesterone, estradiol	Reaction time Calculation time EEG (every alternate day)	Reaction time Calculation time Alpha band EEG frequency	↑	←↑	←↑	↑	→← ←
Lewis & Burns (1975)	2	3	Menses	Dream scoring (twice/week)	Hostility	↑		↑	↑	
Blackett-Smith (1975)	20	1	Menses	Mood question-naire Feminine-test Arm–hand steadiness Rod and frame test Plasma estradiol, progesterone, testosterone, urinary level estrogens: (follicular, mid-cycle, and premenstruum)	Other mood and performance tests Fatigue	NSC		↑		

(*continued*)

37

TABLE 3.1 (Continued)

Study and year	n	Time (months)	Cycle marker	Method	Results	P	M	F	MC	L
Beumont et al. (1975)	32	1	Menses	Beck Depression Symptom check list: psychological and physical	15 menstruating women, Beck physical symptoms	↑	↑			
					psychological symptoms	↑	↑			
			Plasma LH and progesterone for hysterectomized women		Hysterectomized women (all tests)	NSC				
May (1976)	30	2	Menses	Elation–depression scale (on Days 3, 14, 26)	Depression, 50% of women	↑				
					Depression, 40% of women		↑			
					Depression, 10% of women				↑	
Wilcoxon et al. (1976)	11	1	Menses	MDQ Nowlis Mood Check List Pleasant Activities Schedule Personal Stress Inventory	Depression	↑	↑			
					Impaired concentration	↑				
					Stressful event	↑	↑			

Reprinted with permission from Dennerstein L, Burrows GD. Affect and the menstrual cycle. J Affective Disord 1:77–92, 1979.
Note. Abbreviations used: P = premenstruum; M = menses; F = follicular; MC = mid-cycle; L = lateral; NC = no change; NCC = no consistent change; NSC = no significant change

38

showed a sharp and continuing rise until about mid-cycle, and then decreased somewhat and leveled off during the remainder of the cycle. Sexual
arousal was rated relatively high and consistent during the entire cycle
except for the sharp decrease during the menstrual phase. (pp. 38–39)

While this description is largely typical, others have not found the same
relationship between phase of the menstrual cycle and sexual arousal
(see below, p. 49).

Both verbal and physical violence have been noted to increase
during the late luteal phase in women with PMS (Dalton, 1980; Elliott,
1987). This particular problem causes women such considerable distress
that they often seek help. The tendency toward violence can also extend
to oneself, that is, suicidal gestures and acts (see Chapter 4, pp. 88–89).

Sanders and colleagues (1983) studied mood changes in 55 women.
On the basis of information from the Moos Menstrual Distress Questionnaire, they classified women into "clinic PMS" ($n = 19$), "nonclinic PMS,"
($n = 18$) and "no PMS" ($n = 18$). (The "clinic PMS" group were women
from a PMS clinic. Both the "nonclinic PMS" and the "no PMS" women
were other volunteers, recruited for the study from other sources). The
subjects then rated themselves using ten visual analogue mood scales for
one menstrual cycle. Self-ratings of "cheerful–happy" reached maximum in the late follicular phase and declined throughout the luteal
phase in the women with PMS. This pattern was not observed in the
subjects without PMS. Aggression and anxiety reached maximum intensity during the premenstruum in the PMS group. "Clinic PMS"
women and "nonclinic PMS" women behaved similarly in this regard. In
women without PMS, there were no significant statistical differences in
measures of mood across the menstrual cycle. The clinician must therefore be aware of mood changes premenstrually, especially changes in
anger, anxiety, irritability, and lability.

Depression

CLINICAL VIGNETTE: Barbara is 20 years old and describes a severe depressed
mood beginning 2 weeks prior to menses that leaves her progressively drained and
despondent. For 2 to 3 days prior to menses she becomes acutely suicidal, hearing
voices telling her to slit her wrists. She is so impulsive during those days that her
parents have to watch her at all times to prevent her from hurting herself. Her
symptoms remit completely within 24 hours of the beginning of menses.

Depression, like anger, is a symptom that causes women with PMS
such distress that they seek treatment (Blume, 1983; Hallman, 1986).

Accounts may be found in the literature of anecdotal case descriptions of premenstrual depression (Schick, 1953), and research studies have documented the existence of depression in women with PMS (Siegel et al., 1986; Morse et al., 1988).

May (1976) asked 30 healthy, nulliparous young women to rate their moods on Day 3 (menses), Day 14 (midcycle), and Day 26 (premenses) for two menstrual cycles. Fifty percent of this group were most depressed premenstrually, 40% were most depressed during menses, and 10% felt most depressed at midcycle. As McMillan and Pihl (1987) state:

> Significant increases in negative mood during the premenstruum or paramenstruum have been detected in a variety of populations: normal college students (Ivey & Bardwick, 1968, Sheldrake and Cormack, 1976), normal women over 30 (Golub, 1976a, 1976b), women complaining of premenstrual tension (Haskett, Steiner, Osmun & Carroll, 1980; Moos et al., 1969; Sanders, Warner, Backstrom & Bancroft, 1983), hysterectomized women with ovaries intact (Backstrom, Boyle, & Baird, 1981), psychiatric populations (Jacobs & Charles, 1970), and depressed psychiatric populations (Abramowitz, Baker, & Fleischer, 1982). (p. 149)

McMillan and Pihl (1987) went on to study 28 subjects experiencing premenstrual depression and 20 subjects without premenstrual symptomatology as measured by the Premenstrual Assessment Form, a retrospective instrument (Halbreich et al., 1982). These women then completed daily symptom ratings for one menstrual cycle and were assessed before and after menses with self-report depression inventories. Mean depression scores did not vary significantly across the menstrual cycle for the control women. For the women with premenstrual depression by retrospective history, daily ratings revealed two distinct subgroups: 39% were confirmed as experiencing premenstrual depression, and 36% experienced intermittent depression throughout the cycle, that is, no PMS. Only those women with positive daily ratings for premenstrual depression also showed an increase in depression on the specific depression inventories given premenstrually.

Blazer and colleagues (1988) reported the prevalence of depressive symptoms in the Epidemiologic Catchment Area project in North Carolina. Fourteen percent of the 3000 subjects reported sufficient depressive symptoms to be included in further analysis. The investigators were able to delineate a "pure" group of women with "dysphoric affect preceding the menstrual cycle . . . associated with some lability of affect (crying spells), weight gain and other somatic symptoms" (p. 1082). They also found that the symptoms were more prevalent in nonwhites than in whites, an outcome that surprised them. Their concluding statements reflect much of our own view:

> Premenstrual dysphoric symptoms clustered in a type relatively pure of other dysphoric or anxiety symptoms. The clustering of premenstrual symptoms into a pure type, free of a priori assumptions about the interrelationship of premenstrual symptoms, represents an important demonstration of the natural existence of a syndrome representing premenstrual dysphoria that requires further study in community as well as clinical populations. (p. 1083)

Sensory Changes

CLINICAL VIGNETTE: Mrs. Smith is a 38-year-old mother of three children who complained of hearing loss premenstrually. She first noticed a hearing loss during her first pregnancy. Since then, she has noted decreased hearing in her left ear monthly, beginning 10 days prior to menses and improving with the onset of menses. This decreased hearing is accompanied by dizziness, especially on bending or turning her head, ringing in both ears, and feeling miserable and like a different person. Physical examination and serial audiograms were consistent with fluid accumulation in her left middle ear and with hearing loss during the late luteal phase, with remission after the onset of menses.

Subtle threshold differences in the five basic senses (seeing, hearing, tasting, smelling, and touching) have been noted in the literature that describes normal menstrual cycle changes (Parlee, 1985). Parlee emphasizes that these changes do not mean that a woman is impaired. As an example, she uses an anecdote about a physicist who was married to a woman with perfect pitch. He asked her to set the frequency she heard as the note A every day during her menstrual cycle. There were two peaks of change in sensory function related to cycle phase, one premenstrually and the other preovulatory. However, these changes did not impair her performance.

The literature varies in its report of auditory changes. Sommer (1983) reported no significant change in auditory performance during the premenstrual phase. Davis and Ahroon (1982) reported bilateral sensorineural hearing losses that paralleled maximum estrogen levels during the menstrual cycle in normal women. They attributed their findings either to an effect of estrogen on acetylcholine metabolism, since acetylcholine is thought to be the primary efferent neurotransmitter of the auditory system, to fluctuations in arousal state, or to progesterone's effect on electrolyte balance.

A well-designed study of women with PMS, using the technique of auditory evoked EEG potentials, showed no significant change in auditory performance during the premenstrual period (Waldo et al., 1987). Auditory evoked potentials are:

> computer-generated waveforms which are averages of EEG activity following trains of stimuli, and are named by their electrical polarity (P, positive, N, negative) and their nominal latency in milliseconds from the stimulus in a normal population. Each peak presumably represents the activation of a particular neuronal structure involved in the auditory processing, from brainstem auditory structures to the cerebral cortex. (p. 36)

The authors studied 12 women (8 normal controls and 4 women with LLPDD) and 12 men, none of whom had a psychiatric diagnosis. Auditory evoked potentials were measured on Day 9 and one day premenstrually of the same menstrual cycle. Waldo and colleagues found that hormonal changes in the premenstrual period did not affect the gating of P50. All of the women showed suppression of the P50 wave in the test response in a pattern similar to that occurring in the men. The amplitude and latency of the P50 waves in the conditioning response were also comparable to those observed in the men.

It is interesting that no differences were found in women with PMS by Waldo and colleagues, since Franks and colleagues (1983) reported that patients with manic–depressive illness showed significant deficits in the gating of P50 during a manic episode, with a return to normal during euthymic periods. Thus alterations in EEG function present in mania may not be present in normal women or in women with PMS. No studies regarding PMS and senses other than hearing have as yet been reported in the literature.

Fluid Retention

CLINICAL VIGNETTE: Diane is 37 years old, with the complaint of eating binges premenstrually. Primarily, she craves salt during the week prior to menses and may consume a package of tortilla chips at one sitting. She routinely stocks two wardrobes, one for the first 3 weeks of her menstrual cycle and another for the fourth week, when she considers herself 10 pounds heavier. During that week she feels helpless, overwhelmed, and disorganized. At other times of the month she describes herself as "full of beans, capable, organized, and on-the-go." Her difficulties with menses date back to age 18, but her symptoms have grown progressively more severe over the years.

Many women complain of premenstrual symptoms related to fluid retention: headache, mastalgia, bloating, weight gain, and ankle edema

(Monardo, 1974). A series of reports (Thorn et al., 1938; Abramson & Torghele, 1961; Landau & Lugibihl, 1961; Bruce & Russell, 1962; Watson & Robinson, 1965) note premenstrual weight gains associated with sodium retention. On the basis of such evidence, a mineralocorticoid hypothesis of premenstrual change has been proposed (see Chapter 5).

There are only a few well-controlled studies of weight and electrolyte changes (Thorn et al., 1938; Landau & Lugibihl, 1961; Bruce & Russell, 1962; Varma, 1984). Bruce and Russell (1962), for example, hospitalized ten women with premenstrual tension and kept them on fixed caloric, sodium, potassium, and water intake. Despite this controlled regimen, the subjects gained weight and retained sodium premenstrually.

Another research team, however, found no significant changes in weight when they compared 20 women with premenstrual syndrome to 20 women without PMS (Andersch et al., 1978a). Others have also found no significant weight change across the menstrual cycle (Golub et al., 1965; Preece et al., 1975; Faratian et al., 1984).

Wong and colleagues (1972) studied six women with "bloating" prior to menstruation and seven women with no premenstrual complaints. They measured the capillary filtration coefficient (CFC) in the forearm at weekly intervals. Women with "bloating" showed a significant change in CFC across the menstrual cycle, with highest values premenstrually and lowest values immediately after the onset of menses. Women without premenstrual complaints showed no CFC changes across the cycle. They concluded that premenstrual symptoms may be due to a redistribution of body fluid from the intravascular to the extravascular compartment rather than to an absolute increase in body water.

Tollan and colleagues (1987) studied ten women with PMS, confirmed by historical data and daily ratings. The women were examined early in the morning postmenstrually (Days 4–8) and premenstrually (Days 23–28). Their measurement techniques were quite sophisticated, described as follows:

> [Other] methods have made it possible to study transcapillary fluid dynamics by measuring interstitial fluid colloid osmotic pressure, COPi (wick-method), and interstitial hydrostatic pressure, Pi (wick-in-needle-method). Net transcapillary fluid transport can be described by the Starling equation: $F = CFC < (Pc - Pi) - o(COPp- COPi) >$ where CFC is the capillary filtration coefficient, o the reflection coefficient for plasma proteins, Pc the capillary hydrostatic pressure and COPp the colloid osmotic pressure in plasma. (Abstract no. 5)

CFC was measured by strain gauge plethysmography on the leg. COPi was measured both on thorax and at the ankle. Weight, foot volume, COPp and COPi thorax did not change during the cycle. COPi ankle was significantly decreased, and CFC significantly increased during the luteal phase. These findings suggest that some women with PMS have an increased net filtration of fluid from the vascular compartment to the interstitium in the luteal phase. Thus an increase in interstitial fluid volume may account for the sensation of "bloating."

Pain

Findings regarding changes in pain thresholds across the menstrual cycle have been inconsistent and contradictory (Kuczmierczyk & Adams, 1986). In another paper, Kuczmierczyk and colleagues (1986) cite the following results: (1) lower premenstrual pain thresholds (Herren, 1933), (2) no lowering of pain threshold premenstrually (Tedford et al., 1977), (3) greater pain threshold and tolerance premenstrually (Aberger et al., 1983), and (4) no cyclic variation in pain threshold (Veith et al., 1984).

These conflicting findings led Kuczmierczyk and colleagues (1986) to investigate pain responsivity in women with PMS. They studied 21 women (11 diagnosed prospectively as having PMS and 10 control women without PMS) who were between the ages of 20 and 43. Each woman was tested twice, once during the intermenstrual phase (Day 7–22) and once during the premenstrual phase (Day 24–28). A continuous, mounting, aching pain was produced with a pain stimulator. During the pain assessment, a constant force of 45.08 Kgm/sec was applied to the middle phalanx of the index finger of the dominant hand. Each subject determined the length of stimulation. The maximum exposure time was 360 seconds.

Women with PMS did not differ from normal controls on measures of pain threshold and tolerance across the menstrual cycle. However, at *both* phases of the menstrual cycle, women with PMS rated the intensity of their pain experience as significantly more aversive than women without PMS. This result suggests that women who seek treatment may tolerate pain less well and thus receive the diagnosis of PMS more frequently.

Sleep, Fatigue, and Activity Levels

There is a small literature on sleep and the menstrual cycle, and women do report changes in sleep patterns during the premenstruum compared to other phases of their menstrual cycles (Billiard et al., 1975;

Papy et al., 1982). Women describe a greater need for sleep and a sense of feeling better if they sleep longer (Hartmann, 1973). One study (Patkai et al., 1974) asked six healthy women to record their hours of sleep and the quality of sleep nightly, Monday through Friday, for two menstrual cycles. Data were analyzed by comparing four periods of 5 days each: premenses (5 days prior to menstruation), postmenses (Days 6–10), ovulatory (Days 12–16), and postovulatory (Days 16–20). The investigators found that the longest sleep duration was during the premenses, but, according to the women's statements, their sleep was also most disturbed during this period.

Studies using sleep laboratory methods have yielded inconsistent results and suggest that mood may have as much or more effect than menstrual cycle on sleep patterns (Hawkins et al., 1985). Four studies have recorded sleep electroencephalograms (EEGs) of women across the menstrual cycle. Williams and MacLean (1980) studied 11 women every third night over one menstrual cycle. The only changes in sleep pattern occurred during the premenstruum in 2 women whose scores on the Beck Depression Inventory (19.9 and 18.0) were in the mildly depressed range. For these two women, the time from sleep onset to the first rapid eye movement sleep (REM latency) was longer than the REM latency for the other 9 women. This study, however, recorded sleep patterns only every third night and during only one menstrual cycle.

A second study (Hartmann, 1966) recorded sleep in seven women (three normal and four psychiatric inpatients) once a week for 3 months. All seven women had longer REM periods during the premenstruum but no change in total amount of sleep. Hartmann himself noted that the laboratory conditions of the study may have precluded the subjects' increasing their total sleep. Even though this study extended across three menstrual cycles, only 1 night per week was recorded polygraphically.

Another study (Cluydts & Visser, 1980) of four women students (20–24 years old) obtained eight sleep EEGs for each woman, distributed equally over one menstrual cycle. There were no clear cycle effects in sleep variables, with the exception of one woman who scored high on the depression scale of the Profile of Moods States (MacNair et al., 1971). This woman showed a decrease in slow wave sleep and enhanced Stage 2 sleep. No changes were found in the percent of REM sleep. Again, this study observed only one menstrual cycle and recorded only eight nights per woman of sleep EEGs.

One study (Ho, 1972) recorded sleep EEGs on six women (three ovulating and three on oral contraceptives) over three cycles. Six days per cycle were recorded: 2 days of menses (low progesterone and estrogen levels), Days 7–9 (low progesterone, rising estrogen levels), and 2 days premenstrually (falling progesterone and estrogen levels). This study found that the total amount of Stages 3 and 4 (slow wave) sleep was increased in the ovulating women premenstrually and decreased in the women taking oral contraceptives. These findings contradict those of Cluydts and Visser (1980).

Our review of the literature revealed little documentation of sleep changes using daily ratings over consecutive months, despite frequent anecdotal complaints of sleep difficulties during the premenstruum. Furthermore, electroencephalogram studies did not rule out mood changes and other diagnoses, such as PMS, in the women studied. The heterogeneity of the sample might account for the inconsistent findings, since women with affective illnesses, for example, often have sleep changes.

One study of six women with PMS attempted to address this issue (Mauri et al., 1986). They obtained sleep EEGs every third night for one menstrual cycle. Following each recording, blood samples were obtained for hormone levels. On each laboratory night, the Beck Depression Inventory (BDI), the Menstrual Distress Questionnaire (MDQ), and the Premenstrual Tension Self-Rating Scale (PMTS) were administered. Self-report data concerning mood and sleep were obtained daily. Mauri and colleagues divided the cycle into five phases, with Phase V being premenstrual, and compared the differences between low PMTS scorers and high PMTS scorers over these phases. They found that low PMTS scorers showed (1) an increase in sleep onset latency, (2) a decline in total sleep time, and (3) a decrease in sleep efficiency in the early luteal phase. For both groups, Stage 1 (light) sleep was elevated in Phases II, III, and V, while slow wave sleep was increased in Phase IV. No reliable changes in Stage 2 or REM sleep were observed. In other words, all women with PMS had phase-dependent patterns, but the two subgroups showed different patterns.

A subsequent analysis of the subjective measures—that is, the BDI, MDQ, PMTS, and a Post-Sleep Inventory (Webb et al., 1976), revealed a between-group difference in level and intensity of *arousal* and *tension* over the menstrual cycle. They concluded that the intensity of arousal rather than symptom severity may be the factor determining the presence of sleep disturbances in women suffering from PMS.

Mauri and colleagues (1988) have recently reported a new study of 40 women. Fourteen were patients in a PMS clinic ("clinic" PMS); 11 were volunteers who met retrospective criteria for PMS ("nonclinic" PMS), and 15 were volunteers who did not meet criteria for PMS. Subjects completed the Post-Sleep Inventory (PSI) developed by Webb and colleagues (1976) to document their subjective experience of sleep as recalled retrospectively. The investigators do not state when in the menstrual cycle the women completed the inventories.

The "clinic" PMS women reported more restless sleep, frequent awakenings, and difficulty falling asleep again; they also recalled more unpleasant dreams than did either of the nonclinic groups. Both PMS groups, however, recalled a greater amount of dreams than did the non-PMS women. An item-by-item comparison of the PSI revealed that the most disturbed sleep was reported by the "clinic" PMS group, with the least disturbed sleep occurring in the non-PMS women. The "nonclinic" PMS subjects occupied an intermediate range. The authors concluded that sleep complaints form an important component of PMS.

Despite the interruption of sleep and reports of fatigue premenstrually, several studies document increased activity among women premenstrually. Premenstrual peaks in activity were found in women wearing pedometers (Morris & Udry, 1970), in women where arm movement was used as an index of body activity (Stenn & Klinge, 1972), and in women wearing activity monitors (Endicott & Halbreich, 1982). A woman's report of decreased energy may therefore not be reflected in a decreased activity level.

Other Physical Symptoms

Other interesting physical symptoms have also been studied in women with PMS.

Muscle Tension.   Muscle tension levels of the frontalis and trapezius muscles were studied in 16 women, who on a retrospective premenstrual symptom checklist ranged from no to high premenstrual distress (Coyne, 1983). The women were tested on two occasions, 2–4 days preovulatory and 0–4 days premenses. During each session, they completed a copy of the symptom checklist used to select them for the study. They were then asked to relax for 7 minutes. The first muscle tension reading of an electromyogram (EMG) was taken during the final 2 minutes of relaxation. This was followed by a 2-minute EMG reading taken while the subject was solving anagrams. Another relaxation was performed, followed by concentration on a physical symptom of the subject's choice. Two additional relaxation sessions were recorded.

Results of changes in muscle tension in the trapezius muscle across the menstrual cycle were not statistically significant. Differences were seen, however, in the frontalis EMG measures. The PMS subjects showed higher premenstrual EMG levels both in the first relaxation period and while concentrating on a physical symptom, but the results were not statistically significant. The PMS subjects did show significantly higher EMG readings premenstrually compared to their own follicular phase than did the control women.

In this context it should be noted that headaches are recognized as a typical symptom of PMS on daily rating scales. A recent study (Metcalf et al., 1988b) looked at this symptom in 44 women with PMS over 133 menstrual cycles and found that headaches were a peri- rather than a premenstrual phenomenon. In other words, the peak incidence of headaches occurred at the onset of menses, with a symmetrical distribution of frequency before and after.

Hot Flushes.   Casper and colleagues (1987) reported that 72% of their 120 women with PMS listed flushes among their PMS symptoms. They described these flushes in a 26-year-old nulliparous woman with PMS (diagnosed prospectively). On Day 26 of a symptomatic menstrual cycle, skin resistance, finger temperature, and serum luteinizing hormone (LH) were monitored for 8 hours. The woman experienced five hot flushes, each associated with a drop in skin resistance of up to 4,000 ohms followed by an LH pulse. Three of the flushes were associated with a rise in finger temperature of up to 10 degrees Celsius. This large change in skin temperature must represent the extreme of what is physiologically possible, since most postmenopausal women with regularly occurring hot flushes do not experience this magnitude of temperature change (Freddie Kronenberg, Ph.D., Columbia University College of Physicians and Surgeons, personal communication, 1988).

Respiratory Changes.   Some symptoms reported by women with PMS may be related to respiratory changes across the menstrual cycle (Damas-Mora et al., 1980). Such symptoms include dizziness, restlessness, clouding of consciousness, headache, backache, and coldness or numbness of fingertips or toes.

Damas-Mora and colleagues (1980) studied one women with manic–depressive illness and seven women without PMS to compare "the deviation of standardized overbreathing required to produce slow wave activity in the EEG during different phases of the menstrual cycle . . . and changes in carbon dioxide sensitivity of the respiratory system. Normal subjects developed slow waves more quickly and had more sensitive CO_2 responses during the premenstrual/menstrual phases" (p. 492).

Caution should be exercised before extrapolating to PMS symptoms based on this study, because women with PMS were not included. However, it may be a good idea to check respiratory variables in a woman with suspected PMS who complains of any of the symptoms listed above.

Food Cravings.   Food cravings, especially for sugar and salt, are commonly considered symptoms of PMS. This derives from evidence such as that provided by Smith and Saunder (1969), who gave 300 nurses a questionnaire about food cravings and menstrual periods. They found an association between cravings for sweets and premenstrual feelings of tension and depression.

Parlee (1985) has pointed out that even women without PMS almost always mention the presence of cravings during the premenstruum. While the presence of cravings, especially for sweets, would seem to indicate that glucose metabolism would be awry in PMS, in our discussion of etiologies (see Chapter 5), we describe the failure of researchers to find alterations in glucose handling in women with PMS.

A recent prospective study (Both-Orthmann et al., 1988) of 21 women with and 13 women without PMS confirms Parlee's observation that women without PMS experience increases in appetite premenstrually. The study also demonstrates that women with PMS experience significantly greater appetite dysregulation than the control women. The women with PMS, unlike the control women, showed a positive correlation between appetite and depressed mood. Still unknown are answers to why appetite is increased more in women with PMS and what the relationship is between mood and increased appetite in women with PMS. If the positive correlation is substantiated, then women with premenstrual depression would resemble patients with Seasonal Affective Disorder (SAD) (Rosenthal et al., 1984). A hallmark symptom of this cyclically depressed group is carbohydrate craving. Indeed, one investigator is testing the use of D-fenfluramine, an anorectic drug that increases brain serotonin, on women in both the PMS and SAD populations (see Chapter 7, p. 236).

Sexual Activity. Premenstrually, both more and less sexual interest has been reported by Severino and colleagues (1987b), based on the results of prospective daily ratings in women with PMS. Baron and Vargyas (1988) surveyed 23 women with PMS and found that 65% reported an increase in sexual tension/energy premenstrually; 13%, a decrease; and 22%, no change. Ninety-one percent reported a decrease in sexual intercourse premenstrually; 9%, no change; and none reported increased coitus. Additionally, 61% reported increased masturbation premenstrually; 9%, decreased; and 30%, no change. In other words, there was increased sexual activity, but not with a partner. Logue and Moos (1986) reviewed the literature on this topic and concluded from the research that sexual feelings and activity seem to peak biphasically: at ovulation and premenstrually. They suggest that future studies consider the effect of sociocultural factors on this parameter.

Cognitive Behavior

CLINICAL VIGNETTE: Evelyn is a 38-year-old executive secretary who sought an evaluation for PMS at the recommendation of her boss, who was becom-

ing increasingly intolerant of her "bad week" each month. Ordinarily organized, accurate, and efficient, Evelyn becomes disorganized, makes multiple typing errors, spills coffee on important reports, and shows poor judgment for 5 to 7 days preceding each menses. A decade ago her boss was able
to tolerate this week by scheduling work responsibilities around that time.
As his business has grown, however, he is unable to make such allowances.

Not uncommonly, women report changes in cognitive functioning
premenstrually (Paul & Halbreich, 1989). The changes vary from cognitive performance (difficulty concentrating, difficulty with mathematical
calculations), to perceptual–motor performance (clumsiness, impaired
athletic coordination), to psychophysiological and other measures. Findings regarding these symptoms will be described here.

Cognitive Performance.   Most of the studies of cognitive performance across the menstrual cycle have looked at women without PMS.
Sommer (1983) summarized the research up to 1980. She described 11
studies showing menstrual cycle–phase effects and 18 studies showing
no phase differences in performance (see Table 3.2). A risk when
reviewing these data is to conclude that women with PMS have no
change in cognitive performance during the premenstruum. Golub
(1976a), for example, concluded that there is no consistent relationship
between premenstrual mood and impaired cognitive function. However,
none of the 50 women she studied were diagnosed as having PMS.

Perceptual–Motor Performance.   There is an extensive literature on
the effect of menstrual cycle hormonal fluctuations on perceptual–
motor performance. Sommer (1973) provides an excellent review of the
literature prior to 1970 (see Table 3.3). The studies are, however, predominantly of women in general, not studies of women with PMS. She
notes that objective performance measures failed to demonstrate menstrual cycle–related changes. We would expect this to be true of women
who are in no way symptomatic.

In a study of 12 healthy women (20–34 years old) with severe
menstrual distress, physiological and psychological tests were administered once on Day 1 or 2, once during Days 10–18, and once 2–6 days
prior to menses (Gamberale et al., 1975). Heart rate, pulmonary ventilation, oxygen uptake, blood lactate concentration, and perceived exertion
were measured during work on a bicycle ergometer for 6 minutes at
each of two work loads calling for 40% and 70% of their individual
maximal oxygen uptakes. The only physiological measures that changed
over the menstrual cycle were pulmonary ventilation and perceived
exertion, both of which were highest in the menstrual phase. This is
interesting in light of the common symptom report of fatigue premenstrually (see pp. 44–47 above).

TABLE 3.2 Results for Standardized Cognitive Tasks

Studies showing menstrual cycle phase effects	Measures: Results
Kopell et al. (1969)	Time interval estimation: Longer intervals produced premenstrually
Montgomery (1979)	Time interval estimation: Shorter intervals produced premenstrually
Silverman & Zimmer (1975)	Verbal fluency (extemporaneous speech): Premenstrual increase in disfluencies
Komnenich et al. (1978)	Backward subtraction: Poorer performance in preovulatory phase
	Embedded Figures Test: Poorer performance in preovulatory phase
Klaiber et al. (1974)	Rod and Frame Test: Change in response from preovulatory phase to postovulatory phase
Wuttke et al. (1976)	Simple arithmetic: Increased speed in luteal phase, optimum performance premenstrually
Dor-Shav (1976)	Human Figure Drawing: Better in postovulatory phase
	Embedded Figures Test: Better performance in postovulatory phase
Cormack & Sheldrake (1974)	Use of Objects Test: Preovulatory group scored higher than postovulatory group
	Verbal Task: Preovulatory group scored higher than postovulatory group
Jones et al. (1980)	Progressive Matrices: Menstruating group performed better than nonmenstruating group
	Verbal Task: Menstruating group performed better than nonmenstruating group
Komnenich (1974)	Verbal fluency (extemporaneous speech): Menstrual and postovulatory increase in disfluencies
Snyder (1978)	Reflectivity/Impulsivity: Shorter response latency midcycle
Golub (1976a)	Ability to reason Fitting concepts to data Rote memory Ability to think rapidly of appropriate wording Anagrams Ideational fluency Semantic elaboration Ability to produce words from a restricted area of meaning Semantic fluency and flexibility Length estimation Speed of closure Flexibility of closure

(*continued*)

TABLE 3.2 (Continued)

Studies showing menstrual cycle phase effects	Measures: Results
Gamberale et al. (1975)	Letter elimination Perceptual speed Stroop Color Word (without perceptual conflict) Stroop Color Word (with perceptual conflict) Time estimation
Rodin (1976)	Digit symbol substitution Stroop Color Word interference test Anagrams Unsolvable puzzles
Zimmerman & Parlee (1973)	Digit Symbol (WISC) Time estimation
Komnenich et al. (1978)	Stroop Color Reading (noninterference) Stroop Color Naming (noninterference) Digit Symbol (WISC)
Silverman & Zimmer (1976)	Verbal fluence (oral reading)
Little & Zahn (1974)	Time estimation
Wickham (1958)	Mechanical comprehension Assembly of parts using diagram Squares test (spatial task) Spelling Synonyms and rhymes Arithmetic
Sommer (1972a)	Watson-Glaser Critical Thinking
Munchel (1979)	Pursuit rotor with arithmetic Concept formation Unsolvable puzzle
Altenhaus (1978)	Subtraction Solvable and unsolvable puzzles
Sommer (1972b)	Speed of closure Flexibility of closure Addition Visualization
Snyder (1978)	Flexibility of closure Rod and Frame Test Embedded Figures Test
DiNardo (1975)	Letter Series Test
Schwank (1971a)	Time estimation
Lederman (1974)	Cognitive battery
McKenna (1974)	Perceptual-motor tasks
Webster (1979)	Cognitive tasks

Adapted from Sommer B. How does menstruation affect cognitive competence and psychophysiological response? *Women and Health 8*: 58–63, 1983, with permission from Haworth Press, Inc., 12 West 32nd Street, New York, NY 10001.

TABLE 3.3 Perceptual-Motor Performance

Study	Menstrual cycle phases studied	Phase definition	Response measure	Results
Smith (1950a, 1950b)	Premenstrual	5 days prior to onset of flow	Performance based on quality and quantity of production and absenteeism records from three factories	No difference
	Menstrual	During flow		
	Postmenstrual	7 days following cessation of flow		
	Intermenstrual	Remaining days to premenstrual		
Dalton (1960a)	Premenstrual	Within 5 days preceding onset of flow	Performance on academic examinations	More failures premenstrually and menstrually
	Menstrual	Within 5 days following onset		
	Postmenstrual	5 days following cessation of flow		
	Intermenstrual	Remainder		
Erdelyi (1962)	Premenstrual	No further specification	Performance ratings plus self-report of athletes	Poor performances premenstrually, Day 1, Day 2
	Menstrual	2 days after onset of flow		
	Postmenstrual	Unspecified		
	Intermenstrual	Unspecified		
Pierson & Lockhart (1963)	A—premenstrual	2 days prior to menstruation	Performance and movement time on simple reaction time task	No difference
	B—menstrual	2 days after menstruation		
	C	8 days after menstruation		
	D	18 days after menstruation		
Loucks & Thompson (1968)	Days 1, 3, 6, & 20	Days numbered from onset of flow, for two full cycles	Performance on simple reaction time task	No difference

(continued)

53

TABLE 3.3 (Continued)

Study	Menstrual cycle phases studied	Phase definition	Response measure	Results
Kopell et al. (1969)	Days 3, 14, 24, 26 & 28	Days numbered from onset of flow, adjusted for long or short cycles, graphs showed 4 data points—days 24 and 26 combined?	Performance on simple reaction time task, time estimation, two-flash threshold	No difference
Schwank (1971a)	Luteal—Premenstrual	Within 4 days prior to onset of flow	Performance on key press response, card sort and time estimation	Lower performance premenstrually and menstrually
	Menstruation	During flow		
	Follicular	End of flow to estimated time of ovulation		
	Midluteal	11 through 5 days prior to menstruation		
Sommer (1972a)	Premenstrual	Within 7 days prior to onset of flow	Performance on repetitive psychometric measures (timed perceptualmotor tasks)	No difference
	Menstrual	Within 7 days following onset		
	Follicular	Within 7 days after menstrual		
	Luteal	Within 7 days preceding premenstrual (adjusted for long or short cycles)		
Dalton (1968)	Premenstruum	Within 4 days preceding onset of flow	Performance on standardized examination on academic and nonacademic subjects	Lower marks premenses and menses
	Menstruum	Within 4 days following onset		
	Intermenstruum	Remainder		

Study	Phase	Timing	Measure	Result
Diespecker & Kolokotronis (1971)	Premenstrual Postmenstural	Within 5 days prior to onset of flow Within 3 days following cessation of flow	Performance variation in vibrotactile learning	More error in premenstrual group
Sommer (1972b)	Midcycle Premenstrual Menstrual Midcycle	14th day after onset Within 2 days prior to onset Within 2 days after onset Days 14 and 15 following onset (adjusted for long or short cycles)	Performance on the Watson-Glasser Critical Thinking Appraisal and academic examinations	No difference
Smith (1950a, 1950b)	Menstrual Nonmenstrual	During menstrual flow Remainder	Performance based on quality and quantity of production and absenteeism records from three factories	No difference
Wickham (1958)	Period	4 days preceding onset of flow through 4 days following onset (adjusted for long and short cycles) Remainder	Performance on Progressive Matrices and other aptitude tests	No difference
Sloan (1961)	Nonperiod Menstruating Nonmenstruating	During menstrual flow Remainder	Performance of physical exercise (modified Harvard Step test)	No difference
Dalton (1968)	Paramenstruum Intermenstruum	4 days preceding onset of flow through 4 days following onset Remainder	Performance on standardized examinations on academic and nonacademic subjects	Lower paramenstrually
Morris & Udry (1970)	Daily	Adjusted for cycles longer or shorter than 28-day standard	Pedometric measures of activity	Increased activity at midcycle

Adapted by permission of Elsevier Science Publishing Co., Inc. from Sommer B: The effect of menstruation on cognitive and perceptual–motor behavior: a review *Psychosom Med* 35:517–520, Copyright 1973 by The American Psychosomatic Society, Inc.

Psychological tests included tests of attention, short-term memory, perceptual speed, perception of time, and reaction time. Only the test of reaction time was slightly impaired during the menstrual phase. No other changes were noted across the menstrual cycle. In summary, impairment of pulmonary ventilation and reaction time were documented at the phase of the menstrual cycle when distress was high, that is, during menses, not premenses.

Silverman and Zimmer (1976) gave an oral reading task to 20 university students, aged 19 to 36, both at ovulation and 2–3 days prior to menses during one menstrual cycle. Since the women were no less fluent premenstrually than at ovulation, the authors proposed that the principal effect was heightened anxiety on speech fluency (which they had also found in another study) (Silverman & Zimmer, 1975), probably due to an interference with language formulation in brain speech centers rather than a breakdown in motor–speech production.

Since 1980, studies of women with PMS have begun to appear. Hutt and colleagues (1980) studied choice reaction time (CRT) in 12 women without and 4 women with PMS. The CRT apparatus was a console on which eight buttons were mounted so as to fall under the thumb, first, second, and third fingers of each hand. Subjects were asked to press as quickly as possible the buttons corresponding with digits being displayed on a screen. Subjects were tested at four times of the menstrual cycle: menses (Day 2), preovulation (4th day after cessation of menses), postovulation (12th day after cessation of menses), and premenstrual (3rd day before next menses). No significant relationship was found in either group between performance and phase in the menstrual cycle, nor were there any between-group differences.

Jensen (1982) studied 18 women with PMS and dysmenorrhea and 18 women without PMS. Each woman was tested for about 75 minutes on each of 4 consecutive weeks. Six women from each group began the testing on Day 8–12; 6 women began during the premenstruum; and 6 women began on Day 1–2 of the menstrual cycle. Since only one group, the group beginning on Day 1–2, was tested within a single menstrual cycle, the experiment design was flawed. Performance tasks were presented in the following order: simple reaction time, choice reaction time (four stimulus lights/four response buttons), 5-minute rest, then pursuit tracking (irregular step-function input presented at a rate of 1.5 stimuli per second). Only pursuit tracking was dependent on menstrual cycle phase, with mean performance at its worst premenstrually for both women with and without PMS. Simple reaction time showed no significant effects, and choice reaction time results suggested that highly distressed women may perform better at low-demand tasks, whereas asymptomatic women may do better at high-demand tasks.

Some investigators have used such data to conclude that it is a myth that women experience changes in performance associated with menstruation (Brooks-Gunn & Ruble, 1982). It seems to us, however, that it is premature to draw such a conclusion.

Posthuma and colleagues (1987) studied 12 women with PMS (determined by prospective daily symptom ratings over 2 months) and 9 women without PMS. The women completed two paper-and-pencil tests designed to measure perceptual parameters and two tests of fine-motor dexterity at four phases of the menstrual cycle: menstrual, early follicular, early luteal, and late luteal phases. Only the Crawford Small Parts Dexterity Test, Part II (Crawford, 1981), which tests fine-motor function, showed a significant difference between women with premenstrual syndrome and women without PMS. In asymptomatic women, fine-motor function was better in the late luteal phase compared to the early follicular phase. In women with PMS, fine-motor function was worse in the late luteal phase.

Perception of Nonverbal Cues.   The perception of nonverbal cues in women with PMS was reported by Giannini and colleagues (1988). Forty-nine women diagnosed from rating scales and by measures of serum beta-endorphins were age-matched with 15 controls without PMS. Each subject rated the facial expressions of male gamblers at two times during the menstrual cycle (pre- and post-menses), although subjects were blind to the menstrual cycle aspect of the study. Women with PMS were significantly less accurate than control women premenstrually. The PMS women were also significantly better interpreters post-menses. Control women did not differ in their perceptual abilities across the cycle. The investigators suggest that this performance decrement may be related to a decrease in visual perception premenstrually as reported by Ward and colleagues (1978).

Psychophysiological and Other Measures.   Tables 3.4 and 3.5 summarize the literature review by Sommer (1983) of changes in psychophysiological and other measures, respectively, across the menstrual cycle in women not diagnosed as having PMS. Asso (1978) provides a detailed review of the literature on one aspect of these measures, that of arousal (see Table 3.6). She makes a useful distinction between three separate forms of arousal: behavioral, autonomic, and cortical. Her review of the literature suggests an increase in behavioral and autonomic arousal during the premenstruum. The results of measures of cortical arousal are less clear. Again, all of the studies reviewed by Asso (1978) and subsequent studies of arousal across the menstrual cycle (Slade & Jenner, 1979; Chattopadhyay & Das, 1982; Strauss et al., 1983) have looked at women who have not been diagnosed with PMS. Thus much research remains to be done before we understand how cognitive behavior is affected in women who suffer from PMS.

TABLE 3.4 Psychophysiological Measures

Measure: Results	Study
Detection threshold	
Lower during menstrual phase; higher in premenstrual phase	Ward et al. (1978)
Lower in preovulatory phase	Haggard & Gaston (1978)
Lower midcycle and in premenstrual phase	Diamond et al. (1972)
Lowest scotopic threshold (night vision) on day of basal body temperature rise	Barris et al. (1980)
Two-flash fusion threshold	
Lower in perimenstrual phase	Braier & Asso (1980)
Lowest in premenstrual phase	DeMarchi & Tong (1972)
Lowest in premenstrual phase	Kopell et al. (1969)
No phase difference	Wong & Tong (1974)
No phase difference	Clare et al. (1976)
Auditory threshold	
Higher during menstruation	Cox (1980)
No phase difference	Haggard & Gaston (1978)
No phase difference	Schubert et al. (1975)
Olfactory threshold	
Lower midcycle	Doty et al. (1981)
Lower midcycle	Mair et al. (1978)
Lower midcycle and in premenstrual phase	Vierling & Rock (1967)
No phase difference	Amoore et al. (1975)
GSR (galvanic skin response)	
Greater in preovulatory phase	Friedman & Meares (1979)
Greater in preovulatory phase (trend only)	Uno (1973)
Lower in postovulatory phase	Little & Zahn (1974)
No phase difference	Slade & Jenner (1979)
No phase difference	Zimmerman & Parlee (1973)
EEG (alpha frequency)	
Postovulatory increase	Creutzfeldt et al. (1976)
Postovulatory increase	Vogel et al. (1971)
Premenstrual decrease	Sugerman et al. (1970)
Premenstrual increase	Leary & Batho (1979)

Reprinted with permission from Sommer B: How does menstruation affect cognitive competence and psychophysiological response? *Women and Health* 8:76–77, 1983, with permission from Haworth Press, 12 West 32nd Street, New York NY 10001.

Symptom Clusters

For a syndrome to exist, in contrast to separate or individual symptoms, several symptoms should covary in a regular and repetitive way across the menstrual cycle in the pattern described at the beginning of this chapter. Several authors have described clusters of premenstrual symptoms that covary and have postulated that there may be several premenstrual syndromes, each defined by the particular symptom cluster that predominates. Bear in mind, however, that it is *not* necessary for the same symptoms to be present each month for a woman to receive a diagnosis of PMS (see Chapter 6).

The earliest such groupings were based on a factor analysis of the Moos MDQ, a 47-item questionnaire scored on a 6-point scale. Moos delineated eight factors that reflect empirically intercorrelated clusters of symptoms (see Table 3.7): pain, concentration, behavioral change, autonomic reactions, water retention, negative affect, arousal, and control. One of the 47 symptoms did not cluster. That symptom was "change in eating habits" (Moos, 1968b).

Steiner and colleagues (1980a) studied 42 women with severe premenstrual tension syndrome and developed a classification of ten symptom clusters (see Table 3.8): irritability–hostility, tension, efficiency, dysphoria, motor coordination, mental–cognitive functioning, eating habits, sexual drive and activity, physical symptoms, and social impairment. They developed their own symptom rating form using a 4-point severity scale.

TABLE 3.5 Other Measures

Measure: Results	Study
Adrenocortical response to psychological stress: Greater responsiveness premenstrually	Marinari et al. (1976)
Acquisition of conditioned response measured by heartrate: Premenstrual group conditioned more readily	Vila & Beech (1978)
Shock aversion: Greatest sensitivity in preovulatory phase; lowest around ovulation	Tedford et al. (1977)
CNS arousal and responsiveness: Premenstrual increase	Wineman (1971)
Kinesthetic aftereffect: Increase at beginning and end of cycle	Baker et al. (1979)
Aneisokonic body perception: Less distortion through lens as approach menstruation	Fisher & Richter (1969)
Corneal sensitivity to touch: Less sensitivity premenstrually	Millodot & Lamont (1974)
Ratings of pleasantness of sugar solutions: Slightly higher rating in postovulatory phase	Wright & Crow (1973)
Arm–hand steadiness: Greater midcycle	Zimmerman & Parlee (1973)

Reprinted with permission from Sommer B: How does menstruation affect cognitive competence and psychophysiological response? *Women and Health* 8:81, 1983, with permission from Haworth Press, 12 West 32nd Street, New York, NY 10001.

TABLE 3.6 Levels of Arousal

Form of arousal	Author	Response measured	Significant premenstrual change in response measured	Postulated or implied change in level of arousal	Definition of premenstrual phase
I. Behavioral psychological arousal	Moos et al. (1969)	Aggression/hostility (Nowlis Mood Adjective Check List)	Increase	Higher	Unclear. Presume 90–99%ile; approx. Day 27+
	Ivey & Bardwick (1968)	Anxiety (Gottschalk Verbal Anxiety Scale)	Increase	Higher	2–3 days PM*
	Moos et al. (1969)	Anxiety (Nowlis Mood Adjective Check List)	Increase	Higher	Unclear. Presume 90–99%ile; approx. Day 26
	Paige (1971)	Anxiety (Gottschalk Technique)	None	None	Day 26
	Silverman et al. (1974)	Anxiety (frequency of disfluencies in stutterers)	Increase	Higher	2–3 days PM*
	Beumont et al. (1975)	Depression (sections of Beck's Self-Rating Depression Scale)	Increase	Unknown	1 week PM
	Moos et al. (1969)	Depression (Nowlis Mood Adjective Check List)	None	None	Unclear. Presume 90–99%ile; approx. Day 26
	Paige (1971)	Hostility (Gottschalk Technique)	Increase	Higher	Day 26
	Gruba & Rohrbaugh (1975)	Negative affect (menstrual distress questionnaire)	Increase	Labile	1 week PM
	Janowsky et al. (1973)	Negative affect (self-rated, 4-point scale)	Increase	Labile	Within 4 days PM
	Zimmerman & Parlee (1973)	Negative affect (self-rated, 6-point scale)	None	None	4 days PM
	Beumont et al. (1975)	Psychological symptoms (self-rated, 3-point scale)	Increase	Labile	1 week PM

II. Autonomic arousal	Gruba & Rohrbaugh (1975)	Autonomic (self-rated; dizziness, faintness, cold sweats, nausea, hot flushes)	Increase	Higher	1 week PM
	Moos et al. (1969)	Autonomic (self-rated; dizziness, faintness, cold sweats, nausea, hot flushes)	Increase	Higher	Unclear. Presume 90–99%ile; approx. Day 27+
	Asso & Beech (1975)	Conditioned response acquisition (GSR)**	Increase	Higher	Within 4 days PM
	Vila & Beech (1977)	Conditioned response acquisition (GSR)	Increase	Higher	Within 4 days PM
	Little & Zahn (1974)	Heart rate	None	None	2 days PM
	Kopell et al. (1969)	Skin potential	None	None	Unclear. Presume Day 24+
	Little & Zahn (1974)	Skin conductance	None	None	2 days PM
	Zimmerman & Parlee (1973)	Skin conductance	None	None	Days 23–27
	Wineman (1971)	Sympathetic ANS*** (temperature, heart rate, blood pressure, skin conductance, saliva)	Increase	Higher	Within 4 days PM
III. Cortical arousal	Little & Zahn (1974)	Temperature	None	None	2 days PM
	Creutzfeldt et al. (1976)	EEG changes	Increased alpha frequency	Higher	Luteal phase (postovulation to menstruation)
	Vogel et al. (1971)	EEG (driving)	Increase	Lower	Day 15 to menstruation
	Lamb et al. (1953)	EEG (driving)	None	None	1 week PM
	Lamb et al. (1953)	EEG (resting)	Decreased alpha	Higher	From ovulation to 1 day PM

(continued)

TABLE 3.6 (Continued)

Form of arousal	Author	Response measured	Significant premenstrual change in response measured	Postulated or implied change in level of arousal	Definition of premenstrual phase
III. Cortical arousal	Margerison et al. (1964)	EEG (resting)	None	None	1 day PM or day 1 of cycle
	Belmaker et al. (1974)	Monoamine oxidase activity	Increase	Probably lower	4 days PM
	Gilmore et al. (1971)	Monoamine oxidase activity	None	None	1 day PM or day 1 of cycle
	Grant & Pryse-Davies (1968)	Monoamine oxidase activity	Increase	Probably lower	Late secretory phase, presume day 20+
	Klaiber et al. (1972)	Monoamine oxidase activity	Increase	Probably lower	Day 15 to menstruation
	Paige (1971)	Monoamine oxidase activity	Increase	Probably lower	Day 26
	Kopell et al. (1969)	Time estimation	Increase (in time interval)	Lower	Unclear. Presume day 24+
	Schwank (1971b)	Time estimation	None	None	Within 4 days PM
	Zimmerman & Parlee (1973)	Time estimation	None	None	Days 23–27
	Akita (1965)	Two-flash fusion	None	None	Not specified
	DeMarchi & Tong (1972)	Two-flash fusion	Higher threshold	Lower	3 days PM
	Kopell et al. (1969)	Two-flash fusion	None	None	Unclear. Presume day 24+

Adapted with permission from Asso D. Levels of arousal in the premenstrual phase. *Br J Soc Clin Psychol 17*: 47–55, 1978.

*PM = premenses.

**GSR = galvanic skin response.

***ANS = autonomic nervous system.

62

TABLE 3.7 Moos Symptom Clusters

1. PAIN	5. WATER RETENTION
5. Muscle stiffness	1. Weight gain
9. Headache	10. Skin disorders
16. Cramps	30. Painful breasts
22. Backache	34. Swelling
25. Fatigue	
37. General aches and pains	6. NEGATIVE AFFECT
	3. Crying
2. CONCENTRATION	11. Loneliness
2. Insomnia	21. Anxiety
6. Forgetfulness	27. Restlessness
7. Confusion	36. Irritability
24. Lowered judgment	38. Mood swings
29. Difficulty concentrating	40. Depression
33. Distractible	45. Tension
35. Accidents	
42. Lowered motor coordination	7. AROUSAL
	13. Affectionate
3. BEHAVIORAL CHANGE	14. Orderliness
4. Lowered school or work	18. Excitement
performance	31. Feelings of well-being
8. Take naps; stay in bed	47. Bursts of energy, activity
15. Stay at home	
20. Avoid social activities	8. CONTROL
41. Decreased efficiency	12. Feeling of suffocation
	19. Chest pains
4. AUTONOMIC REACTIONS	32. Ringing in the ears
17. Dizziness, faintness	39. Heart pounding
23. Cold sweats	43. Numbness, tingling
26. Nausea, vomiting	46. Blind spots, fuzzy vision
28. Hot flushes	

Hargrove and Abraham (1982) have suggested the subgrouping of patients with premenstrual symptoms into four categories: PMT-A, PMT-H, PMT-C, and PMT-D (see Chapter 5, pp. 122–126). Women with PMT-A most often manifest anxiety, nervous tension, mood swings, and irritability. Those with PMT-H complain of weight gain, swelling of extremities, breast tenderness, and abdominal bloating. The PMT-C cluster of symptoms includes cravings for sweets, increased appetite, dizziness, heart pounding, fatigue, and headache. The PMT-D cluster is composed of symptoms of depression, forgetfulness, crying spells, confusion, or insomnia. According to their system, women must have moderate or severe symptoms from one or more of their categories to receive a diagnosis of PMS.

Halbreich and colleagues (1985) subdivided premenstrual symptoms with an intent to select out groups of women demonstrating primarily psychological premenstrual symptoms. They developed criteria for 18 syndromal categories (see Table 3.9) (Halbreich & Endicott, 1982). There are 6 subtypes of depressive syndrome and 4 subtypes for change in physical condition, as well as 8 other categories. The 18 categories are: major depressive syndrome, minor depressive syndrome, depression with endogenous features, depression with atypical features, depression with hysteroid features, depression with agitated–anxious features, depression with hostile features, depression with withdrawn features, anxious syndrome (not depressed), irritable syndrome (not depressed), impulsive syndrome, increased well-being syndrome, general physical discomfort syndrome, water retention syndrome, fatigue syndrome, autonomic physical syndrome, impaired social functioning, and "organic" mental features.

Three recent studies report the use of some of the scales described above to examine symptom clusters in women. One study used the Halbreich and Endicott Premenstrual Assessment Form (Youdale & Freeman, 1987). They studied 19 self-defined severely symptomatic women and 26 self-defined premenstrually asymptomatic women on ten

TABLE 3.8 Steiner, Haskett, Carroll Symptom Clusters

1. IRRITABILITY–HOSTILITY Irritable Hostile Negative attitude Angry Short-fused Yelling Screaming at others	6. MENTAL–COGNITIVE FUNCTIONING Forgetful Poor concentration Distractible Confused Lower judgement
2. TENSION Tense Restless Jittery Upset High-strung Unable to relax	7. EATING HABITS 8. SEXUAL DRIVE AND ACTIVITY 9. PHYSICAL SYMPTOMS Painful or tender breasts Swelling of abdomen, breasts, ankles, or fingers Water retention
3. EFFICIENCY Decreased efficiency Easily fatigued	Weight gain Headaches Low-back pain, etc.
4. DYSPHORIA Dysphoric mood Distinguish from depression	10. SOCIAL IMPAIRMENT Avoidance of social activities and in- teraction with family, at home, at work, at school, etc.
5. MOTOR COORDINATION Clumsy Prone to accidents Lowered motor coordination	

**TABLE 3.9 Premenstrual Assessment Form
Typological Categories**

 1. Major depressive syndrome
 2. Minor depressive syndrome
 3. Depression with endogenous features
 4. Depression with atypical features
 5. Depression with hysteroid features
 6. Depression with agitated–anxious features
 7. Depression with hostile features
 8. Depression with withdrawn features
 9. Anxious syndrome (not depressed)
10. Irritable syndrome (not depressed)
11. Impulsive syndrome
12. Increased well-being syndrome
13. General physical discomfort syndrome
14. Water retention syndrome
15. Fatigue syndrome
16. Autonomic physical syndrome
17. Impaired social functioning
18. "Organic" mental features

separate occasions: initial session, premenstrual (within 4 days of the onset of menses), menstrual (within the first 4 days of menses), and intermenstrual (within 4 days of the midpoint of the cycle) for three menstrual cycles. The premenstrually symptomatic women reported greater premenstrual changes than the asymptomatic subjects both retrospectively and concurrently. The PMS group also reported more frequent changes during the menstrual phase, suggesting that there is not a dramatic cessation of premenstrual symptoms with the onset of menses. Although this study did demonstrate that retrospective reports of premenstrual symptoms were greater than the number of symptoms confirmed by concurrent data, it also found a group of women who met criteria for premenstrual syndrome on the basis of concurrent data but who had defined themselves retrospectively as asymptomatic. These women would not receive the diagnosis, however, because the symptoms were obviously not causing serious enough impairment in their lives for them to complain or seek help.

The second study (Siegel et al., 1987) administered the Moos MDQ to 156 women who complained of severe premenstrual symptoms. They found two separate clusters of emotional/behavioral symptoms and two of physical symptoms. They described their symptom cluster labeled "withdrawn mood" as being very similar to the cluster that Abraham (1980) described as PMT-D. Their cluster labeled "anxious/tense mood" seemed to them comparable to Abraham's PMT-A cluster. The two physical symptom clusters ("general physical discomfort" and "water retention") also seemed to them to be similar to Abraham's. A final symptom cluster, "arousal," was not a subsyndrome in Abraham's classification.

The third study (Morse & Dennerstein, 1988) used the Moos Menstrual Distress Questionnaire with 75 women prospectively diagnosed as having PMS and no current psychiatric disorder. Factor analysis of 1 month's symptom ratings revealed five factors. One of the factors, follicular distress, accounted for 22% of the total variance. The other four factors together accounted for 30% of the total variance. Those four factors were "follicular anxiety," premenstrual negative feelings, premenstrual activation, and premenstrual stress-pain.

Severino and colleagues (1987b) applied a spectral density analysis to 21 daily symptom ratings of 58 women across two menstrual cycles. This type of analysis looked across days for significant changes in symptom severity that were reliably repeated from cycle to cycle. They found that eight symptoms on the Daily Rating Form (DRF) (Endicott et al., 1986) demonstrated significant premenstrual change: increased enjoyment and efficiency; mood swings; depressed, sad, low, blue, lonely; anxious; irritable, angry, impatient; more sexual interest; less sexual interest; and "drink alcohol, use nonprescription drugs." Importantly, symptoms of mood swings, depression, anxiety, and irritability are the affective symptoms required to meet LLPDD diagnostic criteria in the DSM-III-R research appendix A (see Chapter 6).

Severino and colleagues (1987b; 1989) also looked at the impact of having a psychiatric diagnosis on daily symptom ratings. During the time of symptom ratings, each woman underwent a semistructured interview, using the Schedule for Affective Disorders and Schizophrenia–Lifetime Version (SADS–L) (Endicott & Spitzer, 1978); and all psychiatric diagnoses were determined by applying Research Diagnostic Criteria (Spitzer et al., 1977) to the SADS-L data.

Only two symptoms on the DRF were not affected by the presence of a psychiatric disorder: more sleep and breast tenderness. While a history of, or a present psychiatric disorder introduced clinically negligible effects on the *variability* of symptom severity as a function of menstrual cycle phase, it did appear to have an impact on the average level of symptom *severity* throughout the cycle. Because of this effect, the magnitude of premenstrual change in symptom severity among women with psychiatric disorders was smaller than among women without such disorders. This effect made the detection of significant premenstrual change in symptom severity especially difficult in women with present or past histories of psychiatric disorders, especially as the overall severity of the psychiatric disorder increased.

Coleman and colleagues (1988) have also employed the spectral analysis technique to look at scores on five symptom clusters from the

Moos MDQ over several cycles in women with PMS. Their spectral analysis showed 28-day peaks in most women only for physical symptoms. This differs from the findings of Severino and colleagues, who found premenstrual peaks for affective symptoms.

Timing of Symptoms

The clinical manifestation of PMS symptoms has been said to occur in one of four temporal patterns (Reid, 1985), shown in Figure 3.1. The first pattern is most common and coincides with the onset and duration of symptoms experienced by women who have either PMS or LLPDD. This pattern of symptoms begins during the last week of the luteal phase and remits within a few days after onset of the follicular phase.

The second pattern of PMS symptoms begins at ovulation, with gradual worsening of symptoms across the luteal phase, and remission of symptoms within a few days after the onset of the follicular phase (or menses).

Some women experience a brief, time-limited episode of symptoms

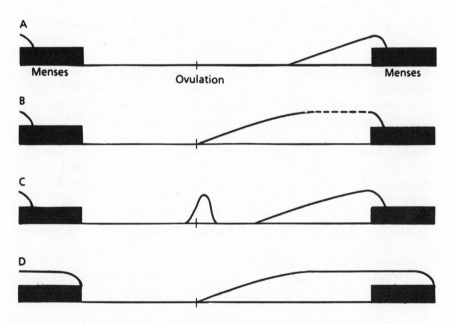

FIGURE 3.1 Patterns of Premenstrual Symptoms.
Reprinted with permission from Reid RL, Yen SSC: Premenstrual Syndrome. *Clinical Obstetrics and Gynecology: A Quarterly Periodical* 26:710, 1983.

at ovulation, followed by symptom-free days and a recurrence of PMS symptoms late in the luteal phase. This constitutes the third pattern.

The most severely affected women (the fourth pattern) have symptoms beginning at ovulation, worsening across the luteal phase, and remitting only after menses ceases. These women describe having only 1 week a month that is symptom-free. If the symptomatic weeks are very disruptive, these women may find that their relationships never fully return to stable, healthy interpersonal relationships during the symptom-free week.

Of course, all of these patterns can be detected by careful prospective ratings. How to differentiate among the patterns is described in Chapter 6. As discussed above on pages 66–67, more sophisticated statistical analyses are also being applied to the daily symptom ratings in the hope of developing more reliable measures of the temporal sequence of symptoms than is possible with the human eye (Severino et al., 1987b, 1989).

CONCLUSIONS

It is clear from the results of research described in this section that certain factors are important to keep in mind when a patient presents her symptoms. Age and family history may influence both the type and severity of symptoms. Prospective ratings are key, since most women, even those who do not complain of PMS, will provide positive retrospective histories when asked to complete questionnaires. While there is no doubt that mood changes occur premenstrually in afflicted women, performance measures may not; this point has implications for working women (see Chapter 9). Commonly held beliefs that women with PMS "bloat" or gain weight premenstrually are not firmly supported by careful research, casting doubt on those treatment strategies based on ridding the body of excess fluid.

The advantage of grouping women into PMS symptom cluster groups has not been established. Perhaps if women fell cleanly into one category, the clusters would be useful from a treatment perspective, but this does not seem to be the case.

Timing of symptoms is, of course, essential in differentiating between PMS and some other syndrome. Diagnostic methods are discussed in Chapter 6.

While this chapter has primarily emphasized negative premenstrual symptoms, Logue and Moos (1987) correctly remind us that not all women perceive the premenstrual phase as negative. They suggest that more research be conducted to identify positive premenstrual changes.

Mills (1988), who writes of "premenstrual awareness (PMA) as a time of cyclic self-integration," would endorse this suggestion.

A list of symptoms that can occur during the premenstruum is provided in Table 3.10.

TABLE 3.10 Representative Symptoms of Premenstrual Syndrome

Psychological	Somatic
Aggression	Proneness to accident
Agitation	Acne
Anorexia	Asthma
Anxiety	Bloatedness (actually)
Confusion	Bloatedness (feeling of)
Contentiousness	Blurred vision
Crying bouts	Breast swelling
Decreased alertness	Breast tenderness
Decreased libido	Clumsiness
Depression	Constipation
Diminished self-esteem	Diarrhea
Drowsiness	Diminished activity
Emotional lability	Diminished efficiency
Energy	Diminished performance
Fatigue	Dizziness
Food craving	Epilepsy
Hopelessness	Finger swelling
Housebound	Flushes
Hunger	Formication
Hypersomnia	Headache
Impulsive behavior	Joint pain
Increased libido	Mastodynia
Insomnia	Migraine
Irritability	Muscle pain
Lack of inspiration	Nausea
Lack of volition	Edema
Lethargy	Oliguria
Listlessness	Pain—iliac fossa
Loss of attention to appearance	Pain—lower abdomen
Loss of concentration	Pain—pelvic
Loss of confidence	Polyuria
Loss of judgment	Poor coordination
Loss of self-control	Premenstrual dysmenorrhea
Malaise	Pruritus
Moodiness	Puffiness
Pessimism	Rhinorrhea
Sadness	Sinusitis
Social isolation	Skin lesions
Suicidal tendency	Sore eyes
Tension	Vaginal discharge
Thirst	Vertigo
Violence	Vomiting
	Weakness
	Weight increase (feeling of)
	Weight increase (actual)

Adapted from O'Brien PMS: *Premenstrual Syndrome*. Oxford, Blackwell Scientific Publications, 1987, p. 7.

CHAPTER 4

Psychological Factors and the Menstrual Cycle

Since mood disturbances are prominent in women who have menstrually related symptoms so severe that they seek treatment, the relationship between psychological factors and experiences of menarche and menstruation deserves investigation. If this were a traditional chapter on psychological aspects of the menstrual cycle, it would include such factors as psychoanalytic concepts, social-learning views, developmental and cognitive theories, and psychiatric epidemiological knowledge. This chapter, of course, includes all these items. However, we also attempt to incorporate *biological* information into our *psychosocial* understanding of women across the menstrual cycle. Such a *biopsychosocial model* integrates the physiology of both the female brain and the menstrual cycle not only with women's cyclic psychological functioning but also with the impact of social factors on women's functioning.

In this chapter, we review various aspects of psychological functioning and the menstrual cycle. Some sections deal with women's attitudes toward events related to the menstrual cycle. Not all of the topics are germane to PMS, but they are important nonetheless in understanding how psychological factors themselves vary or modify other aspects of the menstrual cycle. For the mental health professional in particular, a review of menstrual cycle influences on existing psychiatric disorders is provided.

In addition, throughout this chapter, we will indicate wherever an investigator has used more rigorous subject selection techniques than retrospective histories.

ATTITUDES REGARDING MENSTRUAL CYCLES

Menarche

The onset of menstruation, menarche, is usually a late event in the series of complex changes marking puberty. Gonadotropin cycles probably have a role prior to menarche (Hansen et al., 1975). With the onset of the rhythmic interaction between gonadotropins and ovarian hormones, the female mode of psychosexual functioning is established (Kestenberg, 1967; Notman & Nadelson, 1983).

Early studies of the meaning of menarche to girls focused on perceptions of body changes at puberty and differentiated between the younger adolescent's preoccupation with body parts (breast development, body and pubic hair growth) and the older adolescent's concern with integrating a new body image (Rierdan & Koff, 1980; Grief & Ulman, 1982). Attitudes toward menarche, memories of menarche, timing of menarche (early or late), personality characteristics at menarche, and sociocultural influences on the impact of menarche have all been studied (Brooks-Gunn & Ruble, 1982; Grief & Ulman, 1982; Golub, 1983; Brooks-Gunn, 1984). Brooks-Gunn and Petersen (1984) reviewed the work in these areas, concluding that outcomes of the experience of pubertal events have multiple determinants: biological, cultural, social, and psychological. At a minimum, girls must determine what it means to be a menstruating woman. To do this, they restructure their self-identities to take menstruation into account.

Delaney and colleagues (1976) stated that early psychoanalytic views of menarche emphasized negative meanings of the experience. Deutsch (1944), a proponent of such Freudian views, emphasized women's castration anxiety, feelings of uncleanliness, and penis envy, while Gill (1943) emphasized menstruation as a reminder to the woman of her "deficiency." A contemporary analyst, Malkah Notman (1983), lends a positive perspective to the experience of menarche by delineating the developmental tasks of the adolescent in whom menarche occurs. She describes four tasks:

1. A girl must detach herself from early parental ties. At the time of menarche, a girl is usually shifting back and forth between her infantile attachment to both parents and her moves toward her adult personality. With her mother, she shifts from an infantile longing for maternal closeness to a perception of the mother as a rival. With her father, she seeks closeness, derives pleasure in his interest in her maturation, and partially identifies with him.

2. She must develop a capacity to form peer attachments as a

female. This will ultimately lead to a consolidation of her identity as a woman.

3. She must reestablish a capacity for intimacy and develop the potential for commitment both to another person and to a lifecourse.

4. She must develop a sense of normality as new internal physical sensations occur and as external physical changes appear.

Menarche is only one of the organizers of adolescence. Its importance lies in its ability to be a turning point in a girl's acceptance of femininity in the context of its confirmation of the existence of her internal female organs. These developmental tasks must be understood in the context of the symbolic meaning of menarche for any individual girl. While Notman's perspective on menarche enriches our view of how girls develop into young women, it fails to address the cyclical nature of biological events or the influence of this cycle on the tasks and symbolic meaning of menarche.

Although no author asserts that conflicts about menarche cause PMS symptoms, Shainess (1961) has stated that PMS symptoms recapitulate a devaluation of the self in relation to femininity. Menarche is a crucial point in a woman's development. The subjective context in which it occurs might influence the capacity of some women to respond positively or negatively to the events of the biological cycle (Friedman et al., 1983).

It is unclear how common PMS is in adolescence (Halas, 1987). One survey of 88 white high school students in Utah found that more than half of the girls reported premenstrual depression (Wilson-Larsen & Keye, 1987). The girls also perceived that their premenstrual symptoms interfered with their academic performance, their ability to concentrate and/or take tests, their athletic performance, and their class attendance.

More remains to be known about PMS in adolescence. The Utah survey, for example, needs to be combined with prospective data on teenagers to establish whether these retrospective reports are, indeed, confirmed by daily symptom ratings. Attempts should be made to correlate experiences of menarche with the incidence of PMS. Adolescence is normally a time when coping mechanisms are stressed. One subgroup of teenagers who might be at special risk would be those in whom low-grade impulsivity and lability related to the premenstruum are exacerbated premenstrually by unresolved conflicts of adolescence. In other words, some acting-out behavior of adolescent girls may be due to impaired mastery of the new appearance of biological cycles in their internal environments.

Two additional major categories relevant to adolescent behavior require further study. The first category is adolescent depression and depression-linked syndromes, such as bulimia, and their relationship to premenstrual dysphoria. The second category is stress. What, for example, is the impact of immediate and recent stressors, such as rape, initiation into conflict-laden sexual activity, family conflict, or divorce? What is the impact of past stressors, such as child abuse, incest, exposure early in life to a mother with PMS, or the experience early in life of extreme family stress? The answers to these questions deserve to be the focus of clinicians and researchers, especially since virtually nothing is known about the incidence and experience of PMS in different age groups.

Menstruation

Menstruation, which occurs monthly in most premenopausal adult women, is a biological event that helps define the person as a woman. Since premenstrual syndrome is the result of a dynamic interrelationship between biological and psychological events, it is important to examine various attitudes toward menstruation and how they might determine premenstrual symptom formation.

Early psychodynamic theory hypothesized that menstruation intensified any unresolved unconscious conflicts about the female role, pregnancy, childbirth, uncleanliness, or penis envy (Bertram, 1930; Chadwick, 1932, 1933; Benedek & Rubenstein, 1939a, 1939b; Menninger, 1939; Deutsch, 1945).

> Every woman's analysis shows that with the appearance of menstrual blood, cruel impulses and fantasies of both an active and a passive nature are awakened in her. . . . It is remarkable that so little attention has been paid to the fact that disturbances occur not only during menstruation but even more frequently, though less obtrusively, in the days before the onset of the menstrual flow [p. 99]. . . . I have found without exception and completely independent of the rest of the neurotic structure, the appearance of premenstrual tension in those cases in which one can assume with relative certainty the particularly strong desire for a child, but where there is such a strong defense against it that its realization has never been a remote possibility [p. 104]. . . . The onset of bleeding, however, terminates the fantasies of pregnancy . . . [p. 105] . . . premenstrual tensions are directly released by the physiological processes of preparation for pregnancy. I have now become so certain of this connection that in the presence of the disturbance, I anticipate finding conflicts involving the wish for a child at the core of the illness and the personality. [p. 106] (Horney, 1931)

Current analysts acknowledge the continuing existence of beliefs that menstruation, and hence the menstruating woman, is unclean, harmful, and dangerous; that bleeding means injury, danger, and illness; and that menstruation may also be seen positively as "growing up." These analysts, nevertheless, are more likely to emphasize other issues in women's lives. Notman (1982), for example, states that in her clinical practice, PMS is, at times, an expression of a woman's identification with a mother who was symptomatic. She also postulates that a woman's wish for a direct way to express aggression possibly has something to do with PMS. Girls have been socialized to be quiet, nonaggressive, and passive. If the direct expression of aggression is undesirable, perhaps women develop premenstrual symptoms instead of expressing aggression. Additionally, she hypothesizes that if a woman feels helpless to change her situation, premenstrual tension might reflect problems about control, power, and anger that cannot be expressed otherwise. Menstruation may even reenact an experience from the past that permits the woman to express dependency–autonomy needs that she would otherwise not feel able to express. Nadelson and colleagues (1983) hypothesize that premenstrual symptoms are somatic expressions reflecting body image and self-image concepts of femininity.

While agreeing with Nadelson and colleagues that menstrual cycle symptomatology may correlate with the woman's view of herself, others disagree as to what this correlation means. Some argue that retrospectively reported premenstrual symptoms reflect a woman's stereotyped beliefs about menstruation (Goldschmidt, 1934; Paige, 1971, 1972; Parlee, 1973, 1974).

DiNardo (1975) reported that women with a more positive body attitude experienced fewer menstrual cycle symptoms. Women with negative views of menstruation, perhaps because they expect to feel depressed and physically distressed, may cause themselves to feel worse than they otherwise would. DiNardo, however, did not distinguish between "menstrual" and "premenstrual," nor did she distinguish between premenstrual symptoms and PMS. Other studies can be found to support the belief that women's attitudes toward menstruation may effect their experience of premenstrual tension (Thompson, 1950; Fortin et al., 1958; Paulson, 1961; Shainess, 1961; Levitt & Lubin, 1967; Paige, 1971; Tarpin, 1976; May, 1976). These studies, unfortunately, also suffer from profound methodological flaws.

Woods and colleagues (1982a) studied 179 nonpregnant women residing in five neighborhoods of varying racial composition. They used an adaption of the Moos Menstrual Distress Questionnaire to assess premenstrual symptoms, the Menstrual Attitude Questionnaire to describe women's attitudes toward menstruation, and the Recollection of First Menstruation to measure the women's initial response to menstruation. They found that negative recollections of first menstruation had little effect on current menstrual symptoms. Women with current attitudes that menstruation was debilitating had higher scores on all PMS scales. Consistent with these findings is a study of 46 women with severe PMS (Osmun et al., 1983). Subjects were interviewed on Days 9 and 26 of their menstrual cycles for at least four cycles. Self- and observer ratings for depression, anxiety, irritability, hostility, and physical symptoms were obtained. Subjects also completed daily self-reports and a questionnaire to measure attitudes, superstitions, and misconceptions regarding menarche and menstruation. Results demonstrated that severe PMS also occurred in women with favorable psychosocial backgrounds who did not report negative experiences associated with menarche or menses.

Slade and Jenner (1980a) asked 108 student teachers to complete a questionnaire measuring attitudes to female social roles, the Cattell's 16 Personality Factor Questionnaire, the Neuroticism Scale of the Eysenck Personality Inventory, the Femininity Scale of the California Personality Inventory, and the Moos Menstrual Distress Questionnaire (MDQ). The women scoring at extremes of the attitude scale (very traditional or very egalitarian) reported higher levels of menstrual, but not *premenstrual,* symptoms. High neuroticism scores were associated with premenstrual and menstrual symptoms, but extreme neuroticism scores were associated only with menstrual distress. Similarly, Berry and McGuire (1972) asked 100 women to complete the Moos MDQ and a Role Acceptance Scale. They found negative correlations between role acceptance and menstrual, but not premenstrual, distress. Furthermore, the origin of these symptoms did not appear to be psychological, since the Moos subscales that correlated negatively with role acceptance were dysmenorrhea, concentration, autonomic reaction, and control.

Ruble and Brooks-Gunn (1979) point out that something other than the experience of symptoms accounts for self-reported changes in symptom ratings. They cite studies showing that self-reports are influenced not only by manipulating a woman's level of awareness of her cycle phase but also by the purpose of the study. In a study illustrating this point, Ruble (1977) told 44 female undergraduates at Princeton University that they were participating in contraception-related research in which a new technique for predicting the expected date of menstruation from an EEG, having proven successful in older women, was being tested in young women. Unknown to the subjects, the scheduled day of testing was chosen specifically to correspond to the 6th or 7th day prior to next menses as estimated from menstrual history. On that day, the subject reported to a room containing a large oscilloscope with EEG electrodes. She heard an explanation of the study, completed a short medical history, and had her temperature and blood pressure recorded.

Then a 4-minute simulated EEG was obtained. The experimenter "read" the EEG, and the subject then experienced one of three events: (1) she was told she was premenstrual and her period was due in 1 to 2 days; (2) she was told she was intermenstrual and her period was not expected for 7 to 10 days; or (3) she was given no information. The subject then went to the connecting room, where a second experimentor administered the Moos MDQ. Women were told the nature of the study immediately after completing the questionnaire, and they were contacted later to document actual day of onset of menses. Women who were led to believe that they were premenstrual reported a higher incidence of premenstrual physical symptoms than women who were led to believe they were intermenstrual. On the other hand, women who believed they were premenstrual reported negative moods no more frequently than did women who believed they were not premenstrual. Ruble concluded that learned associations or beliefs may lead a woman either to overstate what she is actually experiencing or to have an exaggerated perception of normally fluctuating body states when she believes she is premenstrual. While we do not disagree with these conclusions, it is not clear how this would apply to women with PMS, since the women in this study were both younger and not complaining of PMS symptoms. It is fascinating that only physical symptoms were over-reported. This may reflect a tendency of that age group and of society in general to find physical symptoms less stigmatizing.

A second group of researchers also disguised the purpose of their studies (Englander-Golden et al., 1977). They presented 12 videotaped vignettes to 78 women (55 normal cycling controls, 18 on combination low-progestin oral contraceptives, 5 on other oral contraceptives) on two occasions, 2 weeks apart. After completing the purported "study," menstrual cycle phase was determined by asking the women where they were in their menstrual cycle and by obtaining the date of onset of the next menses. At the beginning of a debriefing session, the women were asked to complete a questionnaire on menstrual cycle symptomatology. The control women experienced the largest fluctuations in tension ratings across the menstrual cycle when compared to either group on oral contraceptives. The control women scoring in the lower half on pre-menstrual–menstrual symptomatology were, however, more consistent in their ratings of tension across the menstrual cycle than were the women who scored high on symptomatology. Results were interpreted as indicating that physiological symptoms may underly the variability in tension ratings across the menstrual cycle.

Englander-Golden and colleagues (1978) conducted another study where menstrual cycle phase was disguised. Both male and female undergraduate zoology students were asked to participate in a study of biological rhythms. For eleven weeks, subjects completed the Moos

MDQ daily (a condition that made the menstrual cycle not a salient part of the study). At the end of the study, female subjects were asked to complete the MDQ retrospectively (a menstrual-cycle-salient condition) in terms of "how you felt in the most recent premenstrual [5 days prior to menses], menstruating [menses], and midcycle [Days 13 through 7 prior to onset of most recent flow] phases of your menstrual cycle" (p. 79). Data were analyzed from 46 female students (26 taking and 20 not taking oral contraceptives). Only the retrospective questionnaires yielded cyclical variations in symptoms related to the menstrual cycle. Women not taking oral contraceptives reported severe symptoms during *menstruation*. Results were interpreted as supporting the hypothesis that making "the menstrual cycle a salient part of the study may exaggerate possible cyclical variations in moods and behaviors" (p. 76), possibly due to the influence of "broad cultural expectations pertaining to the menstrual cycle" (p. 84).

Others have cited stereotyped beliefs about menstruation as contributing to premenstrual symptomatology (Parlee, 1974; Steege et al., 1985; Au Buchon & Calhoun, 1985). They argue that to the extent that menstruation is viewed as debilitating, unpleasant, and dirty, the premenstruum will be experienced negatively as well.

Arguing against the effect of stereotyped beliefs and for the influence of hormones on the reporting of symptoms is another study in which menstruation was not a factor, since subjects were both postmenopausal and posthysterectomy (Magos et al., 1986a). In a prospective placebo-controlled study, 58 women were treated with subcutaneous estradiol implants or placebo implants. Norethisterone 2.5 or 5.0 mg or placebo was given daily for 7 days. Significant increases in severity ratings for pain, concentration, behavioral change, water retention, and negative affect were found in the group that received 5 mg daily of the progestin. The authors consider this hormonal model as suggestive of the etiology for PMS.

We believe that an individual woman understands her own menstrual cycle physiological changes based on the psychosocial context of the event, on her attitudes and expectations about the event, on her previous experience with menstruation, and on her personality structure. A woman's perceptions of both mood and performance are altered in regular ways across the menstrual cycle in a complex interaction of these relationships.

Caution must be exercised against generalizing from data on normal women to women with psychopathology. With regard to the latter:

> One hallmark of neurosis is the presence of unresolved oedipal conflicts. If intensity of sexual desire fluctuated with the cycle, so, presumably, would symptoms resulting from unconscious anxiety mobilized by desire. The

same type of cyclical fluctuation could be expected to result from aggressive urges, stemming from unresolved oedipal conflicts and resulting in cyclical anxiety and symptom formation. If the hypotheses above are valid, one could expect that the waxing and waning of symptoms would be triggered by physiological changes during the cycle, but the choice of particular symptoms would be determined by the form of the patient's neurosis. (Friedman et al., 1980, p. 734)

This needs to be documented scientifically.

PERSONALITY PROFILES

New understandings of attitudes toward menstruation must take into account the evolution of terms and concepts over time. "Femininity," for example, used to mean the desire to have children, passivity, and domination by hormones. Today, a woman may be considered feminine even though she is ambivalent about having children, is active, and is untroubled by hormonal fluctuations across the menstrual cycle.

Many studies have examined the personality profiles of women with PMS (see Blank et al., 1980, for a review of early studies). Early studies hypothesized that PMS is related to a woman's personality structure (Mira et al., 1985). While some discredit this hypothesis (Kleinsasser, 1976; DiNardo, 1975; Seagull, 1974; Golub, 1976a), others suggest that premenstrual mood changes are related to a woman's psychological adjustment (Wood et al., 1979; Hicks et al., 1986; Mohan & Chopra, 1987). Studies of the relationship between personality and PMS will now be described.

What type of woman complains of PMS? Do these women share any common personality factors? Levitt and Lubin (1967) reported more emotional instability in women who experienced serious premenstrual problems. Ivey and Bardwick (1968) found a greater number of premenstrual symptoms exhibited by women who, as children, had received special gratification from the sick role. The importance of these studies is not what they found, since all of the studies were methodologically flawed. Rather, they are good illustrations of the view of women during that decade. As late as the 1960s, women were viewed as emotionally unstable and as enjoying the sick role.

Taylor (1979b) used the Eysenck Personality Inventory (EPI), Cattell's 16 Personality Factor Questionnaire, and a prospective daily symptom rating scale with 65 "normal" women. He found a strong association between neuroticism and severe premenstrual symptoms. In his study, women with less severe premenstrual symptoms did not score high on neuroticism. While his use of prospective ratings was appropriate (see Chapter 6 for the importance of prospective ratings for the diagnosis of PMS), the women rated only 1 month of symptoms. Furthermore, he does not report whether he screened out women with other psychiatric or medical conditions. In addition, neurotic women may report and/or experience more premenstrual symptoms.

Maloney and colleagues (1982) gave 48 college women selected scales from the Guilford–Zimmerman Temperament Survey and found that negative personality characteristics were not associated with the premenstrual phase of the cycle. However, they used different women at the two cycle phases: 24 women were tested on Days 5–9, and another 24 women were tested on Days 20–25.

Watts and colleagues (1980) compared 25 women with and 25 women without PMS on the State–Trait Anxiety Inventory (STAI) and the EPI, Form B, and found that the PMS women scored significantly higher on the STAI–Trait and the EPI neuroticism scale. The diagnosis of PMS was made by retrospective history, however, and no statement was made of when in the menstrual cycle the inventories were given. Awaritefe and colleagues (1980) attempted "to relate personality to premenstrual tension" (p. 237) by studying 40 parous and 40 nulliparous Nigerian women. The women were divided into two groups. One group of menstruating women was instructed to complete the STAI, the Maudsley Personality Inventory (MPI), and the Premenstrual Symptom Checklist according to how they felt that week and the previous week. The second group, women who were not menstruating at the time they were tested, responded according to how they felt at the time of test administration. The Maudsley Personality Inventory did not discriminate between the groups. State anxiety was reported to be raised during the paramenstruum in both groups. The level of state anxiety seemed to be a linear function of the personality traits of anxiety. However, there were obvious flaws in the study. To begin with, the data on the premenstruum were retrospective. Worse yet, the premenstrual phase of the cycle was equated with the diagnosis of PMS.

Giannini and colleagues (1985) studied 71 women who believed they had PMS. Subjects completed the Peck–Abraham PMS Questionnaire, a self-rating scale of 23 items scored as not present, mild, moderate, or severe. On the basis of the summed scores, women were assigned to mild (26 subjects), moderate (24 subjects), or severe (21 subjects) PMS groups. Trait anxiety in these women was determined from the STAI. Fourteen subjects were randomly selected from among all subjects to obtain serum pseudocholinesterase levels on Day 1 of their menstrual cycles. Pseudocholinesterase, a possible marker for trait anxiety, was elevated in 43% of the severe PMS subjects, in 14% of the moderate PMS subjects, and in none of the mild PMS subjects. Thus a repeated finding seems to be that women with severe PMS are different from women with mild PMS. None of the subjects with mild PMS showed trait anxiety, while 25% of those with moderate PMS and 75% of those with severe PMS did manifest trait anxiety.

One study used prospective daily ratings to confirm that the symptomatic women did have PMS (91 women) and that the control women (33 subjects) were free of the disorder (Mira et al., 1985). The following questionnaires were administered on Days 6 and 21 of the menstrual cycle in a randomly designed fashion: General Health Questionnaire, STAI, and the EPI Neuroticism Scale. Women with PMS (1) scored higher than the normal controls on the State–Trait Anxiety Inventory at both menstrual cycle phases and (2) scored higher when in the luteal phase than in the follicular phase. Control women did not score differently between phases. There were no differences between groups on the General Health Questionnaire or on the Neuroticism Scale.

Stephenson and colleagues (1983) gave the Moos Menstrual Symptom Questionnaire (MSQ) to 423 college women in an initial sample and to 294 college women in a cross-validation study. Participants in the latter also took the EPI. Factor analysis of the MSQ revealed three variables related to the premenstruum: negative affect, water retention, and pain. Neuroticism scores on the EPI were positively related to all three. Again, this work was based on retrospective reporting of women without PMS.

Mohan and Chopra (1987) administered the MDQ and the Eysenck PEN Questionnaire to 32 women immediately before and then again after finishing menstruation. (The PEN is a personality questionnaire consisting of 78 items to measure Psychoticism [P], Extroversion [E], and Neuroticism [N] [Eysenck & Eysenck, 1968].) Those who scored at least one half of a standard deviation above the mean on the MDQ were classified as the high premenstrual tension (PMT) group, and those who scored at least one half standard deviation below the mean were classified as the low PMT group. The low PMT women scored low on both the neuroticism and psychoticism dimensions of the PEN. Conversely, the high PMT women scored high on neuroticism and psychoticism and demonstrated a significant decline in both scores after menses. In the postmenstrual phase, the high PMT women showed an increase in the extroversion/introversion dimension, while the low PMT group showed a decrease. The authors, however, used two separate menstrual cycles for measuring personality variations. A recent study of personality and anxiety variation around menses suffers from the same research design problem (Layton, 1988).

In contrast to the above studies, other researchers, who selected more homogeneous groups of women with PMS and who compared women with and without PMS, have shown that factors usually considered to be trait phenomena seem to change across the menstrual cycle in women with PMS. Halbreich and Kas (1977) administered the Taylor Manifest Anxiety Scale (TMAS) four times during the menstrual cycle (twice during the premenstrual period) to 28 women with PMS (diagnosed with prospective ratings) and 22 women without PMS. Women with PMS had higher scores on the TMAS throughout their monthly cycle, but their scores rose significantly during the premenstrual period.

The patterns observed in the Halbreich and Kas study are consistent with those seen on another scale, in this case a scale designed to measure a personality trait called locus of control (LOC). Locus of control has been defined by Rotter (1966) as a generalized expectancy that events are either more under personal control (internal) or controlled by external forces, such as fate, luck, or others (external). The locus of control scale is a brief, forced-choice questionnaire designed to measure the extent to which rewards are perceived as being internally or externally controlled.

Severino and colleagues (O'Boyle et al., 1988) measured locus of control in 76 women at two times in the menstrual cycle: during Days 5–10 and during the 6 premenstrual days. Based on prospective daily ratings, 55 women met criteria for PMS, while 21 did not. When compared with women who did not meet criteria for PMS, women with PMS had higher LOC scores both at Days 5–10 and premenstrually. Thus the PMS women felt generally more under the control of external forces than did women without PMS. In addition, the LOC scores of women with PMS rose significantly premenstrually, while the LOC scores in the non-PMS group did not. In other words, women with PMS perceived themselves even more under the control of external forces during the premenstruum than during the rest of the month. These authors also examined the relationship between LOC and the presence or absence of psychiatric diagnoses, determined by using the Schedule for Affective Disorders and Schizophrenia–Lifetime Version (SADS–L) in conjunction with Research Diagnostic Criteria. The presence or absence of a psychiatric diagnosis was not related to LOC scores.

Like anxiety and locus of control, women with PMS show mood changes that differ in pattern from women without PMS (Scambler & Scambler, 1985; Morse et al., 1988) (see also Chapter 3). Rubinow and colleagues (1986) studied women in three groups: 20 women with PMS, 20 women who thought they had PMS but were negative on prospective daily ratings, and eight women who knew they did not have PMS. Each participant completed daily visual analogue scale ratings of mood (depression, anxiety) on a twice-daily basis for 3 months following the initial screening. A.M. ratings were completed upon awakening; P.M. ratings were completed in the evening just prior to sleep. Little difference was observed between A.M. and P.M. ratings. However, when ratings were compared across groups, the 20 PMS-positive women showed regular increases of large magnitude in depressed mood prior to menses. In contrast, the 20 PMS-negative women showed mood fluctuations across the menstrual cycle that were not linked to the premenstruum. The normal controls looked very similar to the PMS-negative women. In addition, the PMS-positive group exhibited a postmenstrual elevated mood state that was not observed in women from the other two groups.

The Minnesota Multiphasic Personality Inventory (MMPI), a self-administered 550-item questionnaire widely used as a research tool for personality diagnosis, has also been employed in studies of PMS. Early studies of the MMPI correlates of menstrual distress (Gruba, 1975; Hain et al., 1970) were flawed, however, in the same ways that studies of women with premenstrual syndrome were flawed; that is, diagnoses were based on retrospective reports, and questionnaires were given only once during the menstrual cycle, preventing comparison of cycle phases.

Recent studies of more homogeneous samples of women both with and without PMS have shown menstrual cycle phase changes on MMPI scores. Hammond and Keye (1985) studied 111 women with premenstrual symptoms determined by both retrospective history and prospective charting. The MMPIs were valid in both the follicular and luteal phases. Mean scores on most MMPI scales (hypochondriasis, depression, hysteria, psychopathic deviation, paranoia, psychoasthenia, schizophrenia, social introversion, and anxiety) were significantly higher in the luteal phase. (Elevated scores are suggestive of psychopathology.) Scores on the ego-strength scale were significantly lower during the luteal phase in women with PMS.

Freeman and colleagues (1987) studied 133 women seeking treatment for PMS. In that mixed population, all MMPI scales except masculinity/femininity (M/F) and hypomania were lower in the follicular than in the luteal phase. However, women who met criteria for the diagnosis of PMS had significantly lower MMPI scores in the follicular phase than the remaining women who sought treatment for PMS. This suggests that the other women were more symptomatic during the entire menstrual cycle. These results were again reported by this group in a 1988 article (Trunnell et al., 1988). The authors underscored the importance of evaluating personality characteristics in the follicular phase to distinguish premenstrual syndrome from other psychopathology.

Stout and Steege (1985) also studied 100 women seeking help at a PMS clinic. When evaluated in the follicular phase, most of the women had normal MMPIs. The abnormal profiles were not strongly characterized by any particular personality type. The most common feature of the MMPI profiles was a very low M/F scale, which reflects a strong endorsement of the traditional feminine role.

Two other studies using the MMPI have been reported. Although the populations in both were small, these studies compared the MMPIs of women with and without PMS at both the follicular and luteal phases of the menstrual cycle (as did Freeman et al., 1987, above). Chuong (1986) compared 20 women with and 20 women without PMS, each of whom took the MMPI on Days 7 and 25 of the menstrual cycle. The control women showed no significant changes on MMPI scores between menstrual cycle phases, whereas the women with PMS were markedly more distressed during the luteal phase and showed a lowering of ego strength at that time. He also described two subgroups of women with PMS: (1) those with normal MMPIs in the follicular phase and dysfunctional levels during the luteal phase and (2) those with psychological stress and dysfunction throughout the cycle, with worsening of symptoms during the luteal phase. Hence he was able to differentiate women with PMS from women who had premenstrual exacerbations of other psychological dysfunctions (Chuong et al., 1988a).

The second study looked at 14 women with and 14 women without PMS (Keye et al., 1987). MMPIs of women without PMS were normal in both the follicular and luteal phases of the menstrual cycle. MMPIs of women with PMS were normal in the follicular phase but showed significant increases in depression in the luteal phase.

Severino and colleagues (1988) asked 42 women participating in a PMS study to complete the Personality Diagnostic Questionnaire–Revised (PDQ–R) (Hyler et al., 1986) during Days 5–10 of one menstrual cycle. Ten of these subjects also repeated the PDQ–R rating during the 6 days premenses. The PDQ–R is a self-report questionnaire that assesses personality disorders consistent with DSM-III-R criteria. It has good internal consistency and reliability, and it is considered useful as a screening instrument for efficiently assessing personality dysfunction. Of the 42 women, 64% met criteria for a global diagnosis of personality disorder. Forty-eight percent of the women qualified for a prospective diagnosis of PMS, and 24% of the women met prospective criteria for LLPDD. The presence or absence of a global personality disorder diagnosis was not associated with either the diagnosis of PMS or the diagnosis of LLPDD. Furthermore, a subject was not more likely to receive a personality disorder diagnosis in the luteal phase. The follicular phase PDQ–R total scores accounted for only 17% of the variability in mean symptom severity during the premenstrual phase of the cycle. Thus 83% of the variability in mean symptom severity during the premenstrual phase could not be attributed to the presence of a personality disorder.

In summary, we cannot describe one type of woman who complains of PMS, nor can we say that all women who complain of PMS share the same personality factors. What we can do is underscore several points. First, women seeking help for PMS frequently have other psychiatric problems (see below). Second, specific personality factors, as determined by the MMPI or PDQ–R, do not seem to be differentially related to specific premenstrual syndrome symptoms. Third, evaluating women during the luteal phase alone is of limited value in differentiating PMS from psychiatric disorders.

PSYCHOPATHOLOGY AND THE MENSTRUAL CYCLE

Epidemiological studies have looked at the co-occurrence of premenstrual syndrome and psychiatric disorders (Steege et al., 1985; Roy-Byrne et al., 1986b; Taylor et al., 1986). A recent survey of Swedish women (Hallman & Georgiev, 1987) compared a group of 83 women who reported that they had been absent from work during the previous year because of PMS with a group of 83 women with PMS but no history of absenteeism. The "absentee" group had significantly more severe symptomatology, both mentally and physically. They were also twice as likely to receive a formal diagnosis of "mental disorder." The nature of the relationship between psychopathology and PMS is still uncertain (Rubinow et al., 1987), however, as will be described below.

PMS and Affective Disorders

Women who complain of PMS have shown a high incidence of affective disorder (Schuckit et al., 1975; Wetzel et al., 1975; Halbreich et al., 1983; DeJong et al., 1985; Halbreich & Endicott, 1985; Endicott et al., 1986; Hallman, 1986; MacKenzie et al., 1986; Stout et al., 1986; Hart et al., 1987b; Pearlstein et al., 1987; Severino et al., 1987b; Dennerstein et al., 1988; Endicott & Halbreich, 1988). Severino and colleagues (Hurt et al., 1986) studied 58 women who believed that they had PMS. Thirty-five women (60%) had had one or more lifetime episodes of a psychiatric disorder (derived from the SADS-L interview) (Endicott & Spitzer, 1978). Of these 35 women, 63% had one or more past or current episodes of a depressive or anxiety disorder, and 34% met criteria for a present episode of affective illness. Only 23 of 58 women (40%) had clear histories without past or present episodes of psychiatric disorder. Comparably, Endicott and colleagues (1986) reported a 72% prevalence of any lifetime episode of psychiatric disorder among women recruited for a menstrual cycle study that did not specify premenstrual difficulties. These rates may, however, indicate only the prevalence of psychiatric disorders in women who volunteer for such studies.

Both Severino and colleagues (1987) and DeJong and colleagues (1985) confirmed the diagnosis of PMS in their subjects based on prospective daily symptom ratings. For both studies, it is important to note that the subject pools were comprised of women who believed that they had PMS and were self-referred or referred by a clinician to the research projects. Both observed a difference between the PMS-positive and the PMS-negative women with regard to incidence of psychiatric disorders. Severino found that 54% of the PMS-positive women (i.e., women who thought that they had PMS and were corroborated by the daily ratings) received a diagnosis of a psychiatric disorder, and 90% of the PMS-negative women (i.e., women who thought that they had PMS but who did not have supporting daily ratings) obtained a psychiatric diagnosis. DeJong and colleagues reported that 45% of the PMS-positive women had a significant psychiatric history; 88% of the PMS-negative women had such a history. In other words, there were more psychiatric diagnoses in women who did not have PMS yet had volunteered to participate in PMS research. The prevalence of psychiatric disorders was obviously higher than that in the general public.

The co-occurrence of psychiatric disorders and PMS, especially affective disorders, may in part reflect the lack of differentiation of these two disorders from each other, partially as a result of the evolution of psychodiagnostic nomenclature (Haskett et al., 1984). Beginning in the 1970s, efforts have been directed at standardizing criteria for the identification of homogeneous groups of patients and have been aimed at phenomenology rather than at underlying psychodynamics. Yet only in 1987 has the *Diagnostic and Statistical Manual of Mental Disorders* (DSM-III-R) (American Psychiatric Association, 1987) included a specific diagnostic term in its research appendix to connote a disorder related to the menstrual cycle, i.e., LLPDD. The clinical syndrome is described in terms of its essential and associated features, and inclusionary and exclusionary criteria are specified (see Chapters 2 and 6). Use of DSM-III-R will greatly increase the likelihood that investigators throughout the world, regardless of theoretical orientation, will agree on the category of behaviors represented by LLPDD.

Affective Disorders and PMS

A less extensive literature is available from the opposite perspective. Women with affective disorders have been said to have a higher incidence of PMS than women either with no affective disorder or with another psychiatric diagnosis (Hrbek & Navratil, 1971; Diamond et al., 1976; Kashiwagi et al., 1976; Endicott et al., 1981; Hurt et al., 1982). But the diagnosis of PMS in these studies was based on retrospective histories.

Price and DiMarzio (1986) obtained PMS symptom profiles in 25 patients with rapid-cycling disorder and 25 normal controls. Patients with rapid-cycling affective disorder had an increased tendency to have more severe forms of PMS. Also, those patients with both bipolar illness and more severe forms of PMS tended to cycle more frequently.

Menstrual Cycle Exacerbation of Psychiatric Illness

Women with other psychiatric diagnoses may have disorders that are affected by the phase of their menstrual cycle. Usually this involves an exacerbation of symptoms premenstrually (Malikian, 1987). For example, women with depressive disorders may feel more depressed premenstrually than at other phases of the menstrual cycle but find that their symptoms do not remit regularly and completely with the onset of menses (Roy-Byrne et al., 1987a). The diagnosis of PMS or LLPDD *should not be made* in a women who is experiencing only a premenstrual exacerbation of another psychiatric disorder. However, a woman may have PMS or LLPDD in addition to another psychiatric disorder if she experiences premenstrual symptoms that are markedly different from those she experiences as part of the psychiatric disorder.

The menstrual cycle can modulate symptoms of preexisting psychopathology in several different ways. First, it can result in an exacerbation of psychiatric symptoms. Reports of the exacerbation of symptoms of both schizophrenia (Williams & Weekes, 1952; Glick & Stewart, 1980) and mood disorders (Dalton, 1959a; Mandell & Mandell, 1967; Tonks et al., 1968; Janowsky et al., 1969) are available.

Second, there are anecdotally described clusterings of episodically experienced symptoms of psychiatric disorders, such as bulimia. Leon and colleagues (1986) studied 45 women with bulimia. On the basis of daily ratings of mood and physical symptoms, women were divided into two groups, one with PMS and the other without PMS. The investigators concluded that there were no changes in binge frequency across the menstrual cycle, since the subjects binged often in all menstrual cycle phases. Unfortunately, since they did not compare within subjects, potential differences from the mean across-cycle phases would have been overlooked. They instead compared one subject's level of binge eating to that of the others. In addition, their results were in part obscured by the fact that nearly half of their subjects were taking anti-depressants or tranquilizers.

Another study has looked at premenstrual exacerbations of binge eating in 15 normal-weight women with bulimia (Gladis & Walsh, 1987). These investigators did find a statistically significant premenstrual increase in binge eating. They suggest two possible explanations for this exacerbation: (1) reproductive hormones produce a biological drive to eat in all women, including those with bulimia; and (2) reproductive hormones may lead to mood changes (specifically, increased anxiety or depression), which in turn increase the desire to binge. Consistent with these findings, Price and colleagues (1987b) asked ten women with bulimia to keep weekly records of their binges for 2 months. These ten women binged more during the luteal phase of the menstrual cycle (Days 15–30) than during the follicular phase (Days 0–14).

Early studies of menstrually related fluctuations of anxiety in normal women produced mixed results, a finding that is actually not too surprising (Golub, 1976b; Lahmeyer et al., 1982; Veith et al., 1984; Van Den Akker & Steptoe, 1985). Better correlations were found with psychiatric patients. Yet Sandberg and Endicott (1986) have reported that anxiety patients diagnosed with Panic Disorder or Agoraphobia with Panic Attacks met criteria on the Premenstrual Assessment Form for autonomic physical syndrome, organic mental features, and impaired social functioning more often than did a comparison group. Cameron and colleagues (1986) reported a statistically significant peak in severity of anxiety premenstrually in 20 women with DSM-III defined panic attacks and in 10 women with other anxiety disorders. It is of interest, then, that sodium lactate infusions, which have been shown in many studies to induce panic attacks in approximately 72% of Panic Disorder patients, have been reported to induce panic at the same rate in women with PMS (60–80%) (Sandberg et al., 1987).

Still a third way that the menstrual cycle can modulate symptoms of other psychiatric conditions is as a *Zeitgeber* of periodic psychiatric disorders. This view implies that the expression of the disorder is dependent on menstrual cycle phase (Hatotani et al., 1962; Kolakowska, 1975; Endo et al., 1978). Over the years, case reports have been published of adolescents who experience psychotic episodes during the premenstruum. In 1952, Williams and Weekes described 16 females who had had either manic–depressive–manic or schizophrenic–catatonic psychotic episodes in the 4 days prior to menses. Six of these were teenagers: one 12-year-old, three 13-year-olds, one 18-year-old, and one 19-year-old. The 1960s witnessed the publication of three case reports of periodic psychosis of puberty (Wenzel, 1960; Altschule & Brem, 1963; Janowsky et al., 1967). In 1978, Endo and colleagues described seven cases of periodic psychosis related to the menstrual cycle. Episodes for six of the girls began in adolescence, and for five of these six girls they occurred premenstrually. Episodes for the other adolescent and the one woman occurred during menses. At 11-year follow-up, all of them had recovered completely, displaying no serious residual personality disturbances. Four women reported complete remission of symptoms after only 5 years.

The three most recent case reports (Teja, 1976; Felthaus et al., 1980; Berlin et al., 1982) are similar to each other in that all three young women were treated with oral progesterone, with good remission of symptoms (see Chapter 7, pp. 168–178, for a discussion of progesterone treatment).

While all of these studies underscore the validity of a menstrually related psychiatric condition, it is noteworthy that such a condition has been absent from the psychiatric diagnostic nomenclature (Berlin et al., 1982). In this regard, there are case reports scattered throughout the literature of periodic psychoses in adult women that are very similar to those cited above in adolescents (Blumberg & Billig, 1942; Dennerstein et al., 1983; Schmidt, 1943; Williams & Weekes, 1952; Lingjaerde & Bredland, 1954; Lederer, 1963; Verghese, 1963; Endo et al., 1978; Gerada & Reveley, 1988). Still, the exact relationship between psychopathology and PMS is unclear (Gannon, 1981; Clare, 1983a, 1983b).

Rate of Psychiatric Admissions

Psychiatric emergencies and hospital admissions increase during the premenstrual–menstrual phases of the menstrual cycle (Janowsky et al., 1969; Glass, 1971; Zola et al., 1979; Abramowitz et al., 1982; Dalton, 1984). Luggin and colleagues (1984) assessed menstrual cycle phase at the time of admission to Danish hospitals in 121 women, aged 20–39, and showed that most admissions occurred during menses and were not influenced by age, diagnosis, or tendency for premenstrual symptoms.

Frequency of Suicide and Suicide Attempts

Suicide attempts and completed suicides have also been reported to be highest during the premenstruum (MacKinnon et al., 1959; Tonks et al., 1968; Mandell & Mandell, 1967; Wetzel & McClure, 1972; Birtchnell &

Floyd, 1975; Pallis & Holding, 1976). The most recent study of suicide attempts, however, showed a time of cycle effect, but not a premenstrual one (Fourestie et al., 1986). The latter was a study of 108 women, 35 not on and 73 on oral contraceptives, who were studied within 24 hours of a suicide attempt by overdose on psychotropic medicines. One blood sample was taken from each woman on admission and on discharge from the hospital. This blood sample was assayed for estradiol, progesterone, and prolactin. The authors concluded that in the oral contraceptive nonusers, suicide attempts were associated with low plasma estradiol, with 42% of the attempts occurring during the week of menses and 12% occurring after the fourth week. Frequency of suicide attempts did not vary significantly during the menstrual cycle in women using oral contraceptives. Magos and Studd (1987) criticized the conclusion based on flaws in data analysis and cautioned against assuming etiology when the finding may simply be incidental.

As many authors point out (Lahmeyer, 1984; Shangold & Shangold, 1984; Abplanalp, 1985; Ghadirian & Kamaraju, 1987), it is unclear at this time what the relationship is between affective disorders and PMS or between psychiatric emergencies, including suicide attempts, and the premenstrual phase of the menstrual cycle. We must first distinguish premenstrual phase statistics from premenstrual syndrome statistics, then between PMS and women with a psychiatric disorder, before we can determine whether (and when) women with PMS are at risk for suicide.

Frequency of Deviant Behavior

Other psychopathology has also been associated with the paramenstruum. Violent crime (Morton et al., 1953; Dalton, 1961; D'Orban & Dalton, 1980), shoplifting (Fisher, 1984), and accidents (Dalton, 1960b; Liskey, 1972; Friedman et al., 1978; Patel et al., 1985) have all been reported to be increased during the premenstrual–menstrual phase of the menstrual cycle. These reports need reevaluation in light of current criteria for defining PMS.

Drug Use

There are reports that women with PMS may increase alcohol (Halliday et al., 1986; Bartlik, 1987; Price et al., 1987a) and/or marijuana (Mello, 1986) consumption during the premenstruum. Griffin and colleagues (1986) found that in the absence of severe premenstrual dysphoria, there was no significant covariance between daily marijuana smoking and menstrual cycle phase. Mello and colleagues (1987), however, found that most women cigarette smokers (70–78%) increased tobacco smoking at the premenstruum.

Price and colleagues (1987a) asked 50 alcoholic and 50 nonalcoholic women to fill out the Abraham Menstrual Symptomatology Questionnaire (Abraham, 1983). A significantly greater number of alcoholic than nonalcoholic women were found to suffer from severe PMS. Bartlik (1987) looked at consecutive female admissions to an alcoholism rehabilitation facility. Of 31 admissions over an 11-month period, 10 were admitted during the 4 days prior to menses. This is significantly more than would be expected by chance ($p = 0.05$). An 81% increase in admissions occurred during the 8 days immediately prior to and following the onset of menses ($p < 0.05$). When the menstrual cycles were divided in half and all of the admissions occurring in each half were added together across subjects, 23 admissions occurred in the perimenstrual half and 8 admissions during the other half.

These results contradict the findings of Shen (1984). He looked at the hospital admission date of 33 alcoholic women and found that menses was the phase of the cycle with highest frequency of admissions. Only 2 of the 33 women were admitted during the premenstrual phase. The relationship of alcoholism and other drug abuse to PMS, therefore, remains unclear.

COGNITIVE BEHAVIOR AND THE MENSTRUAL CYCLE

There is an extensive literature on cognitive behavior and the menstrual cycle (See also Chapter 3, pp. 49–58) that has been carefully reviewed (Sommer, 1972a, 1973, 1982, 1983). Sommer reviewed nine studies of menstrual cycle effects on higher-level intellectual functioning. She found that only Dalton reported lower performance in the premenstrual and menstrual phases of the menstrual cycle. The lower performance was reported by schoolgirls regarding their weekly work and performance on standardized academic examinations. Other studies showed no phase differences, indicating that normal, healthy women appear to have stable high-level intellectual functioning independent of menstrual cycle phase.

Sommer reviewed 46 studies of other cognitive functions and perceptual–motor performance. These included studies of rote memory, spelling, verbal fluency, arithmetic, perceptual speed, digit symbol, time estimation, and other functions. Most studies showed no phase differences. One study found a premenstrual increase in verbal disfluency, one reported a premenstrual and a menstrual increase in kinesthetic aftereffect, and one showed a premenstrual lengthening of time interval estimates. Sommer therefore concluded that the evidence did not support the hypothesis that women are cognitively debilitated at menses.

Of 9 studies of cognitive style reviewed by Sommer, none showed menstrual cycle–phase differences. Basing her conclusion on 13 studies of coordination and reaction time, Sommer could find neither an increase nor a decrease in arousal in relation to the menstrual cycle. She concluded:

> Taking all of the reviewed studies in their entirety, the conclusion is that among the general population of women, menstrual cycle variables do not interfere with cognitive abilities—abilities of thinking, problem-solving, learning and memory, making judgments, and other related mental activities. There are indicators that the hormonal fluctuations of the cycle are evidenced in small changes in sensory acuity and sensitivity, and that there may be small effects on motor activity. The data on these sensory-motor effects are neither clear nor consistent. (Sommer, 1983, p. 86)

One study has looked at menstrual cycle effects on task performance, taking into account the particular task and the specific metric employed (Jensen, 1982). The actual results of the report are less important than the conceptual approach that is presented, that is, menstrual cycle effects on performance capacity are not all-or-none phenomena. The question we must begin asking, then, is not whether the menstrual cycle alters behavior, but what behaviors (if any) are altered, in what direction, and why?

BIOPSYCHOSOCIAL MODEL OF PMS

In 1977, Engel described a biopsychosocial model for understanding illness. He argued that understanding any illness solely from a biological point of view could not explain why some individuals experience as "illness" conditions that others regard as "problems of living." The conditions might include emotional reactions to life circumstances as well as somatic symptoms. It is the professional's responsibility to establish the nature of the problem and decide in which framework the problem is best treated. We advocate this model for understanding women with PMS.

No longer can we understand the whole person from only one viewpoint. Physiologically, women are cyclicly functioning human beings (Dyrenfurth et al., 1974). Psychologically, they have a unique development in the context of a sociocultural milieu (Bernsted et al., 1984). The biopsychosocial model applied to PMS would state that a defect in any one factor (biological, psychological, or social) is a necessary, but not sufficient, condition for the development of PMS. A biological defect may determine some features of PMS (e.g., premenstrual timing), but psychosocial factors may determine what symptoms the woman reports, when she reports them, and the severity and impact of her symptoms on her daily functioning. Premenstrual syndrome, according to this concept, would be the result of maladjusted interactions among biological, psychological, and social factors.

To understand women physiologically, one must understand the hormonal changes across the menstrual cycle and how these changes affect body–brain neural and endocrine functioning (see Chapter 1). During the course of the last 20 years, we have come to realize that estrogen and progesterone directly affect nerve cell functioning and thus have profound influences on behavior, mood, and the processing of sensory information (McEwen et al., 1984; McEwen & Brinton, 1987). Each of these factors is known to fluctuate during the normal menstrual cycle (Davis & McEwen, 1982). In addition, the gonadal steroid hormones modulate central neurotransmission through multidirectional processes involving multiple interactions of many different chemical substances. Long-term effects are also produced by estrogen and progesterone through their influence on protein synthesis (Majewska, 1987a, 1987b).

To be more specific, estradiol changes the number of neurotransmitter receptors in very discrete parts of the brain, to which the female brain responds characteristically and differently from the male brain. This sexual differentiation of the brain presumably occurs prenatally. In the absence of testosterone, the brain is "programmed" to cycle by default, leading to the female pattern of hormone release after puberty (Davis & McEwen, 1982). Sexual differentiation of the brain is thought to involve the action of testosterone perinatally on some aspect of the development of the serotonin system, either by its innervation of the basal hypothalamus or by its response to the female hormones, estrogen and progesterone (McEwen, 1985).

The role of these biological events in causing PMS is unclear (Rubinow et al., 1988). It may be that there is no hormonal abnormality in women with PMS; rather, the normal changes of the luteal phase may trigger the physical and emotional symptoms of PMS, depending on a combination of biological, psychological, and social factors as well as the woman's threshold for detecting changes. On the other hand, a single, specific biological cause for PMS has not been ruled out, nor has the possibility that there may be different biological factors underlying subtypes of PMS. These patterns of functioning can be influenced and shaped during development by learning and experience.

Family patterns, small-group relationships, society's expectations, and past and present cultural influences all have an impact on a woman. They do so not only in terms of events but also in terms of the symbolic meaning of an event to a particular woman. Thus the same event can influence two women differently, since each has a unique personality with different defenses and coping mechanisms. To understand PMS symptoms from a biopsychosocial viewpoint, one must realize that the symptoms result from contributions made by biological, psychological and social factors, as well as from interactions among these factors (Notman, 1982; Keye & Trunnell, 1986; Price et al., 1986; Halbreich et al., 1988; Morse & Dennerstein, 1988). This means that we must understand what particular biological events trigger symptoms of PMS, how the woman understands what is happening to her, and how she labels her symptoms. In addition, we must understand the impact of the social setting on how the woman labels her experience. In other words, if a woman is given information about her menstrual cycle phase, how much does this influence her attributing her symptoms to the menstrual cycle rather than to something else? Moreover, we must understand how all of these factors (biological, psychological, and social) are interacting to produce what is being experienced as a premenstrual symptom.

Such an integrated model has been described for understanding menstrual cycle effects on sleep and dreams (Severino, Bucci, & Creelman, in press). Although prior research (Benedek & Rubenstein, 1939a, 1939b; Swanson & Foulkes, 1968; Lewis & Burns, 1975) has demonstrated cyclical fluctuations of psychodynamic themes in dream content, Severino and colleagues (in press) report the existence of a cyclical cognitive pattern that is influenced by gonadal hormone changes across the menstrual cycle. They report evidence that there are psycholinguistic styles characteristic of different phases of the menstrual cycle, and that this variation in verbal expression (social) reflects a correspondence between hormone production (biological) and the ability to access and communicate nonverbal representations (psychological). Severino is currently comparing these changes in women with and without PMS.

The biopsychosocial model allows for the idea that behavior is simultaneously organized at many levels, that causes can simultaneously be effects, and that unitary explanations of etiology are often reductionistic (Severino, 1988).

CHAPTER 5

Proposed Etiologies

It is not known why the menstrual cycles of only some women are associated with severe symptoms. A variety of hypotheses have been proposed and some studied, ranging from biological to psychosocial approaches (Russell, 1972; Abplanalp et al., 1977; Warnes, 1978; Janowsky & Rausch, 1985; Ullman, 1985; Backstrom & Hammarback, 1986; Coulson, 1986; Haskett, 1987). Most of the research, however, has been flawed either in subject selection or in methodology. Only recently has the research community come to appreciate that the diagnosis of PMS must be based on prospective daily ratings (Vila & Beech, 1980; Bell & Katona, 1987). Further, any endocrine study must consider the rhythm of hormone secretion as well as absolute plasma concentrations.

Throughout this chapter, if the subjects were selected for research solely on the basis of retrospective histories, the text will be written "women with PMS." If the investigators used more rigorous selection techniques, we will note it in the text.

In this chapter, we present a comprehensive review of both the biological and the psychosocial hypotheses of the cause of PMS. This chapter provides a useful reference to the chapters on treatment options (Chapter 7) and management of PMS (Chapter 8), since many of the treatment approaches derive directly from specific hypothesized etiologies. The reader should bear in mind, however, that these studies of etiology, like those of symptoms and psychological parameters, are hampered by inadequate subject selection techniques, leading to dissimilar subject populations from study to study. Indeed, it is this point that may explain the plethora of conflicting results mentioned in the sections that follow.

BIOLOGICAL CAUSES

Because PMS typically occurs in women with regular ovulatory menstrual cycles, the *ovaries* must be involved. Cyclic ovarian steroid hormone production must be intimately connected to the syndrome. PMS does not occur in prepubertal girls, during pregnancy and anovulatory lactation, in postmenopausal women, or in oophorectomized women (Reid, 1985).

It is also important to remember that the relative concentrations or patterns of secretion of the ovarian steroids are meaningful only insofar as they relate to the response of target organs. Hormones are, by definition, substances that act as messengers at target organs. For PMS, important primary target organs are the brain, breasts, and uterus. Secondary effects (i.e., directed by the brain) also occur at the thyroid and adrenal cortex.

Thus, in the sections that follow, keep in mind the relationship between dynamic steroid hormone fluctuations and the other hormone or neurotransmitter that is being studied, for example, prolactin. In the absence of the ovaries, the other hormones will not induce PMS.

Furthermore, the ovaries are just one part of the reproductive axis.

> The regulation of the menstrual cycle involves a complex series of interactions between brain neurotransmitter systems, pituitary gonadotropins and ovarian steroids. Instead of representing the cause of the observed psychopathology, altered levels of peripheral hormones may be markers of changes in the central components of the [hypothalamic–pituitary–gonadal] HPG axis and recently, more attention has been directed towards the temporal patterns of circulating peripheral hormones rather than the absolute levels. Changes in peripheral hormone levels may be closely linked to fluctuations in central neurotransmitter systems that not only participate in the regulatory mechanisms of the menstrual cycle, but are capable of altering emotions and behavior (Reid, 1983). Further studies, in carefully characterized populations of women with PMS, should search for abnormal functioning in the dynamic systems that have been shown to be involved in the regulation of the normal menstrual cycle. (Haskett, 1987, p. 133)

Hormones

More than one hormone has been investigated for its relationship to PMS. Each is described below.

Ovarian Steriods

Historically, estrogen and progesterone were the first hormones implicated as the cause of PMS (see Chapter 2). Three theories were proposed: (1) progesterone deficiency (Israel, 1938), (2) estrogen excess (Frank, 1931), and (3) inappropriate ratios of the two steroids (Greene & Dalton, 1953). Other studies have attempted to induce symptoms using exogenous hormones, a technique that implicates progesterone as the hormone behind the syndrome.

Progesterone Deficiency. Israel (1938) proposed that insufficient luteal progesterone led to symptoms of PMS, based on three out of four uterine biopsies from symptomatic women. From this work and that of his contemporaries, the use of progesterone as a treatment began (see Chapter 7).

But is there really a progesterone deficiency in PMS? Research has been done using two approaches: measuring hormone levels and performing uterine biopsies. While many studies of hormones have been performed, the results are contradictory and inconclusive. Of 14 studies measuring progesterone levels in women with PMS, six found low progesterone levels premenstrually (Backstrom & Carstensen, 1974; Smith, 1975; Backstrom & Mattson, 1976; Abraham, 1978; Munday et al., 1981; Dennerstein et al., 1984a), one reported that only 30% of the subjects had low progesterone levels (Munday, 1977), two showed elevated progesterone (O'Brien et al., 1980; Backstrom et al., 1983a), and five found normal progesterone levels (Andersen et al., 1977; Andersch et al., 1979; Taylor, 1979a; Backstrom et al., 1983b).

An even more recent study also contradicts the progesterone deficiency hypothesis (Hammarback et al., 1989). These researchers took daily serum estradiol and progesterone samples for two consecutive months in 18 women prospectively diagnosed as having PMS. High luteal phase plasma estradiol and progesterone concentrations were positively correlated with more severe PMS.

Most of these studies looked at the absolute level of progesterone. This may not, however, be the crucial factor. It may be the turnover of progesterone in a given metabolic pathway that is important. Documentation of such a possible change, however, is difficult because of the variety of metabolic pathways and end products of steroids (Fotherby & James, 1972; Van de Wiele & Dyrenfurth, 1973).

Another major problem with the progesterone theory is that this hormone is also deficient relative to estrogen in the preovulatory phase of the cycle, when premenstrual symptoms are absent in the vast majority of women (see Chapter 3). In fact, it was during the follicular phase that Gillman (1942) was able to *induce* symptoms like those of PMS by injecting exogenous progesterone.

Other evidence arguing against a deficiency of progesterone in the late luteal phase as the cause of PMS stems from the results of a study of 83 infertile women who underwent timed endometrial biopsies for the assessment of luteal phase adequacy. Women with luteal phase defect, defined by the endometrial biopsies, reported the same severity of somatic symptoms of PMS and less severe psychological symptoms when compared to the women with normal luteal phases who were the controls (Ying et al., 1987).

Excess Estrogen. Frank (1931) reported that his patients with PMS appeared hyperestrogenic and suggested various means to rid the body of excess "female sex hormones," such as laxatives, diuretics, and roentgen (X-ray) therapy. Biskind (1943) hypothesized that the estrogen excess was due to decreased hepatic clearance of the hormone as a result of inadequate Vitamin B_6 in the diet.

Since that time, estrogen has been measured in women with PMS to confirm or disprove the hypothesis. Like the results from the progesterone research, studies of circulating estrogen concentrations have been very contradictory. Of the estrogen studies, five reported elevated estrogen levels during the late luteal phase (Backstrom & Carstensen, 1974; Backstrom & Mattson, 1975; Backstrom et al., 1976; Abraham, 1978; Munday et al., 1981) and five reported normal mean estrogen values (Smith, 1975; Andersen et al., 1977; Andersch et al., 1979; Taylor, 1979a; Backstrom et al., 1985).

Even finding the same concentration of estradiol may be misleading. It may be possible that some women have a larger number of receptors for normal levels of steroids, or that their receptors may have a greater affinity for the steroids. One study measured sex hormone binding globulin (SHBG) binding capacity in the plasma of 50 women with PMS and of 50 control subjects (Dalton, 1981). Women with PMS had lower SHBG binding capacity. If this reflects an increase in free estradiol at the tissue level, an estrogen–progesterone imbalance could ensue. An earlier study of 15 women with PMS, however, found no difference from normal in SHBG binding capacity (Backstrom et al., 1976).

Another approach to this problem is to look at ovarian hormone levels in relation to specific symptoms. Plasma estradiol concentrations were measured at the onset of breast tenderness (66 women), migraine (32 women), and depression manifested by suicide attempt (73 women) (de Lignieres, 1987). High estradiol levels were linked to cyclical breast tenderness, and low estradiol levels were linked to headache, migraine, and depression. Casper and colleagues (1987) have also related hot flushes to estradiol withdrawal. It is hard to reconcile the results of these two studies with actual symptom reports, however, since many women complain of both breast symptoms and depression, for example. If absolute amounts of hormone were causal, these two symptoms should not be able to coexist.

In addition, treatment studies using estradiol implants or percutaneous patches have been effective in treating menstrual migraine (Magos et al., 1983; de Lignieres et al., 1986) and PMS itself (Magos et al., 1984, 1986b). These techniques provide constant elevated plasma concentrations of estradiol. It was only when exogenous progesterone was administered in these treatment studies that symptoms began.

Thus the theory that excess or unopposed estrogen causes PMS cannot be supported. Indeed, a recent paper on recurrent premenstrual psychosis (following a puerperal psychosis) suggests that declining estrogen in the premenstruum could affect dopamine neurotransmission (Brockington et al., 1988). Neuroleptic drugs, which are effective in treating these psychotic episodes, act by antagonizing dopamine neurotransmission. Therefore, the *fall* in estradiol premenstrually may precipitate certain psychiatric symptomatology.

Reduced Progesterone/Estrogen Ratio. Proponents of this theory argue that it is not an absolute deficiency of progesterone or an excess of estrogen in the late luteal phase that causes PMS symptoms. Rather, it is an altered progesterone/estrogen (P/E) ratio (Greene & Dalton, 1953; Butt et al., 1983). Facchinetti and colleagues (1983) measured serial estrogen and progesterone concentrations during the menstrual cycle in eight women with PMS (diagnosis questionable) and in four control women. The P/E ratios in women with PMS were significantly lower than in the control women both 9 and 11 days before menses (when the women were asymptomatic) and 2 and 4 days before menses (when the women were symptomatic).

Varma (1984) studied 25 women with PMS (diagnosed prospectively) and 10 women without PMS. Women rated 14 symptoms from 0 (no symptoms at all) to 3 (severe) and could obtain a total score of 0 to 42 (severe on all 14 symptoms). Subjects were then divided into groups comprised of 12 women with severe PMS, 8 with moderate PMS, and 5 with mild PMS (cutoff scores were not stated). Bloods were drawn at 9:00 A.M. on Days 3, 7, 11, 15, 19, 24, and 27 of two menstrual cycles and assayed for estrogen and progesterone. Only 7 of the 12 women with severe PMS had low progesterone/estrogen ratios during the premenstruum. None of the other women showed altered ratios.

One study suggests that the pathophysiology of PMS is related to dynamic, time-related changes in levels of estrogen and progesterone (Halbreich et al., 1986). Seventeen women received a diagnosis of PMS after 1 month of prospective daily ratings. In addition, 4 met diagnostic criteria for a past major depression, 2 had a history of other affective disorders, and 11 met Research Diagnostic Criteria for "never mentally ill." The symptoms of premenstrual depression, anxiety–irritability, and decreased sexual interest in the 17 women were positively correlated with peak levels of progesterone as well as with a rapid decrease of progesterone over time. PMS symptoms were also positively correlated with the ratio between the rates of decrease over time of progesterone in relation to estradiol levels in those instances where progesterone levels rapidly decreased while estrogen levels gradually decreased. "In women in whom the two hormones changed simultaneously and at the same rate, no premenstrual changes were observed" (Halbreich et al., 1988).

Inducing Symptoms with Steroids. Several research approaches have been used to induce or mimic symptoms of PMS. Gillman (1942) injected progesterone during the follicular phase of the menstrual cycle and induced abdominal pain, headache, and other symptoms (see Chapter 7, p. 170).

Two studies have used postmenopausal women as subjects. Hammarback and colleagues (1985) re-created premenstrual symptoms in 22 postmenopausal women who were given replacement hormones. Eleven women were given Oestrogel® cream 3 mg percutaneously daily for 21 days followed by 7 estrogen-free days. In addition to the estrogen, the other 11 women were given lynestrenol (Orgametril®) 5 mg daily during the last 11 days of treatment. Women rated their moods daily for 1 to 6 months. Women who received only estrogen showed no cyclic changes in mood or physical symptoms. Women who took progestin showed significant cyclic patterns, with negative mood changes and physical symptoms starting 1 to 3 days after progestin was added, reaching maximum severity during the final days of treatment.

Similar results were obtained in a prospective study of 58 postmenopausal hysterectomized women who were asymptomatic of medical, psychiatric, or social problems (Magos et al., 1986a). The women received subcutaneous estradiol (50 mg) and testosterone (100 mg) implants (Organon) at regular intervals and remained asymptomatic. Norethisterone, 2.5 mg or 5 mg daily, or placebo was given for 7 days at a defined point. Under these conditions of stable estrogen concentrations, women experienced significant increases in symptoms of pain, decreased concentration, behavioral change, water retention, and negative affect with the 5 mg/day dose of the progestin but not with the 2.5 mg/day dose.

The third technique has been the use of oral contraceptives (see Chapter 7, pp. 181–184). Some women become symptomatic while on oral contraceptives, more so with sequential forms (Moos, 1968a), when progesterone concentrations rise with time (*Physicians' Desk Reference*, 1987; hereafter cited as *PDR*).

The fact that progesterone can induce symptoms argues against both a deficiency theory and the use of progesterone as treatment (see Chapter 7, pp. 168–178).

Impression. From the results of the research presented in this section, it seems likely that the two originally proposed etiologies of PMS, excess estrogen and deficient progesterone, are incorrect. Further, it is likely that progesterone is a major culprit in inducing symptoms. However, there is no consensus as yet. It does not appear conclusive that progesterone alone is responsible for the variety of symptoms that are experienced during the menstrual cycle. More research is required to elucidate fully the role of gonadal steroids.

Androgens

Clinical symptoms of PMS have raised questions about the role of androgens in producing the syndrome. For example, the positive association between testosterone and both sexual drive and aggression, and the exacerbation of acne premenstrually, imply that androgens might be involved.

The stromal tissue of the ovaries produces some androgens, primarily dehydroepiandrosterone (DHA) and androstenedione (Speroff et al., 1984). Stromal tissue normally accumulates at midcycle, leading to a rise in testosterone, DHA, and androstenedione at the same time that estradiol is rising (Abraham, 1974; Persky, 1974; Ribeiro et al., 1974; Vermeulen & Verdonck, 1976).

Backstrom and colleagues (1983b) studied daily testosterone and androstenedione levels across the menstrual cycle in patients at a PMS clinic, in nonclinic patients with PMS, and in women without PMS. They also categorized the groups according to high, medium, and low mood changes. They found no differences in androgen levels among these groups of women. Spironolactone, also known to be an effective treatment for some women with PMS (see Chapter 7, pp. 196–197), has some antiandrogenic properties (Cumming et al., 1982) but is probably not successful as a treatment based on these properties.

On the other hand, historically, testosterone was used to treat premenstrual distress (Greenblatt & Agusta, 1940; Schmidt, 1943; Freed, 1945, 1946; Stieglitz & Kimble, 1949; Rees, 1953a; Lingjaerde & Bredland, 1954). It was thought to be effective because of its ability to "neutralize" estrogens, which would be important according to the excess estrogen theory discussed above.

Recently, testosterone implants have been used in conjunction with estradiol implants as a successful treatment modality for PMS (Magos et al., 1984).

Impression. Since no differences in androgens have been found between women with and without PMS, and since raising androgen concentrations exogenously does not produce PMS symptoms, it seems unlikely that androgens are the cause of PMS.

Prolactin

Prolactin, which stimulates the breasts to secrete milk, is a protein hormone synthesized and secreted by the anterior pituitary gland. Secretion is predominantly under the inhibitory control of the hypothalamus, mediated by the catecholamine dopamine (see Figure 5.1). It has a circadian rhythm of secretion, with a secretory phase that begins during midsleep (Sassin et al., 1972; Nokin et al., 1972; Parker et al., 1973; Ehara et al., 1973). Prolactin release is stimulated by estrogen (McEwen, 1985), stress (Speroff et al., 1984), suckling (Noel et al., 1974), feeding (Quigley et al., 1981), and heat exposure (Mills & Robertshaw, 1981).

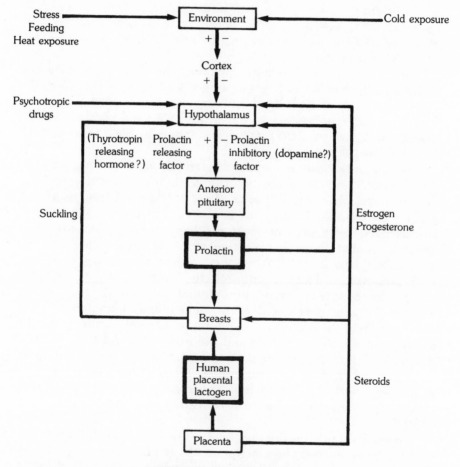

FIGURE 5.1 Prolactin regulation.
Adapted with permission from Speroff L, Glass RH, Kase NG (Eds): *Clinical Gynecologic Endocrinology & Fertility.* Baltimore, Williams & Wilkins, 1983, p. 252.

Horrobin (1973, 1978, 1979) first proposed prolactin as causing PMS on the basis of the effects of prolactin on sodium and water retention. Further, women complaining of fluid retention were often effectively treated with bromocriptine, a dopamine agonist that suppresses the secretion of prolactin. Premenstrual mastalgia improved in particular (Andersch, 1983).

Other characteristics of prolactin that would implicate this hormone in PMS are well summarized by Reid and Yen (1981). These include the following: (1) plasma prolactin reaches a peak level about the time of ovulation (Tamura & Igarashi, 1973); (2) mean prolactin concentrations are higher in the luteal phase than in the follicular phase (Tamura & Igarashi, 1973; Vekemans et al., 1977); and (3) conditions such as postpartum depression occur when prolactin levels are above normal levels (Kellner et al., 1984).

In general, research findings have been contradictory. Some studies report increased prolactin levels in women with PMS (Halbreich et al., 1976; Jeske et al., 1980; Biller & Brandt, 1986), while others report no significant differences between women with PMS and normal controls (Backstrom & Aakvaag, 1981; O'Brien & Symonds, 1982; Steiner et al., 1984b; Casper et al., 1989).

Steiner and colleagues suggested that particular PMS symptom profiles depended on the interaction of prolactin with gonadal steroids in the late luteal phase (Steiner et al., 1984a). High prolactin associated with low estrogen would theoretically result in a premenstrual syndrome characterized by depression, whereas high prolactin but low progesterone would result in a premenstrual syndrome characterized by irritability and hostility. When they studied 37 women with severe PMS, however, and compared prolactin levels on Day 9 and Day 26 of the menstrual cycle, they found no specific relationship between prolactin levels and PMS. Steiner and colleagues (1984b) also measured the circadian secretory profiles of serum prolactin in two women with severe PMS and two women without PMS on Days 9 and 26 of the same menstrual cycle. They found no difference in the hormonal rhythms between groups. Prolactin levels were elevated in the late luteal phase of all four women, suggesting that this is the characteristic pattern of a normal menstrual cycle and not indicative of PMS.

Impression. Prolactin does not seem to be the etiological factor underlying PMS. Further, bromocriptine, the treatment option based on the prolactin etiology, suppresses prolactin quite effectively but does not control the symptoms of PMS (except those associated with the breasts; see Chapter 7, pp. 191–194).

Mineralocorticoids

Aldosterone is a steroid hormone secreted by the adrenal cortex that acts on the distal convoluted tubule of the kidney to promote retention of sodium and excretion of potassium. Urinary aldosterone excretion across the normal menstrual cycle rises slightly at midcycle, continues to rise in the luteal phase, peaks premenstrually, and falls at menstruation (Reich, 1962). Progesterone also causes sodium excretion, which in turn may trigger the release of aldosterone (Sundsfjord & Aakvaag, 1972).

As described in Chapter 3, many studies report that women with PMS experience weight or fluid changes premenstrually. When Janowsky and colleagues (1973) studied 11 women with PMS on a metabolic ward for 15 menstrual cycles, they found increases in (1) anxiety, hostility, and aggressiveness; (2) weight; and (3) urinary sodium–potassium ratios premenstrually. All of these factors dropped dramatically with menses. Since the urinary sodium–potassium ratios were similar to the aldosterone excretion curve described by Reich (1962), Janowsky and colleagues (1973) hypothesized an aldosterone etiology for premenstrual symptoms.

More recent studies, however, have not found any difference in plasma aldosterone levels between patients with premenstrual syndrome and controls (Steiner & Carroll, 1977; O'Brien et al., 1979). Munday and colleagues (1981), for example, measured plasma aldosterone by radioimmunoassay in 20 women with PMS (diagnosed prospectively) and 20 women without PMS on four to six occasions during the luteal phase, between 10:00 A.M. and 3:00 P.M. There were no significant differences in plasma aldosterone levels between PMS and non-PMS women.

On a side note, in Conn's syndrome, a disorder characterized by high aldosterone levels, there are no psychological disturbances similar to PMS (Harrison et al., 1966).

Alternatively, Janowsky hypothesized that angiotensin, a substance whose pattern of secretion is parallel to that of aldosterone, may cause the cyclic symptoms. Both angiotensin and renin are elevated during the luteal phase (Rausch & Janowsky, 1982). Renin is a proteolytic enzyme secreted mainly by the kidney in response to various factors, such as plasma osmolality. Renin catalyzes the production of angiotensin II from its precursor molecule. Angiotensin II then has several actions, including inducing the adrenal cortex to release aldosterone. Results of studies of the role of these hormones in PMS have been contradictory. Although some research showed that a minority of women had highest plasma renin activity as late as cycle Day 28 (Katz & Romfh, 1972;

Kaulhausen et al., 1973, Schwartz & Abraham, 1975), others found that the peak of plasma renin during the luteal phase was followed by a sharp decline 6 days before menses (Steiner & Carroll, 1977). Plasma renin activity, aldosterone levels and atrial natriuretic peptide concentrations do not seem to play a direct role in PMS (Davidson et al., 1988).

Impression. It is not clear that any of the usual hormones associated with fluid retention are responsible for the constellation of PMS symptoms. This has not stopped many clinicians from prescribing diuretics, however (see Chapter 7, pp. 195–202).

Thyroid

Because of the similarity of symptoms between patients with thyroid disorder and patients with PMS (temperature dysregulation, weight gain, lethargy, fatigue, irritability, nervousness, and anxiety), it is surprising that thyroid hormone is one of the most recent hormones to be implicated in the etiology of PMS. Brayshaw and Brayshaw (1987) found that 100% of women with PMS (20 women) exhibited an abnormally high response to thyrotropin-releasing hormone (TRH) challenge. The study, which has been criticized by many because of its methodology (Dalton, 1987b; Hamilton, 1987; Logue & Moos, 1987; Rubinow & Schmidt, 1987b; Steege & Nemeroff, 1987), has nonetheless encouraged others to study this hormone.

Roy-Byrne and colleagues (1987b) measured thyroid-stimulating hormone (TSH) responses to TRH during the follicular and luteal phases of the menstrual cycle in 14 women with prospectively confirmed premenstrual syndrome and in nine control subjects. There were no differences in basal TSH or maximal increases in the TSH values between menstrual cycle phases within or between the two groups of women. However, seven of the ten women with PMS showed significantly greater variability in their TSH response to TRH. Three of the seven women showed blunted responses, and four showed augmented responses. None of the nine control subjects showed this variability.

The abnormal responses were not confined to the luteal phase, however. Some of the seven women with abnormal responses to TRH had a past history of affective or anxiety disorder, compared to none of the controls. Thus an abnormal response to TRH stimulation may define a subgroup of women with PMS and constitute a marker for a more severe course of illness.

Impression. Not enough data have been published either to include or exclude the hypothalamic–pituitary–thyroid axis as a factor in PMS. PMS, however, is not simply masked hypothyroidism (Schmidt et al., 1987b; Casper et al., 1989; Holtz & Halbreich, 1989).

Insulin and Glucose Metabolism

Similarities between certain symptoms of PMS (irritability, nervousness, cravings for sugar, and fatigue) that are also common symptoms of hypoglycemia have led to the hypothesis that premenstrual symptoms may be caused, in part, by abnormalities in glucose metabolism across the menstrual cycle. These abnormalities, in turn, are postulated to be the result of differing estrogen concentrations across the cycle.

Using an oral glucose tolerance test, Morton (1950) found that a majority of women with premenstrual tension had subclinical hypoglycemia premenstrually, as indicated by a low or flat plateau-type curve or a normal curve with a delayed fall in the fourth hour to below initial fasting levels. The premenstrual and postmenstrual oral glucose tolerance curves of these women, compared with a standard normal glucose tolerance curve, can be seen in Figure 5.2. Bear in mind, however, that Morton does not state the population that provided the "normal" curve, a point that is crucial in comparing the PMS data. His findings are consistent with those reported 36 years later in a research abstract by Vliet (1986). The complete data for this recent study, however, did not appear in our literature search.

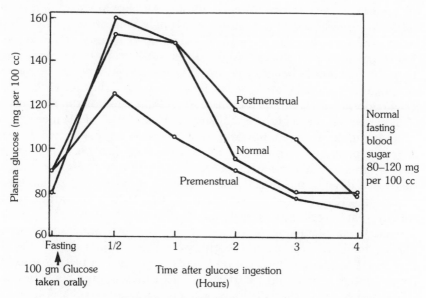

FIGURE 5.2 Glucose tolerance curves.
Adapted with permission from Morton JH: Premenstrual tension. *Am J Obstet Gynecol* 60:343–352, 1950.

In a study of ten women without PMS, Jarrett and Graver (1968) administered oral glucose tolerance tests across the menstrual cycle. They showed that there was a progressive decrease in glucose tolerance (i.e., higher glucose values) following ovulation, with a prompt increase in glucose tolerance near the onset of menstruation, and a return toward normal in the postmenstrual week. They postulated that their findings were the result of modification of carbohydrate tolerance by endogenous estrogen. Thus tolerance would be greatest when estrogen is lowest (during menstruation), with subsequent deterioration of tolerance as estrogen production increases. Other investigators have reported similar data (Okey & Robb, 1925; Asinelli & Casassar, 1936; Roy et al., 1971). These studies suggest changes in glucose metabolism in all cycling women, regardless of whether they have PMS.

One study of 19 women without PMS refutes these findings. Spellacy and colleagues (1967) reported no differences in glucose tolerance across the menstrual cycle using an intravenous glucose tolerance test. However, only two points in the menstrual cycle were measured (Day 5 and Day 25), and such a large dose of glucose was injected (25 gm) that changes in glucose handling may have been masked.

Reid and colleagues (1986) studied changes in glucose, insulin, and glucagon responses to an oral glucose challenge at different phases of the menstrual cycle in five women without PMS and in six women with PMS who complained of premenstrual hypoglycemic attacks. They also looked at the role of endogenous opiates in glucoregulation. They found that responses to oral glucose did not differ significantly between follicular and luteal phases in either group of women. Simultaneous infusions of naloxone (an opiate antagonist) did not significantly alter either the basal concentrations of glucose, insulin, and glucagon or the responses of these measures to a glucose challenge at either phase of the menstrual cycle. It should be noted, however, that the study was conducted across different menstrual cycles. The women were studied on 2 successive days of the follicular phase (between Days 1–6) of one cycle and 2 successive days in the luteal phase (between Days 22–26) of another menstrual cycle. Four of the six women with PMS had symptoms of tremor, diaphoresis, fatigue, palpitation, or headache in *both* the follicular and luteal phases of the cycle during the fourth hour of the oral glucose tolerance test. Although glucose values reached their nadir at that hour, no plasma glucose level fell below 50 ng/dl, a plasma glucose concentration that would be consistent with these symptoms. The authors conclude: "Whether PMS women with alleged PMHA [premenstrual hypoglycemic attacks] truly experience symptoms only during the luteal phase, when cravings for sweets may abruptly increase the amounts of chocolate and refined carbohydrates in their diet, or whether they are merely more aware of symptoms due to heightened anxiety and tension of premenstrual syndrome is not known" (p. 1171). From the failure of naloxone to influence glucoregulation they speculate either: "(1) that the dosage of naloxone [1 mgm/h for the 5-h oral glucose tolerance test] was insufficient to effect receptor blockade within the pancreatic islets . . .; (2) that EOPs [endogenous opiate peptides] act at other types of opiate receptors which are unaffected by naloxone; or (3) that EOPs exert no glucoregulatory actions" (p. 1171). Similarly, Denicoff and colleagues (1987) studied ten women with PMS and found no hypoglycemic changes that were specific to the luteal phase, nor were the hypoglycemic symptoms characteristic of PMS.

Studies of insulin receptor concentrations in women without PMS show that there is a lower specific cell-binding fraction in circulatory monocytes in the luteal phase than in the follicular phase of the menstrual cycle (DePirro et al., 1978). Further data suggest that sex hormones may play a role in the control of insulin receptors. Bertoli and colleagues (1980) have demonstrated an inverse relationship between insulin binding to monocytes and levels of 17B-estradiol, progesterone, and 17A-hydroxyprogesterone. In other words, hormonal control of insulin receptors seems to control affinity and binding, not receptor concentration. What is lacking is information about the premenstruum (i.e., the late luteal phase, when estrogen and progesterone levels are rapidly decreasing) and data to suggest whether women with PMS are the same as or different from women without PMS.

It is also important to remember that what is happening peripherally may not be happening centrally (Both-Orthman et al., 1988). We know, for example, that insulin in the cerebral spinal fluid does not fluctuate following acute changes in peripheral insulin but rather changes more gradually over time.

Estrogen may also modulate other hormones related to feeding and satiety, such as neuropeptide Y (NPY). This 36-amino-acid peptide increases alertness (personal communication from Eric Corp, Ph.D., Westchester Division, The New York Hospital, 1987) and stimulates feeding in rats (Morley & Levine, 1985), the latter by a mechanism as yet not understood. (Insulin, on the other hand, induces sleepiness in rats [personal communication from Eric Corp].) NPY may have a direct effect on neurons involved in eliciting this feeding response. It may release opioid peptides, which in turn lead to feeding behavior, or it may stimulate catecholamine release, resulting in increased food intake (Clark et al., 1984). Both endogenous opiates and catecholamines have been implicated in PMS etiology, as will be discussed later. Estrogen is known to alter NPY concentration in the brain by producing a sequential rise and fall in concentration that parallels the rhythm of luteinizing hormone releasing hormone (LHRH). "These data support the hypothesis that NPY is involved in the regulation of LH secretion either by regulating LHRH secretion or perhaps by a direct action on the pituitary" (O'Donohue et al., 1985). Whether NPY is involved in PMS remains to be determined.

Impression. The results of these studies suggest that while glucose handling may differ according to the phase of the menstrual cycle, these findings may not be specific for PMS. Further, there is no clear evidence that women with PMS have hypoglycemia.

Neurotransmitters

At some time in the future, the brain must gain more attention as an organ that responds to ovarian steroids (Klaiber et al., 1982; Donovan, 1987; Steiner, 1987; Majewska, 1987a, 1987b) and that, therefore, has a role in producing premenstrual symptoms. At this time, studies of estrogen and progesterone effects on brain functions are limited by the need to use animal models. These studies have shown that ovarian hormones have both direct and indirect actions on nerve cell functions (Pfaff & McEwen, 1983; McEwen, 1988). Estrogen, for example, inhibits the synthesis of the enzyme tyrosine hydroxylase, which in turn decreases the production of dopamine in the basal hypothalamus. Dopamine in this part of the brain is involved both in the control of prolactin release and in the control of ovulation. Research has not, however, explained how the individual ovarian hormonal changes during the premenstruum influence the capability of certain neurons to release neurotransmitters. Such a conceptualization may ultimately explain the diversity of symptoms and their timing more satisfactorily.

Both biogenic amines (Rojansky et al., 1989; Spinell; et al., 1989) and endogenous opiates (Chuong et al., 1985) have been implicated in the etiology of PMS. Each will be discussed below.

Biogenic Amines

Interest in the role of monoaminergic neurotransmitters (norepinephrine, serotonin, and acetylcholine) in PMS stems from two sources: (1) the effect of catecholamines on the regulation of salt and water balance (Reid & Yen, 1981) and (2) the role of biogenic amines in determining mood (Asberg et al., 1975). The exact interactions of gonadal hormones and neurotransmitters are unknown (Brush, 1979).

Most research to date has used animal models, which show that both gonadal hormones and neurotransmitters interact with the hypothalamic–pituitary system to regulate sexual behavior and ovulation.

Catecholamines. Two studies, one in women with PMS (Weiner & Elmadjian, 1962) and the other in women without PMS (Patkai et al., 1974), reported increases in urinary epinephrine excretion during the premenstruum. These studies, however, did not discriminate between central and peripheral catecholamine metabolism. In another paper, DeLeon-Jones and colleagues (1978) measured the urinary metabolite of central norepinephrine (3-methoxy-4-hydroxyphenolglycol, or MHPG) (see Figure 5.3) in four healthy women on a daily basis and found a marked increase in MHPG excretion during the late luteal phase, with a rapid decline 2 days before menstruation. This raises the possibility of a link between premenstrual dysphoria and depression, since some individuals with depression have decreased MHPG excretion (Beckman & Goodwin, 1975).

Consistent with the findings of DeLeon-Jones and colleagues, Ghose and Turner (1977) found an increased sensitivity to tyramine premenstrually. Tyramine displaces norepinephrine (NE) from cytoplasmic mobile pools of NE, leading to sympathomimetic effects. Tyramine sensitivity thus reflects increased presynaptic norepinephrine activity. Ghose and Turner (1977) studied five healthy women (aged 23–45) at the beginning of the week between 10:00 and 10:30 A.M. and between 1:00 and 1:30 P.M. for 4 consecutive weeks. Each woman received a rapid injection of intravenous tyramine. From dose response curves, the amount of tyramine required to increase the systolic blood pressure by 30 mm Hg was determined. The women required significantly less tyramine during the premenstrual week. An increased receptor sensitivity to tyramine would compliment the finding of the decreased norepinephrine activity measured by DeLeon-Jones and colleagues and could represent upregulation of receptors due to decreased availability of neurotransmitters.

Schrijver and colleagues (1987) studied urinary excretion of MHPG in 19 women with PMS and 19 women without PMS on Days 5, 11, 17, 21, and 25 of one menstrual cycle. Excretion of MHPG by the PMS women during all 24-hour periods investigated was significantly higher ($p = 0.009$) than that of their matched controls. Schrijver's research group, like DeLeon-Jones and colleagues, observed more MHPG excretion in the luteal phase of the menstrual cycle in women without PMS. Women with PMS did not show this late luteal phase increase.

Serotonin. Serotonin has also been implicated as an etiological factor in PMS (Labrum, 1983), based on the relationship of this neurotransmitter to depression. In depressed patients, decreased sero-

Catecholamines: epinephrine, norepinephrine

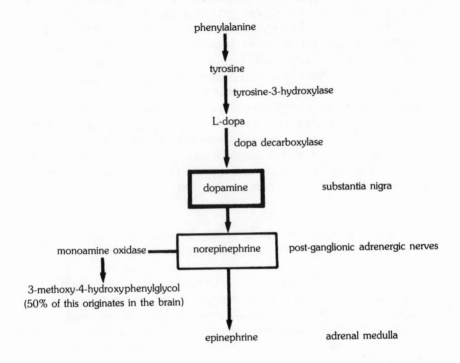

Indoleamine: serotonin

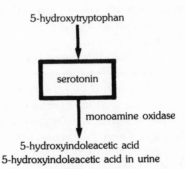

FIGURE 5.3 Metabolism of monoamines.

tonergic activity (Ashcroft et al., 1966; Coppen, 1968; Van Praag et al., 1973; Asberg et al., 1976) and decreased serotonin uptake by platelets (Hallstrom et al., 1976; Tuomisto et al., 1979; Rausch et al., 1981; Stahl et al., 1982) have been reported. Since blood platelets have a high affinity uptake mechanism for serotonin, and since blood platelets can store and release serotonin, platelets have been used as a biological model for serotonergic presynaptic nerve endings (Sneddon, 1973; Stahl et al., 1982). Using this model, Tam and colleagues (1985) hypothesized that if the premenstruum is associated with an increased biological susceptibility to depression, there should be an associated decrease in platelet 5-hydroxytryptophan (5-HT), the precursor to serotonin (see Figure 5.3). This group studied six normal women prospectively across three menstrual cycles, measuring mood and platelet 5-HT uptake on Days 1, 10, and 24. They found a significant linear rise of negative affect across each cycle, peaking on Day 1. However, no significant correlation was obtained between mood scores and platelet 5-HT uptake. In another study of normal women, the urinary metabolite of serotonin (5-hydroxyindoleacetic acid) was found to be highest in the follicular phase, lower in the luteal phase, and lowest during the premenstruum (de Tejada et al., 1978).

Studying symptomatic women, Taylor and colleagues (1984) and Ashby and colleagues (1988) reported reduced platelet uptake of serotonin among women with premenstrual tension in the week before menstruation, and Rapkin and colleagues (1987) reported lower serum serotonin levels during the last ten days of the menstrual cycle in 14 women with PMS compared to 13 women without PMS.

Carr and colleagues (1987) took plasma from PMS patients and controls and extracted lipid soluble substances. Sixty microliters of reconstituted extract (equivalent to 300 microliters of plasma) were incubated with tritiated 5-HT and control platelets. Premenstrual plasma extracts from PMS patients caused a greater inhibition of 5-HT uptake than either postmenstrual extracts from the same patients or premenstrual samples from controls. These findings support the hypothesis that PMS may be related to an endogenous plasma factor that alters platelet serotonergic mechanisms.

One research group postulates that serotonin may be etiologically important in PMS, based on their work with people who crave carbohydrates (Wurtman, 1988; Wurtman & Wurtman, 1989). Carbohydrate craving in obese patients has been successfully treated with D-fenfluramine, a serotonergic drug. This treatment has also been proposed for patients with seasonal affective disorder and with PMS, since both syndromes may involve carbohydrate craving as symptoms (Chapter 7, pp. 236–237). However, not all women with PMS crave carbohydrates, so it is not at all clear how generalizable such a theory or treatment may be.

These studies seem to suggest that women who are symptomatic premenstrually are different from women who are not symptomatic with regard to serotonergic activity. For this reason, these studies deserve replication, with attention given to stringent diagnosis of PMS and to careful exclusion of depressive states. In other words, the following questions remain unanswered: (1) Is serotonin pathophysiologically relevant to PMS? (2) If so, are changes pathognomonic for the late luteal phase mood state? or (3) Is serotonin alteration an epiphenomenon of depressive states in general?

Monoamine oxidase (MAO) is a major enzyme in the catabolism of biogenic amines (see Figure 5.3). Plasma MAO activity has been reported to be significantly greater in the luteal than in the follicular phase of the menstrual cycle in regularly menstruating women (Klaiber et al., 1971; Briggs & Briggs, 1972). Platelet MAO activity was found to peak during the ovulatory interval (n = 13 normal women) and to be lowest 5 to 11 days later in the luteal phase (Belmaker et al., 1974). A recent study compared platelet MAO activity in women with PMS and in normal controls (Hallman et al., 1987). Women with PMS (n = 29) had significantly lower platelet MAO activity than the controls (n = 20). No variation in platelet MAO was found over the menstrual cycle in either group of women, contradicting the report of Belmaker and colleagues. The findings of Hallman and colleagues, however, are consistent with those of Feine and colleagues (1977), who found no significant variation in platelet MAO across the menstrual cycle in 12 women with PMS.

Rapkin and colleagues (1988a), on the other hand, were unable to find a difference in platelet monoamine oxidase B activity in women with PMS compared to normal controls. Diagnoses were given prospectively. They did not detect a phase of menstrual cycle effect on enzyme activity, estradiol or progesterone concentrations at any point across the menstrual cycle. Rapkin and colleagues suggest that their work differs from others (Hallman et al., 1987, for example) in subject selection or platelet isolation techniques.

As with the serotonin studies, these studies suggest differences between women with and without PMS with regard to monoamine metabolism. The same need prevails, however, for replication studies with stringent inclusion criteria.

Neurotensin. Neurotensin (NT) is an endogenous tridecapeptide that interacts with central nervous system dopamine neurons (Nemeroff et al., 1989). It has been suggested that "NT may be an important endogenous modulator of dopaminergic neurotransmission" (p. 17), and therefore the investigators measured cerebrospinal fluid (CSF) NT concentrations in women with PMS. However, the population studied was comprised of psychiatric inpatients who had PMS according to research diagnostic criteria (RDC). Actually, the diagnosis of PMS is not specified by RDC. In any event, this research group did not find any difference in CSF NT concentrations between normal control women and women with PMS. It is also unclear when in the menstrual cycle any of the samples were obtained. Thus, no conclusions about NT in PMS can be drawn from this study.

Acetylcholine. Acetylcholine has also been implicated in PMS as a result of two clinical observations: (1) a hormonal influence on acetylcholinesterase leading to a menstrually related remission of myasthenia gravis (Vijayan et al., 1977) and (2) the mood altering effects of physostigmine, a centrally acting cholinomimetic drug (Janowsky et al., 1972).

Impression. Clearly more research will be required to elucidate fully the role of neurotransmitters in PMS. The serotonin connection is a particularly intriguing one in light of its putative role in major depression.

Endogenous Opiates

The endorphins are one class of brain peptides. The word *endorphin* denotes both their endogenous origin in the brain and their morphine-like action. Beta-endorphin is 5 to 10 times more potent than morphine on a molar basis (Speroff et al., 1984).

Cyclic changes in endogenous opiate activity during the menstrual cycle have been implicated in the pathophysiology of PMS (Cohen et al., 1981; Halbreich & Endicott, 1981; Peck, 1982; Wehrenberg et al., 1982; Reid & Yen, 1983; Tulenheimo et al., 1987). Yet, with the exception of one study (Facchinetti et al., 1987), beta-endorphin levels do not appear to change significantly during the luteal phase (Hamilton et al., 1983; Tulenheimo et al., 1987; Reame et al., 1989). Facchinetti and colleagues (1987) measured plasma beta-endorphin levels every 2 to 3 days for 1 month in 11 women with PMS and in 8 asymptomatic women. No changes of beta-endorphin levels were recorded for the women without PMS. Women with PMS showed a decrease of plasma beta-endorphins in the week preceding menses and during the first days of menstrual flow. The problems with this study, however, were that (1) the diagnosis of PMS was based on retrospective reports, and (2) blood sampling began and ended at midcycle, which meant that the follicular and luteal phases were from two different menstrual cycles.

Facchinetti and colleagues (1988) reported another study of endogenous opiates in PMS. Nine women with unconfirmed PMS and seven women without PMS participated in two naloxone challenges, the first 3 to 5 days after ovulation and the second one 7 to 8 days later than the first challenge. Ovulation was predicted by the rise in basal body temperature. The investigators again inferred transient decreases in opioid tone during the late luteal phase of the menstrual cycle, but only in the women with PMS. In addition, normal women maintained LH release in the presence of naloxone (see next paragraph). Thus, Facchinetti and colleagues (1988) claimed to have supported their previous finding (Facchinetti et al, 1987) that women with PMS have decreased beta-endorphins premenstrually. However, the study had sufficient methodological flaws to warrant additional work in order to substantiate this etiology.

Intravenous beta-endorphin causes a decrease in luteinizing hormone (LH) levels in normal male and female subjects (Reid et al., 1981). A chronic inhibitory effect of endogenous opiates on gonadotropin secretion in humans has been deduced from the finding that naloxone, an opiate receptor antagonist, causes an increase in LH concentration in female subjects (Quigley & Yen, 1980). Naloxone does not stimulate LH release in the early follicular phase, but it does cause a marked increase in LH in the midluteal phase. Since LH level is low at both these times, the differential response to naloxone is accounted for by hypothesizing that endogenous opiate activity is minimal in the follicular phase and maximal in the luteal phase (Quigley & Yen, 1980).

It has also been suggested that the high endogenous opiate activity in the midluteal phase may result in (1) increased appetite, manifesting itself in binge eating, and (2) diminished release of norepinephrine or dopamine, resulting in fatigue and depression (Halbreich & Endicott, 1981). Acute withdrawal of endogenous opiates just prior to menses may lead to rebound hyperactivity of opioid receptors, resulting in symptoms of irritability, anxiety, tension, and aggression (Schwartz et al., 1978; Giannini et al., 1984). Variations in degree or duration of endogenous opiate exposure and the acuteness of withdrawal could explain the differences in symptoms and their severity from month to month.

Impression. At this time, the role of endogenous opiates in PMS is unclear. Even so, two treatment regimens have been proposed based on an endogenous opiate theory: clonidine and naltrexone. These will be described in Chapter 7, pp. 233–234 and 237, respectively.

Circadian Rhythms

Changes in circadian processes may be important in the psychological and physiological symptoms experienced by women who suffer from premenstrual syndrome (Luce, 1971; Hoes, 1980; Watts et al., 1985).

Temporary desynchronization of circadian rhythms is the central mechanism underlying the dysphoria and sleep disturbances experienced by shift workers (Folkard & Monk, 1985) and by travelers suffering from jet lag (Minors & Waterhouse, 1976). Obviously, women do not suffer from PMS because they have traveled across time zones. However, it is plausible that PMS symptoms may be related to a change in the timing of rhythms across the menstrual cycle. This concept is based on many similarities between the symptoms of jet lag and PMS. Both syndromes are transitory, usually lasting from 2 to 7 days. Both include nocturnal sleep disturbance and daytime sleepiness. Mood changes and difficulty concentrating on tasks are common to both. Physical symptoms are also shared by both but differ in nature—jet lag sufferers do not have breast swelling or pelvic discomfort, for example. Both, however, may be characterized by nausea and changes in appetite.

There is some precedent from other psychiatric syndromes for speculating that shifts in phase relationships among circadian rhythms could underlie PMS. In patients with endogenous depression, for example, evidence suggests that several circadian rhythms have abnormally advanced phases relative to the sleep–wake cycle. Most prominent among these are the rhythms of REM sleep and cortisol (Kupfer, 1984; Wehr & Goodwin, 1981; Kupfer et al., 1988).

The gonadal hormones that govern the various events making up the human menstrual cycle are known to have effects on the period, phase, and amplitude of biological rhythms in other mammals. Estrogen has been shown to modulate the period of the rest–activity pattern during the estrous cycle in hamsters (Moline, 1981) and to modify the circadian timing and amplitude of the LH surge in female hamsters (Moline et al., 1986). Estrogen and progesterone modulate the ultradian period and amplitude of LH release in monkeys (Wehrenberg & Dyrenfurth, 1983). Free-running studies of menstruating women conducted in laboratories without time cues where the subjects self-select all events (sleep, meals, etc.) according to their internal biological clocks, also suggest that the sleep–wake cycle lengthens during menses compared to the preceding luteal phase of the cycle (Daniel R. Wagner, M.D., personal communication, 1988). In a recent paper, Lee (1988) showed that the phase of the rectal temperature rhythm was advanced in the follicular phase in one subject when compared to her temperature pattern in the luteal phase.

Melatonin is another hormone with a robust circadian rhythm whose secretion is modified in depression (Rosenthal et al., 1984). Melatonin is an indoleamine produced by the pineal gland. Its usual circadian pattern in women consists of low serum values in the day and high serum levels at night (Arendt, 1985). The hormone has well-described inhibitory effects on the reproductive systems of other species, predominantly in seasonal breeders. It may also be a modulator of menstrual cyclicity in women (Webley & Leidenberger, 1986). Morning melatonin concentrations have been measured across the menstrual cycle and have been found to be highest during the premenstrual–menstrual phases and lowest at ovulation (Wetterberg et al., 1976). The circadian pattern also changes across the menstrual cycle, shown by calculating a melatonin index and then by comparing menstrual cycle phases (Webley & Leidenberger, 1986). The melatonin index represents the total exposure to melatonin in 24 hours that rises above the nadir daytime concentration. The melatonin index increases significantly during the luteal phase and falls significantly before ovulation. Furthermore, there seems to be a positive relationship between melatonin and progesterone (Webley & Leidenberger, 1986), suggesting a mutual reinforcement between the two hormones and menstrual cycle events.

In view of the clinical reports of women with PMS requiring more sleep during the premenstruum, it is interesting to note that melatonin is reported to prolong sleep in humans when given exogenously (Cramer et al., 1974). The only study of melatonin profiles in a woman with PMS found no significant difference in premenstrual versus follicular phase baseline levels of melatonin. However, only one woman was studied, and she also had Seasonal Affective Disorder (Parry et al., 1987).

The circadian rhythms hypothesis states that PMS may be due to changes in period, phase, and/or amplitude of rhythms governed by the circadian timing system that occur in conjunction with the hormonal changes of the human menstrual cycle. In support of this view, one study of women with periodic psychosis recurring in association with the menstrual cycle reported disturbed circadian rhythms of serum 11-hydroxycorticosteroids (Endo et al., 1978). Severino, and colleagues, in a pilot study of one woman with PMS (Severino et al., 1987a), looked at the circadian rhythms of temperature, cortisol, and rapid eye movement (REM) sleep 3 days preovulatory and 3 days premenstrually. Since these three rhythms are thought to be controlled by the same biological clock, the authors predicted that similar phase changes would occur in all rhythms. However, the rhythms did not show consistent phase relationships at both menstrual cycle phases. If this is true only of women with PMS, then the symptoms of PMS may be due to desynchronization of phase relationships among circadian rhythms during the premenstruum. Further research is ongoing in the authors' laboratory to test this proposed etiology.

On the other hand, Steiner and colleagues (1984b) studied the circadian secretory profiles of growth hormone and cortisol in two women with severe PMS and in two women without PMS. Blood samples were obtained every 30 minutes over a period of 24 hours in each woman both on Day 9 (follicular phase) and on Day 26 (luteal phase) of the menstrual cycle. They found no relationship between the hormonal secretory profiles and PMS.

Roy-Byrne et al. (1986a) obtained results somewhat consistent with those of Steiner and colleagues (1984b). Yet they also found menstrual cycle phase-related changes in cortisol response to dexamethasone in 21 *normal* subjects. These subjects had higher post-dexamethasone cortisol values at midcycle compared with the early follicular and late luteal phases. While this abnormal dexamethasone response is reminiscent of the response in depressed patients, it seems inconsistent given that many PMS patients complain of depression, but not around the time of ovulation. However, it is possible that a hypothalamic–pituitary–adrenal axis dysfunction in PMS might be characterized by an *absence* of such a menstrual cycle phase-related pattern or by an abnormal dexamethasone suppression test (DST) at more than one phase. Further, these data do not necessarily contradict the circadian rhythms hypothesis. Only cortisol's pattern was examined, and the circadian hypothesis looks at phase relationships *among* different rhythms.

Impression. At this time, the role of the circadian timing system in the etiology of PMS is unclear. Further research will be needed to define circadian patterns of hormone release as well as the patterns of other rhythms, such as sleep, that appear to be altered in women with PMS.

Prostaglandins

Prostaglandins (PGs) are acidic lipids first identified in fresh human seminal fluid and in a coral *(Plexaura homomala)*. The family of prostaglandins with greatest biological activity have two double bonds and are derived from arachidonic acid (Speroff et al., 1984). Arachidonic acid is found as a constituent of meat (Moncada et al., 1985) or can be formed from its precursor, linoleic acid, which is found in vegetable seed oils, in human milk (Horrobin, 1983b), and in evening primrose oil (Horrobin, 1983a). The rate-limiting step in the formation of the prostaglandin family is the release of free arachidonic acid (Figure 5.4). Afterward, the synthetic path can go in two different directions: the lipogenase pathway or the cyclooxygenase pathway. The cyclooxygenase pathway leads to the prostaglandins (see Figure 5.4). Besides arachidonic acid, the other two precursor fatty acids are linoleic acid, which gives rise to the PG_1 series, and pentanoic acid, the PG_3 series (see Figure 5.5). The numeric subscript refers to the number of double bonds (Speroff et al., 1984).

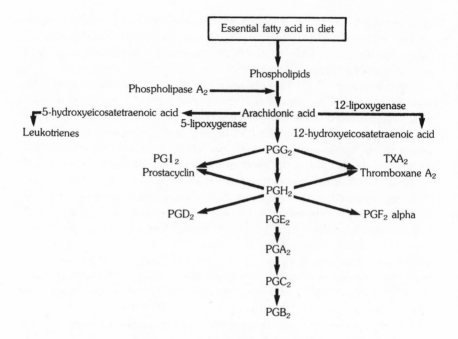

FIGURE 5.4 Prostaglandin biosynthesis.

Adapted with permission from Speroff L, Glass RH, Kase NG (Eds): *Clinical Gynecologic Endocrinology & Fertility.* Baltimore, Williams & Wilkins, 1983, pp. 309–310.

Thromboxanes are not true prostaglandins, due to the absence of the pentane ring (see Figure 5.4), but prostacyclin (PGI_2) is a legitimate prostaglandin. Thromboxane A_2 (TXA_2) is the most potent vasoconstrictor known, while PGI_2 is a powerful vasodilator. Each has opposing effects on platelet function. TXA_2 stimulates platelet aggregation; PGI_2 inhibits platelet aggregation (Speroff et al., 1984).

The 2-series PGs are the prostaglandins important for sufferers from dysmenorrhea. Reducing the conversion of arachidonic acid to 2-series PGs (see Figure 5.6) with nonsteroidal anti-inflammatory drugs (i.e., antiprostaglandins such as Motrin, Ponstel, and Anaprox) brings relief from dysmenorrhea. There is little evidence, however, that the 2-series PGs play a part in PMS. Rather, it may be that PMS is related to a defective formation of PGE_1 (Horrobin, 1983a). Others, however, have hypothesized an excess synthesis of PGE_1 in premenstrual tension (Jakubowicz et al., 1984). (Not surprisingly, then, there are treatments based on raising and lowering prostaglandins! See Chapter 7, pp. 203–205 and 215–218).

Prostaglandins have been implicated as etiological agents in PMS for several reasons (Budoff, 1983; Jakubowicz, 1983): (1) prostaglandins generally increase in the luteal phase and decline during menses; (2) prostaglandin E_1 (PGE_1) seems to attenuate the biological effects of prolactin, specifically fluid retention, irritability, and depression (Horrobin, 1983a); and (3) pyridoxine, known to be essential to the metabolism of fatty acids to prostaglandin E_1, has alleviated symptoms in some women with PMS. The hypothesis is that premenstrual symptoms are the result of abnormal fatty acid metabolism, leading to low levels of PGE_1, which in turn result in an abnormal sensitivity to luteal phase hormones, including prolactin. Support for this view is based on a study of 42 women with PMS (Brush et al., 1984). Blood samples were taken during the follicular phase (Day 12 ± 2) and during the luteal phase (Day 21 ± 1) and analyzed for fatty acids in total plasma phospholipids. The levels of linoleic acid and alpha-linolenic acid were significantly above normal in women with PMS compared to normal controls. Thus there seemed to be no deficit of intake or absorption of the essential dietary fatty acids. However, concentrations of all linoleic acid metabolites were significantly reduced, suggesting a defect in metabolism. There seemed to be no defect in alpha-linolenic acid metabolism. Indeed, metabolites were elevated, possibly in compensation for the linoleic acid metabolism defect. As Brush and colleagues (1987) state, however, the essential fatty acid abnormality was present in both phases of the menstrual cycle and, therefore, cannot itself be the cause of PMS. Other studies have focused on impairment of 6-desaturation of linoleic acid to gamma-linolenic acid (Brush et al., 1987; Horrobin & Manku, 1987). One wonders, however, how the serum levels of prostaglandins

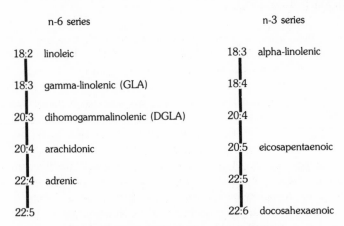

n-6 series   n-3 series

18:2 linoleic   18:3 alpha-linolenic

18:3 gamma-linolenic (GLA)   18:4

20:3 dihomogammalinolenic (DGLA)   20:4

20:4 arachidonic   20:5 eicosapentaenoic

22:4 adrenic   22:5

22:5   22:6 docosahexaenoic

FIGURE 5.5 Essential fatty acid metabolism.
(The first number indicates the number of carbon atoms in the molecule; the second number indicates the number of double bonds.)
Reprinted with permission from Horrobin DF: The regulation of prostaglandin biosynthesis by the manipulation of essential fatty acid metabolism. *Rev Pure Appl Pharmacol Sci* 4:339–383, 1983.

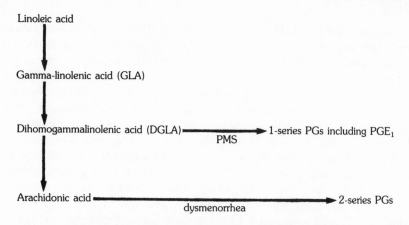

FIGURE 5.6 n-6 series essential fatty acid metabolism.
Adapted with permission from Horrobin DF: The role of essential fatty acids and prostaglandins in the premenstrual syndrome. *J Reprod Med* 28:465–468, 1983.

compare to tissue levels, since prostaglandins are secreted by organs and
act locally.

Impression. Prostaglandins have also been thought to influence hormonal and neurohormonal actions, as well as neurotransmission, in both
the peripheral and central nervous systems (Gross et al., 1977), and they
may play some role in PMS. At this time, however, prostaglandins
remain a very controversial area of clinical research.

Pyridoxine (Vitamin B$_6$)

As noted in Chapter 2, a deficiency of Vitamin B$_6$ was one of the early
theories of the cause of PMS (Biskind et al., 1944). Pyridoxine is one of
the three forms in which Vitamin B$_6$ occurs in natural sources. All three
forms (pyridoxine, pyridoxal, and pyridoxamine) are converted to the
physiologically active form of Vitamin B$_6$, pyridoxal phosphate, in the
body (Goodman & Gilman, 1965). Vitamin B$_6$ is absorbed rapidly from
the gastrointestinal tract, and short-term fluctuation in blood levels is
very likely. The recommended dietary allowance (RDA) for Vitamin B$_6$
is *2–4 mg per day.* RDA is based on the amount needed to prevent
deficiency disease. Pyridoxal phosphate serves an important role in
metabolism as a coenzyme for synthesis of brain monoamines (dopamine
and serotonin), which are hypothesized etiological factors in PMS (Reid
& Yen, 1981). A deficiency in pyridoxine could lead to reduced dopamine and serotonin concentrations (see Figure 5.7).

There are five major theories about the role of Vitamin B$_6$ in PMS.
The first was derived from the view that excess estrogen could lead to
PMS (Biskind, 1943; Biskind et al., 1944). The excess estrogen would be

the result of the failure of the liver to deactivate the hormone due to a Vitamin B_6 deficiency.

Second, dopamine and serotonin are both known to have important effects on mood and behavior. In addition, if dopamine is decreased, increased prolactin levels can lead to breast swelling and tenderness as well as other water retention symptoms characteristic of PMS (Delitala et al., 1976). However, there is no evidence to indicate that women with PMS have altered pyridoxine absorption or metabolism (Mira et al., 1988). In one study of 38 women, 19 with and 19 without PMS (Van den Berg et al., 1986), blood samples were collected in the morning of Days 6, 12, 18, 22, and 26. Twenty-four hour urine samples in separate night and day portions were collected on Days 5, 11, 17, 21, and 25. An oral tryptophan load was given on Days 11 and 25 after the 24-hour urine collection, and another urine collection was obtained during Days 12 and 26 until the next morning. (The oral tryptophan load followed by measurement of xanthurenic acid, an intermediate in the tryptophan–niacin pathway, is used as a functional index of Vitamin B_6 status.) No significant differences were found in plasma pyridoxal and pyridoxal-5-phosphate concentrations, the total erythrocyte glutamate oxaloacetate transaminase activity, the erythrocyte pyridoxine kinase activity, and the urinary 4-pyridoxic acid excretion between the two groups. However, the excretion of tryptophan metabolites before and after the oral tryptophan load was higher in the PMS group. With regard to the biochemical parameters of metabolism of Vitamin B_6, it was concluded that PMS is not related to a "cyclic" Vitamin B status (Van den Berg et al., 1986).

Third, since some women become depressed (iatrogenically) on oral contraceptives, a two-part theory of the depression was proposed. The estrogen component of the contraceptives would be responsible for altering tryptophan metabolism, leading to a functional pyridoxine deficiency (Adams et al., 1973; Winston, 1973; Rose, 1978). If elevated luteal levels of estrogen occur in some women with PMS, a similar functional pyridoxine deficiency could occur, leading to a decrease in

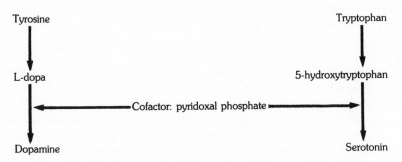

FIGURE 5.7 Pyridoxine and monoamine metabolism.

monoamine synthesis. "To date, however, there is no objective evidence to support the existence of either an absolute or a relative Vitamin B_6 deficiency occurring in women with PMS, nor is there any established link between ovarian function and the levels or activity of Vitamin B_6 that would explain the cyclic nature of symptoms in PMS" (Reid, 1985, p. 28).

Still a fourth reason for hypothesizing pyridoxine deficiency as an etiology for PMS derives from its action as a cofactor in prostaglandin formation from essential fatty acids. This has been discussed in more detail in the section on prostaglandins above.

The last possible role for B_6 in PMS pertains to its place in carbohydrate metabolism. (See the section on nutrition below, with specific references to Figure 5.10 and Figure 5.12).

Impression. None of the five hypotheses for the role of Vitamin B_6 deficiency as the cause of PMS has been proven. Yet support for the pyridoxine hypothesis continues as a result of some treatment studies in which pyridoxine has been shown to be superior to placebo for symptom improvement (see Chapter 7, pp. 207–213). By no means do all of the treatment studies affirm the efficacy of B_6, and we do not endorse this treatment modality. Furthermore, effective therapy does not prove etiology. In the absence of a measurable Vitamin B_6 deficiency, it seems reasonable at this time to consider pyridoxine deficiency as a possible contributor to PMS symptoms rather than as a primary causal agent.

Nutrition

It is unclear what role diet plays in the etiology of PMS. It is possible that diet, both amount and kind, can elicit certain changes that occur during the premenstruum (Reid, 1985). Conversely, the menstrual cycle can affect diet. Indeed, even women without PMS frequently mention changes in food cravings in the late luteal phase (Parlee, 1985).

A study of dietary patterns of women with PMS was conducted by Abraham and his associates (Goei et al., 1982). Fourteen women without PMS and 39 women with PMS were asked to complete a diet questionnaire. Women with PMS reported consuming more refined sugar, refined carbohydrates, and dairy products than women without PMS. Women without PMS reported consuming more vitamins in the B series, as well as more iron, zinc, and manganese.

Abraham studied the women with PMS in more detail and found that those who experience moderate to severe symptoms can be divided into four subgroups, each with its postulated characteristic nutritional deficiencies (Abraham, 1983, 1984). His work is emphasized in a review of nutritional factors in PMS written by Piesse (1984).

The most common subgroup, PMT-A (see Figure 5.8), consists of

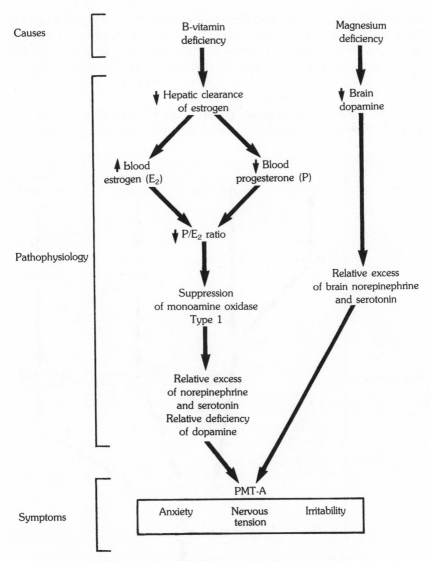

FIGURE 5.8 Postulated pathophysiology of Premenstrual Tension-A.
Reprinted with permission from Abraham GE: Nutritional factors in the etiology of premenstrual tension syndromes. *J Reprod Med* 28:446–464, 1983.

women who experience premenstrual anxiety, irritability, and nervous tension. Abraham has observed elevated blood estrogen and low progesterone in this subgroup, although, as discussed previously (pp. 95–100), many investigators have data that dispute this finding. Women in this subgroup consume an excess amount of dairy products and refined sugar according to Abraham (1983).

The second most common group, PMT-H (see Figure 5.9), is comprised of women who report symptoms of water and salt retention,

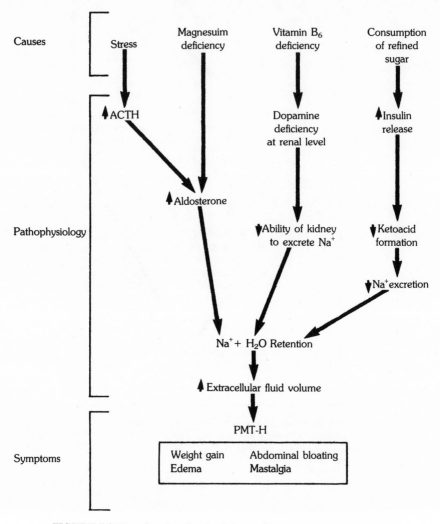

FIGURE 5.9 Postulated pathophysiology of Premenstrual Tension-H.
Reprinted with permission from Abraham GE: Nutritional factors in the etiology of premenstrual tension syndromes. *J Reprod Med* 28:446–464, 1983.

abdominal bloating, mastalgia, and weight gain. The severe form of PMT-H is associated with serum aldosterone levels that are increased manyfold above follicular phase concentrations (Abraham, 1983). This finding is debatable as being relevant to PMS (pp. 103–104).

PMT-C (see Figure 5.10) represents a group of women with premenstrual cravings for sweets, together with an increased appetite for and indulgence in eating refined sugar. These (delicious) habits were

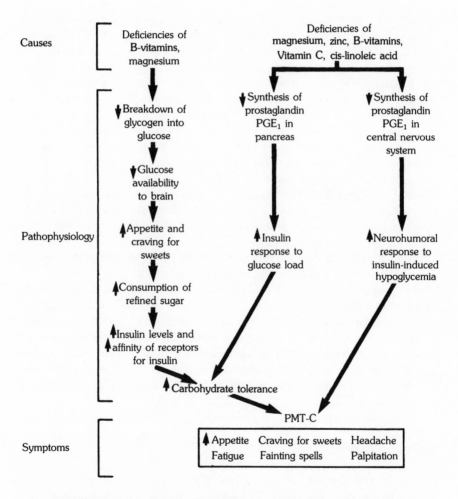

FIGURE 5.10 Postulated pathophysiology of Premenstrual Tension-C.
Susceptibility to PMT-C increases during late luteal phase because of premenstrual increases in insulin-binding capacity. Reprinted with permission from Abraham GE: Nutritional factors in the etiology of premenstrual syndromes. *J Reprod Med* 28:446–464, 1983.

unceremoniously followed by palpitations, fatigue, fainting spells, headaches, and sometimes the "shakes." These women are described as having increased carbohydrate tolerance and low red-cell magnesium (Abraham & Lubran, 1981; Abraham, 1982; Sherwood et al., 1986). Deficiency of prostaglandin PGE_1 may also be a contributory factor (Abraham, 1983), although this finding is also not certain, as discussed in the section on prostaglandins above.

The least common but most severe subgroup is PMT-D (see Figure 5.11). This group consists of women who become so depressed premenstrually that suicide is a risk. The symptoms are depression, withdrawal, insomnia, forgetfulness, and confusion. In ten PMT-D patients, the mean blood estrogen level was lower and the mean blood progesterone level was higher than normal during the midluteal phase (Abraham, 1984). Elevated adrenal androgens were observed in some hirsute PMT-D patients, as they would be for *any* hirsute woman. Two PMT-D patients with normal blood progesterone and estrogen had high lead levels in hair tissue and chronic lead intoxication (Abraham, 1983).

Abraham and colleagues (1981) studied 23 normal female volunteers, using a questionnaire on food intake, and found that on Day 18 through Day 6 of the next menstrual cycle there was a significant positive relationship between day of cycle and protein, fat, carbohydrate, and total energy intakes. They conclude that "the stability and consistency of the relationship between dietary intake and day of menstrual cycle that we have demonstrated, however, suggests that it is probably directly related to factors inherent in the cycle, and is not simply a secondary effect of alterations in mood" (p. 211).

Impression. Although Abraham's studies of dietary patterns are the most comprehensive in the literature, and although his hypotheses regarding nutrition and PMS symptomatology are carefully integrated (Figure 5.12), most of his data were published before prospective daily ratings were required for subject selection. All of his studies need replication using better-controlled methodology. It should be noted that his work has led to the development of a dietary plan and nutritional supplements (Chapter 7, pp. 219–224).

Allergic Reactions

Geber in 1921 and then Urbach in 1939 first described premenstrual urticaria (a skin eruption that itches), which they attributed to a hypersensitivity to some specific substance that appeared in the serum during the premenstruum. They based their conclusion on their observation that premenstrual urticaria could be reduced by injection of

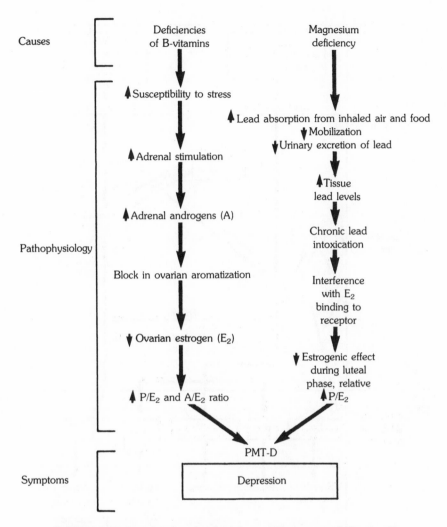

FIGURE 5.11 Postulated pathophysiology of Premenstrual Tension-D.
Reprinted with permission from Abraham GE: Nutritional factors in the etiology of premenstrual syndromes. *J Reprod Med* 28:446–464, 1983.

serum collected premenstrually. Only serum from affected patients resulted in successful desensitization (if administered repeatedly by intracutaneous injection) (Gerber, 1939).

Later, researchers hypothesized that PMS symptoms could be attributed to a hypersensitivity to endogenous hormones or to their metabolites (Zondek & Bromberg, 1947; Hartman, 1947; Meltzer, 1963). This was based on the observation that women with PMS showed a greater

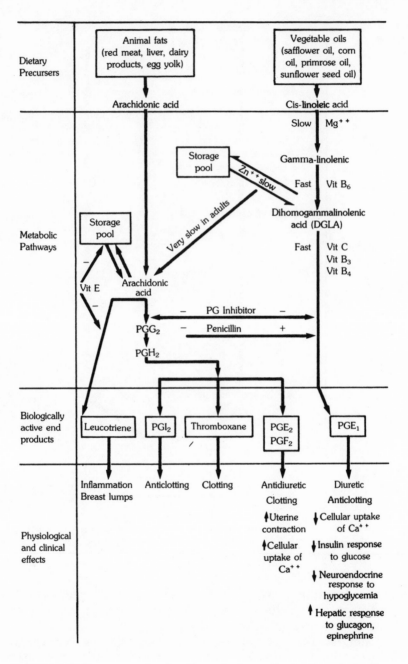

FIGURE 5.12 Precursors of and pathways to the synthesis of prostaglandins.
Dietary sources and physiologic effects of the prostaglandins and related compounds.
Reprinted with permission from Abraham GE: Nutritional factors in the etiology of
premenstrual tension syndromes. *J Reprod Med* 28:446–464, 1983.

frequency and degree of skin sensitivity to subcutaneous injection of steroids than did women without PMS (Heckel, 1951). Rogers (1962) summarized the knowledge lending support to the endogenous allergy hypothesis for PMS:

> *First,* it has been amply shown that many women are markedly allergic to metabolites of progesterone. *Second,* the symptoms of premenstrual tension tend to be most severe in the later years of menstrual life and after long continued exposure to cyclic production of the progesterone metabolites. *Third,* in all of the series of cases treated with hyposensitizing doses of pregnandiol better than average results have been reported. . . . *Fourth,* many of these symptoms we commonly associate with premenstrual tension such as nervousness, irritability, depression, local or generalized edema are present in some degree in many proven allergic conditions; for instance, in hay fever, asthma, and so forth! (Rogers, 1962, p. 101)

In support of this hypothesis are the positive treatment responses to antihistamines used in the second half of the menstrual cycle (Geiringer, 1951; Bickers, 1953). However, these treatment studies did not have adequate experimental designs. Methodological flaws associated with these early reports include the following: PMS was not diagnosed by prospective data, premenstrual symptoms were often lumped together with other menstrual cycle disturbances, and there were no adequate controls.

In more recent careful work, Shelley and colleagues (1964) described one woman with an autoimmune dermatitis related to progesterone. The dermatitis exacerbated regularly premenstrually. The patient was cured by oophorectomy. Farah and Shbaklu (1971) described two women with autoimmune urticaria also caused by progesterone. When given exogenous progesterone, these women developed urticaria. These women had positive skin tests with progesterone, passive cutaneous transfer, and antibodies reactive to the luteinizing cells of the corpus luteum. Inhibition of ovulation subsequently inhibited the urticaria.

A recent study at the National Institutes of Health of four women with recurrent anaphylaxis of unknown etiology demonstrated the efficacy of ovarian hormone suppression for this problem (Slater et al., 1987). Again, it is to be emphasized that although these women reported premenstrual worsening of their attacks some of the time, the episodes occurred throughout the menstrual cycle.

Marshall and Severino (1986) looked at the relationship between PMS and allergies reported in the retrospective histories of women seeking a diagnostic workup for PMS. Women were asked to list any allergies. Of 40 women who thought they had PMS, more than 52%

complained of allergies. However, only 8 out of 40 were diagnosed with PMS on the basis of 2 months of prospective daily ratings. Of those 8 women, 6 reported allergies and 2 did not. Thus, even though 75% of the women seeking a diagnostic workup for PMS reported allergies, most of the women who reported allergies did not meet criteria for PMS.

Impression. Further research is needed to clarify the relationship of allergies to PMS in general and to determine the effects of gonadal steroids on women's allergic responses in specific. Despite the unproven nature of the theory, a treatment based on this putative etiology has been proposed (Chapter 7, pp. 245–246).

Candida albicans

Since it was noted that *Candida albicans* infection was found more frequently in the premenstrual phase than in the follicular or early luteal phase (Segal et al., 1984), *Candida albicans* has been hypothesized to affect the immune system. The relevance to PMS would be in the development of autoimmunity to gonadal steroids. Witkin and colleagues (1983) have detected *in vitro* *Candida*-specific suppressor lymphocytes and a soluble factor that blocks the cellular immune response to *Candida* in some women with recurrent *Candida albicans* infections. Truss (1981) has described the relationship of *Candida albicans* to health disorders in women. Crook (1983) summarized Truss's hypothesis as follows:

> Antibiotics, birth control pills, corticosteroids, and diets rich in yeast-containing foods and carbohydrates promote colonization of Candida. When Candida organisms multiply, they appear to put out a toxin that affects the immune system, leading to a variety of health disorders. (Crook, 1983, p. 21)

Burnhill (1987) also observed the overlap in symptomatology between patients presenting with PMS and those presenting with recurrent vaginal candidiasis. He compared the two groups of patients' responses to *Candida*-specific immune globulin tests. Preliminary results suggested that a subset of PMS patients reacted to cyclic increases in *Candida* within the gastrointestinal tract.

Impression. Whether yeast infections are important in all women with PMS remains to be determined. It could be that *Candida* infections exacerbate existing symptoms. An anti-*Candida* treatment has also been proposed (Chapter 7, pp. 244–245).

Evolution

At least two etiologies have been proposed that are based on principles of evolutionary theory. While they are untestable, they nevertheless deserve to be considered along with some of the other proposed but insufficiently substantiated etiologies.

According to one theory, PMS has survival value (Janowsky et al., 1966). Since premenstrual hostility might serve to thwart mating during the premenstruum, male ardor would be intensified during the next onset of fertility, thereby enhancing the probability of conception (Rosseinsky & Hall, 1974). Morriss and Keverne (1974) present an alternative hypothesis for the survival value of PMS. They postulate that premenstrual hostility promotes the dissolution of infertile male–female relationships and allows for new fertile relationships to be formed. In other words, only infertile women could have frequent enough menstrual cycles so that PMS would be a problem.

Altered Blood Rheology

The most recently hypothesized etiology for PMS is impaired capillary blood flow (Simpson, 1988). This is thought to be due to a hormone-related change in viscosity that occurs in the luteal phase of the menstrual cycle. This change is possibly associated with reduced red blood cell deformability due to one or a combination of the following factors: (1) impaired linoleic acid metabolism resulting in a prostaglandin E_1 deficiency; (2) abnormally high levels of plasma noradrenaline; and/or (3) a hypothyroid state. According to this hypothesis, the women most susceptible to PMS would be women with blood capillaries that are smaller in size than those of non-PMS women.

PSYCHOSOCIAL CAUSES

Psychosocial causes of PMS have been hypothesized by many researchers. Within this view, stress has been examined as a social cause of PMS, and various attributes of women (personality profiles, intrapsychic conflicts, cognitive styles, coping styles, etc.) have been proposed as psychological causes of PMS.

Social Stress

Much time and energy has been devoted to investigating the role of stress in women's health issues (Dickstein, 1984; Lewis & Chatterton, 1987). The concept of stress has been variously defined. Selye (1974) stated that "stress is the nonspecific response of the body to any demand made upon it" (p. 27). Selye further suggested that life stress could be viewed as any event, positive or negative, that requires adaptation. The amount of stress experienced would be expected to be directly related to the intensity of the demand for adaptation or readjustment, with greater stress presumably increasing the probability of illness and disorder. Others have elaborated upon Selye's model, finding certain representative life-change events, such as the death of a spouse, predictably related to onset of illness in the bereaved (Smith et al., 1978). Specifically, individual resources and resistance to disease may decrease with increased demands for adjustment in other areas.

Recently more attention has been paid specifically to stress and women's health issues. An indirect measure of the relationship between menstrual disorders and stress or anxiety was provided by Cox's (1977) study of the Menstrual Symptom Questionnaire (MSQ). Following a systematic desensitization program, daily symptoms were reduced by 49% in previously menstrually distressed subjects. Stephenson and colleagues (1983) reported more direct evidence for the relationship of stress to menstrual disorders. On factor analysis of the MSQ, six factors related to menstrual symptoms emerged: premenstrual negative affect, premenstrual water retention, premenstrual pain, premenstrual gastrointestinal symptoms, menstrual pain, and menstrual backache. Life changes that were described in a negative way by these women were positively related to four of the factors. In other words, stressful life events were associated with menstrual symptoms.

"Negative" or undesirable life changes have also been associated with the number of symptoms of menstrual discomfort (Siegel et al., 1979). Siegel and colleagues' study showed that undesirable life change was the strongest predictor of menstrual discomfort in women who were not using oral contraceptives. Similarly, Wilcoxon and colleagues (1976) found that stressful events accounted for more of the variance than did menstrual cycle phase in terms of negative moods and somatic symptoms. Their data consisted of self-reports of moods from men and women over a 35-day period. Koeske (1981) reanalyzed Wilcoxon and colleagues' data and noted that the most symptomatic group was women in the premenstrual phase of their cycles. Less symptomatic were men randomly assigned to a cycle phase and women taking oral contraceptives. Coincidentally, all the women were under the stress of midterm and final exams. Koeske then suggested that examination stress affected cycle length in women not taking oral contraceptives. Taken together, the studies described above underscore the possibility that there is an interaction of stressful events and menstrual cycle phase.

Several authors have speculated about the relationship between stress and premenstrual syndromes (Ladisich et al., 1978; Sommer, 1978; Ablanalp, 1983; Harrison et al., 1985a; Coughlin, 1987; Dickson-Parnell & Zeichner, 1988; Heilbrun & Renert, 1988). Several of these authors encourage clinicians and researchers to ask patients about their current life situations and stresses. These authors further assert that "general agreement exists that stress exacerbates menstrual discomfort" (Harrison et al., 1985a). This same research group offers possible explanations for the negative statistical correlation of the "symptom" of general well-being with the retrospective reporting of premenstrual dysphoric symptoms (Rosen et al., 1988). They suggest that an absence of a sense of general well-being (which is often a reflection of current life stresses) may influence women to perceive their health negatively, or it may create a state in which women actually experience increased premenstrual symptoms. In addition to the possible exacerbation of premenstrual symptoms by stress, Witkin-Lanoil (1985) suggests that premenstrual symptoms may themselves be a source of stress.

In one unpublished study cited by Ablanalp and colleagues (1980), life changes over the previous 6 months were associated with significantly higher negative affect (tension, anxiety, anger, and depression) when measured prospectively over 2 months. With the highly stressed subjects in this study, there was no relationship between mood state and cycle phase. However, there was a small but statistically significant phase difference in negative moods for those subjects who reported low levels of stress.

Williams and colleagues (1986) reviewed the premenstrual health histories of 51 women who sought a diagnostic evaluation for PMS. While only 54% of them eventually received the diagnosis of PMS, life stress was a major theme for the majority of these women. Life stresses (see below) were spontaneously identified by 41 of 51 women (80%), many avowing a relationship between their increased stress and worse premenstrual symptoms. In contrast, 7 of the 51, or 14%, did not volunteer any information regarding current stressors. The remaining 3 women (6%) identified major life changes but denied that they were stressful.

Types of stressors included conflict with a spouse, difficulty taking care of young children, stressors at work, health problems, and such personal conflicts as turning 35 and feeling upset about "losing" youthfulness. Most women (59%) identified stresses involving relationships with significant others (husband or partner), such as conflict, separation, or divorce. Stresses with children were identified by 35% of the group of 51, with 10 women (20%) citing conflicts with sons. Of this group, 2 women described difficulties separating from their sons.

Conflicts at work concerned 15 women (29%). Nine women (18%) revealed conflicts with their own parents. A final category included 6 women (12%) complaining of depression, irritability, loneliness, dissatisfaction, anxiety, and/or feeling unconnected. Four women (8%) were in psychotherapy, and 3 (6%) had had a recent psychiatric hospitalization.

Sarason and colleagues (1985) have investigated and emphasized the importance of social support in moderating the effects of negative life events and experiences. In their study, the relationship between adverse events and illnesses was higher in people with low levels of social support. High levels of social support may act as a buffer or in some way neutralize the potentially harmful effects of stressful experiences. More on the role of social support in dealing with PMS can be found in Chapter 8.

Given the potentially buffering effect of social support, one could speculate about the dual impact of perceiving a relationship as stressful while experiencing an accompanying decrease in social support. In other words, tension in a close relationship may lower the degree of support previously available in that relationship. A woman who is involved in acute or chronic struggles with her spouse may subjectively experience more stress. In this stressed state, she may feel less able to cope with her usual premenstrual symptoms, or she may actually experience her premenstrual symptoms as more severe (Abrams & Halbreich, 1989).

Given the retrospective identification of stress by these women, it is possible that they were attributing their PMS to those stresses. It would appear, however, that for a large group of women, life stress, especially relational difficulties, plays a role in greater awareness of and complaints about premenstrual symptoms (Woods et al., 1982b; Woods, 1985; Woods et al., 1985; Williams & Severino, 1986).

One study has looked at how a woman's perception of the frequency of occurrence of life events and the degree of associated distress or pleasure are influenced by the hormonal changes that occur across the menstrual cycle (Schmidt et al., 1987a). The investigators studied reports of life events in 28 women with prospectively confirmed PMS and in 20 asymptomatic controls. During the follicular and late luteal phases of the menstrual cycle, subjects completed a schedule for life events, consisting of a 111-item self-report scale that measures their perceptions of how frequently life events occur and the degree of distress or pleasure associated with them. Women with PMS reported more total negative life events than did the control women. In addition, the women with PMS rated the same events as more unpleasant during the premenstruum compared to the follicular phase. These findings support the hypothesis that women with PMS experience (menstrual) phase- and state-dependent changes in their perceptions of themselves. However, the women were obviously not blind to the phase of the cycle, so that the self-reports could have been biased toward their (presumed) expectation of premenstrual worsening.

Impression. Stress appears to be an important factor that can modulate PMS symptoms.

Psychological Causes

Many investigators have sought a psychological etiology for PMS. In this section, we will summarize those proposed etiologies. For a more comprehensive, critical review of the studies that generated these hypotheses, the reader should refer to Chapter 4. This section concludes with the description of three models that organize the psychological hypotheses.

One proposed psychological etiology states that anticipating menstruation intensifies a woman's preexisting conscious and unconscious conflicts about pregnancy, childbirth, uncleanliness, lack of control of body functions, penis envy and masturbation (Deutsch, 1944), aggression (Nadelson et al., 1983), and sexual feelings (Friedman et al. 1982; Friedman & Corn, 1983). In this regard, Benedek and Rubenstein (1939a, 1939b), using psychoanalytic material, suggested that changes in hormones across the menstrual cycle were correlated with changes in the focus of women's psychological conflicts. In the preovulatory phase, when estrogen predominates, fantasies and conflicts centered around heterosexual themes. Premenstrually, when progesterone predominates, conflicts were related to infantile sexual fantasies and homosexual themes. In other words, physiological changes during the menstrual cycle were postulated to trigger particular conflicts resulting in cyclical anxiety and symptom formation in women. Benedek studied neurotic women, however. We do not know if her findings would generalize to women without a psychiatric diagnosis or to women with PMS.

One study seems to indicate that any random sample of women will experience heightened anxiety during the premenstruum (Ivey & Bardwick, 1968). The investigators asked 26 women attending college (aged 19–22) to talk for 5 minutes on any life experience. The subjects were tape-recorded around the time of ovulation and for 2–3 days preceding menstruation for two menstrual cycles. The Gottschalk Verbal Anxiety

Scale was used to rate the verbal samples. For all subjects, the premenstrual anxiety level was significantly higher than that at ovulation. The anxiety related to themes of castration (mutilation, death), separation, guilt, and shame. Another study of fewer women (five), but with more frequent 5-minute samples (daily for one to three menstrual cycles), showed statistically significant rhythmic increases in severity of at least one affective symptom during the menstrual cycle (Gottschalk et al., 1962). The affect involved differed among women. In addition, anxiety and hostility tended to decrease transiently at the time of ovulation. These studies remind us that hormones may have predictable and "normal" effects on emotions. These effects must be distinguished from symptoms of PMS.

Other proposed psychological causes of PMS include (1) the correlation of PMS with personality profiles (e.g., ego strength, guilt, neuroticism); (2) personality style (attributional style, cognitive style, coping style); (3) rejection of the female role; and (4) adoption of the "sick role" (Ehrenreich & English, 1978).

Some researchers report an association between measures of neuroticism and PMS (Gregory, 1957; Coppen & Kessel, 1963; Kramp, 1968; Hain et al., 1970; Taylor, 1979b; Watts et al., 1980), suggesting that women with PMS have personality characteristics of emotional instability, suspiciousness, guilt-proneness, tension, and self-conflict (Taylor, 1979b). In a study of 145 subjects (61 normal women and 84 psychiatric patients), Rees (1953b) had women chart their daily symptoms for a number of menstrual cycles, using a 7-point scale. He diagnosed PMS in 21.4% of the normal women and in 62% of the psychiatric patients. He stressed that neurosis alone was not sufficient to be the cause of PMS.

Several researchers have attributed PMS to a rejection of the female role (Paulson, 1961; Shainess, 1961; Patkai & Petterson, 1975; Slade & Jenner, 1980a). Berry and McGuire (1972) rated women's menstrual and premenstrual symptoms and acceptance of their conventional female sexual and social roles. They found no relationship between PMS and role acceptance. Still other studies report that women who seek treatment for PMS show a strong endorsement of the traditional feminine role when measured by the Minnesota Multiphasic Personality Inventory (Stout & Steege, 1985; Freeman et al., 1987).

Yet another proposed etiology is that preexisting psychiatric disorders predispose a woman to PMS. Therefore, the relationship between psychiatric disturbance and PMS has been studied (Kashiwagi et al., 1976; MacKenzie et al., 1986). Reports abound on mood, the menstrual cycle, and PMS (Moos et al., 1969; May, 1976; Dennerstein & Burrows, 1979; Dennerstein et al., 1984b; O'Neil et al., 1984; De Jong et al., 1985;

Ghadirian & Kamaraju, 1987). The relationship between PMS and depression (Diamond et al., 1976; Abramowitz et al., 1982; Blume, 1983; Halbreich et al., 1983; Hallman, 1986; McMillan & Pihl, 1987), PMS and anxiety (Lahmeyer et al., 1982; Giannini et al., 1985) and PMS and psychosis (Endo et al., 1978; Dennerstein et al., 1983) have all been examined (see Chapter 4).

Some researchers suggest that a woman reports physical or emotional discomforts during the premenstrual phase of her menstrual cycle because she expects to have them (Parlee, 1974; Koeske & Koeske, 1975; Wilcoxon et al., 1976; Ruble & Brooks-Gunn, 1979; Slade, 1984; Bains & Slade, 1988; Kirsch & Geer, 1988). At other times she would interpret her symptoms differently. If this theory is valid and if PMS is related only to expectation and attribution, then taking away physical menstruation (but not the endocrine basis of the menstrual cycle) should confirm it. Hence, hysterectomy, with preservation of the ovaries, provides a means of separating physical causal factors from psychological attributional factors.

Osborn (1981) studied 69 women (aged 45 or younger) with menorrhagia of benign origin. Complete preoperative and postoperative data were obtained on 56 of them. Women were interviewed on four occasions: (1) when they were scheduled for hysterectomy; (2) 3 months later, while they were waiting for surgery; (3) 6 months after hysterectomy; and (4) 9 months post-operative. Women used daily self-report diaries to rate seven common psychological symptoms (anxiety/tension, depression, weepiness, poor concentration, irritability, restlessness, and lability of mood) and six common physical symptoms (tiredness, headache, abdominal pain, abdominal distension, breast tenderness/swelling, and swelling of fingers) on a 3-point scale (absent, present but no interference with function, clear interference with function). Women completed the daily diaries preoperatively, over the 3-month period between interviews 1 and 2, and postoperatively, over the 3-month period between interviews 3 and 4. Before hysterectomy, the premenstruum was defined as 5 days preceding the onset of menses as determined from the daily diaries. After hysterectomy, the premenstruum was defined as 5 days preceding the onset of the menstrual phase determined by twice-weekly plasma progesterone values. Most women with premenstrual symptoms before hysterectomy reported complete relief of symptoms after surgery. A small group of women, however, continued to have premenstrual-like symptoms after surgery, but they were fewer and less severe (Osborn, 1987a). These findings would support the view that some women do experience premenstrual symptoms secondary to attributional factors. Indeed, some women will continue to experience premenstrual symptoms despite hysterectomy and the removal of uterine-related physical cues (Hamilton et al., 1988; Metcalf et al., 1988a).

Osborn (1987b) also measured psychiatric illness in this sample of women. Each woman completed the Present State Examination (Wing et al., 1974) and the Eysenck Personality Inventory (Eysenck, 1962) before and after hysterectomy. Women with premenstrual symptoms were no more likely to be psychiatrically disturbed or to have neurotic personality traits than those without premenstrual symptoms. Keep in mind that Osborn did not make a diagnosis of PMS in either of these studies. She looked at individual symptoms and their relation to personality disturbance.

Two earlier studies used a similar research design. Beumont and colleagues (1975), in a retrospective study of hysterectomized volunteers, reported the absence of cyclical symptoms after surgery. Backstrom and colleagues (1981) found that seven women with PMS continued to have symptoms after hysterectomy although symptoms were less severe.

Impression. The following hypothesized psychological etiologies of PMS have been studied: psychodynamic, social learning, stereotyped beliefs, and psychiatric disturbance (Warnes, 1978; Gannon, 1981; Ablanalp, 1983; Clare 1983a, 1983b, 1983c, 1985; Woods et al., 1985; Isada, 1987). Results have been inconsistent and inconclusive in all studies of the psychological etiology of PMS.

Psychological Models

Despite the lack of evidence for a psychological etiology of PMS, Rubinow (1985) has described three models for organizing our understanding of PMS from a psychiatric perspective. They are the sensitization model, the learned helplessness model, and the state-related model (Frankel & Rubinow, 1988).

Sensitization Model

The sensitization model states that women who repeatedly experience menstrually related dysphoria will be predisposed, or "sensitized," to other dysphoric experiences and, vice versa, other dysphoric experiences may sensitize the woman to her menstrual cycle. This model is based on experiments in rats that had electrodes implanted in their amygdalas (Post & Ballenger, 1981). Stimulating rats with 800 microamps of electricity elicited a brief amygadala after-discharge. Doing this daily for more than 15 administrations caused a limbic seizure. If the animal was not stimulated for a year, and then restimulated at the same subseizure level, the rat would seize again. The nervous system's response to a stimulus had been changed over time by repetitive administration of an initially innocuous stimulus.

When this model is applied to women with PMS, Rubinow (1985) suggests two points: (1) in someone who is genetically predisposed to bipolar affective illness, premenstrual dysphoria could act as a sensitizing factor that alters the development and expression of bipolar illness; and (2) the experience of a menstrually related trauma may sensitize the woman to expect that her menses will be an unhappy event.

Support for this model can perhaps be found from a study of the prevalence of childhood sexual abuse in women with PMS. Hurt and colleagues (1982) looked at the sexual histories of 45 young women on a inpatient psychiatric unit, basing the rationale for the study on the view that menses would remind a woman of the previous sexual trauma. Premenstrual symptoms would occur in anticipation of that cyclic reminder. According to their theory, a sort of kindling would be involved with the recurrence of menses. In their study, they found that of the women with PMS by retrospective history, 57% had abnormal sexual histories. The patients reported previous rapes, sexual molestations, prostitution, incest, ego dystonic homosexuality, and the like. Only 5% of the patients who did not meet criteria for PMS had an abnormal sexual history. The authors concluded:

> The prevalence of the premenstrual affective syndrome is somewhat greater in those groups characterized by both a low level of ego integration and the concurrent presence of severe affective disturbance. We have also presented data indicating that, particularly for these patients, unresolved sexual conflicts, as induced by severe, early sexual trauma, might be of etiologic significance. We would speculate that abnormal sexual experience during early (prepubertal) development creates a specific sense of sexual vulnerability in many women. This vulnerability is evident in the cyclic strain associated with the menstrual cycle and its highlighting of sexual and reproductive conflicts after puberty. The association of an increased prevalence of premenstrual affective syndrome with psychopathologic conditions characterized by the concurrent presence of dysphoric symptoms and poor ego integration is compatible with the model. (pp. 314–315)

Paddison and colleagues (1988) reported that of 174 women who presented for evaluation of their PMS symptoms, 40% described a history of sexual abuse. To date, however, only 34 of the 174 women have been prospectively confirmed as having PMS. Thirteen of those 34 women (38%) had a history of sexual abuse, a number that is not significant. It will be interesting to see whether other investigators find a relationship between PMS and histories of sexual abuse.

Learned Helplessness Model

The learned helplessness model is based on studies of rats placed in two cages and given electrical shocks. The animal placed in cage A can turn off the electric shock by pressing a lever. The animal in cage B, which cannot turn off the shock, receives its shock on the basis of the ability of the rat in cage A to turn off the electricity. In other words, when rat A shuts off the electricity, it goes off in both cages. The rat in cage B has no control over whether or not it gets shocked. The rat in cage B develops learned helplessness and an associated series of neurobiological changes (Swenson & Vogel, 1983). Its brain is depleted of epinephrine, and it develops a poststress opiate-mediated analgesia. The animal also develops immune incompetence (Visintainer et al., 1982). The rat in cage A develops neither learned helplessness nor any of the biological correlates. Furthermore, if the rat from cage A is transferred to cage B, it will not subsequently develop learned helplessness.

How can this model be applied to women with PMS? First, this model suggests that attitude can influence biological alterations. The only difference between the two rats was that rat A could turn off the electricity and rat B could not. Similarly, women who believe that they can control their experiences of premenstrual symptoms may differ significantly from women who believe they cannot, even to the point of influencing physiological changes in their bodies. Second, there may be some protective aspect of mastery of premenstrual symptoms that may generalize and allow a woman to be free of further potentially devastating biological and psychological consequences. In this way, such a woman would be like rat A, who does not develop learned helplessness even when placed in the opposite cage.

State-Related Model

The third model, the state-related model, says that we all occupy experiential behavioral states that are definable. States are characterized by certain attitudes, ideas, memories, and affects, and one state is distinguishable from another. In other words, we each experience ourselves in our worlds differently, depending on the state we are in. Applied to women with PMS,

> the menstrual cycle may biologically choreograph or facilitate state changes instead of causing specific symptoms. Premenstrual syndrome, therefore, would not be conceptualized as a symptom-specific disturbance, but rather as a disorder characterized by a menstrual cycle-linked transition into a specific experiential state, usually, but not exclusively, with dysphoria and/

or irritability as its predominant features. Biological and psychological characterization of the point of premenstrual state transition (the "switch") is likely to foster understanding of the key processes involved in the transition between other experiential states that occur in normal as well as maladaptive human functioning. (Frankel & Rubinow, 1988, pp. 181–182)

Rubinow elaborates this model more completely in a recent article (Rubinow & Schmidt, 1989).

SUMMARY

What causes PMS? We still do not know. However, the clinician should not be discouraged. We now have clearer guidelines for diagnosing PMS, which will be described in the next chapter. These diagnostic guidelines should enable researchers to select more homogeneous samples of women for research purposes. This, in turn, should help us understand the complex interplay of biology and behavior that is manifested in PMS.

CHAPTER 6

Diagnostic Evaluation

Although the specific etiology of PMS remains a mystery, there are methods for determining whether a woman has the disorder according to the definition outlined in Chapter 1. The diagnostic evaluation requires not only a retrospective history of PMS, but a comprehensive medical history and examination, a psychiatric history, and, most importantly, 3 months of prospective daily ratings of common menstrual cycle symptoms.

While many women want immediate treatment, the process of identifying a woman who truly suffers from PMS is more difficult than with many other medical disorders. First, there are no laboratory tests that confirm a diagnosis. Second, lengthy prospective ratings are required, since retrospective histories alone have been shown to be unreliable (O'Brien, 1987; Rubinow, 1987a; Rapkin et al., 1988b). Women should be reassured, however, (1) that confirming the diagnosis is a prerequisite to treatment; (2) that 3 months is a relatively short time compared to the length of time they have suffered from their symptoms; and (3) that they will learn much about themselves from the process of daily ratings.

We need to digress a moment to discuss a point that was alluded to in the preface regarding the use of prospective ratings to confirm a diagnosis of PMS. Magos and Studd (1986) disagree, arguing that retrospective histories are sufficient. They base their position on two factors: (1) early studies included women without PMS, and (2) in their sample of 150 women with retrospective histories of PMS, 97% had positive daily ratings for one symptom cluster, 53% had positive daily ratings for five symptom clusters, and 32% had positive daily ratings for six symptom clusters. Perhaps the disagreement about the validity of a retrospective history rests on how many symptoms must be present to meet criteria for the diagnosis. In support of Magos and Studd, Hart and colleagues (1987a) found that most of the discrepancy between retrospective recall and prospective reporting from a single cycle was due to intercycle variability. They concluded that women's retrospective self-reports did reflect their average or usual experiences. In our research, however, 98% of the women who seek a diagnostic evaluation have PMS according to retrospective history. Only 30% of these women receive a PMS diagnosis (without a concomitant psychiatric diagnosis) when assessed by prospective daily ratings. (Note that 30% is consistent with the percentage of women who showed positive daily ratings on six symptom clusters in the Magos and Studd [1986] sample.) Of these 30%, only 2% to 5% will meet the more stringent criteria for LLPDD (with no other psychiatric diagnosis). A recently published study reported similar figures for the prevalence of PMS in referred populations. Morse and Dennerstein (1988) found that in a group of 200 women seeking help for PMS at the Menstrual Disorders Clinic of the University of Melbourne, 195 (97.5%) met retrospective criteria for PMS, while only 75 women (37.5%) met prospective criteria. We consider, therefore, that prospective daily symptom ratings are mandatory to confirm the diagnosis of PMS or LLPDD.

This chapter contains a guide to the questions that should be asked of each patient and the rationale behind them, decision trees that will aid the clinician in arriving at a final diagnosis, and several practice cases with discussion. The diagnostic process itself has two parts: (1) the PMS interview outlined immediately below and (2) prospective ratings. Ratings should be done only if the results of the PMS interview indicate a high probability that the patient does indeed have PMS. Treatment options will be reviewed in Chapter 7, and management of PMS symptoms will be discussed in Chapter 8.

THE PMS INTERVIEW

A basic outline for the initial PMS interview is provided in Appendix A. Depending on the history given by each individual woman, different aspects of the interview will be the focus of more detailed exploration.

Retrospective History of PMS

It is important (1) to make a list of the woman's symptoms; (2) to ask the woman to describe how each symptom interferes with her life; and (3) to document when each symptom occurs in relation to menses. Do the symptoms occur every month? At what age did each symptom appear? Is there a family history of PMS? As Freeman and colleagues (1988) point out, PMS in a woman's mother may imply a shared biological factor, or it may indicate such psychological factors as shared expectations or self-perceptions.

It is also helpful to inquire about how the woman has managed her symptoms previously. Has she medicated herself? What has she used? Was it helpful? This information is used to corroborate a tentative diagnosis made from the retrospective history regarding the seriousness of the condition.

Medical History

As in all good diagnostic evaluations, taking a medical history is an early step. A woman's age is important. If she is a teenager and within 2 years of menarche, the question arises as to whether her periods are ovulatory. At the other end of the reproductive life cycle, women over 45 may be entering menopause, leading to menstrual cycles not only with differing hormonal pictures but with differing cycle lengths. Although there are references in the literature concerning women who are anovulatory and yet complain of PMS (Adamopoulos et al., 1972; Dalton 1984, p. 24), the diagnosis of PMS should only be given to women with ovulatory menstrual cycles.

Gynecological History

Regularity of cycles: Regularity of menstrual cycles is important at any age and has been mentioned above with regard to teenagers and women approaching menopause. We can be most confident of a diagnosis of PMS in women with regular cycles of 26–32 days in length. With cycles that are short, women may be symptomatic all month. If a woman has a 24-day cycle, for example, she will ovulate on Day 10, just a few days after she finishes her period. She may never be free of either her period or her PMS symptoms for a sufficiently long time to detect a difference in symptom intensity. Women with very long cycles, on the other hand, must document the time of ovulation accurately, not only to make sure that they are ovulating but also to relate the onset of symptoms to menstrual cycle events.

Age of menarche: It is helpful to know the age of menarche and to compare early menstrual cycles with present symptomatic cycles. A physician is most comfortable knowing that the premenstrual complaints correlate with regular ovulatory cycles. Having a history that dates back to the presumed beginning of ovulatory cycles is not a prerequisite for the diagnosis, however, since symptoms can begin at any time during the reproductive years.

Gynecological surgery: A history of surgical interventions should be elicited. Women who have had *both* ovaries removed should suspect causes *other than PMS* for their symptoms, since they will no longer have hormone production with a menstrual cycle periodicity (i.e., approximately 28 days). If a woman has had a hysterectomy without ovariectomy or with only one ovary removed, she may still ovulate and therefore have symptoms of PMS (Backstrom et al., 1981; Backstrom et al., 1982; Reid, 1985).

Pregnancies: The number of pregnancies and births should be elicited. A description of symptoms during pregnancy, if any, should differ from current complaints of PMS. Some undocumented clinical reports attribute PMS symptomatology to women experiencing more lifetime menses, due either to earlier menarche, later menopause, fewer pregnancies, or a combination of factors.

Endometriosis, fibroids: The hallmark of endometriosis is pain preceding the onset of menses. Endometriosis must therefore be ruled out before a diagnosis of PMS is established (Hargrove & Abraham, 1983). A woman with fibroids may experience discomfort premenstrually due to increased engorgement of the intrauterine blood supply. Fibroids, too, must be considered in a differential diagnosis of PMS.

Breast problems: If a woman complains of breast tenderness and engorgement, then the presence of breast masses or cysts must be excluded before a diagnosis of PMS is considered.

Dysmenorrhea: A major differential diagnosis is dysmenorrhea, or pain with menstruation. Dysmenorrhea is not PMS. It usually occurs once menses *has begun* and has different causes and treatment.

Birth control pills and other medications: Women who are taking medications (birth control pills, thyroid medications, tranquilizers) pose a problem in diagnosis. While it is true that women may have more than one condition, it is doubly difficult, if not impossible at this time, to establish a diagnosis of PMS if a woman is taking medications, especially ones that affect moods, kidney function, or hormone levels.

Endocrinological History

Obtain a general health and endocrine history from the patient and ask specifically about the following: thyroid disease, diabetes, and hypoglycemia.

Thyroid disease: Symptoms of thyroid disease, especially those resulting from hyperthyroidism, often resemble those of PMS, for example, increased nervousness or emotional instability. There is also a growing, but inconclusive, literature linking abnormal thyroid function tests with PMS (see Chapter 5).

Diabetes: Many women with PMS complain of polydipsia and polyphagia premenstrually. Since these are also symptoms of diabetes mellitus, a personal and family history of diabetes should be elicited.

Hypoglycemia: Symptoms of hypoglycemia include anxiety, nervousness, weakness, fatigue, headache, restlessness, difficulty with speech and thinking, agitation, prolonged sleep, and temper outbursts. All of these symptoms have been reported by women complaining of PMS. Therefore, the timing of symptoms relative to eating and to phase of the cycle should be documented. Women with true hypoglycemia will not have their symptoms limited to the luteal phase of the menstrual cycle.

Allergies

The allergy system has been implicated in PMS etiology, as has been discussed in (Chapter 5, pp. 126–130). Having allergies does not necessarily preclude a woman's having PMS. However, it is important to know whether her PMS symptoms are related to the specific time of year associated with her allergies or whether they occur throughout the year, independent of season.

Psychiatric History

Both a personal and family history of emotional problems should be obtained. Specifically ask: (1) "Has anyone in your family ever sought help for an emotional problem? Mother? Father? Siblings? Grandparents? Others?" (2) "Has anyone in your family ever been hospitalized on a psychiatric ward or in a psychiatric hospital?" If the answer to either is yes, ask what treatment they received and how they responded to it. This is important information for two reasons. First, the type of treatment may be helpful in a differential diagnosis, since certain psychiatric disorders—such as Major Depression—do have increased familial incidence, and certain conditions respond to specific treatments. Second, if one member in a family responds to a particular medication, other family members with the same disorder may respond in like fashion.

Whether there is a family history, as well as a personal history, of alcoholism should be determined, since women do report an altered response to alcohol across the menstrual cycle. Alcohol use is also associated with self-medication for depression and for insomnia, two symptoms of PMS.

The personal history must attempt to distinguish between premenstrual symptoms that are unrelated to a psychiatric disorder and those that are merely an exacerbation of the symptoms of a mental illness. A personal history, then, of Major Depression, Panic Disorder, Dysthymia, or a Personality Disorder is extremely important. A psychiatric interview and formal mental status examination is mandatory if an emotional illness is suspected (see below).

Stress History

Determine what brought the woman for evaluation at this particular time. Is there a current life stress that accounts for or contributes to her symptoms? Important questions to ask the patient regarding stress include whether there are conflicts in her marriage (or relationships), problems at work, difficulties with children, health problems, or other concerns that might contribute to the severity of her PMS.

All of these above items have been associated with more severe symptomatology (see Chapter 5, pp. 132–135).

MEDICAL AND PSYCHIATRIC EXAMINATIONS

Physical Examination

Other physical illnesses that may mimic PMS must be ruled out. This requires a thorough physical examination, including a bimanual pelvic exam and Papanicolaou smear, a complete blood count, and a chemistry screen. Other hormonal studies, such as thyroid function tests (T_4, TSH) or a lengthy glucose tolerance test, should be pursued only if clinically indicated.

It is not necessary to conduct the physical examination during the premenstrual phase of the month.

Psychiatric Mental Status Examination

The mental status examination should be performed during the follicular phase of the menstrual cycle. If the exam occurred during the symptomatic luteal phase, then it would be extremely difficult to determine which psychological symptoms are the result of an underlying psychiatric condition and which are attributable to PMS.

The mental status examination will assess consciousness, thinking, and mood. If the woman's consciousness is impaired, we would suspect an organic process manifesting itself in mental clouding. If, on the other hand, her thinking is clear, the content of her thinking should be described. Does she have false beliefs, that is, delusions? Does she believe her thoughts are so loud that others can hear them? Does she believe someone else is inserting thoughts into her brain? Is she experiencing hallucinations? What about the rate of her thoughts: Are they racing, slowed down? Are her thoughts logical? These questions are aimed at identifying a thought disorder.

Her mood should be described. Is she feeling "down," and, if so, is her low mood accompanied by a weight change and/or a change in sleep pattern? Is she feeling hopeless and that life is not worth living? Has she made any previous suicide attempts (especially around the premenstruum)? Does she experience unusual elation? Does she have difficulty with anger, and has she ever harmed anyone? Does she show a range of emotions, and are they appropriate to the thoughts she is describing? Such questions elicit information about affective illness.

In other words, does the woman meet criteria for a psychiatric diagnosis? If a diagnosis of Major Depression, Dysthymia, Bipolar Affective Disorder, Cyclothymia, Schizoaffective Illness, Anxiety Disorder, or another psychiatric illness is made, the patient will then fall into one of two categories. In the first category, symptoms will be present at any or all times during the month independent of cyclic hormone changes. In the second, premenstrual exacerbations will be observed. These patterns will be described on p. 151–154 below.

PROSPECTIVE DAILY RATINGS

If the diagnosis of PMS has not been ruled out by any of the factors listed above during the PMS interview, then the patient should be given three months of daily rating forms (see sample Daily Symptom Checklist in Appendix C) and instructed in their use. These rating forms, modified from those of Endicott and colleagues (1986), contain questions about the presence or absence of relevant common symptoms. Menses are also recorded on the form. Patients should be advised to take daily basal body temperature measurements or to use a urine test kit for luteinizing hormone (LH) during each month of rating. Both methods detect ovulation, although the latter is much more specific when performed correctly. Knowing whether a woman ovulates is important, as has been discussed above.

MAKING THE DIAGNOSIS

At the end of the 3-month period, the patient should return the rating forms to the clinician for scoring. The clinician compares symptom presence and mean level during Days 5–10 (6 days) of the cycle to 6 premenstrual days in the same menstrual cycle. While the same symptoms do not have to be present in each of the 3 months, at least *five* symptoms must demonstrate a marked change during each menstrual cycle for the diagnosis to be made. (A quick reference for decision possibilities can be found in the pre-diagnosis decision tree and various decision trees in Appendix B.)

There are four probable *diagnoses* from the three months of ratings: (1) PMS (decision tree B), (2) LLPDD (decision tree A), (3) no PMS (decision tree C), and (4) no LLPDD (decision tree C). There may be other daily rating patterns, but women with these patterns would not receive a diagnosis of either PMS or LLPDD.

PMS

This profile of symptoms shows minimal or absent symptoms from Day 5 of the menstrual cycle until ovulation. After ovulation, symptoms may begin at any time before menses (see Figure 3.1 for patterns). The rating forms will usually show that the six premenstrual days are associated with severe symptoms. Figure 6.1 demonstrates one symptom pattern that can be seen with PMS, that is, a marked increase in severity of symptoms premenstrually, with a remission of symptoms coincident with the onset of menses. Differentiating between PMS and LLPDD is described in the next section.

In summary then, for PMS to be present the following inclusion criteria must be met:

1. A marked change in severity of at least five symptoms premenstrually for two consecutive menstrual cycles.
2. A symptom-free week (usually Days 5–10) for the same cycles.

Patients would not receive a diagnosis of PMS if the following pertain:

1. The two criteria listed above are not met.
2. The above are present but represent merely an exacerbation of another disorder, such as Major Depression.

Subject Code: _____

Scale: 1 = None, 2 = Minimal, 3 = Mild, 4 = Moderate, 5 = Severe, 6 = Extreme

Day	Date	Menst?	Temp.	Mood swings	Depressed, sad, low, blue, lonely	Anxious, jittery, nervous	Irritable, angry, impatient
M	__ / __	N	__	1 2 3 4 ⑤ 6	1 2 ③ 4 5 6	1 2 3 4 ⑤ 6	1 2 3 ④ 5 6
Tu	__ / __	Y	__	1 2 3 ④ 5 6	1 ② 3 4 5 6	1 2 ③ 4 5 6	1 2 ③ 4 5 6
W	__ / __	Y	__	1 ② 3 4 5 6	1 ② 3 4 5 6	① 2 3 4 5 6	① 2 3 4 5 6
Th	__ / __	Y	__	1 ② 3 4 5 6	1 ② 3 4 5 6	① 2 3 4 5 6	① 2 3 4 5 6
F	__ / __	Y	__	1 ② 3 4 5 6	1 ② 3 4 5 6	① 2 3 4 5 6	① 2 3 4 5 6
Sa	__ / __	Y	__	1 ② 3 4 5 6	1 ② 3 4 5 6	① 2 3 4 5 6	① 2 3 4 5 6
Su	__ / __	N	__	① 2 3 4 5 6	1 ② 3 4 5 6	① 2 3 4 5 6	① 2 3 4 5 6
M	__ / __	N	__	① 2 3 4 5 6	1 ② 3 4 5 6	① 2 3 4 5 6	① 2 3 4 5 6
Tu	__ / __	N	__	① 2 3 4 5 6	1 ② 3 4 5 6	① 2 3 4 5 6	① 2 3 4 5 6
W	__ / __	N	__	① 2 3 4 5 6	1 ② 3 4 5 6	① 2 3 4 5 6	① 2 3 4 5 6
Th	__ / __	N	__	① 2 3 4 5 6	1 ② 3 4 5 6	① 2 3 4 5 6	① 2 3 4 5 6
F	__ / __	N	__	① 2 3 4 5 6	1 ② 3 4 5 6	① 2 3 4 5 6	① 2 3 4 5 6
Sa	__ / __	N	__	① 2 3 4 5 6	1 ② 3 4 5 6	① 2 3 4 5 6	① 2 3 4 5 6
Su	__ / __	N	__	① 2 3 4 5 6	1 ② 3 4 5 6	① 2 3 4 5 6	① 2 3 4 5 6
M	__ / __	N	__	① 2 3 4 5 6	1 ② 3 4 5 6	① 2 3 4 5 6	① 2 3 4 5 6
Tu	__ / __	N	__	① 2 3 4 5 6	1 ② 3 4 5 6	① 2 3 4 5 6	① 2 3 4 5 6
W	__ / __	N	__	① 2 3 4 5 6	1 ② 3 4 5 6	① 2 3 4 5 6	① 2 3 4 5 6
Th	__ / __	N	__	① 2 3 4 5 6	1 ② 3 4 5 6	① 2 3 4 5 6	① 2 3 4 5 6
F	__ / __	N	__	① 2 3 4 5 6	1 ② 3 4 5 6	① 2 3 4 5 6	① 2 3 4 5 6
Sa	__ / __	N	__	① 2 3 4 5 6	1 ② 3 4 5 6	① 2 3 4 5 6	① 2 3 4 5 6
Su	__ / __	N	__	① 2 3 4 5 6	1 ② 3 4 5 6	① 2 3 4 5 6	① 2 3 4 5 6
M	__ / __	N	__	1 ② 3 4 5 6	1 ② 3 4 5 6	1 ② 3 4 5 6	1 2 ③ 4 5 6
Tu	__ / __	N	__	1 2 ③ 4 5 6	1 ② 3 4 5 6	1 2 ③ 4 5 6	1 2 3 ④ 5 6
W	__ / __	N	__	1 2 3 ④ 5 6	1 2 ③ 4 5 6	1 2 3 ④ 5 6	1 2 3 ④ 5 6
Th	__ / __	N	__	1 2 3 4 ⑤ 6	1 2 ③ 4 5 6	1 2 3 4 ⑤ 6	1 2 3 4 ⑤ 6
F	__ / __	N	__	1 2 3 4 5 ⑥	1 2 ③ 4 5 6	1 2 3 4 5 ⑥	1 2 3 ④ 5 6
Sa	__ / __	N	__	1 2 3 4 5 ⑥	1 2 ③ 4 5 6	1 2 3 4 5 ⑥	1 2 3 ④ 5 6
M	__ / __	N	__	1 2 3 4 5 ⑥	1 2 ③ 4 5 6	1 2 3 4 5 ⑥	1 2 3 ④ 5 6
Tu	__ / __	Y	__	1 2 3 4 ⑤ 6	1 ② 3 4 5 6	1 2 3 ④ 5 6	1 2 ③ 4 5 6
W	__ / __	Y	__	1 ② 3 4 5 6	1 ② 3 4 5 6	1 ② 3 4 5 6	1 ② 3 4 5 6
Th	__ / __	Y	__	① 2 3 4 5 6	1 ② 3 4 5 6	① 2 3 4 5 6	① 2 3 4 5 6
F	__ / __	Y	__	① 2 3 4 5 6	1 ② 3 4 5 6	① 2 3 4 5 6	① 2 3 4 5 6
Sa	__ / __	Y	__	① 2 3 4 5 6	1 ② 3 4 5 6	① 2 3 4 5 6	① 2 3 4 5 6
Su	__ / __	N	__	① 2 3 4 5 6	1 ② 3 4 5 6	① 2 3 4 5 6	① 2 3 4 5 6

Note. This pattern of symptoms also represents one pattern of PMS. All women with LLPDD have PMS. Not all women with PMS have LLPDD. Menst. = menstruating; Temp. = basal temperature.

FIGURE 6.1 Late Luteal Phase Dysphoric Disorder.

These criteria provide a diagnosis of PMS according to the definition outlined in Chapter 1.

Late Luteal Phase Dysphoric Disorder (LLPDD)

LLPDD is the diagnosis given to that small subgroup of women with PMS who meet criteria for a psychiatric disorder that is related specifically to the menstrual cycle (see Chapter 2 for discussion of LLPDD). For a diagnosis of LLPDD to be given according to DSM-III-R, a woman must have at least a 1-year history of symptoms occurring during the last week of the luteal phase and remitting in the follicular phase (see Table 2.1). She must suffer from at least five symptoms a month, and at least one of those symptoms must be an affective symptom (affective lability, anger, depression, or anxiety). Physical symptoms, such as breast tenderness or swelling, headaches, joint or muscle pain, sensation of bloating or weight gain count as only one symptom, even if all are present in a given month. The symptoms must *seriously* interfere with her life and must not simply be an exacerbation of the symptoms of another psychiatric disorder. In addition, the symptoms must be confirmed by daily symptom ratings for at least two cycles.

The LLPDD group will necessarily be a subset of the PMS group, since all those with LLPDD will also meet PMS standards. Women with LLPDD will have primarily affective symptoms occurring during the late luteal phase. Women with PMS may have only physical symptoms, and their symptoms may begin at different points in the cycle after ovulation (see Figure 3.1).

No PMS or LLPDD

A profile of symptoms in a patient without either PMS or LLPDD can be seen in Figure 6.2. This profile shows only minimal or mild symptoms across the menstrual cycle. The symptoms that fluctuate do so without any relationship to the phase of the menstrual cycle.

Other Daily Rating Patterns

Although the Daily Rating Form is used to confirm the diagnosis of PMS, other patterns of symptoms can be observed. Figure 6.3, for example, is a typical profile of symptom ratings from a woman with a psychiatric disorder, Major Depression. Depression and agitation

Subject Code: _____

Scale: 1 = None, 2 = Minimal, 3 = Mild, 4 = Moderate, 5 = Severe, 6 = Extreme

Day	Date	Menst?	Temp.	Mood swings	Depressed, sad, low, blue, lonely	Anxious, jittery, nervous	Irritable, angry, impatient
M	__/__	N	____	1 ②3 4 5 6	①2 3 4 5 6	①2 3 4 5 6	①2 3 4 5 6
Tu	__/__	Y	____	1 2 ③4 5 6	①2 3 4 5 6	①2 3 4 5 6	①2 3 4 5 6
W	__/__	Y	____	1 2 ③4 5 6	1 ②3 4 5 6	①2 3 4 5 6	①2 3 4 5 6
Th	__/__	Y	____	1 ②3 4 5 6	1 ②3 4 5 6	①2 3 4 5 6	1 ②3 4 5 6
F	__/__	Y	____	1 ②3 4 5 6	①2 3 4 5 6	①2 3 4 5 6	1 ②3 4 5 6
Sa	__/__	Y	____	1 ②3 4 5 6	①2 3 4 5 6	①2 3 4 5 6	①2 3 4 5 6
Su	__/__	N	____	1 ②3 4 5 6	①2 3 4 5 6	①2 3 4 5 6	①2 3 4 5 6
M	__/__	N	____	①2 3 4 5 6	①2 3 4 5 6	①2 3 4 5 6	①2 3 4 5 6
Tu	__/__	N	____	①2 3 4 5 6	1 ②3 4 5 6	①2 3 4 5 6	1 ②3 4 5 6
W	__/__	N	____	①2 3 4 5 6	1 ②3 4 5 6	①2 3 4 5 6	1 ②3 4 5 6
Th	__/__	N	____	①2 3 4 5 6	1 ②3 4 5 6	①2 3 4 5 6	1 ②3 4 5 6
F	__/__	N	____	1 ②3 4 5 6	1 ②3 4 5 6	①2 3 4 5 6	1 ②3 4 5 6
Sa	__/__	N	____	1 ②3 4 5 6	1 ②3 4 5 6	①2 3 4 5 6	1 ②3 4 5 6
Su	__/__	N	____	1 2 ③4 5 6	1 ②3 4 5 6	①2 3 4 5 6	①2 3 4 5 6
M	__/__	N	____	1 2 ③4 5 6	1 2 ③4 5 6	①2 3 4 5 6	1 ②3 4 5 6
Tu	__/__	N	____	1 2 ③4 5 6	1 ②3 4 5 6	①2 3 4 5 6	1 ②3 4 5 6
W	__/__	N	____	1 2 ③4 5 6	1 ②3 4 5 6	①2 3 4 5 6	①2 3 4 5 6
Th	__/__	N	____	1 ②3 4 5 6	1 ②3 4 5 6	①2 3 4 5 6	①2 3 4 5 6
F	__/__	N	____	1 ②3 4 5 6	1 ②3 4 5 6	①2 3 4 5 6	①2 3 4 5 6
Sa	__/__	N	____	1 ②3 4 5 6	1 ②3 4 5 6	①2 3 4 5 6	①2 3 4 5 6
Su	__/__	N	____	1 ②3 4 5 6	1 2 ③4 5 6	①2 3 4 5 6	①2 3 4 5 6
M	__/__	N	____	1 ②3 4 5 6	1 ②3 4 5 6	①2 3 4 5 6	①2 3 4 5 6
Tu	__/__	N	____	1 ②3 4 5 6	1 ②3 4 5 6	①2 3 4 5 6	①2 3 4 5 6
W	__/__	N	____	1 ②3 4 5 6	1 ②3 4 5 6	①2 3 4 5 6	①2 3 4 5 6
Th	__/__	N	____	1 ②3 4 5 6	1 ②3 4 5 6	①2 3 4 5 6	①2 3 4 5 6
F	__/__	N	____	1 ②3 4 5 6	①2 3 4 5 6	①2 3 4 5 6	①2 3 4 5 6
Sa	__/__	N	____	1 ②3 4 5 6	①2 3 4 5 6	①2 3 4 5 6	①2 3 4 5 6
Su	__/__	N	____	1 ②3 4 5 6	1 ②3 4 5 6	①2 3 4 5 6	1 ②3 4 5 6
M	__/__	N	____	1 ②3 4 5 6	1 ②3 4 5 6	①2 3 4 5 6	1 ②3 4 5 6
Tu	__/__	Y	____	1 ②3 4 5 6	①2 3 4 5 6	①2 3 4 5 6	1 ②3 4 5 6
W	__/__	Y	____	①2 3 4 5 6	①2 3 4 5 6	①2 3 4 5 6	①2 3 4 5 6
Th	__/__	Y	____	①2 3 4 5 6	①2 3 4 5 6	①2 3 4 5 6	①2 3 4 5 6
F	__/__	Y	____	①2 3 4 5 6	①2 3 4 5 6	①2 3 4 5 6	①2 3 4 5 6
Sa	__/__	Y	____	1 ②3 4 5 6	①2 3 4 5 6	①2 3 4 5 6	①2 3 4 5 6
Su	__/__	N	____	1 ②3 4 5 6	①2 3 4 5 6	①2 3 4 5 6	①2 3 4 5 6

Note. Menst. = menstruating; Temp. = basal temperature.

**FIGURE 6.2 No Late Luteal Phase Dysphoric Disorder
No Premenstrual Syndrome.**

Subject Code: _____

Scale: 1 = None, 2 = Minimal, 3 = Mild, 4 = Moderate, 5 = Severe, 6 = Extreme

Day	Date	Menst?	Temp.	Mood swings	Depressed, sad, low, blue, lonely	Anxious, jittery, nervous	Irritable, angry, impatient
M	__/__	N	____	1 2 3 ④ 5 6	1 2 3 4 ⑤ 6	1 ② 3 4 5 6	1 2 3 ④ 5 6
Tu	__/__	Y	____	1 2 3 ④ 5 6	1 2 3 4 ⑤ 6	1 ② 3 4 5 6	1 2 3 ④ 5 6
W	__/__	Y	____	1 2 ③ 4 5 6	1 2 3 4 ⑤ 6	1 ② 3 4 5 6	1 2 3 ④ 5 6
Th	__/__	Y	____	1 2 3 4 ⑤ 6	1 2 3 4 5 ⑥	1 ② 3 4 5 6	1 2 3 ④ 5 6
F	__/__	Y	____	1 2 3 4 5 ⑥	1 2 3 4 5 ⑥	① 2 3 4 5 6	1 2 3 4 ⑤ 6
Sa	__/__	Y	____	1 2 3 4 5 ⑥	1 2 3 4 5 ⑥	① 2 3 4 5 6	1 2 3 4 ⑤ 6
Su	__/__	N	____	1 2 3 4 5 ⑥	1 2 3 4 5 ⑥	1 ② 3 4 5 6	1 2 3 4 ⑤ 6
M	__/__	N	____	1 2 3 4 ⑤ 6	1 2 3 4 5 ⑥	1 ② 3 4 5 6	1 2 3 4 ⑤ 6
Tu	__/__	N	____	1 2 3 4 ⑤ 6	1 2 3 4 5 ⑥	1 ② 3 4 5 6	1 2 3 4 ⑤ 6
W	__/__	N	____	1 2 3 4 ⑤ 6	1 2 3 4 5 ⑥	1 ② 3 4 5 6	1 2 3 4 ⑤ 6
Th	__/__	N	____	1 2 3 4 ⑤ 6	1 2 3 4 ⑤ 6	1 ② 3 4 5 6	1 2 3 4 ⑤ 6
F	__/__	N	____	1 2 3 4 ⑤ 6	1 2 3 ④ 5 6	① 2 3 4 5 6	1 2 3 4 5 ⑥
Sa	__/__	N	____	1 2 3 ④ 5 6	1 2 3 4 ⑤ 6	① 2 3 4 5 6	1 2 3 4 5 ⑥
Su	__/__	N	____	1 2 3 4 ⑤ 6	1 2 3 4 ⑤ 6	① 2 3 4 5 6	1 2 3 4 5 ⑥
M	__/__	N	____	1 2 3 4 ⑤ 6	1 2 3 4 ⑤ 6	1 ② 3 4 5 6	1 2 3 4 5 ⑥
Tu	__/__	N	____	1 2 3 4 ⑤ 6	1 2 3 4 ⑤ 6	1 2 ③ 4 5 6	1 2 3 ④ 5 6
W	__/__	N	____	1 2 3 4 ⑤ 6	1 2 3 4 ⑤ 6	1 2 ③ 4 5 6	1 2 3 ④ 5 6
Th	__/__	N	____	1 2 3 4 ⑤ 6	1 2 3 4 5 ⑥	1 2 ③ 4 5 6	1 2 3 ④ 5 6
F	__/__	N	____	1 2 3 4 5 ⑥	1 2 3 4 5 ⑥	1 ② 3 4 5 6	1 2 3 ④ 5 6
Sa	__/__	N	____	1 2 3 4 5 ⑥	1 2 3 4 5 ⑥	1 ② 3 4 5 6	1 2 3 ④ 5 6
Su	__/__	N	____	1 2 3 4 5 ⑥	1 2 3 4 5 ⑥	1 ② 3 4 5 6	1 2 3 4 ⑤ 6
M	__/__	N	____	1 2 3 4 5 ⑥	1 2 3 4 5 ⑥	1 ② 3 4 5 6	1 2 3 4 ⑤ 6
Tu	__/__	N	____	1 2 3 4 5 ⑥	1 2 3 4 ⑤ 6	1 ② 3 4 5 6	1 2 3 4 ⑤ 6
W	__/__	N	____	1 2 3 ④ 5 6	1 2 3 4 ⑤ 6	① 2 3 4 5 6	1 2 3 ④ 5 6
Th	__/__	N	____	1 2 3 ④ 5 6	1 2 3 ④ 5 6	① 2 3 4 5 6	1 2 3 ④ 5 6
F	__/__	N	____	1 2 3 ④ 5 6	1 2 3 4 ⑤ 6	① 2 3 4 5 6	1 2 3 ④ 5 6
Sa	__/__	N	____	1 2 3 ① 5 6	1 2 3 4 ⑤ 6	1 ② 3 4 5 6	1 2 3 ④ 5 6
Su	__/__	N	____	1 2 3 4 ⑤ 6	1 2 3 4 5 ⑥	1 ② 3 4 5 6	1 2 3 4 ⑤ 6
M	__/__	N	____	1 2 3 4 ⑤ 6	1 2 3 4 5 ⑥	1 ② 3 4 5 6	1 2 3 4 ⑤ 6
Tu	__/__	Y	____	1 2 3 4 ⑤ 6	1 2 3 4 5 ⑥	1 ② 3 4 5 6	1 2 3 4 ⑤ 6
W	__/__	Y	____	1 2 3 4 ⑤ 6	1 2 3 4 5 ⑥	1 2 ③ 4 5 6	1 2 3 4 ⑤ 6
Th	__/__	Y	____	1 2 3 4 ⑤ 6	1 2 3 4 5 ⑥	1 2 ③ 4 5 6	1 2 3 4 5 ⑥
F	__/__	Y	____	1 2 3 4 5 ⑥	1 2 3 4 5 ⑥	1 2 ③ 4 5 6	1 2 3 4 5 ⑥
Sa	__/__	Y	____	1 2 3 4 5 ⑥	1 2 3 4 5 ⑥	1 2 ③ 4 5 6	1 2 3 4 5 ⑥
Su	__/__	N	____	1 2 3 4 5 ⑥	1 2 3 4 5 ⑥	1 2 ③ 4 5 6	1 2 3 4 5 ⑥

Note. Menst. = menstruating; Temp. = basal temperature.

FIGURE 6.3 Major Depression.

characterize the entire month. There is never a symptom-free week, and symptoms are severe or extreme throughout.

An example of a patient with both Major Depression and PMS can be seen in Figure 6.4. The patient has depression and mood swings that are worse premenstrually (by 30%) compared to Days 5–10 but are also present at other times of the month. From these symptoms alone, one could not be sure if this is PMS plus Major Depression or merely an exacerbation of Major Depression. However, the patient also demonstrates additional symptoms related to the premenstruum, but not to Major Depression (e.g., physical symptoms). Therefore, the additional diagnosis of PMS can be confirmed.

SAMPLE CASES

The following cases demonstrate arriving at a diagnosis according to the criteria presented in this chapter.

The Constant Caretaker[1]

An overweight 32-year-old woman was brought to the psychiatric emergency room by police escort after she furiously pushed a chair, which hit and shattered a full-length mirror in the principal's office of her child's school. The psychiatrist who examined her diagnosed her as paranoid and dangerous to others and recommended immediate hospitalization, by two-physician certification if she refused to sign in voluntarily.

The patient refused to sign in. She stated that her suspicions of her child's unfair treatment in school were well founded and that she would harm no one. She acknowledged that she was more irritable and angry than usual because she was premenstrual. Her husband supported her decision and took responsibility for her generally and for bringing her to see the psychiatrist the next day. That evening her menses began. When she saw the psychiatrist the next day, she presented as a "different" person. She was relaxed, her anger and irritability had dissipated, and she demonstrated a sense of humor; but her conviction that the school principal owed her an explanation of her child's unfair treatment remained. She gave a history of monthly premenstrual changes dating to menarche, but worsening in her 20s. Symptoms were not the same every month. Some months she would become depressed, with thoughts of suicide; some months she would break out in hives; and some months were symptom-free. Symptoms were always predictable in their timing,

[1]This case is adapted from Severino, 1989. Adapted with permission of the American Psychiatric Association.

bject Code: _____

ale: 1 = None, 2 = Minimal, 3 = Mild, 4 = Moderate, 5 = Severe, 6 = Extreme

y Date	Menst?	Temp.	Mood swings	Depressed, sad, low, blue, lonely	Anxious, jittery, nervous	Irritable, angry, impatient
___ / ___	N	___	1 2 3 4 ⑤ 6	1 2 3 4 5 ⑥	1 2 3 4 ⑤ 6	1 2 3 4 ⑤ 6
___ / ___	Y	___	1 2 3 ④ 5 6	1 2 3 4 5 ⑥	1 2 ③ 4 5 6	1 2 3 ④ 5 6
___ / ___	Y	___	1 2 3 ④ 5 6	1 2 3 4 5 ⑥	① 2 3 4 5 6	1 ② 3 4 5 6
___ / ___	Y	___	1 2 3 ④ 5 6	1 2 3 4 ⑤ 6	① 2 3 4 5 6	1 ② 3 4 5 6
___ / ___	Y	___	1 2 3 ④ 5 6	1 2 3 4 ⑤ 6	① 2 3 4 5 6	1 ② 3 4 5 6
___ / ___	Y	___	1 2 3 ④ 5 6	1 2 3 ④ 5 6	① 2 3 4 5 6	1 ② 3 4 5 6
___ / ___	N	___	1 2 3 ④ 5 6	1 2 3 ④ 5 6	① 2 3 4 5 6	① 2 3 4 5 6
___ / ___	N	___	1 2 3 ④ 5 6	1 2 3 ④ 5 6	① 2 3 4 5 6	① 2 3 4 5 6
___ / ___	N	___	1 2 3 ④ 5 6	1 2 3 ④ 5 6	① 2 3 4 5 6	① 2 3 4 5 6
___ / ___	N	___	1 2 3 ④ 5 6	1 2 3 ④ 5 6	① 2 3 4 5 6	① 2 3 4 5 6
___ / ___	N	___	1 2 3 ④ 5 6	1 2 3 ④ 5 6	① 2 3 4 5 6	① 2 3 4 5 6
___ / ___	N	___	1 2 3 4 ⑤ 6	1 2 3 4 ③ 6	① 2 3 4 5 6	① 2 3 4 5 6
___ / ___	N	___	1 2 3 ④ 5 6	1 2 3 4 ③ 6	① 2 3 4 5 6	① 2 3 4 5 6
___ / ___	N	___	1 2 ③ 4 5 6	1 2 3 4 ③ 6	① 2 3 4 5 6	① 2 3 4 5 6
___ / ___	N	___	1 2 ③ 4 5 6	1 2 3 4 ③ 6	① 2 3 4 5 6	① 2 3 4 5 6
___ / ___	N	___	1 2 ③ 4 5 6	1 2 3 4 ③ 6	① 2 3 4 5 6	① 2 3 4 5 6
___ / ___	N	___	1 2 ③ 4 5 6	1 2 3 4 ③ 6	① 2 3 4 5 6	① 2 3 4 5 6
___ / ___	N	___	1 2 ③ 4 5 6	1 2 3 4 ③ 6	① 2 3 4 5 6	① 2 3 4 5 6
___ / ___	N	___	1 2 3 ④ 5 6	1 2 3 4 ③ 6	① 2 3 4 5 6	① 2 3 4 5 6
___ / ___	N	___	1 2 3 ④ 5 6	1 2 3 4 ③ 6	① 2 3 4 5 6	① 2 3 4 5 6
___ / ___	N	___	1 2 3 ④ 5 6	1 2 3 4 ③ 6	1 ② 3 4 5 6	1 ② 3 4 5 6
___ / ___	N	___	1 2 3 ④ 5 6	1 2 3 4 ③ 6	1 2 ③ 4 5 6	1 2 ③ 4 5 6
___ / ___	N	___	1 2 3 4 ⑤ 6	1 2 3 4 5 ⑥	1 2 3 ④ 5 6	1 2 3 4 ⑤ 6
___ / ___	N	___	1 2 3 4 5 ⑥	1 2 3 4 5 ⑥	1 2 3 4 ⑤ 6	1 2 3 4 ⑤ 6
___ / ___	N	___	1 2 3 4 5 ⑥	1 2 3 4 5 ⑥	1 2 3 4 5 ⑥	1 2 3 4 ⑤ 6
___ / ___	N	___	1 2 3 4 5 ⑥	1 2 3 4 5 ⑥	1 2 3 4 5 ⑥	1 2 3 4 ⑤ 6
___ / ___	N	___	1 2 3 4 5 ⑥	1 2 3 4 5 ⑥	1 2 3 4 5 ⑥	1 2 3 4 ⑤ 6
___ / ___	N	___	1 2 3 4 5 ⑤	1 2 3 4 5 ⑥	1 2 3 4 5 ⑥	1 2 3 ④ 5 6
___ / ___	Y	___	1 2 3 ④ 5 6	1 2 3 4 5 ⑥	1 2 3 ④ 5 6	1 ② 3 4 5 6
___ / ___	Y	___	1 2 3 ④ 5 6	1 2 3 4 5 ⑥	1 ② 3 4 5 6	1 ② 3 4 5 6
___ / ___	Y	___	1 2 3 ④ 5 6	1 2 3 4 ⑤ 6	① 2 3 4 5 6	① 2 3 4 5 6
___ / ___	Y	___	1 2 3 4 ⑤ 6	1 2 3 ④ 5 6	① 2 3 4 5 6	① 2 3 4 5 6
___ / ___	Y	___	1 2 3 4 ⑤ 6	1 2 3 ④ 5 6	① 2 3 4 5 6	① 2 3 4 5 6
___ / ___	N	___	1 2 3 4 ⑤ 6	1 2 3 ④ 5 6	① 2 3 4 5 6	① 2 3 4 5 6

te. Menst. = menstruating; Temp. = basal temperature.

FIGURE 6.4 Major Depression and Premenstrual Syndrome.

occurring the week prior to menses and remitting with the onset of menses.

The patient was the oldest daughter of a chronically depressed and fearful mother and an alcoholic businessman father. She was the caretaker of her family. Her mother recovered significantly during the patient's adolescence, only to fail rapidly and die when the patient left home and married after high school. The patient is the mother of four grade-school children and takes primary responsibility not only for one alcoholic sibling who is dying of cancer but for her virtually handicapped husband, who has himself been severely depressed and vocationally incapacitated since surgery a year ago. She and her family live with her in-laws. Both her husband and his parents have significant alcohol problems.

The patient is the constant caretaker: "I can't live with myself unless I do it all. I feel guilty if I do something for myself." She can cope with the demands of her life and is usually not depressed, except during the premenstruum when "the whole world closes in" and she feels "pulled down."

Discussion. This young woman was apparently diagnosed as having Paranoid Disorder based on her having believed for several months that her child was being unfairly treated at school. Apart from this belief, her behavior was not odd or bizarre. She experienced no hallucinations and had never met criteria for Schizophrenia. Her depressive episodes were limited to the premenstruum, and therefore she had never met criteria for Major Depression.

Another question is whether this woman suffered from a self-defeating personality disorder that rendered her unable to enjoy herself unless she was sacrificing herself for others. Contradicting this diagnosis, however, were the following: (1) She did not habitually reject help from others; (2) she was able to derive pleasure from many social activities; (3) she had many personal achievements to her credit—for example, she was respected for her artistic skills; and (4) she sought the company of people who would treat her well, including her spouse and friends.

Diagnoses: Late Luteal Phase Dysphoric Disorder (Provisional).
               Late Luteal Phase Dysphoric Disorder (Confirmed) by 3 months of daily symptom ratings. (See Figure 6.1 for typical symptom profile of LLPDD.)

Riding the Broom

A 30-year-old divorced mother of three children went to see a psychiatrist because of impatience, irritability, anger, and proneness to accidents. On one occasion, for example, in the midst of preparing a meal for guests, she grew increasingly angry that "no one was helping" her. Impulsively, she stopped cooking, jumped in her car, and, before she knew what she was doing, drove the car through the closed garage door.

The patient's parents had divorced when she was 8 years old, resulting essentially in the loss of her father. Her mother relied on her to cook and care for her younger sibling, a brother. She envied her brother's lack of responsibility and attributed it to the fact that he was a boy. She herself was shy and lacked confidence in herself as a women.

Although she attributed the failure of her own marriage to her husband's old-fashioned expectations that she remain at home to care for their children, she was also aware that she could find no man suitable for remarriage. Indeed, she wished she were in the position of her ex-husband, free of the day-to-day responsibilities of childcare. She returned to work looking for a source of self-esteem. In doing so, however, she found herself chronically tired and overwhelmed. Like her mother, this woman had divorced, gone to work, and relegated care of her children to her oldest daughter. Because of what appeared to be a repetition of unresolved conflictual issues, psychodynamically oriented insight therapy was recommended as the treatment of choice.

Over the course of psychotherapy, it became apparent that the patient's symptoms were present only during the premenstruum. In her words, she developed a "warp" in her thinking at that time over which she had little control. She experienced herself as "crazy," a "witch riding the broom." It seemed, in retrospect, that the difficulties with her husband had not been constant but had occurred only during the premenstruum. She wondered how this could have gone unnoticed by all concerned: her husband, her friends, and herself.

Discussion. This women was apparently diagnosed as suffering from a psychoneurosis, at the core of which was an unresolved oedipal conflict. The components of the oedipal conflict were a wish for and fear of appealing to her father as well as a wish for and fear of triumphing over her mother. The presence of this conflict plus behavior that suggested a repetition compulsion—that is, the fact that this woman had seemingly repeated the trauma of her parents' divorce by divorcing her own husband—led the psychiatrist to recommend insight-oriented psychotherapy to resolve the core conflicts.

Over time, however, the therapist observed that the patient's symptoms were present only during the premenstruum. Her symptoms were not so severe that she was suicidal, homicidal, or manifesting a thought disorder. This women would meet criteria for a provisional diagnosis of PMS, with additional damage to her self-esteem requiring psychotherapeutic intervention.

Diagnoses: Premenstrual Syndrome (Provisional).
              Premenstrual Syndrome (Confirmed) by three months of
              daily symptom ratings.

See-Saw of Emotion

This 30-year-old woman felt that there were only a few days each month
when she did not have PMS symptoms. Those few days were the days of
her menses. Over the past 6 months, her menstrual cycle had changed
from every 28 to every 23 days. As a result, the patient felt that the week
she lost was "my one good week."

Eight months ago her mother died, resulting in a serious depressive
reaction characterized by sleep disturbance, psychomotor retardation,
low energy, extremely depressed mood, and somatic pains not attributable to another cause. The depression persisted, requiring the help of a
pastoral counselor for several months. Although her mood, in general,
lifted, she continued to be subject to extreme mood swings from deep
despondency, when she felt like it was "the end of the world," to euphoria, when she felt that "everything is solved." Just prior to coming for
a PMS evaluation, she had been so despondent when visiting her counselor that he suggested she seek a psychiatrist who could prescribe medication. She did not want to do this and sought a second opinion by coming
for a PMS evaluation.

Five years ago, after the birth of her daughter, she suffered a
postpartum depression of moderate severity lasting several months.
Following this, she would become nauseated for a week prior to menses.
Mood swings during that time began to increase and have continued to
do so over time. In general, all her PMS symptoms (depressed mood,
irritability, and sleep disturbance) have increased with time.

Her family history was positive for Major Depressive Disorder
(maternal grandmother and maternal aunt).

Discussion. This young woman had a personal history of postpartum
depression and a family history that was strongly positive for Major
Depressive Disorder. Her presentation was more indicative of Major
Depressive Disorder exacerbated premenstrually than of PMS. There
was also the possibility that she was developing a rapid-cycling Bipolar
Disorder.

Such a patient should be evaluated for PMS. However, only if she
has affective symptoms restricted to the premenstruum would she meet
criteria for PMS or LLPDD. If her affective symptoms occur all month,
but she has other symptoms (breast tenderness and swelling, headaches,
back or joint pain, for example) that are restricted to the premenstruum,
she would meet criteria for both Major Depression and PMS.

Diagnosis: Major Depressive Episode Recurrent. (See Figure 6.3 for typical symptom profile.)

Intense and Unstable

This 40-year-old woman was very blunt, direct, and immediately quite open and familiar in discussing her life and problems. She stated that she was premenstrual and would probably cry. She was, in fact, quite tearful and somewhat pressured. She described her premenstrual symptoms as short (24 hours) but intense. She reported withdrawal, extreme fatigue, and feelings of helplessness, which she typically responded to with rage and feelings of depression so strong that "I can't get out of bed." She usually called in sick on these days, because she was easily provoked to start with and found it hard to control her temper at these times.

Her personal history was characterized by its apparent instability. As a child, she was sexually abused over many years by her brother. She completed high school but was often truant. She initiated fights with other girls and ran away from home frequently. After graduating from high school, she had five husbands and as many as 17 jobs. Her description of how and why she moved between jobs and relationships was puzzling. In her words, "life seems very arbitrary." One husband "suddenly" turned abusive right after the marriage; another decided to work extensive hours, and so they split up; another, who sounded like an unrooted individual, moved to Puerto Rico for warm weather and gave up on the marriage; still another was 15 years her senior, had no income, and was an extravagant spender when she married him. She also spoke of friends who arbitrarily dropped her. Although she felt that she had a network of longstanding women friends, it was difficult to believe that these were sustained reciprocal relationships. Rather, she seemed to attract women from whom she could borrow money to pay off her debts. She, in turn, never repaid these "friends" and felt no remorse over her abuse of them.

Discussion. This woman never completed her daily symptom rating forms or any other part of the diagnostic workup except for the structured psychiatric interview, which was done at the time she made her initial contact since she seemed to be in such crisis. Her psychiatric evaluation, however, was consistent with the diagnosis of Antisocial Personality Disorder in the following respects: current age over 18, onset of antisocial behavior before 15 (truancy, fighting, and running away from home), and manifestations of the disorder since age 18 (unable to sustain consistent work behaviors, failure to honor financial obligations, impulsive planning with no clear goals, inability to sustain a monogamous relationship for more than a year, and lack of remorse for mistreating others).

Diagnosis: Antisocial Personality Disorder.

Chronically Depressed

This well-dressed, 30-year-old woman spoke clearly and articulately. As she described her marital history, her affect became more obviously sad and she began to cry. She described feelings of chronic fatigue and depression, which under stress became unmanageable except with the help of antidepressants. She had been treated with antidepressants on two occasions in the past, with improvement in her mood after 6 weeks and discontinuation of the medication after 6 months. Never, however, was she completely free from fatigue and depressed mood.

These chronic symptoms were tolerable all month except for the week prior to menses, when she would "blow up" at her husband and children. As a result, she became even more self-critical over her loss of control as well as more depressed. Once menses began, she returned to her usual ongoing depressed state.

Discussion. The patient's history of two treatments for depression without total relief of her symptoms suggests an enduring depressive characterological picture with intermittent episodes of Major Depression. Her history also suggests either a premenstrual exacerbation of depression or PMS plus depression.

Her Daily Rating Forms (see Figure 6.4) revealed chronic depression, with an exacerbation of her depression premenstrually. In addition, she had several symptoms premenstrually that were absent the rest of the month and were unrelated to her depression. Those symptoms were bloating, edema, headaches, breast pain, and back pain.

Diagnosis: Major Depression—Past.
             Dysthymic Disorder—Present.
             Premenstrual Syndrome.

The New Bride

This 23-year-old, well-dressed, articulate, slightly hirsute, professional woman complained of 10 to 14 days a month of irritability, moodiness, tearfulness, anxiety, depression, and physical clumsiness. Situations that she usually handled with a degree of perspective became "devastating" before and during her menstrual periods, which were irregular in their frequency.

She was the older of two children. When she was 2 years old and her brother was 8 months old, her parents divorced. Her father and a homemaker reared the children, who had no contact with their mother. The father was extremely strict and severely limited her social life throughout high school. She complied until the age of 18, when she left home, found a good job, and created a new life for herself. She struggled with her PMS symptoms and even sought psychotherapy for them. She married 1 year ago and found that her symptoms put a severe strain on the marital relationship. There was no family history of mental illness.

Discussion. This woman's retrospective history was consistent with PMS, and she was instructed to begin charting her daily symptoms. However, because of her irregular menstrual cycles and the hirsutism, this woman was referred for consultation to a gynecologist who specialized in endocrinology. The gynecologist's physical exam was normal except for the hirsutism. Pelvic exam and Pap smear were normal. Complete blood count and blood chemistry screen were within normal limits. She did, however, have a persistent elevation of 17-hydroxy-progesterone.

A structured psychiatric interview was negative for a psychiatric disorder. Prospective daily ratings showed no pattern of symptoms consistent with PMS or LLPDD (see Figure 6.2 for a typical symptom rating).

Diagnosis: "Cryptic" balanced adrenal hyperplasia.
Her hirsutism was treated with spironolactone for its anti-androgen effect. When pregnancy becomes an issue, she will be treated to induce ovulation.

CHAPTER 7

Treatment Options

There are more than 50 proposed treatments for PMS, and we have attempted to present each treatment option completely and fairly, based primarily on the research, pro and con. When reading the chapter, several points are worth keeping in mind. First, subject selection technique for any study, especially for a treatment paradigm, is critical.

> Advances in our understanding of premenstrual symptoms and their treatment may yet be made if different treatments are applied in a controlled manner to specific premenstrual symptoms and if as much attention is paid to the problems of rating premenstrual complaints as is currently paid to the measurement of plasma and endometrial enzyme and hormone levels. (Clare, 1979, p. 578)

In the discussion of studies in which subject selection was not based on prospective ratings, the phrase "women with PMS" will be used. If the investigators went further than retrospective histories in selecting subjects, it will be so noted in the text.

Second, study design is key.

> Any drug trial for the premenstrual syndrome must be rigorous. It should be randomized, controlled, and double blind. Patients with relevant pelvic disease or current psychiatric disorder should be excluded, and diaries should be used to select patients and assess outcome. A parallel design is preferable, but crossover may be used if the sample is small. (Gaith & Iles, 1988, p. 237)

Third, it is interesting to examine the history behind treatments that are today promoted in the scientific and lay literature as the treatment(s) for PMS. Many times, the original subject group was unique, unlike the population for which later proponents recommended a particular treatment. Thus the general applicability of a treatment may not pertain except to the specialized circumstance.

Treatments for PMS that are based on the popular etiology of the moment are often later discovered to be unsafe. A primary example is one of the first treatments: roentgen therapy to the ovaries and anterior pituitary (Frank, 1931; Israel, 1938). In those days, the "safety and value of radiation" (Israel, 1938, p. 1723) were accepted without question. Today, we have concerns not only about radiation but also about side effects of other treatments, such as excess Vitamin B_6.

Finally, it is clear from actual practice that although treatments are made available to a patient by her clinician, they may not be *endorsed* by the clinician (Lyon & Lyon, 1984).

The chapter is organized as follows: (1) "simple," commonly suggested first approaches to treatment, (2) hormonal treatments, (3) drugs that affect water balance, (4) treatments based on locally active substances, such as prostaglandins or histamine, (5) nutritional supplements, (6) psychotherapy and psychoactive drugs, and (7) miscellaneous treatments. Each section has a description (if warranted), a critique of the research conducted on the treatment modality, and our impression of the treatment. It is hoped that this chapter will provide a useful and comprehensive basis upon which to advise patients regarding the plethora of choices for treating this disorder. This chapter is meant to be used in conjunction with the next one on management, where we present our guidelines for managing PMS.

EDUCATION AND SUPPORT

Description. This section concerns education and supportive counseling, which may overlap psychotherapy, described later on pages 224–226.

Research. It is generally accepted that

> discussing the premenstrual syndrome with the patient and allowing her to discuss her problems and symptoms is of great therapeutic value. Understanding that the symptoms only occur in the premenstrual phase, that she is not "going mad," and that they will be relieved by menstruation is often of great help. She should know that many other women suffer similar problems. However, this will rarely be sufficient to relieve her symptoms completely. (O'Brien, 1982, p. 147)

Several papers have been written on the use of family and group support in the treatment of PMS (Long, 1985; Frank, 1986; Levitt et al.,

1986). Although each claims good outcome, none was a research study.

One study (Walton & Youngkin, 1987) compared two populations of women with PMS, selected prospectively, who were assigned either to group therapy ($n = 5$) or not ($n = 6$). Each subject completed a self-esteem inventory before therapy and again after 8 weeks. There were no significant differences in response between groups before or after group therapy. Women were permitted to use any other form of treatment during the study, and most did. This confound, plus the relatively short duration of the study (2 months) and small sample size, hinders the interpretation of the results. It may be that group therapy does not work, although it may provide secondary benefits, such as

> (1) comfort in knowing one is not alone; (2) increased knowledge from educational material . . . (3) validation of symptoms; (4) sharing treatments and life-style changes used to reduce symptoms; (5) support and understanding from others experiencing the same problems; (6) recognition that premenstrual syndrome is a disease and that one is not lazy, crazy, or possessed; and (7) help in better understanding oneself so that one can forgive oneself. (Walton & Youngkin, 1987, p. 177)

Impression. Clearly, any women who seeks help for PMS deserves information and support (See Chapter 8). There is no obvious contraindication to support groups if a woman likes them, but there is no evidence to date that support groups can alter the course of the syndrome.

EXERCISE

Research. Based on a consensus of opinion that sports and gymnastics have a "favourable effect" on PMS, Timonen and Procope (1971) sent a survey to women attending an institute of physical education and to control women attending other institutions of higher learning. According to this retrospective study, students of physical education reported significantly less premenstrual headache, nervousness, irritability, anxiety, depression, and fatigue; they also consumed fewer analgesics. No influence on any parameter related to fluid balance was found.

A paper asserting that regular aerobic exercise should provide relief for PMS (Canty, 1984) provides no supporting data. The exercise program that the author advocates takes into account a postulated impairment of physical performance during the luteal phase of the cycle. This "impairment," however, does not bear up under the type of critical evaluation discussed in Chapter 3.

One study examined the intensity of premenstrual symptoms (*not* PMS) during an aerobic training program (Prior et al., 1987). Previously sedentary women began a 6-month exercise program consisting of running. Other subject groups included normally active (nontraining) women and marathon runners. Women who began training had shorter luteal phases and significantly fewer breast, fluid, and stress complaints at Cycle 6 (at the end of the training program) than at Cycle 1 (before the training program). Exercise had no effect on depression or anxiety in this group. Marathon runners in training showed significant decreases in fluid symptoms and luteal depression but did not show a decrease in anxiety. Control women did not differ across the 6 months.

There has been some work on the effects of exercise on depressed mood in general (e.g., Brown et al., 1978). In a study of young normal and depressed subjects undergoing a fitness program, psychometric tests taken before embarking on the program and at the end of the study indicated that physical fitness was associated with feelings of well-being as well as decreased depression and anxiety.

Impression. While the benefits of exercise for PMS have been extolled in virtually all lay articles and books written recently, very little evidence has been published to support this view (Prior & Vigna, 1987). Even the prospective study by Prior and colleagues (1987) cited above was of premenstrual *symptoms*, not PMS.

That exercise can influence plasma endorphin concentrations (Carr et al., 1981) is potentially important for PMS, since endorphins have been implicated in the etiology of the disorder. (See Chapter 5, pp. 113–114.)

In summary, while exercise has not been shown to be an effective treatment for PMS, it is sensible to advocate it for most patients. First, it may help those symptoms related to bloatedness, such as breast fullness. Second, many women may find that regular physical exercise improves their self-esteem, especially in the context of our current fitness-oriented culture. Third, depression and anxiety may be reduced as a result of a fitness program.

SIMPLE DIETARY CHANGES

Increasing Meal Frequency

Description. Most lay articles and many reviews of PMS recommend that women consume a hypoglycemic diet in which meal frequency is increased, meal sizes are proportionately decreased, and complex carbohydrates predominate (Hunter, 1985; Smith & Youngkin, 1986). The rationale is that glucose metabolism during the premenstruum is altered. However, as described in Chapter 5, pages 105–108, this is still an area of controversy.

The hypoglycemia idea is based on the work of Morton (1953), who attempted to show increased glucose tolerance premenstrually in symptomatic women. It is not clear from his paper what population provided the "normal curve" for comparison purposes. At any rate, he advocated a high-protein, low-carbohydrate diet, with frequent feedings to control the "hypoglycemia."

Morton and colleagues (1953) tested their dietary plan with and without diuretic or placebo in a prison and reformatory population. This study is discussed in detail on pages 198–199 below. The conclusion by the investigators that the diet was successful cannot be supported, however, since the study design was seriously flawed by the choice of subject populations in different locations, of different ages, and with different pretreatment symptom profiles. Further, detailed records of the diet actually consumed were not made. There are no other research articles demonstrating the effectiveness of such a diet plan (Keye, 1985; Pariser et al., 1985; Haskett, 1987).

Impression. Modifying one's diet to include more healthful foods and less refined sugar and other simple carbohydrates makes sense for everyone. While this countermeasure for PMS remains to be proven, it is an easy first step. Women should understand, though, that PMS is *not* due to hypoglycemia.

Limiting Caffeine Consumption

Description. Caffeine is a member of the methylxanthine family, which also includes theophylline and theobromine. These compounds, commonly found in coffee, tea, colas, and chocolate, inhibit the enzyme that degrades cyclic AMP (cAMP) within cells. Higher levels of cAMP are associated with the development of fibrocystic breast disease (Minton et al., 1979). Caffeine is also a well-described central nervous system stimulant. In excessive amounts, caffeine intoxication can occur. According to the definition found in DSM-III-R, caffeine intoxication is associated with at least 250 mg of caffeine (2.5 cups of coffee) and can lead to nervousness, diuresis, and various gastrointestinal problems. In extreme cases of excess consumption (over 1 g/day), psychomotor agitation, thought disorder, and cardiac arrhythmia can occur.

Research. Higher levels of caffeine consumption have been associated with both increased prevalence and more severe symptoms of PMS in a retrospective study of college sophomores (Rossignol, 1985). Women who consumed 4.5–15 drinks containing caffeine per day were 7.5 times more likely to have moderate or severe symptoms of PMS than women who did not consume caffeinated beverages. It is therefore somewhat ironic that an early suggested treatment for PMS was increasing coffee intake, presumably for its diuretic properties (Frank, 1931).

Rossignol and colleagues (1989) recently reported that higher rates of tea consumption were associated with a higher prevalence of premenstrual syndrome in women in the People's Republic of China. The study was conducted using a retrospective questionnaire, but still supports Rossignol's early work on the relationship between premenstrual symptoms and methylzanthine consumption.

Impression. Since caffeine can induce many of the symptoms associated with PMS, such as difficulty in sleeping and irritability, it makes sense to limit the intake of caffeinated substances during the premenstruum.

Limiting Salt Intake

Description. Women with PMS are often advised to limit salt intake, thereby theoretically decreasing bloating and edema symptoms (Morton, 1950; Cerrato, 1988). As early as 1940, Thorn and Emerson (1940) were advocating (1) total restriction of sodium chloride for 7–10 days before expected menses and (2) potassium therapy (as a diuretic presumably), but *only* in women with generalized premenstrual edema whose weight exceeded normal. Thorn and Emerson reported that the number of such patients was small. Further, they did not present data about these women; they merely said that the select group responded well to this treatment regimen.

To date, there have been no controlled studies, well designed or otherwise, to substantiate this treatment (Keye, 1985). Further, as will become clear from the section on diuretics below (pp. 197–202), women who report these symptoms may not only *not* gain weight premenstrually, but they do not categorically benefit from medical treatments that induce diuresis.

Impression. Women who relate their symptoms to dietary components may very well benefit from advice to control salt intake, especially in light of recommendations from the U.S. Public Health Service to avoid too much sodium (NIH Publication No. 87-2878). A woman should be made aware, however, that limiting salt has not clearly been shown to be effective for treating PMS.

STEROID HORMONE–RELATED TREATMENTS

Progesterone

Description. Progesterone is a C-21 steroid hormone produced by the corpus luteum and adrenal cortex. It has a variety of biological actions (see Chapter 1), among the most important of which are inducing a secretory endometrium; inhibiting gonadotropin secretion from the anterior pituitary; limiting uterine contractility during pregnancy; stimulating breast alveolar development; and facilitating sodium and water excretion, probably by antagonizing aldosterone (Glick & Bennett, 1981).

Progesterone is quickly degraded by the liver following oral administration (Chakmakjian & Zachariah, 1987). As a result, "natural" progesterone is usually administered as injections (Progesterone 50; Legere) or in rectal or vaginal suppositories. Only the injectable form is readily available; suppositories need to be compounded by a pharmacist.

Synthetic hormones with progestational action have been developed for oral use. The synthetic progestins are C-19 (norsteroid) and C-17 (hydroxyprogesterone) derivatives. The orally active progestins are used to treat secondary amenorrhea and abnormal uterine bleeding due to hormonal imbalances that are not the result of pathologies, such as fibroids or uterine cancer (PDR, 1987). Progestins are essential components of oral contraceptives. They have been associated with thrombotic disorders, such as thrombophlebitis and pulmonary and cerebral embolisms. Progestins may cause birth defects, bleeding, spotting, edema, amenorrhea, depression, nausea, and sleep problems.

The pattern of absorption of progesterone from vaginal suppositories has been examined (Myers et al., 1987). Subjects were recruited from a hospital PMS center. In 17 women studied after 1–9 days of using progesterone suppositories, the net increment in progesterone following a 400 mg suppository in the luteal phase showed a significant inverse relationship between progesterone concentrations achieved and day of treatment. In a second study, using the same six women on Days 1 and 8 of treatment during the luteal phase, a similar relationship was found: A significantly smaller response to the eighth suppository was measured. There were no significant differences in peak concentrations achieved with the suppositories, which suggests a "floor effect" on progesterone concentrations that can be reached with this technique of administration.

Many women find the use of oily suppositories, vaginal or rectal, to be unpleasant. Thus the search for oral forms of progesterone was launched. Since the side effects of synthetic progestins mentioned previously are problems that could be avoided through the use of a "natural" hormone, a new oral form of progesterone, micronized progesterone, was developed.

Maxson and Hargrove (1985) examined the bioavailability of micronized progesterone in nine postmenopausal women and one man. Subjects injested 200 mg of micronized progesterone in a gelatin capsule. Peak concentrations of hormone were reached after about 3 hours (average 17 ng/ml) and were comparable to luteal phase progesterone concentrations. Elevated progesterone levels were measured for at least 6 hours after a single oral dose. No complications were reported except for minor drowsiness.

Chakmakjian and Zachariah (1987) also studied the bioavailability of progesterone in different forms. Using three types of oral micronized progesterone as either a sublingual form, capsule, or tablet, they found significant elevations in serum progesterone concentrations within 30 minutes to 1 hour. They then compared serum concentrations of progesterone in response to 100 mg of progesterone in sublingual and capsule forms and to vaginal and rectal suppositories of 100 mg progesterone. The suppositories sustained the serum concentrations longer, but peak concentrations did not differ. The investigators noted that some women did not absorb the hormone well, judged by low mean peak progesterone. They concluded that oral forms of progesterone may be useful therapeutically, but that the optimal dose, frequency, and duration of administration remained to be determined.

A second recent paper (Sitruk-Ware et al., 1987) reviews research using oral micronized progesterone. It is clear from the review that this form of progesterone is physiologically active.

Thus, when reading the section that follows, keep in mind that oral forms may be substituted for progesterone suppositories in the near future for research and treatment. Currently, however, micronized progesterone is not readily available in the United States.

Research. Both "natural" and synthetic progesterone have been evaluated in women with PMS. Each will be described in this section.

Natural Progesterone

Israel (1938) was apparently the first to use progesterone, based on the finding that three out of four uterine biopsies from women with premenstrual symptoms suggested decreased progestational stimulation. A case report showed that his patient improved markedly after receiving daily injections of progesterone from the 18th through 30th day of the menstrual cycle for 3 months. When she relapsed without progesterone, Israel treated her with low-dose irradiation to the pituitary and ovaries.

He later treated seven women with progesterone intramuscularly every day or every other day from midcycle to menses. Five of seven became symptom-free, and the other two improved. Six of seven relapsed after progesterone was discontinued; four patients then received low-dose irradiation treatment. Only one of the seven women was "cured" by progesterone. This work, and Israel's luteal phase-deficiency theory, spawned the use of progesterone therapy.

Gray (1941) reported the use of injections of progesterone in 38 women with nervous tension. Included in the subject population were women with hysterectomy (4), agitated depression (2), and problems relating to sex (15). Gray stated that the majority of these women had nervous tension constantly during the month rather than only during the premenstrual phase. However, each woman received 1–5 mg progesterone in daily, twice-weekly, once-weekly, or once- or twice-monthly injections, with more frequent and larger injections premenstrually. Thirty-five of 38 improved: 13 markedly, 14 moderately, 8 slightly, and 3 not at all. (One patient committed suicide, but we do not know which of these groups she was in.)

Gillman (1942) injected 10–30 mg of progesterone intramuscularly on one to three occasions in the follicular phase of the cycle of 14 women. He was able to induce certain "premenstrual" symptoms in several of the woman, such as low-abdominal pain (4 women), rhinorrhea (5 women), headache (3 women), and malaise (2 women). Based on these observations, he criticized Israel's (1938) work, since the symptoms he induced could not have been the result of progesterone deficiency. Gillman stated:

> That it is plausible to treat cases of premenstrual tension with progesterone scarcely seems logical, nor is this remark supported by Israel's results in 10 cases, as the administration of corpus luteum cured one and temporarily relieved six; four of the six and two additional patients were subsequently cured by low dose irradiation to the pituitary gland and the ovaries; one malnourished patient was benefited by a gain in weight aided by insulin therapy. This does not seem to be an impressive basis for inspiring the continued use of progesterone in alleviating premenstrual tension. (p. 159)

Yet it was!

Schmidt (1943) successfully treated a recurrent menstrual-related psychosis that occurred in the luteal phase of a woman who had had a postpartum psychosis. Injections of progesterone, 10 mg daily, were given at the probable onset of the next psychotic episode and continued until 2 days before the expected menses. That month's psychosis was averted. Follow-up was not reported.

Greene and Dalton (1953) treated women with severe cases of PMS with either 10 mg progesterone injected daily intramuscularly or 25 mg injected on alternate days starting, in both cases, at midcycle. Of 61 women so treated, 83.5% became symptom-free and another 6.6% improved. Greene and Dalton also used progesterone implants (200–500 mg) in 28 women, with complete relief in 27. They suggested that the implant technique was more effective as treatment with less labor for the patient.

Rees (1953a) injected progesterone intramuscularly on alternate days for 12 days before menses in five patients. The treatment regimen was "effective" but had "practical disadvantages." Rees went on to use ethisterone, a synthetic progestin, which will be described later.

Since that time, others have reported case histories or open trials showing improvement with progesterone (Norris, 1983; Freeman et al., 1985), but the champion of this treatment is Dalton. She has treated thousands of women over the years (Dalton, 1984) but has yet to report the results of a double-blind placebo-controlled study from her research and clinical practice. She does, however, have long-term data and average-dose information that she recommends to clinicians.

Smith (1975) administered 50 mg progesterone intramuscularly in a controlled study of 14 women with premenstrual depression. Treatment began on or about Day 19 and continued every other day until menses. During a different month, women received placebo injections. Three women improved, three became worse, and eight found no difference with progesterone. Smith does not report his subject selection criteria or research tools, and he studied spironolactone during the study as well (with no improvement in symptoms from that drug), making data interpretation difficult.

Sampson (1979) reported a double-blind controlled trial of progesterone. Following one cycle with prospective daily ratings, 35 women with PMS were randomly assigned to either 200 mg progesterone twice daily (as vaginal or rectal suppositories) or placebo for one cycle starting approximately 12 days prior to menses. Crossover occurred during the second cycle. A subsequent 26 women continued in the study, but they received either 400 mg progesterone twice daily or placebo for one cycle, then crossed over. In the first study (200 mg twice daily), 31% preferred progesterone, 43% preferred placebo, 20% were helped by neither, and 6% were helped by both. Global results from the second study (400 mg twice daily) indicated that 27% preferred progesterone, 35% preferred placebo, 23% found neither helpful, and 15% were helped by both. Regardless of treatment, 60% reported improvement during the first month. In addition to obtaining global assessments, Sampson looked at the daily ratings during treatment. Only the lower dose of progesterone

(200 mg twice daily) and placebo lowered the values for pain, concentration, behavioral change, negative affect, and control scales. At 400 mg twice daily, progesterone was significantly better than placebo for pain but did *not* produce statistical improvement when compared to the untreated cycle. Thus this study did not demonstrate the superiority of progesterone over placebo.

Van der Meer and colleagues (1983) reported a small double-blind crossover trial with progesterone. Twenty women with PMS as well as low midluteal progesterone (less than 30 nmol/l) began a random course of 200 mg progesterone or placebo twice daily rectally from midcycle to menses for 2 months, then were crossed over to the other treatment. Daily ratings and global assessments were obtained. Only 13 out of 20 subjects completed the study. Overall, four felt better on progesterone, four on placebo, and five had no preference. There were no differences in mean daily symptom scores premenstrually between progesterone and placebo treatments. The rectal mode of progesterone administration raised plasma progesterone concentrations significantly (39 ± 9 nmol/l compared to 19 ± 7 on placebo), thus "correcting" any luteal phase defect. The authors concluded that progesterone was not beneficial but were concerned about the large dropout rate and the low dose used, even though it was the dose recommended by Dalton (1977b).

Richter and colleagues (1984) conducted a 4-month double-blind study but used inadequate subject selection techniques (retrospective history, concurrent use of vitamins or antiprostaglandins). Daily ratings were obtained during the 4-month study. Twenty-two women received either 400 mg progesterone or placebo twice daily as rectal suppositories beginning 15 days before menses. Four orders of treatment were used, for example, placebo–progesterone–progesterone–placebo, to which subjects and investigators were blinded. Overall, seven preferred progesterone, eight preferred placebo, two each did somewhat better on progesterone or placebo, and three found no difference between treatments. However, the nine women who improved on progesterone had more striking cyclical symptomatology than the women who preferred placebo. In fact, that placebo group may not be eligible for a diagnosis of PMS at all, a point that reinforces the need for prospective selection of subjects. Although the results of this study were not totally negative regarding progesterone, the uncontrolled concomitant use of other putative PMS treatments (e.g., vitamins) and less-than-rigorous selection techniques render interpretation difficult.

Andersch and Hahn (1985) also conducted a crossover study of women with PMS, judging the results against a 1-month reference cycle. For the second month, each of the 15 women who completed the protocol received randomly either 100 mg progesterone vaginally twice daily or placebo for 10 days preceding menses. A third treatment month was comprised of the crossover. The results indicated that both physical (e.g., swelling) and psychological symptoms improved compared to the reference cycle with both placebo and progesterone, with no differences between treatments.

Dennerstein and colleagues (1985) assessed women prospectively for one cycle, then applied strict criteria in selecting subjects with PMS for their double-blind crossover trial using oral, micronized progesterone. Twenty-three women received 300 mg progesterone per day or placebo for 10 days starting about 3 days after ovulation for 2 months, then crossed to the other treatment. Women improved on both progesterone and placebo. During the first month of treatment, progesterone was superior to placebo for control factors, stress, anxiety, depression, swelling, and hot flushes. These effects were not continued in the second month of treatment, however. While the authors' concluded that "an appreciably beneficial effect of progesterone over placebo for mood and some physical symptoms was identifiable after both one and two months of treatment" (p. 1617), they recanted this position in a reply to a critical letter to the editor of the *British Medical Journal* by Magos and Studd (1985) as follows: "at no time was it suggested that the totals across treatments were significantly different from each other" (Gotts & Dennerstein, 1985, p. 214). Basically, this study shows favorable trends with oral progesterone but no clearly consistent effectiveness.

Maddocks and colleagues (1986) reported on a study of 20 women who completed an 8-month protocol of vaginally administered progesterone or placebo. After 1 month of prospective ratings and quite rigorous subject selection, women received 3 months of progesterone, 200 mg twice daily, or placebo, beginning on Day 16 until menses. After 3 months, crossover occurred and treatment continued for another 3 months. The eighth month was a posttreatment control. Results indicated that women improved both on placebo and on progesterone, with no differences between treatments for depression, anxiety, irritability, or global scores. The eighth month showed that there was a true placebo response, since scores tended to increase (i.e., symptoms worsened) without treatment.

Dalton (1987a) criticized the work of Maddocks and colleagues (1986) on the grounds that not enough progesterone was administered to parous women in that study. Maddocks and colleagues (1987) then rebutted by reporting a "plateau" effect of progesterone concentrations produced by vaginal suppositories of different doses. This point has been discussed earlier in this section.

Progesterone has been used recently to treat premenstrual exacerbation of bulimia (Price & DiMarzio, 1988). Five women who met criteria for both bulimia nervosa and LLPDD received either oral micronized progesterone (300–600 mg/day) or placebo on Days 14–28 for one cycle, then crossed over to the other treatment for an additional cycle. During the cycle on progesterone, subjects reported fewer premenstrual binges and calories consumed than when on placebo. These results were considered preliminary and may not have reached statistical significance (not stated in the article).

Progesterone has also been prescribed (openly) to treat premenstrual exacerbation of asthma (Beynon et al., 1988). Three women with severe recurrent worsening of asthma premenstrually received intramuscular injections of progesterone—600 mg of depomedroxyprogesterone acetate twice weekly (one subject) or 100 mg progesterone daily (two subjects)—to control the symptoms. In a letter to the editor of *Lancet,* Dalton (1988) suggested that the mechanism of action of progesterone for asthma relief may be due to stimulation of progesterone receptors in the nasopharyngeal passages and lungs. If so, it is curious that these women reportedly did not have problems throughout the follicular phase of the cycle, when progesterone concentrations are also low.

Dydrogesterone: Progesterone's Stereoisomer

Taylor (1977) reported an open trial of dydrogesterone (6-dehydro-retro-progesterone) in 50 women selected on the basis of low luteal progesterone. Each subject received dydrogesterone, 10 mg twice daily, from Day 12 to Day 26. Fifty percent or more of women complaining of the following symptoms reported being cured or greatly improved: depression, irritability, tension, headaches, bloating, and edema. Overall, 72% reported global improvement or "cure," while 10% were "disappointed" and 18% had no change. The investigators also reported on the use of dydrogesterone in eight women with normal luteal progesterone; only four were greatly improved.

In a single-blind trial of dydrogesterone, Day (1979b) reported an overall improvement of 73% in 67 women who received dydrogesterone for 3 months according to the schedule used in the previous study. However, 43% improved on placebo. Twenty-two reported side effects with dydrogesterone, with nausea (6), irregular bleeding (5), and worse symptoms (3) heading the list. Six women reported side effects on placebo, but there was no consistent complaint. Again, depression, irritability, and bloating responded, but breast tenderness did not.

Taylor and James (1979) reported on the results of their clinical practice, in which they used dydrogesterone as an initial treatment (10 mg twice daily from Day 12–26). Overall, the first 293 women had a 70% rate of being cured or greatly relieved. It is interesting to report on their view toward treatment, since they correctly point out that open and single-blind trials are

> not ideal, as we all know, but we are concerned with the end-result in patients. We consider it unreasonable to await the results of double-blind, crossover studies when we are dealing with urgent problems and a form of management is available which gives very good results and is free from side-effects. (p. 51)

Fortunately, the dydrogesterone was apparently not an expensive form of treatment.

In an expansion of the data presented by Day (1979b), Kerr and colleagues (1980) added that there were no differences in pretreatment luteal progesterone concentrations between responders and nonresponders to dydrogesterone. Dydrogesterone treatment suppressed progesterone by about 17%. If the luteal deficiency theory is correct, then by lowering total progestin concentrations (endogenous plus exogenous sources of progestin), each woman's symptoms should have become worse, not better.

Dennerstein and colleagues (1986) reported a double-blind crossover trial with dydrogesterone using carefully selected subjects. Twenty-four out of 30 women completed the study, which consisted of 2 months of dydrogesterone (10 mg twice, Day 12–26) and 2 months of placebo. Greatest improvement in symptoms occurred between pretreatment and the first 2 months of treatment, regardless of whether it was hormone or placebo. There were no clearly beneficial effects of dydrogesterone over placebo; placebo, in fact, was better than dydrogesterone for a few symptoms, including negative affect as self-reported on the Menstrual Distress Questionnaire.

Sampson and colleagues (1988) selected women from a PMS clinic and a self-referral health clinic for a double-blind study of dydrogesterone. After one month of daily prospective ratings, 108 women received either dydrogesterone (10 mg orally every 12 hours for the 14 days ending 2 days before predicted menses) or placebo for 4 months. Treatment crossed over each month. Sixty-nine women completed the study. Both treatments decreased symptoms in the premenstrual phase. Dydrogesterone treatment was found to decrease pain associated with menstruation (significant for both severity and frequency of pain) but was significantly more likely to be associated with increased frequency of breast tenderness. There were no other statistically significant differences between treatments.

Medroxyprogesterone Acetate

Jordheim (1972) tested medroxyprogesterone acetate (Provera, Upjohn) alone and in combination with a flumethiazide diuretic in 365 women with PMS. Doses were 2.5 mg progestin and 2 mg diuretic three times daily beginning 10 days before menses. After two months, the treatment crossed over. He found that 26% improved globally (good or very good outcome) with the combination of drugs, but only 19% improved on progestin alone (not statistically different). Next, a double-blind trial of the combination drug or placebo was attempted. Nineteen percent and 21%, respectively, were improved.

In contrast to these negative reports, Glick and Bennett (1981) reported the successful use of medroxyprogesterone acetate in the treatment of a woman with severe PMS, using 10 mg daily for 10 days before menses. The investigators also referred to their unpublished work with medroxyprogesterone acetate and PMS, which led to global improvement over two to four cycles using 10 mg for 10 days prior to menses.

Depomedroxyprogesterone acetate has also been used in an open trial (Keye, 1985). Fifteen of 20 women reported a decrease of symptom severity by more than 50% following 150 mg depomedroxyprogesterone acetate every one to three months. Similar results from 30 mg medroxyprogesterone acetate orally every day were reported by six women in a different trial. Of surprise to the Keye group was that symptoms abated for only one cycle with the depomedroxyprogesterone acetate in some women. However, this is consistent either (1) with a placebo response, since symptoms usually decrease in the first month regardless of treatment (see Dennerstein et al., 1985, 1986) or (2) with a role of progesterone in *initiating* symptoms (see Gillman, 1942; Magos et al., 1984).

Ethisterone

Greene and Dalton (1953) reported the first (according to them) series of patients treated openly with ethisterone. Of the 46 women with mild to moderate symptoms who received oral doses of 30–150 mg daily for 12 days beginning on Day 14, 48% became symptom free and 17% improved. Thirty-one percent had no relief from this treatment.

Rees (1953a) used ethisterone, 5 mg twice daily, in an open trial for 12 days prior to menses. He reported an 85% success rate, with improvement in bloating, tension, anxiety, depression, fatigue, and headache. The drug delayed the onset of menses in a few patients and *increased* dysmenorrhea in some.

Appleby (1960) tested ethisterone and dimethisterone in patients with severe to moderate PMS. He also studied women on chlorothiazide, meprobamate, and placebo in the same study. Each of the five treatments was given for three cycles to 30 women. Drugs began 9 days before (expected) menses as follows: ethisterone, 25 mg twice daily; dimethisterone, 5 mg three times daily; chlorothiazide, 500 mg twice daily; meprobamate, 400 mg three times daily; placebo, once daily. Both of the progestins led to marked or complete improvement in only 10% of the women; placebo, in 7%. Appleby found that women rarely responded to more than one treatment. Meprobamate helped 53% and chlorothiazide 33%, but only five women responded to both. In this study as well, the synthetic progestins exacerbated dysmenorrhea.

Norethisterone

Ylostalo and colleagues (1982) studied norethisterone (a 19-norsteroid progestin), bromocriptine, and placebo in a four-cycle protocol of women with PMS. Norethisterone, 5 mg twice daily, began on Day 15 and continued until Day 25. To make the duration of treatment consistent with the bromocriptine and placebo groups, placebo was given to the norethisterone group on Days 12–14 and Day 25 to menses. Placebo was given from Day 12 to menses in the placebo-only group. Active hormone was given during Cycles 2 and 4, placebo during Cycles 1 and 3. Norethisterone significantly improved breast tenderness (over placebo) during the second treatment cycle but was not as effective as bromocriptine for breast symptoms. Norethisterone caused headache in two women and nausea in two others. From hormone measurements, norethisterone was found to decrease mean serum luteinizing hormone (LH), follicle stimulating hormone (FSH), and progesterone concentrations, as expected from negative feedback.

Coppen and colleagues (1969) reported a parallel treatment study of norethisterone, dytide (a combination diuretic), and placebo. Women with severe to moderate symptoms participated for 1 month. The norethisterone group was given 7.5 mg per day from Day 16 to 25, then placebo until Day 28. Placebo was taken for 13 days. Norethisterone was not superior to placebo for any symptom. The diuretic was statistically better than norethisterone for symptoms of depression.

Impression. From all of the research studies presented, the overwhelming majority suggest that progesterone is ineffective in treating PMS when compared to placebo, whether used in the "natural" form or as a synthetic. Maddocks and colleagues (1987) summed up the antiprogesterone view as follows:

> Proponents of progesterone therapy have used the arguments of inappropriate patient selection criteria, insufficient numbers of patients, and/ or treatment duration, and the concept of too little progesterone too late to downplay the results of a growing number of double-blind trials, each of

which has failed to document a salutory effect of vaginal progesterone in the treatment of premenstrual syndrome. (p. 1555)

In addition to the lack of effectiveness in appropriate clinical trials, progesterone has been shown to *induce* symptoms of PMS (Gillman, 1942; Magos et al., 1984). Further, the etiological basis for using progesterone, that is, luteal phase deficiency or excess estrogens, has not been proven.

Yet on the other hand, PMS clinics around this country and others use progesterone routinely and, reportedly, quite successfully. Whether this success is due solely to the placebo response is worth further study; one would become suspect if patients needed to increase their dosages of the hormone with time to achieve relief in light of the papers that show a limit to blood levels reached even with increasing doses of progesterone suppositories. Further, progesterone is expensive: A local (Westchester County, New York) pharmacy that formulates suppositories charges $4 per 100 mg. If a woman needs 400 mg daily for 14 days, the cost would be $224. That works out to $2,912 per year (13 menstrual cycles). According to Dalton (1987), 400 mg is a relatively low dose. There are less expensive distributors, however. Madison Pharmacy Associates in Madison, Wisconsin, formulates many types of progesterone, including oral micronized progesterone capsules and tablets. Their price (as of the writing of the book) was $1.10 per 400 mg suppository ($200.20 per year), 86¢ per 200 mg oral tablet ($313.04 per year), and 54¢ per 100 mg oral capsule ($393.12 per year).

A point to consider if one decides to prescribe progesterone for PMS is that this use of the hormone is not "labeled" or "approved" as such by the Food and Drug Administration (FDA). However, the FDA does not determine how a physician prescribes an approved drug (Archer, 1984). Even so, Norris (1983) suggests that patients be advised that this use of progesterone has not been approved by the FDA as yet (and may never be approved).

Our view, then, on this therapy is this: If a clinician candidly tells the patient who "demands" progesterone that there is no clear rationale for its use and that research studies have not validated its efficacy for PMS, but that it may help her, albeit as a placebo, then he or she may prescribe the hormone. The "natural" form is preferable, since few side effects have been noted. The synthetic forms of progesterone that have been used in research, such as dydrogesterone, ethisterone, and norethisterone, are not available in the United States; but they are of questionable utility anyway. Medroxyprogesterone acetate (Provera) is available, but not very effective.

Estradiol

Description. Estradiol-17B is the major physiologically active estrogen produced (primarily) by the ovaries. In unconjugated forms, it cannot be administered orally, so it must either be injected, implanted or applied percutaneously. Estradiol is typically used in the treatment of postmenopausal symptoms, such as hot flushes. Risks are discussed below in the "Impression" section.

Research. The use of estradiol as a treatment for a premenstrual symptom (in this case, premenstrual headache) was first reported by Rubenstein (1942). In that paper, he presented six case studies of young women with several characteristics in common:

> a) severe incapacitating premenstrual headache; b) nervous, highstrung, active women; c) childbearing age; d) vaginal smears consisting predominantly of fragmented cells and cells from deep layers of the mucosa . . . suggests the existance of an abnormally low gonad hormone production; such smears are never found in young adult women unless there is vaginitis; e) prompt amelioration of the symptoms occurring with moderate estrogen dosage; f) dosage and timing of the therapy seem to require individual adjustment, although in the cases so far studied, 1 mg. of estradiol dipropionate intramuscularly about a week before the onset of menses is adequate, if not optimal. (p. 702)

In addition, one of the six patients received placebo or 5 mg progesterone intramuscularly on different months. Only when estradiol was added did the headaches remit.

Interest in the use of estradiol as a treatment for PMS reappeared in 1983, when Magos and colleagues published a report on the treatment of menstrual migraine with estradiol implants. Of the 24 women studied, all had had regular attacks of classical or common migraine before or during menstruation for at least two years. Sixteen women also had PMS, but no description was provided as to the criteria used in establishing that diagnosis. Initially, implants of 100 mg estradiol, a dose that inhibits ovulation sufficiently to be classified as a contraceptive, were inserted into the subcutaneous fat of the lower abdominal wall. Approximately every 6 months a new implant was given, in a dose between 50 and 100 mg. Subjects were also given oral progestin (norethisterone, 5 mg) monthly for 7 days to induce endometrial shedding and to prevent the development of endometrial pathology. All but one patient (23 of the 24) improved, most either completely (46%) or almost completely (37.5%).

A second study has also shown the efficacy of estradiol, this time by percutaneous administration, in the treatment of menstrual migraine (de Lignieres et al., 1986). Twenty women with regular menstrual cycles and migraine limited to two days prior to menses or during menses participated in a double-blind placebo-controlled crossover trial for 3 months. Estradiol (1.5 mg in 2.5 g gel) or placebo (2.5 g gel) was administered to the skin 48 hours before the earliest predicted onset of migraine and continued for 7 days each month. Women reported headaches, their severity, and any side effects, such as breast soreness or mood changes. This treatment regimen prevented a significant number of attacks: Attacks occurred in 8 of 26 estradiol cycles (30.8%) but in 26 of 27 placebo cycles (96.3%). Headaches occurring during active treatment were milder and shorter than those during placebo. No breast tenderness or mood change was observed.

Magos and colleagues (1984) then went on to test estradiol implants in 92 women with PMS. In that study, it was not clear whether the women received the diagnosis retrospectively. Implants of 100 mg were made subcutaneously, as with the menstrual migraine study. However, 87% of the women also received a 100 mg testosterone implant at the same time, "especially when reduced libido was a problem." Participants usually received 7 days (range, 5–13 days) of norethisterone (5 mg daily) to promote endometrial sloughing. Eighty-four percent reported either complete or almost complete relief of symptoms following the implant procedure, usually within 3 to 6 weeks. There was no difference between the combined estradiol–testosterone implant group and the estradiol-only implant groups with respect to efficacy of treatment. Symptoms began to reappear after about 5 months, leading to a mean interval between implants of 5.7 months. PMS symptoms were reproduced by the treatment regimen in 45% of the women, with symptoms occurring at the time that progesterone was administered, but they were reported to be much milder and shorter than before implant treatment in all but one subject. Plasma estradiol concentrations were found to be elevated in 13% of the women, all of whom had received seven to eight consecutive 50 mg estradiol implants. Plasma testosterone was raised in 32% with the combined implants, but no virilization occurred. Thus, while this implant treatment appears to work for PMS, a placebo-controlled prospective study would be required to validate the treatment.

In 1986, Magos and colleagues (1986b) again reported on estradiol implant treatment for PMS, this time in a placebo-controlled study. Women with PMS were carefully selected prospectively for the study. Each of the 68 subjects received either (1) a 100 mg estradiol implant with 7 days of 5 mg oral norethisterone (33 women) or (2) a placebo implant and oral placebo for 7 days (35 women). All women were interviewed, and they filled out health questionnaires, and recorded daily symptoms. New implants were administered every 3 months as needed. Symptoms improved at the start of treatment in both the active and placebo groups, but only in the estradiol group was the benefit sustained significantly after 2 months. The efficacy of estradiol applied to pain, water retention, and negative mood, among other symptoms. The placebo response rate was initially 94% (33 of the 35 women), but the daily symptom ratings returned to pretreatment levels by six months. Side effects from the active treatment were minimal and transient.

Impression. Although only one research group has performed studies using estradiol implants with cyclic oral progestin, the treatment appears to be useful for a variety of important PMS symptoms. Unfortunately, implants are not available in the United States at this time, except for specified research purposes. It is to be hoped that drug treatment trials will commence shortly or are underway.

A word of caution, however. No matter how promising this treatment may be, it carries with it the same risks that other gonadal steroid hormone treatments do, including the induction of malignant neoplasms, gallbladder disease, effects similar to those caused by oral contraceptives (thromboembolic disease, hepatic adenoma, increased blood pressure, decreased glucose tolerance), hypercalcemia, and risks associated with estrogen administration during pregnancy (*PDR*, 1988).

On a different note, these studies point to the etiology of PMS. First, PMS was prevented or greatly lessened in severity by maintaining consistent plasma concentrations of estradiol. Adding the monthly and necessary course of progestin brought on symptoms. This estrogen/ progesterone treatment regimen has also been shown to cause PMS-like symptoms in postmenopausal women (Hammerback et al., 1985). Thus it appears that progesterone is involved in the *onset* of PMS symptoms. It also suggests that progesterone replacement therapies may be fundamentally incorrect from the etiological point of view.

Second, a high placebo response rate of 94% was found by Magos and colleagues (1986b). While the placebo effect was not sustained, it nevertheless underscores (1) the need for several months of follow-up for any potential treatment for PMS and (2) the impact of psychosocial factors on PMS that may be amenable to supportive treatment, be it active or placebo.

Oral Contraceptives

Description. Oral contraceptives contain a combination of various synthetic estrogens and progestins that prevent conception by inhibiting the ovulatory surge of gonadotropins. Typically, a 3-week course of the pill is taken, followed by a week of withdrawal culminating with menses.

While oral contraceptives are highly effective in preventing pregnancy, they are not without risk, especially to women who smoke (*PDR*, 1987). Thromboembolism, stroke, and myocardial infarction are more common in women who take oral contraceptives. These drugs can also cause depression, fluid retention, gastrointestinal distress, breast changes, and vaginal bleeding.

Research. An early report on the effects of oral contraceptives on premenstrual symptoms appeared in 1968 (Moos, 1968a). In a subject population of 718 wives of graduate students, 420 were taking oral contraceptives and 298 were not. Participants retrospectively filled out the Moos (1968b) Menstrual Distress Questionnaire, estimating how they felt during the menstrual, premenstrual, and intermenstrual phase of the most recent menstrual cycle. Symptoms reported by oral contraceptive users and controls were not different intermenstrually. However, on average, women on oral contraceptives complained less of such premenstrual (and menstrual) symptoms as difficulty concentrating, water retention, behavioral change, and negative affect. Women on sequential preparations reported greater change in symptoms across the cycle than those on combination pills, as well as greater variances on all symptom scales.

Oral contraceptives were studied prospectively by Herzberg and Coppen (1970). Women about to begin a course of oral contraceptives (152 women) or a barrier method (40 controls) filled out questionnaires about the prevalence of menstrual symptoms. Follow-up questionnaires were given at 5 weeks, 5 months, and 11 months while the subjects were on oral contraceptives. Using oral contraceptives significantly alleviated premenstrual symptoms of depression and irritability, beginning at 5 weeks. Headache and swelling (type not specified) were not improved. However, some women discontinued the oral contraceptives due to depression and irritability (20.4%). Interestingly, 47% of those women who discontinued had complained of moderate or severe premenstrual depression prior to beginning oral contraceptive use.

In a double-blind crossover study of women on Enovid for two cycles (5 mg norethynodrel plus 0.075 mg mestranol) or placebo for two cycles, use of the oral contraceptive led to decreases in irritability and anger but not necessarily at the premenstrual phase (Silbergeld et al., 1971). The Enovid also caused drowsiness, increased water retention and nausea/vomiting.

Kutner and Brown (1972) reported on a large-scale survey study of women in a major health plan who completed the Minnesota Multiphasic Personality Inventory (MMPI) and self-rating mood scales of moodiness, premenstrual moodiness, and premenstrual irritability at the time of their yearly physical examinations (apparently irrespective of phase of the menstrual cycle). Current oral contraceptive users ($n = 1,989$) reported significantly less premenstrual moodiness and irritability than past users ($n = 1,436$) and those who had never used them (n) = 1,726). Overall depression and moodiness were not related to oral contraceptive use. In addition, combination oral contraceptive users had significantly less premenstrual moodiness and irritability than sequential preparation users. The authors also found an inverse correlation between amount of progestin and severity of depression.

Cullberg's (1972) study of different progestin and estrogen combinations did not show significant improvement on premenstrual irritability or depression in women on oral contraceptives.

Andersch and Hahn (1981) also conducted a large random survey study of women currently taking oral contraceptives (26%) or not (74%). Age was a variable in data analysis. They found that women over age 18 reported a beneficial effect of oral contraceptives on symptoms such as sadness, irritability, anxiety, and breast swelling. In addition, the investigators found that oral contraceptive users were less likely to be absent from work premenstrually.

Andersch (1982) studied the 191 women from the survey reported above who were taking oral contraceptives. He subdivided the subjects according to the progestin "potency" of the particular oral contraceptives. He found that the average (retrospective) symptom score for premenstrual depression and abdominal swelling was greater in women taking pills with "weaker" progestin, although the difference between groups for the sadness symptom was small. Other common symptoms were not different.

Oral contraceptives have also been used to treat psychiatric disorders. Kane and colleagues (1966) treated a patient with suicidal ideation and self-mutilation with oral contraceptives, with good success. A 21-year-old woman with premenstrual psychosis dating from 1 year post-menarche was also treated successfully with oral contraceptives (Felthous et al., 1980). Her psychosis had been refractory to both lithium and antipsychotic medications.

Two case reports demonstrated the effectiveness of oral contraceptives in treating affective disorders. Roy-Byrne and colleagues (1984) prescribed an oral contraceptive for a 20-year-old woman with monthly severe premenstrual depression as well as insomnia, anorexia, irritability, and edema. While this woman was found to have concurrent hypothyroidism, after thyroid replacement was administered she still required the oral contraceptive to maintain symptom remission.

The second case report was of a 35-year-old with Bipolar Disorder dating to the time of menarche (Price & Giannini, 1985). The patient noticed that affective episodes often began premenstrually and recalled that she had felt better in the past when she had taken oral contraceptives. Thus the clinicians began a treatment trial of an oral contraceptive, which successfully controlled her mood swings. While it should be noted that she was taking imipramine (200 mg four times daily) concurrently, the antidepressant had not been effective before she began the oral contraceptive.

Impression. Research on the effectiveness of oral contraceptives in minimizing premenstrual symptoms appears to be equivocal. While several large-scale survey studies suggest that certain symptoms, such as depression and irritability, may be reduced with oral contraceptive use, other studies showed that women discontinued oral contraceptives *due to* depression. There was general agreement that combination pills were associated with less severe symptoms than sequential pills. Clearly, more long-term prospective studies are required to critically test oral contraceptive use for PMS.

There does seem to be a role for oral contraceptives in treating menstrually related affective illness and psychosis, especially when the patient has been refractory to more conventional psychoactive medications.

Antiestrogen (Tamoxifen)

Description. Tamoxifen (Nolvadex; ICI Pharma) is an oral nonsteroidal antiestrogen. It presumably acts by competing for estrogen binding sites on receptors in target organs such as the breast (*PDR*, 1988).

Tamoxifen is used to treat metastatic breast cancer in postmenopausal women. Side effects include hot flushes, nausea, vomiting, menstrual irregularities and vaginal bleeding. The drug should not be used during pregnancy since fetal harm may ensue.

Research. Tamoxifen has been used by one group as a treatment for premenstrual mastalgia (Messinis & Lolis, 1988), based on the premise that estrogens are involved in the development of PMS. Thirty-six women with principal complaints of longstanding severe premenstrual mastalgia were selected to participate. Affective symptoms, if present, were not severe, and no subject complained of bloating or weight gain. Women were assigned randomly either to tamoxifen (10 mg daily from Day 5 to Day 24) or to placebo for six menstrual cycles. No crossover occurred.

At the end of the 6-month treatment period, 89% of the women in the tamoxifen group reported complete remission of the mastalgia, compared to 0% in the placebo group. The improvement persisted during the next 12 months in the majority of women even though treatment had been discontinued.

Tamoxifen did not alter menstrual cycle lengths significantly.

Impression. This is the first study using a specific antiestrogen for the treatment of a premenstrual complaint. A clear superior effect of tamoxifen over placebo for premenstrual mastalgia was demonstrated in this study. However, the investigators selected a group of women with only one major symptom, which does not allow any generalizations to be made regarding the efficacy of the drug for any other premenstrual complaints. Further, the parameters of treatment do not seem to be fully resolved. For instance, the duration of treatment (Days 5–24) seems excessive. This drug may become an alternative for the management of premenstrual mastalgia as long as the patient is aware of the potential toxic effects on a pregnancy.

Danazol

Description. Danazol (Danocrine; Winthrop Pharmaceuticals) is a synthetic androgen derived from ethisterone (*PDR*, 1988). It acts to suppress the hypothalamic–pituitary–ovarian axis by inhibiting the release of the gonadotropins LH and FSH. Danazol may also have direct inhibitory effects at the ovary by binding at gonadal steroid receptor sites.

Danazol is successful in treating endometriosis and hereditary angioedema. It is also used in the treatment of fibrocystic breast disease when simpler measures have failed. Danazol should not be prescribed to women contemplating pregnancy; already pregnant or nursing; or with hepatic, renal, or cardiac abnormalities. Side effects of treatment include weight gain due to fluid retention and symptoms related to androgenization (hypoestrogenic state), such as mild hirsutism, decreased breast size, flushing, and vaginitis.

Research. Danazol was first used as a treatment for PMS by Day (1979a), on the premise that suppressing ovulation with this potent antigonadotropin would prevent menstrual cycling and therefore the symptoms of PMS. Day divided his subjects into two groups: (1) women whose PMS was refractory to other treatments and (2) women who were newly referred by general practitioners to an OB/GYN department. Subjects kept diaries of symptoms while they received either 200–800 mg danazol per day (Group 1) or 400 mg danazol per day (Group 2). Three women from Group 1 had endometriosis and did not show improvement with danazol, and two others discontinued treatment due to weight gain or nausea. Of the six remaining patients in Group 1, four described improvement in their major symptom (breast tenderness and swelling). In Group 2, five patients discontinued the 400 mg danazol within the first week, with three complaining of faintness and two reporting weight gain. Of the remaining patients, three out of six reported some improvement in their chief complaints, either depression, breast tenderness, or migraine headaches. This study was obviously flawed by a lack of placebo controls and prospective ratings in Group 2, but it was presented as a pilot project.

Another report (Labrum, 1983) suggests that low-dose danazol can be effective (10–50 mg daily), although Labrum decided upon this course of treatment "by accident" (p. 444) and is planning a double-blind, placebo-controlled study for the future. It is interesting that Labrum refers to work by Day (1979a) as support for the use of full-dose danazol to suppress menstrual cycles in women "in serious difficulty premenstrually, with recurrent suicidal ideation or worsening of a psychotic illness" (p. 444). Day (1979a) does not make this claim.

Two additional placebo-controlled trials of danazol for PMS have been reported recently. In the first (published in preliminary form by Watts et al., 1985), Watts and colleagues (1987) selected 40 subjects on the basis of prospective daily ratings and randomly assigned 10 women each to one of four groups (double-blind): placebo, 100 mg, 200 mg, or 400 mg danazol per day. Treatment continued for 3 months. As with a previous study (Day, 1979a), many subjects failed to complete the drug trial (13/40; 1 from placebo, 5 from 100 mg, 2 from 200 mg, and 5 from 400 mg groups): 5 of those 13 reported no improvement, while the others complained of nausea, drowsiness, pain, or skin rash. In the patients who remained, breast pain decreased significantly ($p < 0.05$) in all danazol groups. Irritability declined significantly in the 200 mg and 400 mg groups when compared to the placebo group. By the third month, seven symptoms (depression, aggression, lethargy, anxiety, tearfulness, irritability, and breast pain) were significantly improved in the 200 mg group compared to two symptoms (lethargy and clumsiness) in the placebo group. Danazol did not control abdominal bloating.

The second double-blind study with placebo or danazol employed a cross-over design (Sarno et al., 1987). Seventeen women were selected to participate on the basis of 1 to 2 months of prospective daily ratings. Exclusion and inclusion criteria were rigorous. Subjects received danazol (200 mg/day) or placebo from the onset of symptoms to the onset of menses. In this respect, this study differed from the others. The initial drug regimen continued for 2 months, then was crossed over. Subjects were interviewed monthly and continued self-ratings. Fourteen women completed the study, but the 3 who did not dropped out during the placebo phase. While no symptom improved significantly in the remaining 14, 11 women had lower overall symptom scores on danazol ($p <$ 0.035). This treatment regimen did not alter cyclicity, and the cycles were ovulatory, as detected from progesterone assessments. Further, no side effects were reported.

Impression. Danazol appears to be of limited utility in the treatment of PMS. Women do not seem to tolerate it very well when it is given daily, and there are general concerns about its use in otherwise normal women of childbearing age because of its androgenic properties. Few symptoms were convincingly ameliorated, except for breast pain. More research using appropriate techniques and larger sample sizes is required before danazol can be accepted as a mainstream treatment.

Testosterone

Description. The major male reproductive steroid secreted by the testes, testosterone is also produced by the adrenal glands and ovaries of women. In men it is responsible for sperm production, male secondary sex characteristics, and libido. In women, testosterone also modulates libido.

Research. Testosterone has been used as a treatment for PMS since 1940 (Greenblatt & Agusta, 1940) on the premise that the important etiological factor was either hyperestrogenemia (Frank, 1931) or unantagonized estrogens (Israel, 1938). Since male sex hormones were thought to "neutralize the action of estrogens" (Greenblatt & Agusta, 1940, p. 121), testosterone should theoretically have worked if either etiology were correct. Greenblatt and Agusta reported on two cases with severe premenstrual symptoms, each of whom received injections of testosterone propionate (10 to 50 mg per month). This dose did not eliminate menstruation but was reported to alleviate symptoms of "tension."

The second report used two methods to administer testosterone: (1) by injection of the propionated form (30 women) or (2) by mouth, using methyl testosterone (30 women) (Freed, 1945). Freed selected his patients from referrals and included only those women who could not tolerate their symptoms. Injections of testosterone were given 10 and 3 days before the expected menses in doses of 10–25 mg per injection, depending on the severity of the symptoms. Oral testosterone began 7 to 10 days before menses at 10 mg daily. In both groups, the majority of women improved.

Freed published a second study of testosterone in 1946. He compared an aqueous suspension of testosterone to testosterone propionate in oil and to placebo. All active treatments were more successful than placebo. The oil or water suspension did not matter.

Rees (1953a) treated 10 women with methyltestosterone in doses of 10 mg daily for 12 days before menses. Symptoms of tension, irritability, anxiety, depression, and bloating were improved. In some women, menses was delayed and dysmenorrhea increased.

Testosterone implants have also been used in conjunction with estrogen implants and cyclic oral progestins (see p. 180, above; Magos et al., 1984).

Impression. Testosterone has not been tested in a rigorous way, although it intuitively seems that it should work (and appears to) by virtue of its interference with the hypothalamic–pituitary–ovarian axis. However, it is not advisable for women of childbearing age to take androgens because of the risk of birth defects due to excess androgens. Further, in women taking anabolic steroids (synthetic forms of testosterone) it may not be possible "to reverse masculine traits once they appear—including facial hair, a deep voice, and a male physique" (Marshall, 1988, p. 183). Therefore this treatment should not be prescribed routinely.

GnRH Agonist

Description. Gonadotropin releasing hormone (GnRH) analogs are small peptides that bind at pituitary GnRH receptors. Potent agonists of GnRH that have been chemically modified to increase their half-lives, the analogs have a paradoxical effect on reproduction (Andreyko et al., 1987). While LH and FSH release is stimulated initially, continuous activation of the pituitary GnRH receptors causes desensitization of those receptors and decreased gonadotropin secretion. With the decline in LH and FSH, estrogen concentrations are reduced to postmenopausal levels within 2 to 4 weeks of treatment (*PDR*, 1987). Of course, menstrual cycles cease during treatment.

GnRH analogs are usually administered subcutaneously or nasally by a patient on a daily basis. Currently, one analog, leuprolide acetate (Lupron; TAP Pharmaceuticals), is available for the treatment of advanced prostatic cancer (*PDR*, 1987). There are no indicated uses of this hormone for women at this time according to the *Physicians' Desk Reference*.

Research. GnRH analogs have been used in several studies of PMS (Muse et al., 1984; Bancroft et al., 1987; Hammarback & Backstrom, 1988) on the premise that eliminating menstrual cycles by "medical ovariectomy" would lead to a cessation of PMS symptoms. In the study by Muse and colleagues (1984), eight women were selected to participate in a double-blind crossover study based on prospective daily ratings. Women self-administered either placebo or GnRH agonist (50 micrograms) daily by injection for 3 months, then were crossed over to the other treatment. As expected, GnRH treatment led to a loss of menstrual cycling; and while this could have affected the blind study, since placebo did not cause this effect, the women assumed that they had just missed their periods. When compared to placebo, symptoms from the second and third months of treatment were completely abolished ($p <$ 0.05). The authors attribute the success of this treatment to the decrease in ovarian steroid hormones.

In a commentary on the paper by Muse and colleagues (1984), Edelson and colleagues (1985) suggest that there are alternative hypotheses that could be invoked to explain the efficacy of GnRH on PMS symptoms, including a direct effect of GnRH on the brain or the alterations in the pattern of release of the gonadotropins themselves. Certainly, these are viable possibilities.

A recent paper (Bancroft et al., 1987) studied a nasal-spray form of GnRH, buserelin, in 20 women. Clear diagnoses of PMS were not documented. Ten women showed improvement in bloating and breast tenderness on a daily dose of 600 micrograms but less striking changes in negative mood. The other 10 women had adverse responses to the same dose of agonist and discontinued treatment by 11 weeks.

Hammarback and Backstrom (1988) reported the use of nasal GnRH agonist for PMS. Women were selected to participate based on prospective daily ratings, but 14 of 26 subjects had "premenstrual aggravation" (p. 160) since their symptoms were present before ovulation as well as premenstrually. Women with PMS and those with premenstrual exacerbations were not differentiated in the treatment phase or in most of the data analyses. GnRH agonist (buserelin, 400 micrograms) or placebo was used daily for 3 months then crossed over for an additional 3 months. This dose was selected so that regular menstrual bleeding would occur in a majority of women even following anovulatory cycles. Both affective and physical symptoms improved significantly on both placebo and GnRH, although GnRH was superior to placebo as well. Three of the 26 women experienced a worsening of symptoms. Better responses to GnRH were observed in the women whose symptoms were limited to the premenstrual phase. Hammarback and Backstrom did not find that this dose of buserelin lowered plasma estradiol to postmenopausal levels, even though ovulation was prevented.

Finally, GnRH analogs may be useful in the treatment of relatively rare medical illnesses that can be exacerbated by the menstrual cycle (Andreyko et al., 1987), such as acute intermittent porphyria and premenstrual high-frequency hearing loss.

Impression. GnRH analogs may be useful in some cases of PMS. However, the subcutaneous method of administration is difficult, and the loss of menstrual cycles, while reversible, may have long-term consequences that have not yet been studied. The intranasal method of administration was associated with only a 50% success rate in relieving symptoms of PMS, even when ovulation had ceased (Bancroft et al., 1987). Hammarback and Backstrom (1988) reported better success, but the study was hampered by poor subject selection. Certainly, reducing estrogens to postmenopausal concentrations by either technique could lead to a risk of osteoporosis. Thus this treatment regimen should not be prescribed hastily.

Ovariectomy

Impression. Removing the ovaries from women with PMS will certainly cure the symptoms in the vast majority of women. Dalton (1984, p. 24) has reported, however, that a few women remained symptomatic after bilateral oophorectomy. Her finding seems counterintuitive, though; symptoms of PMS occur neither prepubertally nor during pregnancy and usually cease with menopause, strongly suggesting that ovarian cycles are required for the syndrome to exist. It may be, however, that these women had become so sensitized to their menstrual cycles that the symptoms persisted after removal of the original cause of their symptoms.

This radical treatment also causes premature menopause and, therefore, the possibility of unwanted symptoms as a result of low estrogen production. Surgical menopause may cause even greater bone loss than that which occurs naturally after natural menopause (Riggs & Melton, 1986), leading to osteoporosis. Thus many other treatments should be attempted before resorting to surgery.

Glucocorticoid-Synthesis Blocker (Trilostane)

Trilostane is a drug that blocks an enzyme in the steroid biosynthetic pathway, thus lowering cortisol, aldosterone, and deoxycorticosterone production (Barnes & Thomas, 1983). It has apparently been prescribed to treat PMS based on its ability to "alter the sex hormone balance." We have not seen any subsequent reports in the literature on the use of this drug, so recommendations cannot be made. Further, it appears to be a drug still under investigation that may not be available by prescription in the United States.

PROLACTIN-RELATED TREATMENT: BROMOCRIPTINE

Description. Bromocriptine (Parlodel; Sandoz) is an ergot derivative and dopamine receptor agonist, binding at postsynaptic dopamine receptors. It is highly effective in decreasing plasma prolactin concentrations due to pituitary tumors or physiological lactation (*PDR*, 1987). It is also used as an adjunctive treatment for acromegaly and Parkinson's disease. Side effects noted with this drug include nausea, headache, dizziness, and fatigue.

Research. Benedek-Jaszmann and Hearn-Sturdivant (1976) reported on a double-blind placebo-controlled study of bromocriptine, a treatment based on the theory that prolactin can alter fluid and electrolyte balance (see Chapter 5, pp. 100–102). Ten women, most of whom were attending an infertility clinic, had symptoms of PMS (diagnosis unclear). In their first study, each subject received 2.5 mg bromocriptine or placebo for one cycle, beginning on Day 10 and continuing until menstruation. Treatment then crossed over. Symptoms that improved with bromocriptine but not with placebo included breast symptoms, weight gain, and mood. In a second group of women with PMS, 42 subjects openly received 2.5 mg bromocriptine twice daily, from Day 10 until menses. All 34 who completed the study "showed a marked improvement in or complete relief of premenstrual symptoms" (p. 1097). It should be noted that the infertile women had prolactin concentrations close to or above the upper limit of normal.

In another placebo-controlled study (Ghose & Coppen, 1977), women were recruited from general practitioners' offices and asked about PMS symptoms. (They were not consulting their general practitioners because of PMS.) Women ($n = 13$) who reported moderate or severe symptoms on a questionnaire received bromocriptine (2.5 mg/day) or placebo for one cycle, beginning 10 days before the expected menses, then crossed over. No statistical improvement with bromocriptine was observed.

The next placebo-controlled study (Andersen et al., 1977) selected women with severe PMS complaints by history, but the investigators included a control month. Then each of 26 subjects received 2.5 mg bromocriptine twice daily or placebo, from (expected) ovulation until menses. Five women did not complete the study, four due to side effects of bromocriptine. The investigators found a placebo response as well as improvement on bromocriptine; bromocriptine was superior overall, but only significantly for mastodynia. Interestingly, placebo was better than bromocriptine for edema and abdominal distension, two fluid-related symptoms that prompted the use of bromocriptine in the original studies.

Barwin (1980) compared bromocriptine to Bellergal (see p. 235 below) and to placebo in a triple crossover study of 30 women. Bromocriptine was superior to Bellergal and to placebo, but the details are lacking in the published abstract.

Andersch and colleagues (1978a) compared body water and weight changes across the menstrual cycle in women with PMS (by history) who were taking either bromocriptine (1.25 mg twice daily) or bumetanide (a diuretic, no dose stated) or nothing. The drugs were given from Day 19 until menses. The researchers found no effect of either bromocriptine or the diuretic on mean weight or body water. Further, mean weight and body water in the untreated luteal phase did not differ in PMS women compared to the control women without PMS. There was, however, a statistically significant higher water/potassium ratio in the luteal phases (treated or not) compared to follicular phases in PMS subjects. This was interpreted as "a small but real accumulation of water in the later luteal phase" (p. 548). How any of this related to PMS symptoms is unclear, since no mention was made of ratings or improvement with either treatment.

To this end, the authors performed a second study using the same groups of women (Andersch et al., 1978b). Women with PMS received either bromocriptine (1.25 mg twice daily) or bumetanide (1 mg daily). Treatment was double-blind and started on Day 19. Psychiatric interviews were conducted during a control premenstrual phase and during the premenstrual phases of the 2 treatment months. Psychiatric symptoms decreased significantly during treatment with bromocriptine and with the diuretic ($p < 0.01$ vs. $p < 0.05$, respectively). The diuretic subjectively improved symptoms of swelling and bloating, while bromocriptine improved breast symptoms and irritability. Overall, 10 of 19 subjects judged a good outcome with bromocriptine and 5 of 19 with bumetanide. Physician assessment was 12 of 19 and 6 of 19, respectively.

The next double-blind study selected women who complained of either breast tenderness or weight gain as part of their symptoms (Graham et al., 1978). Eight subjects participated in a 5-month study: control month, bromocriptine or placebo for 2 months, then crossover for 2 months. Bromocriptine treatment began on Day 14 at 2.5 mg/day and was increased to 5 mg/day from Day 17 until menses. Symptoms that improved more with bromocriptine than with placebo included bloated ness, depression, anxiety, insomnia, and irritability. Breast symptoms were not improved, nor was a placebo response noted. Weight and breast size increases were prevented by bromocriptine. The investigators suggest that to be effective, sufficient bromocriptine must be given in order to suppress prolactin by more than 50% of control or placebo concentrations.

Kullander and Svanberg (1979) studied ten women with PMS, diagnosed somewhat prospectively in control cycles. Then each subject received either bromocriptine (2.5 mg twice a day) or placebo from Day 14 until menses. Symptoms improved with both bromocriptine and placebo, but there were no statistical differences between treatments. Bromocriptine was better than placebo for mastodynia. Seven patients reported side effects, but not of sufficient magnitude to end the study.

Elsner and colleagues (1980) improved on subject selection and set up a placebo-controlled study without crossover. Twenty-four women with PMS were assigned to one of four treatment groups for three cycles: one placebo group and three bromocriptine groups using different doses depending on the day of the cycle. These different regimens are not listed here because they were apparently not a source of distinction in the data analysis. According to physician evaluation during the premenstruum, significant placebo effects were observed for breast and abdominal tenderness and for physical discomfort. Even so, bromocriptine was superior to placebo for breast tenderness ($p = 0.06$), according to the physician raters. Patient diaries then revealed a significant improvement in breast tenderness, abdominal bloating, and depression comparing bromocriptine with placebo, but a positive placebo effect on general discomfort and tension.

Andersch and Hahn (1982) studied 35 women with "a combination of mental symptoms and symptoms of swelling" (p. 107) that required medical attention. Using a rating scale of 0–3, only abdominal swelling and irritability were rated at about 2 (other common symptoms listed below were rated lower). Women were treated randomly with bromocriptine (1.25 mg twice daily) for three cycles and placebo for one cycle. Both treatments significantly decreased mean scores for abdominal swelling, irritability, sadness, anxiety, and swelling of fingers and legs. However, bromocriptine was significantly superior to placebo only for swelling of fingers and legs.

Ylostalo et al. (1982) tested bromocriptine versus placebo and norethisterone in 32 women with PMS. Seventeen women received 1.25 mg bromocriptine twice daily on Days 12–14 and 2.5 mg twice daily from Day 15 to menses during Cycles 2 and 4 of the 4-month study. Placebo was given during Cycles 1 and 3. Bromocriptine significantly reduced breast tenderness, depression, and need for sleep when compared to placebo. Women also gained less weight. However, some subjects complained of nausea and vomiting. Global improvement with respect to placebo occurred only in the second bromocriptine cycle, suggesting that any placebo response had been overcome.

Steiner and colleagues (1983) used quite rigorous selection criteria to study 28 women with dysphoric symptoms of PMS. Each subject was assigned to one of four groups for three treatment months (following a control month): placebo and bromocriptine 2.5 mg/day, 5.0 mg/day, or 7.5 mg/day. Medication began on Day 10 and continued until menses. In this study, all dysphoric symptoms improved, with no difference found between bromocriptine and placebo. The investigators suggested that their work was preliminary and that a crossover design would be preferable to their parallel one.

Ylostalo (1984) selected 268 women with PMS who suffered from breast symptoms, among others. Subjects in Group A received 1.25 mg bromocriptine daily from Day 1–5, then 2.50 mg daily from Day 6 through menses. Group B began 1.25 mg bromocriptine on Day 11, increasing to 2.50 mg on Day 14. Treatment continued for three cycles. Bromocriptine improved breast symptoms in 86 to 89% of the subjects. The cyclical treatment regimen given to Group B was more effective than continuous treatment for swelling and pain of the breasts. Global marked improvement was reported by 49.6% in Group A and by 44.9% in Group B. Twenty-one percent of the subjects dropped out due to side effects.

Impression. As of 1984, when the last study discussed in this section was published, bromocriptine had been in use for 6 years (Vance et al., 1984). Despite the plethora of double-blind and open studies using this agent, it is clear that the definitive study has yet to be done. As with studies of other treatment modalities, these reports using bromocriptine were not carried out long enough to separate placebo response from actual responses to treatment. But even with inadequate trials and less than rigorous subject selection, the majority of these reports suggest that breast symptoms do respond well to bromocriptine. Two reviews (Andersen & Larsen, 1979; Andersch 1983) advocate bromocriptine as the drug of choice for premenstrual mastodynia. The dose should be 2.5 mg twice daily to be effective and should be administered only in the luteal phase. However, it should be noted that every study using this dose reported adverse side effects.

More work is required to determine the effect of bromocriptine on other symptoms of PMS. At least at this point, the prolactin hypothesis of PMS is not supported by treatment trials of bromocriptine.

THYROID HORMONE

Description. Levothyroxine sodium (Synthroid; Flint) is synthetic l-thyroxine, the major hormonal product of the thyroid gland. It is used as specific hormone replacement therapy for reduced or absent thyroid function as a result of any etiology (*PDR*, 1987).

Research. Thyroid extracts were used by Lederer (1963) to successfully treat a woman with premenstrual kleptomania. (She also had mild hypothyroidism). Other symptoms that improved included depression, level of activity, and libido. The positive response required 4 months of treatment to become apparent.

Brayshaw and Brayshaw (1986) reported that women with PMS responded well to levothyroxine sodium. However, in this open study, women were apparently diagnosed with PMS not only by retrospective symptom reports but also by abnormal response to thyroid-stimulating hormone (TSH). In addition, 94% of the subjects with PMS had one or more symptoms of thyroid dysfunction.

Brayshaw and Brayshaw (1987) later expanded on their 1986 report. More details concerning the subject population were published; the authors had included women with major depression, irregular and/or anovulatory cycles, and anorexia nervosa in the PMS group (diagnosed retrospectively and loosely in the first place). Further, some of the subjects had symptoms that persisted throughout the month. Despite good success with thyroid treatment (average daily dose of 0.13 mg), their conclusion "that PMS may be merely a symptom of underlying thyroid dysfunction" (p. 179) cannot be supported.

Impression. A PMS diagnosis cannot be given to a woman who presents with an untreated thyroid disorder. Thus it is important to treat the endocrinopathy first, and then see if symptoms of PMS persist. Whether the thyroid-releasing hormone challenge test used by Brayshaw and Brayshaw (1986, 1987) indicates that all of their PMS patients had subclinical thyroid dysfunction is not clear. Wholesale prescribing of Synthroid for women with PMS does not seem warranted at this time.

DIURETICS AND ANTIHYPERTENSIVES

Several types of diuretics that have been used to treat PMS will be described below. Recently, clonidine and verapamil, drugs most widely known as an antihypertensive and an antiarrythmia agent, respectively, have been tried as treatments for PMS. The premise for the use of both clonidine and verapamil is based not on their effects on blood pressure or cardiac function, but on their psychoactive properties as antimania drugs. Therefore, the sections on clonidine and verapamil appear below (pp. 233–234) with the other putative therapeutic agents that are psychoactive.

Spironolactone

Description. Spironolactone (Parke-Davis, among others) is a synthetic steroidal antagonist of aldosterone and, as such, is a diuretic and antihypertensive agent (*PDR*, 1987). It is indicated in the management of primary hyperaldosteronism, edema associated with congestive heart failure, cirrhosis of the liver, essential hypertension, and hypokalemia. Spironolactone can cause gastrointestinal disturbance, central nervous system depression, and irregular menses. It has been shown to be tumorgenic in rats. Spironolactone should not be used during pregnancy.

This drug also is an antiandrogen by virtue of its ability to alter both the synthesis of androgens and their binding at the nuclear level of target cells (Cumming et al., 1982).

Research. Research on the use of spironolactone for PMS began on the premise that aldosterone could be responsible for PMS as a result of its sodium-retaining properties (O'Brien et al., 1979). Twenty-eight women, 18 with premenstrual symptoms according to a mood index and 10 without, participated in a four-cycle double-blind crossover study of spironolactone (25 mg) or placebo four times daily from Day 18 to Day 26. Crossover occurred randomly during the 4 months. Scores on the mood index were significantly lower during the active treatment months in the symptomatic group, indicating that symptoms of depression, tension, bloatedness, loss of libido, and anxiety, among others, had improved. In both groups, active treatment months were associated with weight loss. Interestingly, aldosterone concentrations were not related to symptoms.

In a report based on clinical experience, spironolactone was successful in treating 80% of 50 patients (Simmons, 1983). Depression, crying, and abdominal bloating were treated by spironolactone administered four times per day, 25 mg per dose, Day 14 through menses.

Hendler (1980) selected seven women with two or more psychological symptoms (e.g., depression, anger, irritability) and one or more fluid-related symptoms of PMS for his study. Five women with regular cycles received spironolactone openly, 25 mg twice daily for 7 days before the expected menses and throughout the menstrual period. Two women with irregular cycles took spironolactone daily. After 3 months, all seven were withdrawn from the drug. Six of seven reported subjective improvement, especially in irritability (5 of 6) and depression (4 of 6). All six asked to be continued on the drug at the end of the six month study period.

In a recent double-blind placebo-controlled study (Vellacott et al., 1987), subjects with (1 month) prospectively documented PMS were selected. Women were excluded if they had a history of psychiatric illness. Symptoms were constrained to end by two days of menses. After charting Cycle 1, the 63 participants received either spironolactone (100 mg daily in one dose) or placebo from Day 12 of the menstrual cycle until the first day of the next menses for two cycles (no crossover). By Cycle 3, 9 of 12 symptoms tended to be better with active treatment, but only reduction in bloatedness reached statistical significance. By global assessment, 60% of the women improved on spironolactone, while only 30% did on placebo.

Impression. Despite the inability of several groups to find significant changes in body fluids that correlate with PMS symptoms (Vellacott & O'Brien, 1987), two controlled studies have shown a reduction in symptoms, especially in bloatedness. These effects may be mediated by spironolactone's diuretic properties. Thus spironolactone may be used by women whose predominant somatic symptoms include weight gain and bloatedness. In addition, if a diuretic is to be used, then spironolactone is a good choice, since it spares potassium and does not cause secondary aldosteronism. Further, any tendency to aldosteronism should be minimized by using the diuretic only from Day 12 to menses.

Diuretics

Drugs in this category promote the excretion of water and salts from the kidney by various modes of action. Diuretics were among the first treatments for PMS. Frank (1931) suggested using calcium lactate, theobromine sodiosalicylate, or coffee to promote excretion of excess "female sex hormone," his etiology for the cause of PMS being hyperestrogenemia. Several other diuretics have been used: ammonium chloride, thiazide diuretics, chlorthalidone, metolazone, and triamterene. Spironolactone has already been described above in a separate section for two reasons. First, much research on its use in PMS has been published, and second, its mechanism of action is via aldosterone, not directly on the kidney. Potassium ion is also a diuretic, but it is described under nutritional supplements (pp. 221–222).

A methodological problem with most of the studies that follow, however, which is not addressed by the investigators, is the identification of an active cycle by the supposedly blind subject. One would expect that if a subject is undergoing significant diuresis, she will know it. Further, she need only to stand on her scale to note a difference between a treatment cycle and a placebo cycle by the presence or absence of her usual weight gain. Thus one wonders whether expectation factors play a role in the success of this treatment. The reader should bear this point in mind when considering the study of any diuretic.

Ammonium Chloride

Description. Ammonium chloride is no longer used as an acid diuretic but is a component of other medications, such as cough syrups.

Research. Ammonium chloride was used by Greenhill and Freed (1941) to treat women with premenstrual "distress or tension" based on their proposed etiology that the syndrome was the result of electrolyte and water imbalances due to cyclic ovarian activity. It is interesting that these authors made a distinction between "distress" and "tension," the latter being more serious because of the intensity of symptoms. Forty women received 3 gm of ammonium chloride daily, starting 10–12 days before menses. Thirty-four reported "definite" relief, especially those women with more serious symptoms. While ammonium chloride treated edema successfully, it did not affect menstrually related migraine or painful breasts.

Stieglitz and Kimble (1949) treated 67 women with ammonium chloride for 10 days before menses, using a dose of 1 gm three times per day. Ninety-one percent responded favorably, but maximum benefit often took two or three months of treatment to become evident.

Rees (1953a) used enteric coated ammonium chloride in the dose of 0.5–1.0 g three times daily for 12 days before menses. The majority of his 30 subjects (actual number not stated) felt more comfortable and were relieved from their symptoms of bloating. However, "the method was not always effective in relieving the nervous tension, irritability, depression and anxiety. This suggests that hydration is not responsible for all the symptoms of the syndrome" (p. 1015).

Ammonium chloride was also used in combination with other ingredients, such as caffeine, homatropine methylbromide (an antispasmodic), and Vitamin B complex (Pre-mens, now not available) (Morton et al., 1953; Fortin et al., 1958), and just with caffeine (Aquaban, Thompson Medical Co.) (Hoffman, 1979).

Morton and colleagues (1953) studied prison and reformatory inmates divided into four groups. Each subject received either two tablets of Pre-mens or placebo three times daily for 10 days before menses. In addition, the diets of one group each of Pre-mens and placebo were supplemented with high-protein snacks. These women were also advised to limit their salt and sugar intake, and substitutes for both were available. After one month, 79% reported improvement on active medication and diet and 39% improved on placebo plus diet. In the drug-only group, 61% improved on medication versus 15% on placebo. While Morton and colleagues wanted to make a case for the diet's causing the difference among groups, it should be pointed out that the women in the diet group came exclusively from the prison and were older than the reformatory inmates. Further, pretreatment symptom profiles differed in percentages (> 12%) reporting pain, fatigue, appetite and cravings, low abdominal pain, and dysmenorrhea. These points are important, since this is the work that led to the advocacy of the hypoglycemia diet and of sugar and salt restriction. While the diuretic may have helped, the effect of the diet is certainly unproven. The study also suffers from its short duration.

Fortin and colleagues (1958) administered Pre-mens openly to 13 subjects with PMS. Nine reportedly improved, two did not, and two became worse.

Hoffman (1979) tested Aquaban in 22 women who gained at least two pounds premenstrually. Some were taking oral contraceptives. Half of the women received one tablet daily containing either 325 mg ammonium chloride and 100 mg caffeine or placebo for 1 month during the 6 days prior to menses. Crossover occurred in the second month. Weight was the outcome measure. Not surprisingly, using a diuretic led to statistically superior control of premenstrual weight gain.

Impression. Use of ammonium chloride with or without other ingredients promotes diuresis and limits the symptoms of bloating. However, most of these studies were open, used less than rigorous subject selection and were short in duration. It is not clear from this work whether long term use is either safe or advisable.

Aquaban is still available over-the-counter (see pp. 238–242).

Thiazide Diuretics

Description. Thiazide diuretics used in research on PMS include chlorothiazide, flumethiazide, and benzthiazide. Chlorothiazide (tablets by Lederle and others) is a diuretic and antihypertensive acting on the renal tubule to decrease electrolyte reabsorption, thereby promoting salt and water excretion. Patients need to be evaluated periodically for serum electrolyte composition, since hypokalemia may develop. Weakness, orthostatic hypotension, and gastrointestinal problems may occur.

Benzthiazide (Exna; Robins) is also a diuretic and antihypertensive used for the treatment of edema associated with congestive heart failure, corticosteroid and estrogen therapy, and renal disease. The same cautions mentioned above for chlorothiazide apply.

Flumethiazide is not available in the United States, but it is probably similar in most respects to other thiazide diuretics.

Research. Jungck and colleagues (1959) reported an open trial of chlorothiazide in 50 women with typical premenstrual complaints. Chlorothiazide was administered in doses of 500–1,000 mg for 7–10 days before menses. Of 42 women with severe nervousness and tension, 21 were relieved with chlorothiazide alone. The other 21 received a mild sedative, such as meprobamate, in addition to the diuretic, with good outcome. Thirty-three women had complained of swelling; all 33 responded "excellently," as did 8 out of 8 women with breast tenderness.

Winshel (1959) reviewed the literature on diuretics up to 1959 and stated that they "have found a useful place in the management of premenstrual tension" (p. 541). His own clinical experience supported his view, but no details were given. He favored chlorothiazide since it could be given once per day instead of three times as with ammonium chloride.

Appleby (1960) compared chlorothiazide to synthetic progestins, meprobamate, and placebo. Using chlorothiazide in a dose of 500 mg twice daily for 9 days before menses, 33% of the study participants reported complete relief or marked improvement after 3 months, compared to 7% on placebo. Six women had earlier onset of menses while on chlorothiazide. No correlation between loss of weight and relief of symptoms of irritability and depression was found. Interestingly, those who responded to chlorothiazide tended not to respond to meprobamate, and vice versa, suggesting the presence of subgroups of women with PMS.

Benzthiazide (25 mg), in combination with triamterene (50 mg) (see p. 202 below), was used in a parallel treatment trial to norethisterone and placebo in women complaining of PMS (Coppen et al., 1969). After one month of drug taken on Days 22–28, the diuretics significantly improved irritability and depression scores over both placebo and norethisterone, but did *not* change the rating of body swelling.

A derivative of flumethiazide was assessed with medroxyprogesterone acetate by Jordheim (1972). Only 26% of women with PMS reported good or very good results with the combination of drugs (2.5 mg medroxyprogesterone acetate and 2 mg diuretic, thrice daily starting 10 days before menses), as compared with 19% on progestin alone. The difference was not significant. No group received only a diuretic.

Impression. There certainly is a lack of consensus about the efficacy of this treatment. In open trials, women seem to do well with regard to swelling symptoms. However, Appleby (1960) could not relate diuresis to improvement in depression or irritability. Further, Coppen and colleagues (1969) could not show that using diuretics improved swelling; but they did show that mood symptoms improved.

Since these thiazide diuretics can cause electrolyte imbalances, it seems more reasonable to use a potassium-sparing diuretic such as spironolactone if the symptoms of swelling warrant treatment.

Metolazone

Description. Metolazone (Diulo; Searle Pharmaceuticals) is a diuretic/saluretic/antihypertensive drug in the sulfuramide group. It acts at the cortical diluting site and proximal convoluted tubule. Metolazone is used for edema due to congestive heart failure and for renal disease. Precautions are the same as with the thiazide diuretics.

Research. A double-blind placebo-controlled study of metolazone was conducted by Werch and Kane (1976). Women who gained at least three pounds on each of two successive premenstrual phases were selected for study. Treatment began 7 days before menses and continued through menses for two cycles before crossover to the other treatment occurred. Doses of active diuretic were either 1.0 or 2.4 mg daily.

Metolazone significantly decreased premenstrual weight gain over placebo, as well as symptoms of irritability, depression, tension, anxiety, edema, breast swelling, and abdominal swelling. Metolazone also lowered postmenstrual scores for irritability, tension, depression, edema, abdominal swelling, and headache. However, premenstrual headaches, insomnia, and tiredness were not improved, suggesting that diuresis may not clear up everything.

Impression. This study suggests further that diuretics may be of use to women who gain weight premenstrually. Some mood symptoms may also be improved in those women when water retention is eliminated.

Chlorthalidone

Description. Chlorthalidone (Hygroton; Rorer Pharmaceuticals, among others) is an oral hypertensive/diuretic that differs from the thiazides in its structure and duration of action. This long-acting diuretic acts at the ascending loop of Henle. The uses and precautions are the same as for the thiazides.

Research. Kramer (1962) used chlorthalidone to treat 24 women with PMS who had pronounced features of edema. The dose was not stated, but "results were very impressive" (p. 6). Both physiological and psychological symptoms improved.

Mattsson and von Schoultz (1974) tested chlorthalidone in a double-blind study in comparison with lithium and placebo (see p. 232 below). The diuretic was not satistically better than placebo.

Impression. This very sketchy case report suggests that women with severe edematous features may benefit from a diuretic such as chlorthalidone. The double-blind study by Mattsson and von Schoultz (1974) also did not show the superiority of chlorthalidone over placebo. More research is required on the effect of this particular drug on PMS.

Triamterene

Description. Triamterene (Dyserium; Smith Kline & French) is a potassium-sparing diuretic. It acts on the distal renal tubule to inhibit sodium ion reabsorption in exchange for potassium and hydrogen ions. This action is not related to aldosterone secretion or antagonism, and triamterene thus differs from spironolactone in this regard. Triamterene can lead to hyperkalemia and cannot be used in conjunction with other potassium-sparing drugs, such as spironolactone. Other adverse effects are rare.

Research. This diuretic is advocated by Dr. Penny Wise Budoff for women with symptoms of bloating who are not sufficiently helped by salt restriction (Klein, 1988). We were unable to find any case reports or papers on its use as a solo agent. It was used in combination form with benzthiazide by Coppen and colleagues (1969; see p. 200 above).

Impression. As with the other diuretics and spironolactone, it is not clear whether any benefit will be realized from a majority of women who feel "bloated" but do not gain weight. Clearly, more research is required on this particular diuretic before its use can be advocated as being helpful for PMS.

Atenolol

Description. Atenolol is a beta-adrenergic receptor blocker that decreases heart rate and lowers both systolic and diastolic blood pressure. Thus it is used in the management of hypertension. Few side effects are associated with the drug, but it is toxic in high doses to rat fetuses. Hence atenolol should be used with caution in women of childbearing age.

Research. One research group has reported the use of atenolol for PMS (Rausch et al., 1987, 1988). The investigators hypothesized that symptoms of irritability would improve with atenolol since the drug decreases plasma renin activity and inhibits urinary aldosterone excretion, thereby improving sodium and water changes that might produce irritability. They also suggested that anxiety might improve since other beta blockers such as propranolol have been used to treat anxiety disorders.

Rausch and colleagues selected 16 women with provisional diagnoses of LLPDD. Subjects completed one month of prospective daily ratings, then were assigned either to atenolol (50 mg) or placebo once daily starting 10 days before expected menses. After one cycle, the treatments were crossed over. Blood samples for estradiol and progesterone measurement and a battery of psychological tests were administered during the two treatment months.

Atenolol treatment was superior to placebo for decreasing irritability and for preventing the usual decrease in vigor, elation, and friendliness. Interestingly, women who had had PMS for more than 5 years responded more favorably to the drug than women with shorter durations of the syndrome.

The investigators also found that atenolol did not inhibit luteal phase increases in aldosterone or plasma renin activity. However, women with more moderate PMS symptoms showed a larger decrease in plasma renin activity than women with more severe symptomatology. Progesterone concentrations were higher luteally during atenolol treatment, especially in those women with longer histories of PMS.

Impression. The investigators concluded that "the data from this study indicated that atenolol blunted symptoms of premenstrual tension to a limited extent in the subject group as a whole. This alleviation was much more dramatic in subjects who had premenstrual tension for more than 5 years" (p. 146). More research will be required to validate this treatment option.

PROSTAGLANDIN-RELATED TREATMENTS

Prostaglandin Inhibitors—Mefenamic Acid (Ponstel)

Description. Mefenamic acid is a member of the fenamate family. Drugs of this class are nonsteroidal, with anti-inflammatory, analgesic, and antipyretic activity (*PDR*, 1987). Their mode of action is not precisely known, although they are nonspecific prostaglandin synthetase inhibitors (Jakubowicz et al., 1984).

Mefenamic acid is indicated for the treatment of primary dysmenorrhea, IUD-induced (secondary) dysmenorrhea, menorrhagia (Fraser, 1985), and other moderate pain when therapy will not exceed 1 week. The drug is known to cause rash, diarrhea, and other gastrointestinal disturbances (*PDR*, 1987).

Research. The first published report on the use of mefenamic acid in women with PMS appeared in 1980 (Wood & Jakubowicz, 1980), on the theory that metabolic products of prostaglandins might cause PMS.

Women aged 25–50 were recruited by phone and screened for a history of premenstrual complaints. Following a control month during which subjects completed a daily check list, the women were assigned randomly to either a placebo or mefenamic acid group using double-blind technique. Crossover occurred after the second month. The dose of mefenamic acid was 500 mg three times daily. Of the 37 subjects, only 3 were symptomatic solely during the premenstruum; the other 34 had combinations of premenstrual and menstrual symptoms. Twenty-three subjects preferred the month with mefenamic acid, 6 preferred the placebo, and 8 had no preference. None of the women with only premenstrual complaints improved. Symptoms that were relieved in 8 to 10 women (not identified as to the timespan of their usual symptoms) included tension, irritability, and depression. Breast symptoms and fluid retention were not altered by treatment. The authors concluded that antiprostaglandins should not be used in women with only premenstrual symptoms, in women whose major problem is breast symptoms, or in women who may become pregnant.

In 1984, Jakubowicz and colleagues reported an expanded study using mefenamic acid. Although 80 women participated, only 19 women were assigned to a 3-month double-blind crossover trial (one control month followed by two treatment months). The subject population included women with menorrhagia and dysmenorrhea (47%) and with previous psychiatric illness (11%). Thirteen of 19 preferred the month with mefenamic acid (500 mg three times daily), 4 preferred placebo, and 2 were relieved by both. In the larger group of 61 women, 86% reported substantial or complete improvement with mefenamic acid. However, 26% of the subjects complained of side effects, which included dyspepsia, nausea, diarrhea, and rash within 1 to 6 months of treatment.

Budoff (1983) reported the results of an 8-month double-blind crossover study using mefenamic acid. Subjects had a variety of PMS complaints and were also being treated for dysmenorrhea. The women were instructed not to begin medication until 4 days prior to the (expected) onset of menses. Her subjects reported statistically significant relief from premenstrual breast tenderness, abdominal bloating, and ankle swelling. There was no improvement in tension, lethargy, or depression, which contradicts the two studies discussed previously.

Gunston (1986) also conducted a 5-month double-blind prospectively randomized placebo-controlled trial of mefenamic acid. Thirty women participated for 1 month of control self-reports and 4 treatment months. Few characteristics of the patient population were reported, such as the severity or types of PMS complaints, and Gunston's definition of PMS was broad. Sixteen reported subjective improvement on mefenamic acid (250 mg three times daily) only, 3 improved on placebo only, and 11 found no difference. The difference in improvement between mefenamic acid and placebo was statistically significant. When individual symptoms were analyzed from the self-report checklists, only gastrointestinal symptoms improved significantly with mefenamic acid. Gunston also showed a large placebo effect on management, since 5 to 10 subjects improved on either placebo or mefenamic acid for the following symptoms: irritability, depression, bloating, breast tenderness, and tension.

Another recent study of mefenamic acid was designed to improve subject selection (Mira et al., 1986). Like the other studies, it used a prospective, randomized, double-blind crossover technique with placebo. However, the subject population was much more rigorously defined to avoid any factor that could lead to a misdiagnosis of the syndrome. The investigators selected women with PMS as determined by 3 months of daily ratings. They excluded any woman who (1) had a history of psychiatric illness, (2) took any medication (including vitamins), or (3) had a gynecological disorder, such as dysmenorrhea or menorrhagia. The authors also determined the date of ovulation by using luteinizing hormone measurement and confirmed this with a serum progesterone assay. During the study, mefenamic acid or placebo treatment was changed every 2 months for 6 months. Treatment began each month 12 days before the predicted onset of menses. Mefenamic acid was then administered at 250 mg three times daily for 3 days followed by 500 mg three times daily until menses. The investigators found that a number of physical, mood, and behavioral symptoms were improved significantly, including fatigue, general aches and pains, sadness, irritability, and bad and slow performance. However, breast and abdominal symptoms as well as tension, confusion, inability to concentrate, difficulty sleeping, and appetite changes and cravings were not affected.

Impression. The research studies suggest that mefenamic acid may be preferred more than placebo in some women with PMS. However, there are inconsistencies among the research groups regarding the symptoms that are treated effectively, including such major common problems as depression, breast tenderness, tension, irritability, and fluid retention. Since mefenamic acid can cause side effects and may be useful for only a few selected symptoms related to pain, it appears at this time to have limited utility in the treatment of PMS.

Prostaglandin Precursors

Prostaglandin precursors are free fatty acids. Some of these are found in evening primrose oil. This dietary supplement is described below on pages 215–218.

HISTAMINE-RELATED TREATMENTS

Antihistamines

Description. Two common antihistamines, promethazine hydrochloride (Phenergan; Wyeth) and pyrilamine maleate (component of Histalet; Reid-Rowell and others), are H_1 receptor blockers. They are commonly used to treat various forms of rhinitis and anaphylactic reactions. In addition, Phenergan is used to treat nausea, vomiting, and motion sickness and to sedate adults and children.

Research. Use of antihistamines to treat PMS is recorded in the early literature. A case report using Phenergan for PMS was reported in 1951 (Geiringer, 1951). This antihistamine was tried since Geiringer had noted a similarity between PMS symptoms and allergic attacks. After one asymptomatic month on the antihistamine, the subject became pregnant, thus ending the experiment.

In 1953, Bickers used a combination drug, bromaleate, composed of pyrilamine maleate and bromtheophyllinate, to treat women with PMS. As with the report on the use of Phenergan, the premise for trying the antihistamine was the theory that "allergy to the ovarian steroids is a factor in the etiology" (p. 876) of PMS. The bromtheophylline was added to act as a diuretic. Bickers administered the drug to 56 women with moderate to severe PMS and menorrhagia, beginning 4–12 days before the expected menses, the interval to be determined by the onset of symptoms. He reported that weight gain was less during drug treatment than before (4.2 lbs vs. 1.6 lbs, respectively) and that symptoms were relieved. More detail is lacking.

Impression. Antihistamines are common additions to over-the-counter medications for PMS (see pp. 238–242 below). However, there is little supportive evidence in the literature for the efficacy of these agents.

Histamine

Description. Histamine is an imidazole derived from the amino acid histadine. It causes vasodilation, gastric acid secretion, bronchoconstriction, headache, and the skin wheal and flare response to local irritation (pain and itch) among others. Histamine is also involved in anaphylactic reactions.

Research. One report has appeared in the literature on the use of histamine to treat PMS (Atton-Chamla et al., 1980). The histamine was administered as part of a gamma globulin/histamine complex (2 microliters containing 12 mg gamma globulin plus 0.15 micrograms histamine hydrochloride), based on a report that migraine had been treated successfully with the complex (Teitelbaum et al., 1970). Either the complex or placebo was given to 86 women with PMS (no definition of subject selection criteria was given). Both groups received injections on Days 6, 13, and 20 of the first cycle, Days 13 and 20 of the second cycle, and Day 20 of the third cycle. The response to the complex was significantly better than to placebo, even at follow-up several months later. The authors also found a positive correlation between elevated levels of serum IgE and response to treatment with histamine complex.

Impression. This study is interesting, but it is not clear whether histamine itself has any role in the pathology of PMS. This study does not determine whether the histamine, the gamma globulin, or the complex was the factor responsible for the improvement in symptoms. Further, since rigorous subject selection techniques were not used, no firm conclusions can be drawn regarding efficacy. The gamma globulin/histamine complex is not available in the United States at this time.

NUTRITIONAL SUPPLEMENTS

Pyridoxine—Vitamin B_6

Description. Vitamin B_6 is actually a group of compounds including pyridoxine, pyridoxal, and pyridoxamine (Garrison & Somer, 1985). When converted to its coenzyme form, pyridoxal phosphate (PLP), the vitamin is essential in the metabolism of proteins. PLP is also required for the biosynthesis of important neurotransmitters, such as serotonin, gamma-aminobutyric acid, norepinephrine, acetylcholine, and histamine. PLP is involved in hemoglobin synthesis, lipid and carbohydrate metabolism, and the conversion of glycogen to glucose.

Symptoms of B_6 deficiency "are vague and hard to reproduce" (Garrison & Somer, 1985). Weakness, confusion, irritability, insomnia, anemia, and skin lesions are some of the deficiency symptoms reported.

The adult Recommended Daily Allowance for women over age 15 is 2 mg. Women on birth control pills may require more vitamin since the oral contraceptives may interfere with either the concentration of the vitamin or its coenzyme form.

Consuming this essential water-soluble vitamin is not without risk, however, when taken in large doses. Schaumberg and colleagues (1983) reported a series of patients with ataxia and sensory nervous system dysfunction resulting from daily consumption of 2–6 g B_6 for 2 to 40 months. The seven women had begun the megavitamin regimen either as a self-imposed supplement or for edema. (Edema did not sub-

sequently improve.) Patients had unstable gait, numbness and clumsiness of the hands, and perioral numbness. Nerve biopsy demonstrated
nonspecific axonal degeneration of large and small myelinated fibers.
Within 2 months of discontinuing the vitamin, gait and discomfort in the
extremities both improved. Vibratory sense did not recover completely,
however, even after 2 to 3 years.

An additional 16 patients with similar neuropathies were described
by Parry and Bredesen (1985). Their patients consumed between 0.2
and 5.0 g/day, less than Schaumberg and colleagues (1983) reported.
The investigators noted an inverse relationship between dose and duration that led to the appearance of symptoms. From the "pure sensory,
length-dependent, axonal neuropathy," Parry and Bredesen (1985) concluded that B_6 may be toxic to the dorsal root ganglia.

Dalton (1985) reported the prevalence of symptoms in 27 women
taking 50–300 mg B_6 daily. In the sample of older women with PMS (43
years old on average), 40% had sensory neuropathies associated with
serum B_6 concentrations greater than the 3–18 ng/ml norm. In addition
to neurological problems, these women also complained more frequently of tiredness, bloating, irritability, depression, and headache when
taking B_6. Note that these are common symptoms of PMS.

Brush and Perry (1985) criticized Dalton's (1985) report on the
grounds that B_6 levels are difficult to measure. They also questioned
whether the age of the subjects was important. They mentioned that in
630 women taking 80–200 mg B_6 daily for PMS between 1976 and 1983,
no neuropathies were seen.

Dalton and Dalton (1987) reported recently on low-dose B_6 "intoxication." Their subjects were women who came to a PMS clinic
already taking B_6. The investigation measured serum B_6 concentrations
and asked about neurological symptoms. Sixty percent (103) of 172
women with B_6 concentrations above 18 ng/ml complained of neurological symptoms. The average daily dose was 118 mg in the neurotoxic
group versus 117 mg in the 40% of women with elevated B_6 but with no
neurological complaints. The neurotoxic group had used B_6 for an
average of 3 years, while the controls had for only 1.6 years, a significant
difference. Symptoms reported by the 103 afflicted women included
paresthesia, bone pain, hyperesthesia, muscle weakness, fasciculation,
and numbness. After abstaining from B_6 for 2 months, most had serum
concentrations in the normal range. By 3 months, 55% of the neurotoxic
group reported partial or complete recovery, and all had recovered by 6
months. The investigators suggest that other studies reporting less than
complete recovery were of women consuming higher doses of B_6 per
day than in this sample (see Schaumberg et al., 1983; Perry & Bredesen,
1985).

Research. Reports of the use of Vitamin B$_6$ for PMS began in the 1940s (Biskind et al., 1944), based on the premise that deficiencies in B vitamins were associated with conditions of "excess estrogen." This hyperestrogenism was, in turn, correlated with a variety of menstrual complaints, including menorrhagia, metrorrhagia, painful breasts, and premenstrual tension. Biskind and colleagues (1944) reported a series of cases using oral and parenteral B vitamin complex. The concentration of B$_6$ in the oral preparation was not stated but was 5–8 mg in the parenteral solution administered every second or third day. The women treated in this study frequently had signs of B avitaminosis, such as atrophic glossitis and cheilosis. None of the women had only PMS; most also had breast problems, dysmenorrhea, or profuse flow. Following oral and/or parenteral treatment, prompt positive responses were obtained. The authors did find, however, that relapses occurred in some women as soon as the parenteral or oral dosages were decreased. One wonders whether there may have been a placebo effect at work here, since by the end of a few months of treatment vitamin levels had presumably been restored.

A report on a controlled study on the use of B$_6$ appeared in 1972 (Stokes & Mendels, 1972). After successfully treating two women with PMS and "self-loathing" in an open trial, the investigators designed a double-blind long-term study of 13 women with PMS. B$_6$ (50 mg) or placebo was prescribed for 18 days over the premenstrual and early menstrual phases. Nine of 13 improved, but 5 were "spontaneous remissions" (i.e., placebo responders). The other 4 subjects tended to show improvement on B$_6$ but not on placebo, but the difference was only significant in 1 subject. Three of the 13 responded to neither treatment; 1 became worse on B$_6$. It would have been useful to have more details on subject selection and symptoms that improved.

A paper often cited as the rationale for using B$_6$ in PMS appeared in 1973 (Adams et al., 1973). This group studied women taking oral contraceptives who became depressed as a result. Twenty-two women participated in a 4-month crossover study with placebo (2 months) or active treatment (2 months) after their B$_6$ nutritional status was assessed. Active treatment was 40 mg B$_6$ daily. Half of the sample (11 women) had evidence of absolute B$_6$ deficiency, as detected by analysis of ratios of urinary metabolites of tryptophan that are dependent on B$_6$ concentrations. Symptoms of depression improved significantly only in the B$_6$-deficient group, as measured by the Beck Depression Inventory, a questionnaire filled out by the subjects. Interestingly, if a subject received B$_6$ first, the good outcome persisted through both placebo cycles, that is, no relapse occurred.

Kerr (1977) reported an open study of 70 women in his clinical practice who were started on B_6 as the first treatment. With doses beginning at 40 mg (up to 100 mg in subsequent cycles) from 3 days before typical symptom onset to menses or shortly thereafter, good results were obtained after two cycles of treatment. "Cures" in 40% or more of the women were achieved for depression, irritability, bloating, breast tenderness, and headache.

Abraham (1978) presented anecdotal reports of premenstrual symptoms that were improved by 200–800 mg B_6. Women on the vitamin had decreased appetite, less premenstrual weight gain, increased energy, better sleep, and decreased susceptibility to stress. Side effects noted were headache, dizziness, and nausea.

Taylor and James (1979), from the same hospital as Kerr (1977), reported on the results of open use of B_6 in 217 women who had presented with symptoms but who were cured or greatly relieved with B_6. The dose utilized was 40 mg twice daily from Day 12 to Day 26. Depression, edema, irritability, tension, abdominal distention, and breast discomfort were those symptoms that responded to treatment in 50% or more of the patients.

Day (1979b), from the same hospital as Kerr and Taylor and James, reported preliminary data from a six-cycle double-blind study of 100 mg B_6 daily or placebo from Day 10 to Day 3 of the next cycle. The placebo was given during Cycles 1, 5, and 6, and B_6 during Cycles 2, 3, and 4. The only result provided was that 63% of the 40 subjects who completed the trial improved overall. In a parallel study of dydrogesterone, the placebo response was 43%. Since subjects for this B_6 study were from the same patient pool, it is likely that the placebo response was equivalent. We could not find a more recent reference from Day to confirm the percent of placebo responses.

Abraham and Hargrove (1980) studied 25 women with PMS in a double-blind crossover study of 500 mg B_6 daily or placebo. Each treatment regimen lasted 3 months. Symptom scores rated prospectively were compared in individual women (1) between follicular and luteal phases during placebo cycles and (2) between luteal phases on placebo or B_6. Twenty-one of 25 women showed improvement during the luteal phase on B_6 when compared to placebo. However, close examination of the data revealed that scores also improved during the follicular phase on B_6 in 21 out of 25 women. This suggests that the B_6 effect may be nonspecific for the menstrual cycle, since women felt better at both phases.

Harrison and colleagues (1984) screened 30 women very carefully for PMS before conducting their treatment trial. Unfortunately, 60% of the women had a prior history of depression, so the subject group was not clean in that respect. However, they instituted one month of placebo prior to active treatment, the latter consisting of Vitamin B_6 plus tryptophan. Their selection of a combination treatment was based on the premise that higher concentrations of B_6 could increase tryptophan's conversion to serotonin, which in turn would alleviate premenstrual depressive symptomatology. Harrison and colleagues found that 11 women (41%) initially responded to placebo; 6 continued to do so for an additional three cycles. Placebo nonresponders and placebo relapsers received 1.5 g tryptophan and 50 mg B_6 for one cycle. If a woman did not respond, the doses were doubled in the second cycle and increased again in the third cycle. The average maximum dose was 3.7 g tryptophan and 110 mg B_6. However, side effects of daytime sleepiness occurred in 7 subjects using 3 g of tryptophan and 100 mg B_6. Only 2 women reported improvement on the treatment regimen.

Barr (1984) was one of the first to use intermittent B_6 therapy. His 36 subjects, some of whom were taking oral contraceptives (a design flaw), received 100 mg B_6 or placebo from Day 10 of one cycle to Day 3 of the next. After 2 months, the treatments crossed over. Global assessment showed that 20 women preferred B_6 to placebo, 10 improved on both, and 6 improved on neither. This was not how Barr presents the data, but we do not think that his analysis was appropriate.

Brush and Perry (1985) reported a success rate of 70% to 80% for mood, breast, and headache symptoms in 630 women taking 80–200 mg B_6 daily for PMS. No further details were provided.

Hagen and colleagues (1985) selected 34 women with PMS by retrospective history for a double-blind placebo-controlled test of B_6. Each woman received 100 mg B_6 or placebo daily for two cycles, then crossed over. No significant effect of B_6 was measured. Further, the investigators observed a period effect: Women preferred the second drug of the trial, whether it was B_6 or placebo.

Another placebo-controlled double-blind study was reported by Williams and colleagues (1985). This study was large: 724 women began the screening process; 434 women eventually completed three months on B_6 or placebo (no crossover). Global improvement occurred in 82% of women on B_6 and in 70% of placebo controls. Unfortunately, 74 women were concurrently taking anxiolytics and/or antidepressants, 60 were on analgesics, 33 were on diuretics, and 100 were using oral contraceptives or other gonadal hormones. That B_6 was superior to placebo, given the high placebo response and frequent use of other treatments for PMS, is a conclusion that is not supported by this work.

Kendall and Schnurr (1987) recently reported a B_6 versus placebo trial. They selected 55 women on the basis of retrospective history of PMS, but then used 1 month of prospective ratings to match the treatment groups by age and symptoms. The dose of B_6 was 50 mg three times daily. The investigators found a significant effect of treatment on autonomic reactions, such as nausea and dizziness, and on poor performance and social withdrawal. Subjects taking B_6 seemed to improve on autonomic reactions across the entire menstrual cycle. The researchers noted that women in both treatment groups "reported a substantial degree of premenstrual symptomatology despite the relative reduction in negative autonomic reactions and behavior changes seen in the B_6 group" (p. 148).

In addition to presenting their own data, Kendall and Schnurr (1987) reanalyzed those of Abraham and Hargrove (1980), a study criticized above by us. Kendall and Schnurr found that Abraham and Hargrove's data not only supported a main effect of therapy (B_6 versus placebo) but also a main effect of cycle phase. The latter indicates that symptoms persisted with B_6 treatment but that their severity decreased.

At the 2nd International Symposium: Premenstrual, Postpartum and Menopausal Mood Disorders, held in September 1987, Hallman and Oreland reported positive results with Vitamin B_6 using higher doses than did Kendall and Schnurr (1987) or Hagen and colleagues (1985). Selection criteria were unclear. Out of 50 women who were screened, 44 began the study, 12 dropped out, and 32 women with PMS completed the double-blind cross-over study using placebo and B_6. Subjects rated 13 common PMS symptoms for the 11 months of the study: one cycle to become familiar with the self-rating technique, four cycles on placebo or B_6, two cycles of wash out, and four cycles on the other treatment. B_6 (300 mg) or placebo was given daily from Day 12 until the first day of menstruation. When the mean symptom scores during the last seven days before menses were compared, significant improvements ($p < 0.05$) were found for irritability, depression, hyperactivity, clumsiness, swelling, changes in skin/hair, and headache. No significant difference was found for the symptoms of tension, anxiety, apathy, sleeplessness, tiredness, and increased appetite. Only headache was improved by placebo. No side effects were reported.

Malmgren and colleagues (1987) studied the effect of B_6 treatment on PMS in relation to platelet serotonin kinetics. The subjects were selected based on 1 month of prospective ratings in the follicular and luteal phases. Women with a psychiatric history or those taking hormones were excluded. Vitamin B_6 (300 mg) or placebo was taken daily from Day 15 to Day 1 of the next cycle. Treatments then crossed over for another month. While symptoms did not improve in the PMS group, B_6 treatment led to an increase in the rate of serotonin uptake in both the control women and the women with PMS (no difference between groups). The investigators were unable to explain this finding.

Impression. Vitamin B_6 is often cited as "the first-line drug treatment for PMS" (Rubinow, 1987b). However, the research presented in this section leaves one skeptical at best. There is no hard evidence for any of the proposed etiological factors underlying the use of B_6 (hyperestrogenemia, depletion of neurotransmitters, etc.). For example, Schrijver and colleagues (1987) were unable to show any change in urinary 3-methyl-4-hydroxyphenolglycol (MHPG) excretion in women with PMS who were treated with 120 mg B_6 daily for one menstrual cycle. Problems in subject selection and data analysis hamper the interpretation of results from many of the "controlled" studies, whether they advocate or oppose the use of the vitamin.

Further, some of the early work supporting a role for B_6 found that symptoms improved in women who were *deficient* in the vitamin (Biskind et al., 1944; Adams et al., 1973). Dalton and Dalton (1987) measured plasma concentrations of B_6, but they were not looking at treatment effects, only at neurotoxicity. None of the other papers on treatment assessed B_6 nutritional status. Further, recent work by Mira and colleagues (1988) found no difference in B_6 status in women with prospectively diagnosed PMS who either had never taken B_6 or had improved with B_6 in the past, when compared to control women without PMS.

Reynolds and Leklem (1985) reported that plasma concentrations of pyridoxine-1-phosphate reach a plateau after 25–50 mg B_6 per day. They question the use of higher supplement levels, given that neurotoxicity is associated with them.

That brings us to the last point. Contrary to the much-promoted view that "Vitamin B_6 therapy is inexpensive, well tolerated, without side effects and at least a safe placebo" (Chakmakjian, 1983, p. 534), this clearly is not the case. Since several investigators found a dose versus time relationship to the onset of neurological symptoms, it may be that long-term use of megadose B_6 cannot be advocated at all. Even 100 mg daily is 25–50 times the recommended daily dose. One cannot prescribe a treatment regimen whose outcome may be worse than the initial symptoms.

Vitamin E

Description. Vitamin E, alpha tocopherol, is a fat-soluble vitamin. Members of the tocopherol family are anti-oxidants. Vitamin E prevents the oxidation of essential cellular components by free radicals by acting as a cofactor of glutathione peroxidase in regions within the cell with high lipid content (Bland, 1985). Vitamin E has been shown to be of value in the treatment of fibrocystic breast disease (FD) and cystic mastitis; it may also improve intermittent claudication (Bland, 1985).

The recommended daily allowance of Vitamin E is 30 IU. Vitamin E has no clearly defined deficiency state, and its toxicity has not been established (Bland, 1985). However, when excessive daily amounts are consumed (over 8,000 units per day), thrombophlebitis, pulmonary emboli, fatigue, gynecomastia, (both sexes), and breast tumors have been reported (Roberts, 1982).

Research. Research into the effects of Vitamin E on PMS symptoms began as a result of its use in treating FD (London et al., 1983a). Patients with FD ($n = 42$) were administered questionnaires and divided into Abraham's (1983) four categories (see Chapter 5, pp. 122–126) of PMS. Women received either placebo or 150, 300, or 600 units/day of d,l-alpha-tocopherol using double-blind technique. Vitamin E decreased symptoms of headache, fatigue, insomnia, depression, and food cravings (PMT-C and PMT-D).

London and colleagues (1983b) expanded the subject population in a second report. Again, each subject had benign breast disease. All subjects completed questionnaires and were assigned to one of the four PMS groups. The doses of Vitamin E were the same as before, as was placebo. After two treatment months, subjects reassessed their symptoms. In this study, the symptoms listed previously as improving were also better (PMT-C and PMT-D), as were symptoms of anxiety (PMT-A) in the 150 and 300 unit/day groups. Symptoms of bloating, weight gain, and breast tenderness (PMT-H) were not improved. These treatments did not alter circulating testosterone, estradiol, progesterone, or dehydroepiandrosterone sulfate concentrations when measured in samples drawn once at the beginning of treatment and once again after 2 months of Vitamin E therapy (London et al., 1984). This study suffers from including women with breast disease and from a lack of prospective assessment of PMS.

This research group went on to improve subject selection (London et al., 1987). The MMPI was used to rule out significant psychopathology, but they again failed to use sufficient prospective ratings. After being assigned to one of four PMS groups, women were then assigned either to placebo ($n = 19$) or to alpha tocopherol ($n = 22$; 400 units/day) for three menstrual cycles. While tocopherol treatment did reduce symptom severity in each PMS category in this study, differences before and after active treatment did not reach statistical significance ($p > 0.05$).

Impression. The results from the most recent work by this group show encouraging trends toward the efficacy of Vitamin E as a treatment, but the data are not very compelling at this time.

Vitamin A

Description. Vitamin A is one of the fat-soluble vitamins. It is required for visual adaptation to darkness, for growth, and for the integrity of epithelial cells. It is stored in the liver and metabolized slowly. The daily recommended dose is 4,000 units in nonpregnant, nonlactating women. Chronic toxicity can occur at doses of 50,000 units per day for longer than 18 months or 500,000 units daily for 2 months (*PDR,* 1987).

Research. The use of Vitamin A as a treatment for PMS began with a serendipitous observation that a woman with premenstrual symptoms in addition to a diagnosis of hyperthyroidism improved on both counts with the administration of high daily doses of Vitamin A (400,000 IU) (Simkins, 1947).

Following the case report, two studies examined the use of Vitamin A in a larger subject population with PMS. In the first, Argonz and Abinzano (1950) reported on the results from 30 women, 80% or more of whom complained of mastalgia, bloating, and "nervous tension." The women were treated with 200,000 units daily, beginning on Day 15 and continuing until menses. Treatment continued for 3–4 months. Vitamin A treatment reduced breast complaints in 23 of 30 women. Bloating and the "bizarre symptoms . . . grouped under the denomination of nervous tension" (p. 1585–1586) also improved in 22 of 22 and 23 of 23, respectively. Improvement continued after therapy ended and persisted for several months.

The second study used Vitamin A daily (200,000–300,000 units) only during a subject's usual symptomatic period (Block, 1960). In his subjects, Vitamin A treatment produced a good or moderate response in 80.5% of women with nervous symptoms (agitation, irritability, depression); in 79.5% of women with symptoms of "heaviness" in the breasts, abdomen, or other places; and in 92.7% of women with headaches. Placebo was employed in 20 out of 218 patients, and there was a 25% placebo response rate.

Impression. These studies were performed prior to the development of rigorous subject selection techniques and were not performed double-blind with placebo. However, a variety of symptoms were reportedly improved. Clearly, more research should be done to validate these tantalizing reports.

Fatty Acids—Evening Primrose Oil

Description. Fatty acids are component parts of lipids. Two fatty acids, linoleic and linolenic, are polyunsaturated (two or more double bonds between carbon moieties) and are mandatory dietary components, since mammals cannot synthesize them. Thus they are called "essential fatty acids" (Lehninger, 1979). Essential fatty acids (EFA) are precursors of prostaglandins and are involved in normal phospholipid membrane functions. There is currently no recommended daily dose of EFA. EFA are abundant in human breast milk and in most vegetable oils except coconut and palm (Taylor & Anthony, 1983). Evening primrose oil is an especially good source (Horrobin, 1983a).

Research. Horrobin (1983a) and his research team began to test the effect of supplying EFA to treat PMS based on their theory that women with PMS may be abnormally sensitive to prolactin at the cellular level. His alternative theory was that the first enzyme in the metabolism of linoleic acid, delta-6-desaturase, was defective in women with PMS (Horrobin, 1983b). Prostaglandin E_1, formed from EFA, would "switch off some of the biologic effects of prolactin" (p. 466).

In his paper, Horrobin (1983a) reviews the work of others, some of which has not been published in peer-reviewed journals. In an open study of 68 treatment-refractory women with PMS, 61% improved completely and 23% had partial remission using 2–4 gm evening primrose oil per day in the luteal phase. Physical and psychological symptoms improved. Two double-blind studies of women with cyclic breast problems also reported significant improvement using 4 gm primrose oil per day. Nodularity and tenderness of the breasts, well-being, and irritability responded to the oil. Primrose oil was also successful in another large open trial of 196 women selected "after careful scrutiny of menstrual cycle records" (p. 467).

Puolakka and colleagues (1985) selected 30 women with "severe, incapacitating PMS" for their 4-month study. Each subject received 2 months of primrose oil (1.5 g twice daily) or placebo from Day 15 through menses. Overall assessment by the patients indicated that 62% improved at least slightly using primrose oil, and 40% improved on placebo. Of the individual major symptoms, only depression improved more with primrose oil than with placebo.

Three treatment studies using evening primrose oil were reported at the 2nd International Symposium: Premenstrual, Postpartum and Menopausal Mood Disorders in 1987. The first study (Massil et al., 1987) began by measuring polyunsaturated fatty acid levels in 20 women with PMS and in 20 asymptomatic controls. The levels were the same in both groups. Eighty women with PMS were then studied in a double-blind crossover trial of evening primrose oil versus placebo. Linear visual analog scales were used to assess symptoms. Six symptoms showed significant improvement after 3 months of treatment with evening primrose oil: headache, bloating, clumsiness, depression, breast discomfort, and irritability. Methods of diagnosing PMS, length of treatment, and dose of evening primrose oil were not stated in the presentation.

The second study (Casper & Powell, 1987) asked 92 women to complete 3 months of prospective self-rating scales every third day. Women with 2 positive months were diagnosed with PMS (66 women), and women with no cyclic elevation of symptom scores (26 women) were the non-PMS group. These women entered a double-blind placebo-controlled crossover study lasting 6 months, followed by a 6-month open period. Forty-four PMS subjects and 17 controls completed the study. Day 8 scores were subtracted from Day 23 scores to give a delta score for each cycle. A reduction of 24% and 33% in Day 23 and in delta scores, respectively, were seen with placebo. No difference was observed with evening primrose oil treatment for 3 months. However, after 6 months of treatment, Day 23 and delta scores were reduced 53% ($p < 0.01$) compared to placebo. Scores in the control subjects were not affected by either the primrose oil or placebo. Dose of evening primrose oil was not stated.

The third study (Mansel et al., 1987) was a randomized double-blind single crossover trial of evening primrose oil in 37 women with cyclic mastalgia. Women either received six capsules of evening primrose oil for 4 months or placebo for 2 months followed by evening primrose oil for 2 months. The investigators concluded that 51% of the women experienced improvement of breast pain, heaviness, and tenderness in response to primrose oil. However, the placebo trial was short, a scale of only 3 points was used to rate symptoms, and the subjects were also given Vitamin C with the evening primrose oil.

Recently, Callendar and colleagues (1988) reported a double-blind study of evening primrose oil for women with primarily affective premenstrual symptoms. Using 2 months of prospective ratings and detailed clinical assessments, they selected 12 women with PMS from an initial pool of 45 women referred to a PMS clinic. (This percentage is close to that found by Severino and colleagues for women who actually have PMS from a referred population—see page 143.) The women were constrained to have at least mild to moderate premenstrual anxiety and depression. The subjects were assigned either to a combination of two capsules of Efamol and two tablets of Efavit (both supplied by Efamol Ltd.) (see Table 7.1) or placebo three times daily beginning on Day 1 through Day 7 of menses for two menstrual cycles. After two washout cycles, the treatments were crossed over. Of the 40 menstrual cycles from the 10 subjects who completed the study, the subjects reported that, overall, 6 cycles were better on placebo, 14 were improved on Efamol/Efavit, 14 were worse or no different on placebo, and 6 were not improved on the combination therapy. During both placebo and active drug months, significant decreases in depression and anxiety were observed by the clinicians. No differences between placebo and drug were found. Further, 80% of the women had a skin rash following the ingestion of the combination drugs, presumably due to the niacin in the vitamin tablet. Decreasing the dose eliminated the problem. The investigators were concerned that the rash might have broken the double-blind, leading to more favorable global assessments than predicted from the other data. Their conclusion was that Efamol/Efavit was not more effective than placebo in treating depression and anxiety.

Jones (1987) examined the effect on menstrual symptoms of high- and low-fat diets containing different ratios of polyunsaturated and saturated fats. The degree of saturation had no effect on symptoms. Women on the low-fat diet perceived that weight gain was less premenstrually, but no significant weight changes were measured. This finding was discussed above on pages 197–202.

Impression. The views on the use of evening primrose oil for PMS range from suggesting that "the evening primrose promises to take its place in the hall of fame of plants with important medicinal properties" (Graham, 1984, p. 13) to a quote by an author of a health guide in regard to "a purported PMS panacea dubbed 'evening primrose oil' . . . I don't know what it is, or the therapeutic rationale for it. But there have been several reports of poisoning in the literature" (quoted in Gonzalez, 1984, p. 471). We checked out the toxicity aspect with a poison control center, and they were unable to substantiate this claim. We also could not find these reports.

Even though the oil may not be toxic, it is clear that more definitive research using primrose oil is necessary. If primrose oil indeed promotes production of prostaglandin E_1 (PGE_1), this might be dangerous premenstrually, since PGE_1 can elevate AMP in platelets, thus inducing a tendency toward hemorrhage. If the oil also blocks thromboxane formation, this would place women in double jeopardy of severe bleeding during menstruation (Marcus, 1984; Moncoda et al., 1985). Clinically, however, no reports of hemorrhage in women taking Efamol have appeared in the literature.

There are further research concerns about primrose oil. To begin with, none of the studies, except perhaps that reported in the abstract by Casper and Powell (1987), was carried out long enough to remove placebo response as a factor. Indeed, Callendar and colleagues (1988) did not find improvement in excess of the placebo rate. Further, the rationale behind the use of the oil is rather weak, at least in the case of prolactin. Last, it should be noted that Horrobin, a major proponent for the use of primrose oil, is employed by its major manufacturer.

Mixed Vitamin and Mineral Supplements

Description. The definition of a substance in this category is either a preparation available over-the-counter (OTC) with multiple vitamins and minerals, or a recommendation to use multiple vitamins and minerals for PMS (Berger, 1987). Three OTC preparations are available as specific PMS supplements: PMS Balance–Premenstrual Nutrition Supplement (Rexall Nutritional Products), Efamol PMS (Nature's Way Products), and Windmill Premenstrual Supplement (Windmill Vitamin Company) (see pp. 238–242 for details). Optivite (Optimox) and ProCycle Multivitamin–Mineral Supplement (Madison Pharmacy Associates) are not listed in the same section of the nonprescription drugs version of the Physicians Desk Reference (1987) as are the first three, but they are the only ones that have been the subject of some research, as described below. Optivite and ProCycle have nearly the same formulation, down to the digestive enzymes, so the research performed using Optivite presumably applies to ProCycle as well.

Research. Goei and Abraham (1983) reported an open study of Optivite in 31 women. They used Abraham's four category classification system (PMT-A, PMT-H, PMT-C, PMT-D) to divide women into subgroups (see Chapter 5). Women with moderate or severe symptoms in one or more categories participated. Some of the women apparently had persistent symptoms of depression. Subjects were given Optivite on Day 1 and told to take up to 12 tablets daily to relieve symptoms. This would provide 25,000 units of Vitamin A and 600 mg of Vitamin B_6. Total scores on the (retrospective) rating scales used in the study decreased during both the follicular and premenstrual phases. Side effects were minimal. The authors go on to suggest the need for double-blind placebo-controlled studies.

A second open study of 16 women also showed an efficacious response (Fuchs et al., 1985). The treatment regimen was the same as before: up to 12 tablets per day. Fourteen out of 16 subjects improved after several treatment cycles. From single blood samples taken during the luteal phases of a control (pretreatment) cycle and from months 3 and 6 following therapy, the investigators found significantly lower serum estradiol, higher progesterone, and nonsignificantly lower aldosterone. Serum glucose, alkaline phosphatase, serum glutamic oxaloacetic transaminase (SGOT), serum glutamic pyruvic transaminase (SGPT), and glucoglutamic pyruvic transaminase (GGPT) were all significantly elevated in women who consumed the supplement, but it is not at all clear whether the values were outside the normal range of values measured in their particular laboratory.

Abraham's group also reported a double-blind placebo-controlled crossover study of 31 women with moderate to severe PMS (Chakmak-jian et al., 1985). After two control cycles, women consumed either six Optivite or six placebo tablets (with riboflavin, since Optivite turns urine yellow due to the riboflavin). Only symptoms in the PMT-A (anxiety) and PMT-C (somatic symptoms of headache, increased appetite) groups improved more with Optivite than with placebo. The most severely affected group, PMT-D, was not affected by treatment, nor were symptoms associated with fluid retention and weight gain. On global assessment, 7 women preferred placebo, 16 preferred Optivite, and 8 could not differentiate between treatments.

Abraham and Rumley (1987) provided a comprehensive dietary program and supplement schedule in a report on the role of nutrition in managing PMS. Among the dietary recommendations were the following: (1) to limit intake of refined sugar, salt, red meat, dairy products, alcohol, coffee, tea, and chocolate; (2) to limit fat intake, especially saturated fats; (3) to limit or eliminate tobacco use; and (4) to increase intake of fish, poultry, whole grains, legumes, green leafy vegetables, and fresh fruits. They went on to test this diet as part of a four-group open study of a daily multiple vitamin ($n = 5$), diet alone ($n = 13$), Optivite alone (6 tablets; $n = 20$), or diet and Optivite (6 tablets; $n = 19$). After 3 months, mean symptom scores from the groups on diet or Optivite alone were the same or slightly lower than the group on diet plus vitamin supplement. However, since women were not assigned randomly to groups before the study began, pretreatment scores differed. Thus the percentage decrease in mean symptom scores was better for the two groups receiving Optivite, either alone (58.5%) or with dietary instructions (56.6%), than for the group undergoing dietary change alone (50.4%). Taking a multivitamin daily decreased scores by 15.4%, but the control group had begun with fewer symptom complaints.

Abraham and Rumley (1987) also conducted a survey by mail of 313 women with PMS. Women used their supplement and nutritional program for 2 to 60 months. The scores on the questionnaire improved when women consumed between 2 and 12 nutritional supplement tablets per day. Twenty-two subjects had side effects: 20 with gastrointestinal symptoms and 2 with diuresis. The investigators suggested that women try the nutritional plan and supplement for 3 months before being considered as nonresponders. Nonresponders would presumably seek other forms of treatment.

Stewart (1987) performed two placebo-controlled parallel trials using Optivite in high or low doses. Women were selected prospectively over 2 months but were allowed to continue any current treatment for

PMS during the study, including other nutritional supplements, diuretics, antidepressants, and hormones. Women in the high-dose group took four tablets daily for the first 2 weeks of the cycle and then eight tablets until menses. Women in the low-dose group took two and then four tablets, using the same pattern. Placebo in each case was 500 mg of mineral oil once per day. By overall assessment done by questionnaire through the mail, 55% improved substantially and 60% were cured by placebo in the two studies. Using the high dose, 71% were substantially better; and 63% were much better or cured with the low-dose regimen. Stewart reported that the high-dose response (71%) was statistically better than the placebo response (55%) but that the low-dose response did not differ.

Impression. These studies on the use of nutritional supplements do not demonstrate unequivocally that dietary manipulations are the answer to PMS. The open trials were at best suggestive, but the subject groups were either poorly chosen or the number of tablets consumed uneven. Even with the double-blind crossover study (Chakmakjian et al., 1985), only 52% of the women preferred the nutritional supplement.

Using Abraham and Rumley's (1987) dietary advice is a good idea, since it emphasizes wholesome foods and adheres well to the National Cancer Society's nutritional guidelines. As for Optivite, it is important to remember that five of the six studies reported in this section were coauthored by Abraham, who is employed by the company that produces it. Considering the high Vitamin B_6 content in 12 tablets (600 mg) and the lack of convincing evidence from well-designed studies, we would hesitate to recommend this supplement.

Potassium

Research. Two reports on the use of potassium salts for the treatment of PMS have appeared in the literature (Thorn & Emerson, 1940; Reeves et al., 1971). Thorn and Emerson (1940) suggested that both women with severe generalized premenstrual edema and women who exceeded their normal weight (according to idealized tables) be placed on a diet that completely restricted sodium and chloride. In addition, these patients were to receive potassium citrate, 10 cc of a 20% solution in fruit juice, two to three times daily. While no data were provided, the investigators reported that the treatment was of "great benefit."

Like the first study, the rationale for the more recent trial was the effectiveness of potassium in controlling edema (Reeves et al., 1971). In a well-designed study using placebo controls and prospective ratings (an unusually good technique for that time), women with and without PMS were administered either 1 gm potassium chloride three times daily or placebo. They remained on the drug regimen for two cycles and then crossed over to the other group. When the total number of symptoms was compared across groups in the five days premenses, no differences were found between the placebo or potassium groups in either women with or without PMS. Further, potassium treatment did not alter weight gain, as would be expected based on its diuretic properties.

Impression. Potassium does not appear to be effective in controlling symptoms of PMS.

Magnesium

Several researchers advocate the use of magnesium supplements for the treatment of PMS (Abraham & Rumley, 1987), based on the premise that magnesium concentrations are lower in women with PMS. This finding is disputed by Mira and colleagues (1988), who did not find differences in plasma magnesium between women with PMS (diagnosed prospectively) and control women without PMS.

There are no studies of magnesium supplements used as a single treatment modality. Rather, they are components of several over-the-counter mixed vitamin and mineral preparations (see pp. 219–221 above and 238–242 below). The effectiveness of magnesium remains to be determined.

Tryptophan

Description. L-tryptophan is an essential amino acid. It is a precursor for the synthesis of serotonin, a central neurotransmitter. It is also used as an over-the-counter sedative, since exogenous tryptophan causes sleepiness (George et al., 1988).

Research. Only one case report of the use of L-tryptophan by itself for the treatment of PMS appears in the literature (Price et al., 1984–85). The authors tried tryptophan in an effort to increase serotonin levels in their patient, on the premise that decreased serotonin could account for depression and other symptoms of PMS. The patient had suffered from severe PMS for 11 years, since age 14, and had both physical and psychological symptoms. It was the severity of the latter that brought her to the attention of the investigators, a team of psychiatrists. She was given tryptophan 1,000 mg orally, five times daily. After 1 month, she still complained of the physical symptoms, but her anxiety, depression, and tension levels had decreased, and she was sleeping better.

Harrison and colleagues (1984) tried tryptophan in combination with Vitamin B_6, since B_6 is intimately involved in the conversion of tryptophan to serotonin. The methodology of the study is described on pages 210–211 above. The results were, however, disappointing, since only 2 of 27 women who completed the study improved.

Impression. The case study is interesting since it suggests an underlying role of serotonin in PMS. However, the controlled study seems to indicate that trying to increase brain serotonin concentrations by oral routes may not be the answer for PMS, assuming that serotonin is indeed the key factor. Clearly, much more research will be required to validate this treatment option. Further, on the basis of the limited case report, tryptophan may only be useful in treating some psychological symptoms of PMS.

Despite the lack of evidence from a well-controlled treatment trial, tryptophan has recently been promoted as a treatment in a pamphlet on PMS entitled "Premenstrual Syndrome—Breaking Through the PMS Cloud" and published by Kramer Communications. This pamphlet implies that the etiology of PMS is a disruption of normal serotonin secretion, a fact that is not yet proven (see Chapter 5). Further, no references are provided for a motivated reader to seek additional information.

Dietary Fiber

Research. Part of the PMS diet proposed by Abraham and Rumley (1987), often cited in lay articles on PMS, involves increasing dietary fiber consumption to 20–40 g/day. The premise is that by increasing fiber, fecal excretion of estrogens would be increased. Since some women with PMS symptoms reportedly have high plasma estrogen, this increased excretion might prove helpful.

The view that increasing estrogen elimination through the gut would be helpful for PMS is not new. Frank (1931) advocated the use of laxatives, such as magnesium citrate, to increase the excretion of estrogens, an excess of which Frank believed caused PMS. The more recent promotion of dietary fiber uses the same rationale.

However, the reasoning is somewhat faulty. First, excess estrogen as a cause of PMS is not proven, even for Abraham's subtype PMT-A. Second, the paper by Goldin and colleagues (1982) regarding fecal and plasma estrogens (and cited by Abraham and Rumley [1987] as support for increasing fiber to eliminate estrogens) does not state or show that increasing fiber intake will lower plasma estrogen concentrations, since it was not a prospective study. Goldin and colleagues (1982) found that plasma estrogen concentrations in omnivorous and vegetarian women were equivalent, even though the vegetarians ate much more dietary fiber, produced more fecal mass, and excreted significantly more estrogens in their feces. Conversely, urinary excretion of estriol by the vegetarians was significantly lower than by the omnivores. Even so, the urinary route of estrogen excretion is much more important than the fecal route. It should also be noted that the total excretion of estrogens (urinary plus fecal routes) was approximately the same in omnivorous and vegetarian women. Thus a balance between routes of excretion occurs, leading to equivalent plasma concentrations.

Impression. Abraham and Rumley (1987) are correct in advocating adequate consumption of dietary fiber for good health. Indeed, the National Cancer Institute of the National Institute of Health (NIH) advocates consuming 20–30 g of fiber per day. However, it should be understood that fiber does not clear the circulation of estrogens: A prospective study would be needed to prove this point. Further, since fecal excretion represents a much smaller percentage of total daily estrogen excretion, a recommendation to consume 20–40 g per day may prove to be more uncomfortable than useful for many women.

Fruits, Vegetables, and Herbs

Mindell (1988), in his *New and Revised Vitamin Bible,* suggests that women with PMS increase their consumption of (1) "strawberries, watermelon (eat seeds), artichokes, asparagus, parsley and watercress" (p. 242) since they are "natural" diuretics, (2) foods rich in potassium, such as bananas and sunflower seeds, and (3) *Dong Quai,* an herb. He also suggests that women use Vitamins B_6, E, and pantothenic acid, magnesium and calcium supplements, evening primrose oil, and exercise. Finally, he advises women with PMS to eschew salt and salty foods, licorice, cold foods and beverages, caffeine, astringent dark teas, alcohol, and spinach. Some of his plan seems sensible (exercise, low salt, and minimal caffeine), as has been discussed previously. For the most part, however, he is promoting an exotic plan with no proven efficacy for PMS.

PSYCHOTHERAPY

Description. The term "psychotherapy" refers to an interaction between a patient and a therapist that promotes positive change in disturbed thoughts, moods, and behaviors. There are many approaches to psychotherapy. This section describes active interactions that complement the supportive and educational approaches described above (see pp. 163–164).

Research. Rees (1953a) reported that PMS was not amenable to psychotherapy alone, based on his experience with 16 patients attending a psychiatric clinic for the treatment of neurosis. When some patients recovered from the neurosis, the premenstrual symptoms persisted. Others treated with hormones (type unknown) improved premenstrually without change in the neurotic symptoms. Rees (1953a) did suggest that "psychotherapy of a simple kind can help the patient in understanding the condition and can improve her attitude and reaction to it" (p. 1015). This is similar to what was discussed on pages 163–164 above.

Fortin and colleagues (1958) used an introspective approach to treatment, emphasizing anamnestic data, conscious attitudes about menarche and menstruation, and unconscious associative material. Out of 25 subjects with PMS, 14 improved, 8 did not, and 3 became worse after the psychotherapy. Of the 20 control women studied who did not have PMS at the outset, one became persistently symptomatic after revealing "traumatic and disturbing material."

Currently work is being done by Hamilton and colleagues (1984), who suggest a metacognitive approach to psychotherapy that would deal with issues arising from two postulated etiologies: the state-dependent learning model and learned helplessness model. The authors suggest that this metacognitive approach needs to be expanded and tested.

The Trimble Model TM (Trimble, 1987) employs a therapeutic process to help a woman with PMS alter her perception of herself. This abstract does not describe the details of how this is accomplished. It does report that since 1982 it has been used with more than 3,500 patients. Measured responses (these are not specified) showed that 80% of the women achieved control over their PMS symptoms. Their use of medications decreased from 90% to less than 9.8% of what they stated they were using. More descriptive references by Trimble have not been found by us.

Impression. From the limited amount of research, it seems unreasonable to conclude that psychotherapy can cure PMS. As O'Brien (1982) points out in his review of treatments, a 50% success rate (Fortin et al., 1958) is similar to the response rate to placebo. However, we would hasten to add that the field of psychotherapy, in general, suffers from a lack of good treatment outcome studies. Furthermore, the difference between "cure of" and "improved coping with" PMS needs to be specified in future research studies.

One should bear in mind, however, that only if PMS were caused by unresolved unconscious conflicts (which we do not believe) would we expect psychotherapy to cure it. Psychotherapeutic interventions, such as support, education, the Trimble Model TM, cognitive psychotherapy, introspective psychotherapy, and other methods, may, however be very beneficial in helping a woman cope with her symptoms.

PSYCHOACTIVE AGENTS

Anxiolytics (Aprazolam, Meprobamate, and Buspirone)

Alprazolam

Description. Alprazolam (Xanax; Upjohn) is a triazolo analog of the benzodiazepine class of psychoactive drugs. It is used in the treatment of anxiety disorders (*PDR*, 1987). Since the drug causes sedation, driving and consuming alcohol are potential problems. Further, benzo-diazepines can cause birth defects. Withdrawal symptoms can occur following acute discontinuation of the drug; it should therefore be tapered gradually under supervision (Ayd, 1989b).

Recently, serious side effects have been associated with the drug that are similar to withdrawal symptoms but occur when patients are *still on* the medication (*Psychiatric News*, July 15, 1988). Further, tapering patients has been found to be difficult, although necessary, and often requires the use of a second benzodiazepine to prevent withdrawal effects. A suggestion was made in the article to limit the daily dose to 1 mg per day, which is less than the approved therapeutic dose.

Research. Discussion of alprazolam in the treatment of PMS first appeared in the literature as a case report (Freinhar, 1984). A 29-year-old woman with marked dysphoria, generalized tension, decreased appetite and sleep as well as some physical complaints was given alprazo-lam 0.25 mg twice daily at the time that symptoms began. Treatment continued for 7 days. Her symptoms remitted within 3 days. She prevented symptoms for the next 7 months by using the same 7-day treatment. Note that there was no tapering of the dose. The author of the case report was surprised at the rapid onset of action and suggested further investigation.

Two recent studies of alprazolam have been reported. In the first, women were diagnosed with PMS prospectively (Harrison et al., 1987). They were constrained to have regular menses, no current psychiatric disorder (76% had prior history), and clear symptoms of premenstrual anxiety, depression, or irritability severe enough to cause moderate social or occupational impairment. Each subject who fit inclusion criteria was treated with placebo for one or two menstrual cycles. Women who responded in both months were excluded from the active drug study. Placebo nonresponders and those who relapsed entered the drug trial

(52 women). Each received either alprazolam or placebo for 3 months. Medication began 8 to 12 days before menses, then was tapered by 25% per day during menses to avoid withdrawal effects. Doses ranged from 0.25 to 4 mg/day. Only global ratings were reported in this paper: 73% rated alprazolam superior to placebo, 12% rated placebo superior, and 15% reported no difference. The doctors' impressions were that 60% responded to alprazolam, 6% responded to placebo, and 34% did not respond to either treatment. Drowsiness was the only significant side effect, leading 6 who were taking alprazolam to discontinue participating in the study.

The second study also used rigorous subject selection techniques in a 5-month, double-blind placebo-controlled crossover study (Smith et al., 1987). The 19 women selected rated their symptoms daily. After a baseline month, each subject received either placebo or alprazolam for 2 months, then crossed over. The drug (0.25 mg) was administered three times daily starting from Day 20 through the second day of menstruation, followed by a tapering of one pill per day. Subjects were allowed to decrease the daily dose if they experienced daytime sedation (2 did so). Fourteen out of 19 women completed the study. Alprazolam was found to cause significant improvement compared to control and placebo cycles in nervous tension, mood swings, irritability, anxiety, depression, fatigue, forgetfulness, crying, craving for sweets, abdominal bloating, abdominal cramps, and headache. Interestingly, this research group did not find many placebo responders, which they attribute in part to their method of analysis.

The use of alprazolam was also reported at the 1987 annual meeting of the Pacific Coast Fertility Society (*OB/GYN News*, August 1–14, 1987). A research group at UCLA School of Medicine found that alprazolam was more effective than placebo for decreasing anxiety, tension, irritability, and headache in 17 women. Placebo or alprazolam was administered 10 days prior to and 2 days during menses for three monthly cycles and then crossed over. The women were diagnosed with PMS by psychometric testing for anxiety and depression and by 2 months of prospective daily ratings. It is interesting that depression and physical complaints responded both to placebo and to active drug, a finding that suggests a need to increase the duration of treatment trials in an effort to eliminate placebo effects. Again, in this study women complained of drowsiness.

Impression. Taken together, these studies suggest that alprazolam may indeed be a useful treatment for PMS, especially in women for whom anxiety, tension, and insomnia are predominant symptoms. However, the medication does cause sedation, is unsafe during pregnancy, and has recently been associated with side effects, such as bone or joint stiffness, excessive lacrimation without accompanying affect, labored breathing, visual problems, profuse sweating, and rapidly alternating mood swings (*International Drug Therapy Newsletter*, September 1988). Further, tolerance/dependence can develop. What is needed now is a longer-term study of alprazolam in the PMS population to test both efficacy and safety of an intermittent treatment regimen.

Meprobamate

Description. Meprobamate (Miltown; Wallace and others) is a carbamate derivative that is used for the management of anxiety (*PDR*, 1987). Dependence, both physical and psychological, can occur with this drug. In addition, mental and/or physical abilities can be impaired. Since meprobamate interacts with alcohol and other central nervous system (CNS) depressants, drug use must be carefully monitored. Adverse side effects include drowsiness, weakness, nausea, headache, tachycardia, and allergic reactions, among others. Meprobamate can cause birth defects in the first trimester and thus must be used with caution by women of childbearing age.

Research. Meprobamate has been used alone (Pennington, 1957; Appleby 1960) and in combination with the diuretic Tenavoid (Carstairs & Talbot 1981) (see p. 237 below). When it was given alone (Pennington, 1957), women between ages 16 and 42 were selected based on reports of PMS and primary dysmenorrhea since menarche. Twenty-eight received meprobamate 400 mg three times daily beginning at the onset of symptoms each month. Another 14 received the same dose daily for 2 months, then intermittently as with the first group. Each woman received placebo at some point during the study for at least 1 month. All of the patients in each group experienced either a substantial reduction (22%) or complete remission (78%) in premenstrual symptoms. Many attributed this to an improvement in sleep patterns. There was no apparent advantage to daily administration of the medication.

Appleby (1960) tested women with moderate to severe symptoms of PMS with 400 mg three times daily of meprobamate, starting 9 days before menses. After 3 months on medication in this (at least single) blind study, 53% of the women reported complete relief or marked improvement from meprobamate, compared to 7% from placebo. This is the same study that examined synthetic progestins and chlorothiazide (p. 176 above). Meprobamate was the most successful of all the drugs tested.

Impression. Considering that the first study of meprobamate was reported in 1957, the study design was quite good for the time. However, it is now known that meprobamate does cause dependency, contrary to Pennington's declaration to the contrary. Since the response to meprobamate is noteworthy, however, further research is warranted.

Buspirone

Description. Buspirone (BuSpar; Mead Johnson Pharmaceuticals) is a new anxiolytic that is not related to the benzodiazepines, barbiturates, or other sedative drugs. It is indicated for the treatment of Generalized Anxiety Disorder (*PDR*, 1988). There is some concern that long-term use of buspirone may lead to motor dysfunctions similar to those caused by neuroleptics (dystonia, tardive dyskinesia), since the drug binds to dopamine receptors. Several years of marketing the drug will determine whether this is a significant risk.

Research. Buspirone was tested openly in outpatient women with symptoms of anxiety of sufficient intensity to warrant pharmacological treatment (David et al., 1987). Retrospective PMS histories were obtained, and women were classified as having marked, moderate, mild, or no PMS (the rating system was not described). Treatment began at 5 mg buspirone three times daily and was titrated as needed to an end dose of 2–12 5 mg tablets per day (total dose of 10–60 mg). A consistent relationship was found between anxiolytic effect and intensity of premenstrual symptoms. Further, women with the most marked PMS reported fewer adverse reactions. The investigators provided a useful critique of the strengths and weaknesses of their study and concluded that a controlled trial would be worthwhile. We agree.

Buspirone is also currently being tested in women with PMS by Tammaro (1988). The drug was reported to be successful in treating symptoms of persistent anxiety.

Impression. This drug is new, and the reports mentioned above are preliminary. Thus, while the studies are encouraging, we have to reserve judgment until a methodologically adequate study has been published.

Antidepressants (Nortriptyline and Monoamine Oxidase Inhibitors)

Tricyclic Antidepressants (Nortriptyline)

Description. Nortriptyline (Pamelor; Sandoz Pharmaceuticals) is a tricyclic antidepressant. It is thought to interfere with central catecholamine transport, release, and storage as its antidepressant mechanism of action (*PDR*, 1988).

There are a variety of warnings and precautions associated with this drug, including the dictum to avoid alcohol and to be extremely careful when driving a car or operating machinery since mental and physical abilities may be impaired. The safe use of this drug during pregnancy has not been established. Side effects that have been reported with other tricyclic antidepressants include, among others, confusional states, insomnia, paresthesias, palpitations, dry mouth, skin rash, nausea, breast enlargement, urinary frequency, and fatigue. Toxic overdoses have been reported.

Research. Harrison and colleagues (1989) recently reported on the use of nortriptyline for the treatment of women with LLPDD. Subjects were selected for the study based on prospective daily ratings. Women with DSM-III-R Axis I psychopathology within the past 6 months were excluded.

Subjects received (openly) daily doses of 50–125 mg nortriptyline daily at bedtime starting 4 weeks before the premenstrual assessment period to allow for the well-established therapeutic lag in response to tricyclic antidepressants. Eleven out of 13 subjects completed at least one month of the study.

According to physician ratings, 8 of the 11 subjects were better on nortriptyline (much or very much improved). Seven of the 8 elected to continue on nortriptyline, with good results. Subject rated themselves as significantly better on all premenstrual assessment form (PAF) measures except "increased well-being." (The PAF is retrospective self-report.) Daily rating scores also showed a significant treatment effect.

Side effects were noted by all 11 subjects, and included dry mouth (11 subjects), constipation (10), insomnia (5), and overstimulation (5). The side effects were severe enough in two of the original 13 subjects to cause withdrawal from the study.

Impression. The results of the study indicate that some subjects with premenstrual dysphoric changes may benefit from antidepressants. It would have been useful to know each woman's duration of symptoms and to have some index of the degree of depression (Hamilton Rating Scale Score, for example). We agree with the investigators that "the efficacy of tricyclic antidepressants in women with premenstrual depression needs confirmation with double-blind, placebo-controlled studies" (p. 139).

Monoamine Oxidase Inhibitors

There has been a suggestion that "premenstrual depression can be alleviated by means of monoamine oxidase inhibitors like isocarboxazid [Marplan; Roche] and phenelzine [Nardil; Parke-Davis]" (Warburton, 1975, p. 65). However, we have not found any literature supporting this view. In light of the efficacy of monoamine oxidase inhibitors in treating clinical depression, a treatment trial should be instituted. However, drugs of this category can induce serious increases in blood pressure, and patients require a carefully controlled diet limiting cheese, yogurt, smoked meats, and alcohol, among other foods. Further, the safe use of monoamine oxidase inhibitors has not been established during pregnancy, and thus they should be used with caution by women of childbearing age. Clearly, these drugs cannot be recommended for treatment of PMS at this time.

Antimania Drugs (Lithium, Clonidine, and Verapamil)

Lithium

Description. Lithium (Eskalith; Smith Kline & French, among others) is used in the treatment of manic episodes in Bipolar Disorder. Maintenance therapy on lithium diminishes or prevents these manic episodes (*PDR*, 1987). Usually, 1 to 3 weeks of treatment are required to normalize symptoms. Lithium is effective only within a narrow therapeutic range, and plasma levels must be monitored closely to prevent accidental toxic overdose.

Side effects of lithium include fine hand tremor, polyuria, diarrhea, drowsiness and muscle weakness. Lithium can cause birth defects and thus should be used with caution by women of childbearing age.

Research. The first case report on the use of lithium for the treatment of PMS appeared in 1966 (Sletten & Gershon, 1966), its use based on the clinical similarity of PMS to some features of mania and "schizophrenic excitement." Eight patients (two described) received 5 grains of lithium carbonate tablets three times per day beginning 8–10 days prior to (expected) menses. All eight improved substantially and remained so for the 12–18 months of the treatment trial.

Fries (1969) treated five women with premenstrual tension of an "unusually severe type." Two women improved, each of whom had cyclothymic personality and endogenous-type depressions. One woman improved on a daily regimen of lithium, the other on intermittent use (10 days before menses to onset of menses). Tupin (1972) also lists a case in which a woman partially improved on lithium. No details regarding symptoms that responded or the precise treatment that was effective were published.

A paper purporting to be a controlled evaluation of lithium (Singer et al., 1973), and often referenced as such by others, used unacceptable subject selection according to today's standards. Nineteen women, 12 of whom had concurrent psychiatric disorders, participated in a study of lithium or placebo. Dosages were flexible and aimed at maintaining plasma lithium concentrations at 0.8–1.3 mEq/1 throughout the month.

Subjects were allowed to take oral contraceptives. Women improved on both lithium and placebo, with no clear advantage to the lithium.

The next published study used a double-blind placebo-controlled crossover design to compare lithium and a common diuretic, chlorthalidone, both to the placebo and to control cycles with no treatment (Mattsson & von Schoultz, 1974). Twenty-five women with mild to moderate symptoms participated; only 18 finished. After 2 control (no treatment) months, each woman received either lithium (6 mEq four times per day starting 14 days before menses) or chlorthalidone (25 mg daily for 1 week, then 50 mg for another week before menses) or placebo for two cycles each (total = 8 cycles). Subjects improved on all three treatments, with placebo preferred by most and chlorthalidone and lithium preferred about equally. Women who gained more weight premenstrually than others responded well to lithium, and did not gain weight on those cycles. The authors stress (1) that their findings are valid only for women with mild or moderate symptoms, (2) that there is a large placebo effect, and (3) that it is difficult to understand how lithium could have been effective while acting as a diuretic (in preventing weight gain) when the known diuretic did not.

Another study of lithium treatment for PMS selected women based on prospective ratings (Steiner et al., 1980b). Although not stated explicitly, the 15 participants probably did not have a current major psychiatric disorder. Each was treated with lithium (openly), 600 mg or 900 mg daily for three cycles. Only 9 women completed the study; 6 dropped out (3 due to side effects). While 5 patients showed some benefit, only 3 of those 5 continued on the lithium. Physical symptoms were not improved in any of the 9, and in 5 they became worse. It is interesting that the 3 women who continued on the drug after the study were suspected of having subclinical affective disorder. Two of the three had first-degree relatives with affective illness. The investigators, therefore, postulated that a subgroup of women with PMS may benefit from lithium as a result of a change in cyclothymic features.

A woman with severe psychological premenstrual symptoms received enough lithium to achieve a plasma concentration of 0.6–0.8 mEq/1, with good success in controlling her symptoms (DeLeon-Jones et al., 1982). This group concurrently measured her urinary 3-methoxy-4-hydroxyphenolglycol (MHPG) excretion. They found that the usual elevation in MHPG that occurred in association with her florid premenstrual symptoms was absent when she was treated with lithium.

Lithium, in combination with antipsychotic medication and either medroxyprogesterone acetate or oral contraceptives, has been used to treat premenstrual exacerbations of schizophrenia (Glick & Steward, 1980).

From a different perspective, the premenstrual phase can affect plasma lithium levels, despite a constant daily dose (Kukopulos et al., 1985). Plasma lithium was highest during a recurrent premenstrual depression and lowest during the subsequent premenstrual mania. Treatment was altered to supplement the plasma level during the manic periods.

Impression. The studies on lithium once again point out many of the methodological problems that are associated with PMS research. While several case reports suggest that lithium may be useful in subgroups of women with PMS, its overall effectiveness has not been clearly demonstrated. Even the papers concluding the opposite have serious design flaws. At any rate, "lithium is certainly not a first-line drug for the treatment of PMS" (Barklage & Jefferson, 1987). It may be tried, however, when an underlying affective illness is diagnosed, or for women with treatment-resistant severe psychological symptoms.

Clonidine

Description. Clonidine (Catapres; Boehringer Ingelheim) is an antihypertensive agent that works by stimulating alpha-adrenergic receptors both centrally and peripherally (*PDR,* 1987). Clonidine may also decrease plasma renin activity and promote aldosterone excretion. Use of the drug has been associated with drowsiness and sedation, and withdrawal symptoms (high blood pressure) can occur if the drug is discontinued abruptly.

Clonidine also has antimanic effects (Price & Giannini, 1984), but it is not usually used for mania except in refractory cases.

Research. The use of clonidine to treat PMS was based on (1) the similarity between some symptoms of opiate withdrawal (for which clonidine is used) and of PMS and (2) its reported use in treating dysmenorrhea (Price & Giannini, 1984). Price and Giannini used clonidine hydrochloride to treat two women with PMS. The women's scores on using the Brief Psychiatric Rating Scale (BPRS) increased between Day 10 and Day 25 pretreatment, indicating that they had more affective and psychotic symptoms premenstrually. After clonidine treatment for 2 months, Day 25 scores fell by 22.5% and 21.4% in the two cases. Anxiety, tension, and depression were most affected. The women reported mild sedation and orthostatic changes.

A second report was also a case study (Nilsson et al., 1985). This group had noted that women participating in a study of clonidine's effect on affective disorders reported relief from PMS. When the authors administered clonidine (25 micrograms three times daily) to a 33-year-old woman with a 3-year history of PMS, her main symptoms of irritability and aggressiveness were attenuated, and the effect lasted for 15 consecutive cycles. In this study, clonidine began 15 days before and ended 2 days after menstruation.

The most recent study employed a random design with placebo controls (Giannini et al., 1988). An interesting subject selection technique was used: The investigators required a moderate to severe decrease in beta-endorphin levels during the "preluteal" phase in addition to the report of PMS symptoms. Clonidine (17 micrograms/kg four times daily) or placebo was administered for two cycles and then crossed over. The BPRS was again used to rate symptoms during each premenstrual phase. Clonidine and placebo both decreased symptoms, but only clonidine led to statistically significant improvement.

Impression. Clonidine is a very interesting therapeutic candidate based on the proposed endogenous opiate etiology of PMS. The case reports and the small double-blind crossover study strongly suggest that this drug is worth exploring in larger prospective studies of longer duration. At this time, however, there is no indication about the range of symptoms that clonidine may affect, for example, physical symptoms, since none of the three reports commented on this point.

Verapamil

Description. Verapamil (Isoptin; Knoll and others) is a calcium antagonist and slow channel inhibitor. It has antiarrhythmic properties and is a vasodilator. It is indicated for treatment of sinus or ventricular arrhythmia (intravenous form) or for angina (tablet form).

Research. The use of verapamil to treat symptoms of PMS is based not on its effects on the cardiovascular system but on its antimanic properties (Price & Giannini, 1986). A similar rationale exists with clonidine, a well-known antihypertensive drug (see previous section). The discovery of verapamil's effects on PMS was made in one woman with mitral valve prolapse and PMS. While on verapamil (50 mg three times daily), she self-reported improvement in irritability, agitation, depression, guilt, and emotional outbursts. The verapamil did not effect physical symptoms, such as bloating, breast swelling, or abdominal cramping.

In a recent case report (Deicken, 1988), verapamil was successfully used to treat a woman with marked irritability, affective lability, agitation, and hostility that were limited to the premenstrual phase. She was titrated over 3 weeks to a dose of 320 mg/day, more than Price and Giannini (1986) used (150 mg/day). Mild symptoms of edema and headache were not affected by verapamil.

Impression. These papers are only case reports exploiting the psychotropic properties of verapamil in the treatment of PMS. Clearly, verapamil should be tested in a larger, well-designed study for its possible effectiveness in those subjects with primarily psychological symptoms.

Antipsychotics (Molindone)

Description. Molindone (Moban; DuPont) is an antipsychotic agent used to treat schizophrenia. It also may have antidepressant and anxiolytic properties (Shader & Harmatz, 1975). As with other neuroleptics, serious adverse side affects can occur, including tardive dyskinesia, akathisia, drowsiness, and altered hormonal secretion (mainly increased prolactin) (*PDR*, 1987).

Research. One paper that appears in the literature addresses the effectiveness of molindone on symptoms of anxiety and depression during the premenstruum (Shader & Harmatz, 1975). These researchers selected women who were on oral contraceptives and who had anxiety and depression scores on standardized tests that were above average but not high enough to warrant a psychiatric diagnosis. Molindone (1 mg three times daily) was prescribed for one week, from Day 21 to Day 28. Subjects were assessed before and after for anxiety, depression, and various measures of psychosocial functioning. Molindone produced a significant decrease in anxiety but no consistent change in depression, hostility, or premenstrual impairment.

Impression. While this antipsychotic agent may be effective for treating anxiety symptoms around the premenstruum, it will be necessary to perform more rigorous studies using women with PMS before any recommendation can be made for its use as routine treatment. In addition, since the anxiolytic properties of molindone were exploited here, it makes sense to turn first to other classes of anxiolytics that would not have the same propensity toward causing movement disorders.

Tranquilizers (Bellergal)

Description. Bellergal (Sandoz Pharmaceuticals) is a combination drug comprised of phenobarbital, ergotamine tartrate, and belladonna alkaloids. The preparation is thought to act by decreasing the activity of both the parasympathetic and sympathetic nervous system (*PDR*, 1987). It has been used to treat menopausal symptoms such as hot flushes, cardiovascular disorders with palpitation and tachycardia, and gastrointestinal disorders such as hypermotility and "nervous stomach." Since this preparation contains a barbiturate, it may be habit-forming. Side effects include paresthesias of the extremities, blurred vision, urinary retention, and dry mouth, among others. Bellergal can change the tone of the uterus and should not be used during pregnancy.

Research. Two reports on the use of Bellergal for PMS appear in the literature. In the first (Robinson et al., 1977), Bellergal was chosen to "shield" the autonomic nervous system from the effects of imbalance. Thirty-two subjects who complained of fatigue, insomnia, nervousness, irritability, dysmenorrhea, or headache began a 3-month double-blind trial of active drug or placebo. Medications were administered three times per day, starting 10 days before the next expected menses, and subjects rated their symptoms daily. (No dose of Bellergal was reported.) At the end of 3 months, symptoms of fatigue, nervousness, and tender breasts had significantly improved over placebo according to the researchers' assessments. By self-report, subjects on active drug improved on irritability, lethargy, and listlessness as well.

Barwin (1980) published an abstract based on a triple crossover study of 30 subjects who participated for 3 months each on placebo, Bellergal, or bromocriptine. Bellergal was superior to placebo, but whether this conclusion was based on global or specific symptom improvement is not clear.

Impression. Here is another case where more extensive research is warranted, since many psychological symptoms appear to be improved by the intermittent use of Bellergal. In addition, subjects experienced fewer breast symptoms, a reaction not generally found with other psychoactive drugs. However, the drug should not be prescribed hastily for women of childbearing age, since the uterus can be affected.

Anorectics (Fenfluramine)

Description. Fenfluramine hydrochloride (Pondimin; Robins) is a sympathomimetic amine related to amphetamine that is used in the short-term treatment of exogenous obesity (*PDR,* 1987). Its mechanism of action is thought to relate to brain concentrations or turnover of serotonin; fenfluramine raises serotonin levels and increases glucose utilization. This drug may cause diarrhea, sedation, and depression, and it should not be used with antihypertensive agents or alcohol. It is a controlled, Schedule IV drug, and has the capacity for abuse. High doses are toxic. A recent concern was raised about the neurotoxicity of the drug, since fenfluramine was reported to deplete serotonin uptake sites in rats, an effect whose reversibility is not known (Barnes, 1989). In response to that paper, the manufacturers of the drug disputed the neurotoxicity claim (Derome-Tremblay & Nathan, 1989), and suggested that mode of administration, as well as species and dose factors make comparisons of drug effects difficult between rats and humans.

Research. Dr. Richard Wurtman, a professor at the Massachusetts Institute of Technology, has used fenfluramine to treat women successfully for premenstrual depression. In a personal communication, he stressed that his data are preliminary and that D-fenfluramine is the active drug (often racemic mixtures are sold).

Impression. This information is very new, and, of course, the details will need to be published before we or anyone else can assess their worth.

Opiate Antagonists (Naltrexone)

Description. Naltrexone hydrochloride (Trexan; DuPont) is a pure opioid antagonist (*PDR*, 1987). It reversibly blocks the subjective effects of exogenously administered opioids, such as heroin. It is used as an adjunctive treatment in detoxified, formerly opioid-dependent persons. Naltrexone is hepatotoxic and can also lead to insomnia, anxiety, cramps, nausea, and headache.

Research. Chuong and colleagues (1988b) conducted a well-designed double-blind crossover trial of naltrexone or placebo, based on the premise that a fall in endogenous beta-endorphins causes symptoms of PMS and that this decline could be prevented with naltrexone. After 3 months of prospective ratings, each of 20 subjects with PMS was assigned either to naltrexone (25 mg twice daily) or to placebo for 3 months. Treatment lasted from Day 9 to Day 18. After a 1-month drug-free washout, the treatments crossed over. Scores on the Moos Menstrual Distress Questionnaire (1968b) significantly decreased on naltrexone when compared to placebo. Significant changes in individual symptoms were not reported. Side effects of naltrexone were mild and included nausea, decreased appetite, and dizziness/fainting.

Impression. This treatment seems to be effective in treating women with PMS. The treatment regimen used—that is, medication on Days 9–18—leads to questions regarding the rationale behind the study, however. At a dose of 50 mg/day, the opiate receptor blockade lasts 24 hours (*PDR*, 1987). Thus the effect of the drug is over by Day 19, before the time that Facchinetti and colleagues (1987) demonstrated a decrease in plasma beta-endorphins. It is therefore difficult to understand how this treatment regimen can be effective based on the mechanism proposed by the investigators.

This drug is not without risk. Its known hepatotoxic potential should lead one to prescribe it with caution. Further study is required to validate this treatment option.

Anxiolytics/Diuretics (Tenavoid)

Description. A combination drug, Tenavoid (Edwin Burgess Limited, Great Britain) is composed of 3 mg benzthiazide and 200 mg meprobamate. Thus it possesses both diuretic and anxiolytic properties and side effects, both of which have been described in previous sections (pp. 228–229, above).

Research. In an effort to treat both psychological and somatic symptoms (fluid retention specifically) using one medication, a combination drug (Tenavoid) was used in a PMS trial (Carstairs & Talbot, 1981). One hundred five women with premenstrual complaints and regular menses began a four-cycle randomized study. For two cycles, a woman received either Tenavoid (see description above for daily dose), benzthiazide (2.5 mg three times daily), or meprobamate (200 mg three times daily). Only the Tenavoid/placebo groups were double-blind. Treatment began at the occurrence of symptoms and lasted until the onset of menses. Subjects rated the severity of symptoms before the study began and at subsequent visits (frequently not listed in the paper).

Subjects improved on all treatments, including placebo. For individual symptoms, Tenavoid was statistically superior (1) to placebo only for irritability and tension; (2) to meprobamate only for irritability, tension, and "bloated feeling"; and (3) to benzthiazide not at all. Overall, however, Tenavoid was rated significantly better than both placebo and meprobamate.

Side effects were encountered, mainly on Tenavoid, and included nausea, constipation, fatigue, and headache, among many others. Ten women (about 10%) withdrew from the study as a result of side effects. However, as the authors point out, many of the side effects are also symptoms of PMS, so attributing them to the medication may be difficult.

Impression. Let us start by mentioning that Tenavoid is not available in the United States. Its components are, but since the medication was not superior to the diuretic, and since the combination drug was associated with many undesirable side effects, it does not make sense to suggest that women receive two prescriptions to mimic the combined form.

MISCELLANEOUS TREATMENTS

Over-the-Counter Medications for PMS

Over-the-counter medications that are marketed specifically for PMS (and dysmenorrhea in some cases) fall into three major categories: (1) combination drugs, (2) diuretics, and (3) nutritional supplements. Combination drugs are comprised of an analgesic, a xanthine diuretic (Pamabrom), and an antihistamine (see Table 7.1). The diuretics are either ammonium chloride and caffeine, or Pamabrom. The nutritional

TABLE 7.1 Over-the-Counter PMS Preparations

Drug	Manufacturer	Day/dose	Active ingredients	Concentration	Action of drug
Prēmsyn PMS	Chattem	up to 8	Acetaminophen Pamabrom* Pyrilamine maleate	500 mg 25 mg 15 mg	Analgesic Xanthine diuretic Antihistamine
Maximum Strength Midol PMS	Glenbrook	up to 8	Same as Prēmsyn PMS	500 mg 25 mg 15 mg	Analgesic Xanthine diuretic Antihistamine
Pursettes PMS Tablets	Jeffrey Martin	up to 8	Same as Prēmsyn PMS	500 mg 25 mg 15 mg	Analgesic Xanthine diuretic Antihistamine
Pamprin Extra Strength Multi-Symptom Pain Relief Formula Tablets	Chattem	up to 8	Acetaminophen Pamabrom* Pyrilamine maleate	400 mg 25 mg 15 mg	Analgesic Xanthine diuretic Antihistamine
Lurline PMS	Fielding	up to 8	Acetaminophen Pamabrom* Pyridoxine	500 mg 25 mg 50 mg	Analgesic Xanthine diuretic Essential nutrient
Aqua-Ban	Thompson	up to 6	Ammonium chloride Caffeine	325 mg 100 mg	Diuretic Stimulant, diuretic
Aqua-Ban Maximum Strength	Thompson	up to 3	Ammonium chloride Caffeine	650 mg 200 mg	Diuretic Stimulant, diuretic

(continued)

TABLE 7.1 (Continued)

Drug	Manufacturer	Day/dose	Active ingredients	Concentration	Action of drug
Ordinil Water Pill	Fox Pharmacal	up to 8	Pamabrom*	25 mg	Diuretic
Trendar	Whitehall	up to 6	Ibuprofen	200 mg	Analgesic
PMS Balance—Premenstrual Nutrition Supplement	Rexall Nutritional Products	1	Vitamin B$_6$	100 mg	Essential nutrient
			Vitamin E	300 IU	Essential nutrient
			Magnesium	200 mg	Essential nutrient
Efamol PMS	Nature's Way Products	4–6	Vitamin B$_6$	21 mg	Essential nutrient
			Vitamin E	12 IU	Essential nutrient
			Vitamin C	100 mg	Essential nutrient
			Calcium	20 mg	Essential nutrient
			Magnesium	30 mg	Essential nutrient
			Zinc	3 mg	Essential nutrient
			Natural oil base	—	Prostaglandin precursor
Windmill Pre-Menstrual Supplement	Windmill Vitamin Company	3	Evening primrose oil**	500 mg	Prostaglandin precursor
			Vitamin B$_6$	300 mg	Essential nutrient
			Magnesium	250 mg	Essential nutrient
			Calcium	125 mg	Essential nutrient
			Potassium	99 mg	Essential nutrient
			Folic acid	400 mg	Essential nutrient
			Herbal complex base	150 mg	Unknown rationale
Optivite	Optimox, Inc.	6–12	Vitamin A***	25,000 IU	Essential nutrient
			Vitamin E	200 IU	Essential nutrient
			Vitamin D$_3$	200 IU	Essential nutrient
			Folic acid	400 mcg	Essential nutrient
			Vitamin B$_1$	50 mg	Essential nutrient
			Vitamin B$_2$	50 mg	Essential nutrient
			Niacinamide	50 mg	Essential nutrient
			Vitamin B$_6$	600 mg	Essential nutrient
			Vitamin B$_{12}$	125 mcg	Essential nutrient
			Pantothenic acid	50 mg	Essential nutrient
			Choline bitartrate	625 mg	Unknown rationale
			Vitamin C	3,000 mg	Essential nutrient
			Magnesium	500 mg	Essential nutrient
			Iodine	150 mcg	Essential nutrient

Product	Company	Concentration	Ingredient	Amount	Notes
			Iron	30 mg	Essential nutrient
			Copper	1.0 mg	Essential nutrient
			Zinc	50 mg	Essential nutrient
			Manganese	20 mg	Essential nutrient
			Potassium	95 mg	Essential nutrient
			Selenium	200 mcg	Essential nutrient
			Chromium	200 mcg	Essential nutrient
ProCycle	Madison Pharmacy Associates	2–6	Vitamin A****	12,500 IU	Essential nutrient
			Vitamin E	100 IU	Essential nutrient
			Vitamin D_3	100 IU	Essential nutrient
			Folic acid	200 mcg	Essential nutrient
			Vitamin B_1	25 mg	Essential nutrient
			Vitamin B_2	25 mg	Essential nutrient
			Niacinamide	25 mg	Essential nutrient
			Vitamin B_6	300 mg	Essential nutrient
			Vitamin B_{12}	62.5 mcg	Essential nutrient
			Biotin	62.5 mcg	Essential nutrient
ProCycle	Madison Pharmacy Associates	2–6	Panthothenic acid	25 mg	Essential nutrient
			Choline bitartrate	312.5 mg	Unknown rationale
			Inositol	25 mg	Unknown rationale
			Paraamino benzoic acid	25 mg	Unknown rationale
			Vitamin C	1,500 mg	Essential nutrient
			Bioflavonoids	250 mg	Unknown rationale
			Rutin	25 mg	Unknown rationale
			Calcium	125 mg	Essential nutrient
			Magnesium	250 mg	Essential nutrient
			Iodine	75 mcg	Essential nutrient
			Iron	15 mg	Essential nutrient
			Copper	0.5 mg	Essential nutrient
			Zinc	25 mg	Essential nutrient
			Manganese	10 mg	Essential nutrient
			Potassium	47.5 mg	Essential nutrient
			Selenium	100 mcg	Essential nutrient
			Chromium	100 mcg	Essential nutrient

*Pamabrom is 2-amino-2-methyl-1-propanol-8-bromtheophyllinate
**Concentration in 3 tablets
***Concentration in 12 tablets
****Concentration in 6 tablets

supplements listed in the table contain Vitamins B_6 and E as well as magnesium. Optivite for Women (Optimox) and ProCycle (Madison Pharmacy Associates) are also nutritional supplements. Although they are not listed in the Over-the-Counter *Physicians Desk Reference* under the Product Category Index as menstrual preparations as most of the others are, at least Optivite is described as being useful for PMS in the indication section.

The combination drugs use the same antihistamine (pyrilamine maleate) and xanthine diuretic (Pamabrom or bromtheophyllinate) as Bickers (1953). Bickers's (1953) study was inadequate to support the efficacy of the drugs (see p. 206 above). Adding acetaminophen as an analgesic may help some pain symptoms, but its use is based on empirical evidence since it has not been studied in a treatment trial.

Ammonium chloride and caffeine are known diuretics. However, considering that caffeine is a stimulant drug that can exacerbate irritability, a common symptom of PMS, it seems out of place in a PMS preparation. The rationale and research studies underlying the use of diuretics in general have been discussed above on pages 197–202.

The use of nutritional supplements has been examined on pages 219–221.

Most of the over-the-counter preparations described above and in the table probably do not work except as placebos. Day (1968) provides an interesting discussion on whether pharmacists should knowingly sell a "worthless product" with a placebo response. He leaves the decision up to the pharmacist, and we leave it up to you, the clinician.

Sleep Deprivation

Research. One research group has tried sleep deprivation as a treatment for PMS (Parry & Wehr, 1987), based on the ability of sleep deprivation to improve major depression (Gillin, 1983), albeit temporarily. Women with PMS were selected rigorously and were also constrained to meet DSM-III criteria for Major Depression in the premenstrual week. Ten women out of 40 recruited met all selection criteria. Following a night of total sleep deprivation, 8 of 10 had improved significantly, as measured by changes in Hamilton Depression Rating Scale.

A second study examined "partial sleep deprivation" in five of the original ten subjects using a crossover design. Actually, the sleep periods were either phase advanced ("late sleep deprivation," women slept from 8 P.M.–2 A.M.) or phase delayed ("early sleep deprivation," women slept from 2 A.M.–8 A.M.). Only women who were phase advanced showed improvement on the Hamilton scale.

Impression. This study is interesting because it suggests a common link between severe forms of PMS and prominent depressive features, including Major Depression itself. However, as the authors themselves point out, the study was not blind and used relatively few subjects. In addition, while "partial sleep deprivation" may be feasible repeatedly, it is not clear whether it is the advance in the timing of sleep or the total duration of sleep that is the important factor in the success of this technique.

Light Treatment

Description. Recently, a subgroup of patients with seasonal Major Depression have been described (Rosenthal et al., 1984). Typically, the periods of depression begin in the fall and remit spontaneously in the spring. These patients with Seasonal Affective Disorder (SAD) are characterized by depression and lethargy, as in nonseasonal Major Depression, but tend to gain instead of lose weight, sleep more in lieu of having insomnia, and crave carbohydrates. The preferred treatment for this group of seasonally depressed patients is bright, full-spectrum light.

Research. A case report of a patient with seasonal PMS appeared recently (Parry et al., 1987). Her depressions were limited to the luteal phases of her menstrual cycles in the fall and winter. She was treated with 5 hours of bright (2,500 lux), full-spectrum light from 6:00 P.M. to 11:00 P.M. starting at the onset of symptoms through menses. Within a week, her degree of depression had decreased considerably as assessed by conventional scales.

Impression. As the authors state, both PMS and SAD are disorders related to cycles in affect. Thus, it was interesting to find a patient with a seasonal form of PMS. Whether light treatment would be useful in nonseasonal cases of PMS remains to be determined.

Antibiotics

Description. Doxycycline (Vibramycin; Pfizer) is a broad-spectrum antibiotic derived from oxytetracycline (*PDR,* 1987). It is useful in treating bacterial infections caused by both gram positive and gram negative microorganisms. Doxycycline is also used in the treatment of *Chlamydia* and gonorrheal infections.

Use of any tetracycline can cause side effects, such as supergrowth of yeast or other fungi, photosensitivity, and some gastrointestinal distress. Doxycycline can permanently discolor teeth and thus should not be used by a pregnant woman, since the developing teeth of the fetus may be affected. Further, animal studies suggest that tetracyclines are embryotoxic (which is actually a more compelling rationale to avoid them in the PMS population than is teeth discoloration).

Research. A report by Toth and colleagues (1988) studied the use of doxycycline in the treatment of PMS. Although subjects were selected prospectively, the criteria for inclusion were rather loose. After 1 month of ratings, women received either doxycycline (15 women; 100 mg twice daily) or placebo (15 women) for an entire cycle. While both groups improved significantly, antibiotics were superior to placebo. At 6 months, there was still improvement, although by that time there was no longer a placebo group since all women had received antibiotics. The authors also found a higher than expected rate of previously treated lower genital tract infections in women with PMS.

Impression. This study is interesting but suffers from methodological flaws. Whether the efficacy of treatment has to do with treating existing genital infections or with some other mechanism remains to be established. Further, we question whether the use of an antibiotic for longer than ten days is wise, especially in women of childbearing age.

Anticandida Treatment.

Description. Nystatin (Mycostatin; Squibb, among others) is an antifungal antibiotic active against yeast and other fungi (*PDR*, 1987). Taken orally, it is effective against oral and intestinal yeast infections. Vaginal treatment is also available for infections there. Oral nystatin is safe to use during pregnancy.

Research. A study using two anticandida techniques, oral nystatin and/or a yeast-elimination diet has been reported (Schinfeld, 1987). Thirty-two women with PMS who had not responded to prior treatments—including B$_6$ (18 women), progesterone (2), psychiatric (24), or other (10) treatments—were recruited. Twelve had never had a candida infection; 20 had. Study groups were arranged as shown in Table 7.2.

Global improvement was reported by 10 of 15 women on medication plus diet and by 1 of 3 women on oral treatment. Depression was not successfully treated yet was the major symptom of most groups.

Impression. The investigator sums up his own work as follows: "This therapy remains unproven until the results of a large, prospective, carefully monitored study can be evaluated" (p. 74). We agree.

TABLE 7.2 Anticandida Treatment

	No candidiasis		Previous candidiasis			
Group	A	B	C	D	E	F
N	7	5	7	9	3	1
Nystatin		yes-o		yes-o	yes-o	yes-v
Yeast-elimination diet		yes		yes		yes
B$_6$	yes					
Nothing			yes			

Note. o = oral nystatin; v = vaginal nystatin.

Allergy Management Techniques

Description. Allergy management techniques involve using minute quantities of antigen to "neutralize" symptoms (Mabray et al., 1982).

Research. Miller (1974) proposed a new treatment for relieving "progesterone-related symptoms" in women with PMS or on oral contraceptives. He prepared serial dilutions (1 : 5) of aqueous progesterone, beginning with 50 mg/ml. Women were tested on symptomatic days with 0.05 ml of a dilution. Symptoms either "cleared" within 20 minutes, or another weaker or stronger concentration was tried until they remitted. Miller reported that headache, tension, cramps, nausea, depression, heavy flow, fatigue, and other symptoms were successfully relieved by this technique. Overall favorable responses were achieved in 80% of 53 women tested, but their diagnoses were not stated. Of interest is part of the instruction given to the patients with their take-home doses: Neutralizing doses may change at any time, necessitating more evaluation in the office.

Using the technique of Miller (1974), Mabray and colleagues (1982) tested serial dilutions of aqueous progesterone in women complaining of PMS. (Verification of PMS was not provided.) When women were symptomatic, they received a set of injections until one was found that led to complete or marked relief of the symptom. They then went home with the effective concentration in a vial to self-administer. Twenty-nine women participated in an open study: 96% improved completely or markedly. In a second, single-blind test of 20 additional women (four with endometriosis as well as PMS), 18 chose progesterone and 2 chose placebo as the preferred "neutralizing" dose.

Impression. These studies are provocative but leave many issues unresolved, such as the length of time that symptoms remit and the role of expectation. Certainly subject groups need to be more clearly defined.

We will reserve judgment on this technique until more research is published.

Biofeedback and Relaxation Techniques

Research. Biofeedback and other relaxation techniques—such as progressive relaxation, meditation, yoga, and "alpha training" (Lovesky, 1978)—all lead to a state of relaxed wakefulness and, usually, drowsiness. Pain response may be lessened (Daniel R. Wagner, M.D., neurologist, personal communication, 1988). Several authors suggest that women with PMS be taught these techniques (Lovesky, 1978; Coyne, 1983). Coyne (1983), for example, based her recommendation on her finding that muscle tension varied across the menstrual cycle (See Chapter 3, pp. 47–48).

In one study of women with PMS (diagnosed retrospectively), subjects were trained either to warm or to cool their hands (Mathew et al., 1979). Those trained to warm showed an improvement in premenstrual concentration but increased pain. Those trained to cool their hands had decreased negative affect but, again, increased pain. None of these changes were reported to be significant.

Impression. Here is another proposed therapy that, like exercise and limiting salt intake, has been promoted frequently and is unsupported by research. However, there is nothing wrong with relaxing. We cannot think of any negative side effects, and it may be useful for women who are anxious. Thus, while biofeedback has not been shown to be effective, it can be suggested as an adjunctive treatment.

Acupuncture

Acupuncture has been reported to be effective in treating menstrual disorders, including PMS, but no data or references are provided (Boston Women's Health Book Collective, 1985, p. 65). In keeping with the well-recognized placebo response to any treatment, we will remain skeptical until controlled studies demonstrate the efficacy of this treatment.

CHAPTER 8

Management of Premenstrual Syndrome

Given the uncertainty about the cause of PMS, a clinician may adopt a hopeless attitude toward the management of women with this condition. We would caution against any pessimism regarding management and treatment. The risks of missing the condition in a diagnostic workup can be devastating to a woman not only in terms of her view of herself but also in terms of her interpersonal relationships. The risks of missing another medical condition because of premature treatment before careful evaluation can be life threatening (Vigliani, 1988). In addition, even though we cannot pinpoint the one and only single treatment at this time, there is much that the clinician can do to help a woman cope with her symptoms. With this in mind, let us begin.

Management of a patient who has come for a PMS evaluation begins with a review of the results of the diagnostic workup and daily ratings (if they were indicated) with her. At this point, the clinician will have assigned the patient into one of five categories: (1) women with PMS, (2) women with LLPDD, (3) women with both a psychiatric diagnosis and PMS (or LLPDD), (4) women with only a psychiatric diagnosis (not LLPDD), or (5) women with neither PMS nor a psychiatric diagnosis. This chapter is therefore organized into sections on the management of patients in each group.

The rating process itself is of fundamental importance. First, it defines each woman's symptom pattern, thereby validating or negating the retrospective history of PMS that prompted the woman to seek an initial evaluation. Second, it serves as a visual adjunct for the clinician who needs either to refer a woman to another health professional—an endocrinologist, for example (see Chapter 6, p. 161, for a case sample)—

or to help a woman understand that her symptom profile is not consistent with the diagnosis of PMS. Third, through the rating process, an important first step in management may already have been taken. As they chart their daily changes, many women gain a sense of control over their problems. The precise identification and quantification of the severity and timing of symptoms can make them seem more manageable. This sense of control can be enough to relieve some women's distress and make other interventions unnecessary (Osofsky et al., 1988).

However, further management may be needed and/or desirable. But just as there are no definitive tests for PMS at this time, there are no routine treatments. We, like others (Massil & O'Brien, 1986; Keye, 1988b) are recommending symptom-oriented approaches, as can be found in the following sections.

It is also important for clinicians who see women for PMS to prepare themselves beforehand for the fact that many of these women probably have read about the condition, diagnosed themselves, and know what to expect as treatment. In such instances, clinicians must be clear about the pros and cons of each type of treatment and insist that the therapeutic plan be designed specifically for the particular patient based on her symptom history and prospective ratings.

WOMEN WITH PMS

This section deals with the treatment of women whose prospective ratings indicate a pattern consistent with PMS, as defined in Chapters 1 and 6. This group of women is still heterogeneous and will be comprised of patients whose symptoms begin at different points of the cycle (after ovulation) and are of varying severity and type. We favor subdividing women with PMS into three broad groups: (1) women with predominantly psychological symptoms, (2) women with mainly physical symptoms, and (3) women with symptoms of both types. The majority of women with PMS will undoubtedly fall into the third category.

Many women with PMS may benefit from some or all of the suggestions in the section that immediately follows. More options can be recommended for managing some of the common physical symptoms than for the psychological ones, as will be discussed on pages 250–255.

Most Women with PMS

For most women with PMS, we suggest four initial interventions: (1) education, (2) caffeine restriction, (3) limiting salt consumption, and (4) exercise.

Education

Education and support are very important factors in helping a women to understand what PMS is so that she can begin to modify her lifestyle. Having kept daily ratings, she can learn to plan her monthly schedule ahead of time. In this way, she can prepare her family, herself, and, if necessary, her co-workers for her symptomatic times. She should attempt to limit external stresses as much as possible during the premenstruum.

Women can benefit from social support relationships (Sarason et al., 1985). Management focuses on three specific goals: (1) improving coping mechanisms, (2) reducing stress by stress management techniques, and (3) improving support systems by utilizing available interpersonal resources.

These aims can be accomplished by a number of different techniques. One approach is brief couple or family therapy, the purpose of which is to educate family members about the cyclic nature of the woman's symptoms. During this type of therapy, family members can learn about the syndrome and learn not to view it as a reflection on them personally. They can also be encouraged to plan ahead for the woman's symptomatic intervals; for example, they can help her by limiting demands for extra work from her during that time.

Another approach is group therapy (see Chapter 7, p. 163). Reid and Maddocks (1987) describe an eight-session group program that has apparently been quite helpful clinically, even though the approach in general has not been the subject of research. The group meets for 2-hour sessions weekly, and each week has a different focus. In the first week, the women share their experiences. Of limited use as a goal in and of itself, this nevertheless enhances group cohesion. It also allows the group therapist to set a tone of optimism for obtaining long-range benefit from the group experience. The goal of the second week is to learn how to use daily symptom charts to develop constructive methods of managing their symptoms during the premenstruum. Stress reduction techniques are taught during the third week. This particular group program teaches progressive muscle relaxation. The fourth week is devoted to improving patterns of communication, so that women can feel better about themselves in terms of assertiveness and competence. Assertiveness training techniques are employed. During the fifth week, the women organize their individualized nutrition and exercise programs. Time management is a focus, so that the women can schedule their exercise sessions within their busy weekly routines. The symptoms of depression and withdrawal are addressed during the sixth week. Negative views of themselves that can lead to depression are restructured. Women are taught to make fewer demands on themselves during those days rather than to isolate themselves from others. The seventh week is devoted to the symptoms of anger and guilt, with an emphasis on teaching techniques for the adaptive expression of anger. To the extent that women can be taught to channel their anger in constructive ways, they feel less guilt and more self-esteem. The final group session is used for discussing and evaluating the group. While this is not the only group approach, it serves as a good example of what can be designed for those women with PMS who might benefit from this type of education and social support in a group treatment setting.

Restricting Caffeine

As discussed in Chapter 7, pages 166–167, caffeine intake has been retrospectively associated with more severe premenstrual symptoms (Rossignol, 1985; Rossignol et al., 1989). Since caffeine can cause irritability, insomnia, and gastrointestinal distress at any time of the month, it makes sense to limit the consumption of caffeine or related compounds (tea, colas) during a patient's usual symptomatic days.

Limiting Salt Consumption

Symptoms associated with fluid retention are very common complaints. As has been discussed in the etiology and treatment chapters, not all women who complain of bloating and swelling actually gain weight premenstrually. However, most American women (and men) consume more salt than necessary according to the American Cancer Society Guidelines. Since overconsumption of salt can lead to temporary weight gain (MacGregor et al., 1979), it seems reasonable to recommend watching, and if necessary limiting, one's salt consumption at least prior to and during the usual symptomatic interval each month. Those women who gain substantial weight monthly may also benefit from a diuretic (see p. 252 below).

Exercise

The data from the studies of the effects of exercise on PMS symptoms are at best equivocal. Even so, we recommend that women engage in moderate levels of physical activity throughout the month. Aerobic exercise, except for women with obvious medical contraindications, may improve some symptoms associated with fluid retention (see Chapter 7, pp. 164–165) and may also increase a person's self-esteem.

Women with Predominantly Psychological Symptoms

Included in this group will be women with psychological symptoms whose severity does not warrant the diagnosis of LLPDD. Three therapeutic options are available that have some data supporting their effectiveness in treating women in this category: oral contraceptives, alprazolam, and meprobamate. None has been identified as the drug of choice. Two additional drugs (clonidine and buspirone) should be labeled as promising but in need of further clinical trials (see Chapter 7, pp. 233–234 and 229, respectively).

Oral Contraceptives

Both retrospective and prospective treatment studies suggest that oral contraceptive use may minimize symptoms of PMS, including the psychological ones (see Chapter 7, pp. 181–184). However, oral contraceptives have also been shown to induce PMS-like symptoms, for example, depression. Thus a woman should be asked if she has used oral contraceptives in the past. If the answer is affirmative and she remembers that her symptoms improved during that time, then they may be tried again (unless medically contraindicated or if she wants to become pregnant in the near future). If the patient has no experience with oral contraceptives, then a trial is possible. Patients with adverse reactions to previous oral contraceptive use should obviously not be prescribed the same type of oral preparation.

In all cases, if oral contraceptives are to be utilized, then combination forms should be prescribed. Although the sequential formulations that seemed to make symptoms worse are no longer on the market, triphasic oral contraceptives have appeared and are popular. These have not been tested on women with PMS.

Alprazolam

Some women may be averse to taking psychotropic medications. For those who are more sanguine about the idea, a trial of alprazolam may be attempted. However, there are many problems with this benzodiazepine, such as its propensity toward causing tolerance and dependence and the recent reports of unusual side effects (see Chapter 7, pp. 226–228). Only women who clearly have no tendency toward manifesting addictive behavior should receive this drug. More details on prescribing alprazolam are found below on page 255.

Meprobamate

While there is less research supporting the use of meprobamate than the use of alprazolam in the treatment of PMS, none of those studies has been negative (actually not too surprising, considering the nature of most treatment trials). Meprobamate has also stood the test of time, since it has been used clinically for decades. However, the same concerns about the addictive potential of the drug that we raised regarding alprazolam are relevant here as well.

Meprobamate can be prescribed during the patient's usual symptomatic interval and should help with symptoms of anxiety, fatigue, and insomnia. Recommended dosage is 200 mg in the morning and 200 mg in the late afternoon prior to the patient's self-reported stressful activities, for example, dinnertime with small children. This dose may be increased up to 400 mg twice daily (which is still in the pediatric dose range). No tapering of the drug during menses is required. This management regimen has worked well for John W. Schelpert III, M.D., a gynecologist in private practice in New Rochelle, New York, who shared his experience with us.

Women with Predominantly Physical Symptoms

Women in this group will have quite heterogeneous symptoms. If one of the following is the patient's major complaint, then a treatment trial with the suggested medication is in order (see also Table 8.1).

Fluid Retention

Fluid retention is an interesting symptom, because not all women who complain of bloating actually accumulate fluid, that is, gain weight. We have already recommended regular aerobic exercise for women with PMS, in part because there has been the suggestion that exercise can ameliorate some symptoms related to fluid retention. For those women who do gain weight, a diuretic may be prescribed. The diuretic of choice is spironolactone. While all the research data are not conclusive regarding the efficacy of spironolactone in treating symptoms of PMS other than bloating (see Chapter 7, pp. 196–197), this drug spares potassium while acting as an effective diuretic. Further, aldosteronism can be avoided. Spironolactone should be started after midcycle and discontinued with the onset of menses. The recommended dosage is 25 mg four times a day.

TABLE 8.1 Management of PMS: Physical Symptoms

Fluid retention with weight gain: Spironolactone
Mastodynia: Evening primrose oil, Vitamin E, bromocriptine
Fatigue and/or insomnia: Sleep hygiene
Headaches: Over-the-counter analgesics
(Pre)menstrual migraine: Cafergot, Fiorinol, or Midrin
Food cravings: Diet plan

Mastodynia

Women with symptoms of breast swelling or pain can first try one of the over-the-counter remedies that have shown some efficacy in treating these problems. Vitamin E (see Chapter 7, pp. 213–214) and evening primrose oil (Chapter 7, pp. 215–218) have some data supporting their usefulness in treating breast symptoms.

The PMS Medical Group in New York City recommends Efamol (evening primrose oil; Nature's Way) at a dose of one capsule (500 mg) twice daily with meals in the luteal phase only. If there is no improvement, the dose should be increased slowly up to 1,000 mg three times daily with meals for the whole cycle (Joseph Mortorano, M.D., personal communication, 1984). Improvement may require three or four cycles. Over a period of a year, the dose required usually decreases.

For serious cases of breast problems, bromocriptine will often be successful (Chapter 7, pp. 191–194). Use of this drug should not be routine, however, since numerous unpleasant side effects are common with the dosages that are usually prescribed to control the symptoms.

Fatigue and/or Insomnia

Women whose primary complaints include fatigue and/or insomnia should be instructed about sleep hygiene. The following are recommendations made by the Sleep-Wake Disorders Center of the Westchester Division, The New York Hospital:

1. Sleep on a very regular schedule, *including weekends.*

2. Do not spend too much time in bed. One-half hour more than your average amount of sleep per 24 hours is sufficient. To figure out your baseline average sleep time, each morning jot down your best estimate of how many hours and minutes you slept during the previous night. After 14 nights, add up the column of numbers and divide by 14.

3. Avoid caffeinated beverages after noontime, and if this doesn't help, avoid them altogether.

4. Avoid alcohol within 4 hours before bedtime, if not altogether.

5. Exercise, but do so in the morning or afternoon, not in the 3 or 4 hours before bedtime.

6. Do something relaxing in the hour or so before getting into bed. Avoid arguments, excitement, and bill-paying during this time.

7. A light bedtime snack is OK, but avoid eating a full meal just before bedtime.

8. An occasional sleeping pill is OK but should be reserved for very special circumstances. More than one per week is too many.

9. Stop trying to make sleep happen. You have to *let* it happen.

Prescribing a sedative hypnotic for premenstrual insomnia is probably not a good idea since (1) tolerance and dependence occur and

(2) residual daytime sedation is common. Alternatively, tryptophan is also sedating for some people and is available over-the-counter. If tryptophan is suggested, then the dose should be 2–3 grams (mixed with applesauce to be palatable) 30 minutes before bedtime (Charles P. Pollak, M.D., Head, Sleep–Wake Disorders Center, Westchester Division, The New York Hospital, personal communication, 1989).

Headaches

Women with premenstrual headaches should try any of the usual over-the-counter analgesics (aspirin, acetaminophen, ibuprofen) at the onset of the headache. One of the most common mistakes people make is waiting too long to begin the medication.

(Pre)menstrual Migraine

Treatment for (pre)menstrual migraine is the same as treatment for migraine at any other time of month. This type of headache is acute, unilateral, throbbing, and accompanied by photophobia and nausea. It may last for 4 to 12 hours. Often the patient becomes irritable and may withdraw or isolate herself due to the *headache*, not to the PMS.

Several combination drugs are available for treating migraine: (1) Cafergot (Sandoz), a combination of ergotamine tartrate and caffeine; (2) Fiorinal (Sandoz), comprised of butalbital, aspirin, and caffeine; and (3) Midrin (Carnrick), consisting of isometheptene mucate, dichloralphenazone, and acetaminophen. Each of these drugs can cause side effects, including nausea. In addition, the number of days for which Cafergot can be prescribed is limited.

If migraine headaches occur more frequently than once a week, then the patient will need prophylactic treatment (Daniel R. Wagner, M.D., neurologist, Westchester Division, The New York Hospital, personal communication, 1989). A variety of drugs are available for this purpose, including Bellergal-S (Sandoz) and Inderal (Ayerst). It is interesting that Bellergal has been the subject of some research in treating PMS (Chapter 7, p. 235).

Food Cravings

Women who have cravings first need to learn to regulate their food intake. One of the best means of doing so is to have the patient follow a diet plan. The plan that we are suggesting incorporates frequent small meals and adequate nutrition. By taking control of one aspect of their lives, such as food intake, women often feel that they have taken control of their PMS, thereby increasing well-being and self-esteem. In addition, as the Tufts Nutrition Letter (Volume 6, Number 8, October 1988) points out, women can try the diet "because, if nothing else, it is certainly a healthful prescription for eating that will at least help insure optimal nutrition" (p. 5).

This diet plan should not be confused with the hypoglycemia diet that is often recommended for all women with PMS. The rationale behind hypoglycemia as an etiology of PMS is extremely weak, and the diet itself has not been tested critically (Chapter 7, p. 165).

A sample diet is provided in Appendix D.

Women with Mixed Symptoms

As mentioned earlier, no panacea for mixed PMS symptoms exists as yet. Thus, for women who fit into this category, we recommend a trial of oral contraceptives for those who have either no experience with them or can remember that their symptoms improved when they took oral contraceptives in the past.

Suitable candidates may also receive alprazolam or meprobamate on a trial basis. Despite the fact that these are psychotropic medications, research suggests that, when effective, both psychological and physical symptoms are improved. Due caution should be exercised when prescribing either of these drugs (see p. 251 above and the section immediately below).

WOMEN WITH LLPDD

Women in this category have, by definition, psychological symptoms that are rated as more severe than those in women with PMS, since the LLPDD patient's daily life must be seriously disrupted to qualify her for the diagnosis. These patients will need intensive management, since the symptoms are so debilitating. Any of the management approaches for PMS described above may be indicated for women with LLPDD if their symptom profiles correspond. A major problem, however, is that the diagnosis is new. Thus no previous large treatment study has selected subjects with LLPDD. Any management approach with these patients will be breaking new ground.

A woman who is depressed to the point of being suicidal, or so angry that she might harm someone, should be protected from herself. This can be done by increasing family vigilance and support throughout the premenstrual days. In addition, medication is strongly indicated.

In general, short-term use of a benzodiazepine such as alprazolam may be tried first for treating depression (with or without anxiety). A problem with this class of drugs is that dependence and tolerance occur quickly (see Chapter 7, pp. 226–228). Thus, before a benzodiazepine is prescribed, the clinician should be familiar enough with the patient to know whether she manifests any sign of an addictive personality. Women who clearly show no such tendencies or are reluctant to take any unnecessary medication should do well in a clinical trial of such a drug. Another potential caution, though: Depressed women can become so disinhibited on benzodiazepines that the depressive symptoms actually worsen (Klerman & Deltito, 1986; Ayd, 1989a).

Since there is a wide variation in individual susceptibility to drowsiness produced by alprazolam, the proper dosage must be determined for each individual woman (Vargyas, 1982). Harrison and colleagues (1987) suggest beginning treatment in the early luteal phase at the onset of premenstrual symptoms with 0.25 mg at bedtime and 0.125 to 0.25 mg three times daily. They increase the dose daily up to 4 mg until either a satisfactory effect is obtained or side effects preclude further dosage increases. Smith and colleagues (1987) do not exceed 0.25 mg three times daily.

It is important to taper the dose, beginning on Day 2 of menses, by no more than 25% daily to avoid withdrawal symptoms. Withdrawal symptoms can include exacerbation of anxiety, shakiness, palpitations, tremor, and seizures.

If the initial intermittent use of the benzodiazepine is successful, the patient should be monitored regularly to ascertain whether continued use remains effective and to prevent habituation to the medication. After about a year, the drug should be discontinued to determine whether the LLPDD is in remission.

For women with LLPDD who suffer from a thought disorder limited to the premenstruum, major tranquilizers, such as Navane (thiothixene; Roerig), in small doses for symptomatic days can be effective. This use is based on clinical experience, since major tranquilizers have not been tested specifically for patients with either PMS or LLPDD.

WOMEN WITH A PSYCHIATRIC DIAGNOSIS AND PMS (OR LLPDD)

Women with a psychiatric diagnosis and PMS (or LLPDD) will often have premenstrual exacerbations of their present psychiatric illness as well as other symptoms, such as physical ones. It is important to treat the underlying psychiatric disorder first before tackling the premenstrual symptoms. This is analogous to treating hypothyroidism or fibroids before proceeding to treat the PMS.

Affective illness may worsen premenstrually. The type of psychotherapy, as well as the prescription of psychoactive drugs, will be based on the nature of the individual patient's affective symptoms. However, there are cases in the literature in which the amount of medication clearly needed to be increased to control a patient's symptomatology (see Chapter 7, pp. 231–233, on lithium, for example). One should bear this possibility in mind when designing a treatment program.

For those women with bipolar illness and marked premenstrual affective lability and dysphoria resulting in serious functional impairment, we concur with the treatment recommendations of Harrison and colleagues (1985b), who prescribe daily doses of lithium in the 600–900 mg range to achieve serum lithium concentrations of between 0.5–0.6 mEq/L. If premenstrual symptoms do not improve within two to three menstrual cycles, lithium should be discontinued.

As discussed in Chapter 4, unconscious conflicts may be expressed in symptoms premenstrually. For example, in a woman who has not satisfactorily resolved her oedipal conflicts, sexual and aggressive urges can lead to anxiety. To the extent that these urges and other behaviors fluctuate with the phases of the menstrual cycle (Benedek & Rubenstein, 1939a, 1939b; Adams et al., 1978), one would expect that symptoms resulting from anxiety mobilized by these unconscious conflicts would be manifested accordingly. In other words, symptoms would wax and wane depending on the phase of the menstrual cycle. The nature of the symptoms manifested would be determined by the form of the woman's character structure or neurosis (Friedman et al., 1980). For example, a woman with an obsessive–compulsive character structure might spend greater time cleaning or become more worried about time commitments premenstrually. The phobic woman might become more phobic at that time of month. These psychodynamic aspects of PMS or LLPDD would be managed most effectively with insight-oriented psychotherapy or psychoanalysis. As Gold (1987) points out, "psychotherapeutic intervention will, of course, depend upon the psychodynamics uncovered in each instance" (p. 118).

Women with panic attacks usually experience them throughout the month; only seldom are they limited to the premenstruum. Premenstrual exacerbations of panic disorders do occur, however, and not rarely. For these patients, a tricyclic antidepressant such as imipramine or a monoamine oxidase (MAO) inhibitor (if the woman could be careful about her diet) should be prescribed for the whole month. The baseline dosage may need to be increased during the premenstruum (Joseph A. Deltito, M.D., Head of the Anxiety and Depression Clinic, Westchester Division, The New York Hospital, personal communication, 1988).

WOMEN WITH ONLY A PSYCHIATRIC DIAGNOSIS (NOT LLPDD)

These women should be shown how their daily ratings differ from those of women suffering from PMS. They should understand that their symptoms occur throughout the month and are in no way consistently related to the menstrual cycle. Should they need treatment for their symptoms, they should be referred to an appropriate mental health professional.

Women with psychiatric diagnoses who have premenstrual exacerbations of symptoms have been discussed in the immediately preceding section.

WOMEN WITHOUT PMS

As with the patients in the previous group, women without PMS should be shown both (1) that their daily symptom ratings do not meet criteria for PMS and (2) that their workup is not consistent with any other medical diagnosis. In many instances, a life stress can be found to account for their symptoms. Some women need help identifying ways to cope with these life stresses.

At other times, nothing can be found to explain why the women sought treatment. Often women are relieved to discover that their symptoms are not as severe as they had thought and that they have no diagnosable condition. On the other hand, some women are unhappy to learn that they do not have PMS. These women may need help accepting this fact and in reaffirming their self-worth. Short-term supportive psychotherapy may be helpful in this regard.

Another possibility is that women in this category are in the incipient months of developing PMS. Thus symptoms may be present but not severe enough to meet criteria for a definitive diagnosis. If this is suspected, the patient should be encouraged to return in 6 months to a year to repeat her workup. Alternatively, she can be supplied with several more months of daily rating forms so that she can continue to chart at home.

SUMMARY

Clear guidelines are available for a thorough diagnostic evaluation for PMS (Chapter 6). Initial management approaches include education, support, proper diet, and exercise. Drug therapy should be used with caution and with the dictum to do the least harm. The severity of impairment must be weighed against short-term and possible long-term side effects of medications.

What is firmly recommended at this time is an evaluation/management program that establishes individual symptom baselines and tailors individual symptom management. As Keye (1988) and McDaniel (1988) suggest, a biopsychosocial management program is required. Using such an approach, health care providers will select medical, psychological, and social interventions as appropriate to each particular woman.

CHAPTER 9

Premenstrual Syndrome and Women's Issues

As alluded to in Chapter 2, PMS and LLPDD remain controversial diagnoses today. This is due in part to mass media and lay magazines that have stirred the interest of the general public about them. With women comprising a substantial and increasing proportion of the work force, medical problems that could have a bearing on performance and productivity or that could be used to discriminate against job placements or promotions for women have become "hot potatoes." Sometimes such attention is beneficial, since public pressure can lead to increased research dollars, as with AIDS research, for example. On other occasions, misinformation in the nonmedical community causes more damage than help and can result in women being treated incorrectly or seeking help from disreputable specialty clinics.

The aim of this chapter is to discuss some of the contemporary issues regarding women and PMS. The following section is a discussion of the rationales behind creating the diagnosis of LLPDD, a *psychiatric* diagnosis. The subsequent section covers the use of PMS in the courts, since PMS has been used successfully as a defense in criminal cases in England. The final section before the closing note concerns the impact of PMS on families and women's health issues.

DIAGNOSING PMS (OR LLPDD) AND WOMEN'S RIGHTS

Currently, PMS is a controversial disease entity. Many women welcome professional legitimization for longstanding and troubling symptoms which have been either dismissed as unimportant signs of "weakness" or "hysteria" by a male-dominated medical culture, or popularized as the central features of antifeminist jokes. The women's rights movement is understandably ambivalent about PMS, not wanting to deny its existence and the importance to women of research and treatment, while attempting to prevent social discrimination on the basis of sexual differences. But by asserting the reality of PMS, the existence of far-reaching biobehavioral differences between the sexes is implied. (Johnson, 1987, p. 341)

Particularly within the feminist community, debate continues about PMS.

PMS has been characterized as a double-edged sword. If denied or treated lightly, researchers will ignore it and women whose symptoms could be treated will continue to suffer. On the other hand, since the menstrual cycle is one of the few real biological differences between women and men, when we do acknowledge menstrual problems, they are alleged to be evidence of our biological inferiority. (Chait, 1986, p. 271)

Historically, there was some objection to the classification of PMS as a gynecological illness. This was voiced, for example, by Laws (1983):

If we [women] are to reintegrate ourselves we have to own all our states of being as part of ourselves, even, or perhaps especially, the painful ones. . . . Why women's lives should involve cyclic changes, and often unpleasant or painful feelings which recur cyclically, is a philosophical and political problem for us all. It is not a problem which we can safely hand over to doctors to deal with. (p. 30)

When attempts were made to delineate a subgroup of women with PMS and classify them as having a psychiatric illness (LLPDD), debate escalated (Spitzer et al., 1989). Criticisms of LLPDD were voiced by the Committee on Women of the American Psychiatric Association and by the Association of Women Psychiatrists. Essentially, these groups were concerned both that not enough is known about the disorder and that classifying PMS as a mental disorder would stigmatize women and undermine gains that have been achieved to better women's rights. It seems to us that the issue of stigmatization really reflects the continuing stigmatization of mental illness, not the stigmatization of women. Thus women would fear being associated with an illness that did not carry the respect of a physical malady.

It is worthwhile to review in detail the scientific and social (potential harm to women) issues that were raised in 1987 since the debate over the inclusion of LLPDD in the Research Appendix of DSM-III-R continues even after its publication (Spitzer et al., 1989).

Scientific Issues Raised by the LLPDD Diagnosis

The scientific issues can be summarized as follows:

(1) Is too little known about the disorder to classify it?
(2) Isn't the International Classification of Diseases (ICD) classification sufficient?
(3) How valid can the diagnosis be when the requirement of "functional impairment" is based on subjective reports?
(4) Doesn't the name "LLPDD" imply that something is biologically wrong with the menstrual cycle?
(5) Since all women experience some premenstrual changes, how can LLPDD be considered a disorder?
(6) Doesn't the diagnosis reflect gender bias?

It is true that little is certain about the etiology and treatment of this condition. This also happens to be true for most DSM-III-R categories. However, there *is* a general consensus about the descriptive features of the disorder, including the common symptoms and the timing of their appearance during the menstrual cycle. Specifying these in DSM-III-R facilitates subject selection, thereby increasing the quality and comparability of research on LLPDD conducted by different research groups. As we have stated earlier (Chapters 5 and 7), a major problem with research has been unclear and retrospective criteria used to select women for research studies, thus resulting in heterogeneous populations that are not necessarily representative of women with PMS.

With regard to the second issue, it is true that there is a category, (625.4) Premenstrual Tension Syndromes, that is included in the genitourinary section of the ICD. However, no definition is given, nor are diagnostic criteria provided. The central issue here is whether LLPDD, whose definition requires a disturbance of mood and functional impairment, should be classified as a physical disorder or as a mental disorder. The DSM-III-R definition of a mental disorder is "a clinically significant behavioral or psychological syndrome or pattern that occurs in a person and that is associated with present distress (a painful symptom) or disability (impairment in one or more important areas of functioning)." (American Psychiatric Association, p. xxii). To this extent, LLPDD meets this definition. Furthermore, differentiating a diagnosis of LLPDD from other mental disorders requires the special skill of a mental health professional. Thus, having the criteria in the manual encourages the training of mental health professionals to recognize LLPDD when they evaluate women who are symptomatic. This does not necessarily mean that LLPDD must be treated with psychotherapy. LLPDD, like other mental disorders in which biological factors play a central role (such as Major Affective Disorder), may require biological therapy.

Many women attending PMS clinics fear that they would lose insurance coverage were their condition reclassified as a "mental disorder." This is a legitimate concern. It is unclear what the effect on third-party reimbursement will be, particularly since LLPDD appears only in the appendix of DSM-III-R and therefore is not an official DSM-III-R category. In any case, such fiscal considerations should not be the basis for excluding the disorder from a classification whose primary concerns are clinical and scientific.

The issue of the subjectivity of symptom reports is a problem that exists for other diagnoses as well. For example, the diagnosis of Obsessive Compulsive Disorder or of a Simple Phobia may also require a clinical judgment that the symptoms significantly interfere with a person's functioning. The clinician may sometimes have access to more objective confirming data, such as a spouse's report or job performance records. Without these, the clinician must rely solely on the subject's assessment of whether the symptoms are so severe that they "seriously interfere with work or with usual social activities or relationships with others."

In response to the question of biological malfunction, research has not revealed any biological abnormality in women with severe premenstrual symptoms. Therefore, LLPDD may be not a disorder *of* the menstrual cycle, but rather one *associated with* the menstrual cycle. All possible causes of this disorder must be explored, including biological, psychological, and social etiologies.

Some of the opponents of LLPDD argued that premenstrual changes in women are ubiquitous and that therefore LLPDD is only an arbitrary selection of the extreme expression of a "normal" phenomenon. The same argument could be made for many well-established diagnoses. For example, one extreme of the distribution of intelligence in the population is recognized as mental retardation. Extreme forms of sadness or grief are recognized as depressive disorders, and extreme concern with body weight, size, or shape is recognized as an eating disorder. What this issue underscores, however, is the importance of defining the boundary between normal and pathological, both for research purposes and for good clinical care. In the case of LLPDD, the diagnostic criteria assure that only a relatively small percentage of women with premenstrual symptoms will qualify for the diagnosis.

Because LLPDD can only be diagnosed in women, the question of gender bias arises. Many mental disorders, however, are prevalent differentially according to gender. Just as there are many diagnoses in DSM-III and DSM-III-R that are more common in women (e.g., Depressive Disorders), there are many that are far more common in men (e.g., Antisocial Personality Disorder, Psychoactive Substance Use Disorders) and some that are hardly ever seen in women (e.g., the Paraphilias). One DSM-III-R disorder, Premature Ejaculation, by definition can only be diagnosed in men, and there is no analogous category in women. The implication of gender bias in the diagnosis of LLPDD, then, is simply not true.

Social Issues Raised by the LLPDD Diagnosis

The social issues in the debate included the following concerns about potential harm to women:

(1) Will the diagnosis reinforce negative myths about women?
(2) Given the potential for stigma, why include the diagnosis in DSM-III-R?
(3) Will the diagnosis harm women in the workplace?
(4) Will the diagnosis be used against women in the courts?

The negative myths, described in Chapter 2, include the view of women as cyclically unstable and defective as a result of their "raging hormones." The recognition that *some* women have a cyclic disorder associated with the menstrual cycle certainly does not imply that *all* women who menstruate are ill. In fact, most women do not have mood fluctuations associated with the menstrual cycle (Van den Boogaard & Bijleveld, 1988). Do women have a special vulnerability? Yes; just as men are vulnerable to developing certain disorders, so too are women. It is not "anti-women" to recognize LLPDD any more than it is "anti-men" to recognize the large number of illnesses that are more common in men.

Those who are concerned about gender bias (Gallant & Hamilton, 1988) and those who fear stigmatization have questioned including the diagnosis in DSM-III-R, especially when there is no single treatment for the disorder. It is true that research has not yet indicated a consistent benefit from one particular form of treatment in double-blind controlled studies (See Chapter 7). However, there are many other mental disorders (as well as physical disorders) that are included in official classification systems for which effective treatments have yet to be developed. Researchers need standard criteria in order to evaluate various treatments of LLPDD and to investigate the causes of the disorder.

In the workplace it is true that an employer might be reluctant to hire a woman who acknowledges that she suffers from LLPDD. However, an employer might well be reluctant to hire a women who acknowledges *any* mental or physical disorder that could impair her job functioning. If the woman truly is job-impaired, the employer's rejection is not unfair discrimination. If the woman is not impaired, then the solution to the problem of unfair discrimination in the workplace is certainly not to pretend that the disorder does not exist.

It is also true that many women with LLPDD are or would be uncomfortable with the idea that they suffer from a "mental disorder" and that some of these women might be reluctant to seek help if they knew that the disorder was regarded as such. Nevertheless, large numbers of women throughout the country seek help from many clinics in departments of psychiatry that specialize in the study and treatment of this condition. This indicates that the stigma of "mental illness" does not discourage at least many of them from seeking clinical care.

The issue of PMS or LLPDD in legal conflicts is an issue that deserves special attention and will be described in more detail in the next section. In general, however, if a woman has LLPDD or any disorder that results in her harming her children, the legal issue is the same as for any mental disorder. Hence the diagnosis might be a relevant issue in child custody cases. The insanity defense is a separate issue; in most states it requires demonstrating that the individual suffers from a psychotic disorder. Because LLPDD rarely involves psychotic behavior, it is unlikely that it would frequently be used successfully as a psychiatric defense in criminal cases in this country. In the rare instance in which LLPDD is associated with psychotic features, it would be up to the jury to decide if the presence of the condition was relevant to an insanity defense or if it should be used as a mitigating factor in sentencing (see below).

PMS AS A LEGAL DEFENSE

Some state that PMS is making its way into our courts (Oleck, 1953), and some are fearful that as a result all women are going to be on trial (Sommer, 1984). This is obviously a simplistic view, since using PMS as the basis for a claim or as a defense is fraught with many problems, such as: (1) lack of consensus about a definition of the condition, (2) lack of a diagnostic test for PMS, and (3) lack of agreement about causes or treatment. Furthermore, to date in the United States, PMS has not successfully been asserted as a defense in a criminal action (Benedek, 1988).

The fact that the DSM-III-R lists LLPDD in the research appendix has stirred fears that LLPDD will be recognized as a mental illness. Elissa Benedek, a forensic psychiatrist, states:

[A]ll DSM-III-R diagnoses are not equivalent to mental illnesses. Some states contrast mental illness with emotional disorders. Mental illness is generally defined as a substantial disorder of thought or mood which significantly impairs judgment, behavior, capacity to recognize reality, or ability to cope with the ordinary demands of life. A diagnosis listed in the Appendix could be considered an emotional disorder. (Personal communication, December 12, 1988)

However, Meehan and MacRae (1986) point out that a problem in presenting a defense of PMS based on its being a disease of the mind is that there is little evidence that women with PMS fail to appreciate the nature of an act or to know that it is against the law. Rather, they know and appreciate the nature of the act but fail to control themselves. D'Orban (1981) also recognized the need to prove an abnormal mental state if PMS is to succeed as a defense. Further, neither LLPDD nor PMS can meet any of the known insanity tests, that is, the McNaughton test, the Durham test, and the irresistible impulse test (Chait, 1986).

Some research does indicate that women with PMS feel less in control of their emotions and behavior in general than women without PMS (O'Boyle et al., 1988) and that they feel even less in control premenstrually than at other times of the menstrual cycle. This finding may have important implications, since grounds might be made for a "diminished capacity" or a "lack of intent" defense. However, "lack of control" that is not due to a primary psychiatric disorder or to an altered state of consciousness is not likely to be the basis of a substantial defense (Weiss, 1985).

Specific Difficulties with PMS as a Defense

At this point in time there are several problems associated with using PMS as a defense.

Difficulty proving that the defendant suffers from PMS. One must prove each of the following: (1) that the defendant has PMS, (2) that she was suffering from it at the time of the incident, and (3) that it caused the incident. Given the fact that diagnosis depends on a minimum of 2 months documentation of cyclic symptoms, there may not be enough time to establish the diagnosis. Furthermore, how can one prove that the woman had a menses within 2 weeks of the crime (Heggestad, 1986)? And how can one prove that the months the defendant rated her symptoms were like the month when the incident happened?

Difficulty documenting the defendant's history. Since the defendant's retrospective history of PMS may be subject to question, other-factors must be considered in establishing a definitive diagnosis of PMS. In this regard, Riley (1986) makes several suggestions. If a woman is a previous offender and the timing of previous incidents can be linked to the premenstruum, this would help establish the defense. First-time offenders could document premenstrual work impairment or social or marital problems, or they could produce corroborative medical records. But a woman who states that she was under the influence of analgesics for dysmenorrhea at the time of the incident probably was not suffering from PMS.

Difficulty using expert witnesses. Generally, experts may testify in courts only as to matters that are generally accepted in the scientific field (Oakes, 1986). Since there is no agreement about what causes PMS and no diagnostic test, there is still medical uncertainty about the condition (Benedek, 1985). While clarity and simplicity of PMS diagnostic techniques seem to be improving, the reliance on subjective determinations may result in divergent opinions among experts. Furthermore, the validity of LLPDD is not yet accepted in the scientific field, since it appears in the appendix of the psychiatric diagnostic manual, not as a "sanctioned" diagnostic category.

Esoteric Points

> Court-ordered treatment of PMS may, by itself, create an array of difficult legal, ethical and social questions. Specifically, what should be done with the PMS offender who fails or refuses to obtain court-ordered treatment? Does a woman have a right to refuse treatment on religious or moral grounds? What should be the liability of the physician who fails to diagnose or treat premenstrual syndrome in a woman who later is involved in a crime as a result of PMS? What happens if the recognized treatment is not approved by the Federal Food & Drug Administration? What is the liability of the court or treating physician if the patient claims an adverse reaction? Qualified physicians have proposed treatment for PMS other than progesterone. Should these treatments be considered or allowed by the court? How should the criminal justice system react if the patient commits another crime while she is under proper treatment? Can an individual use PMS as defense more than once? (Riley, 1986, p. 201)

Thus it can be seen that many legal questions remain unanswered. One cannot claim that PMS is a "mental disease or defect" or that a person suffering from PMS totally lacks the capacity to understand her action. Instead she may suffer a diminished capacity to control her behavior, so that PMS may be considered a "mitigating circumstance" or a factor to be considered in sentencing (Meehan & MacRae, 1986).

We were unable to find any literature concerning the use of PMS or LLPDD *against* a woman, as in a child custody case. It will be interesting to see whether cases are reported that involve either diagnosis and, if so, how they are treated by the courts.

NEGLECTED AREAS OF RESEARCH

This chapter has attempted to describe several of the more political issues surrounding PMS today. The debates over both the legitimacy of the diagnosis of PMS and LLPDD as well as the use of them in courts of law are not likely to end in the near future.

In the meantime, two other issues concerning PMS need special mention and additional research: (1) PMS and the family and (2) PMS and women's health.

PMS and Family Systems

There is a paucity of scientific literature on the ramifications of PMS on the family system. How does PMS affect marital relationships and relationships with children? How does the family environment influence a woman's susceptibility to the development and maintenance of PMS symptoms?

Only two studies of these issues appeared in our literature search (Rattray, 1986; Siegel, 1986). Both studies found marital dissatisfaction and problems with dyadic intimacy that correlated positively with the severity of PMS. Each study was methodologically flawed, however, because of lack of confirmation of PMS by prospective daily ratings. In addition, neither study ruled out psychiatric diagnoses in their subjects. Thus, given the problems with this research, the results will have to be confirmed.

There is one anecdotal account in the literature of a husband whose asthma was exacerbated premenstrually by the change in his wife's odor premenstrually (Palomaki, 1988). We do not know whether this had an impact on their relationship.

Certainly, understanding family dynamics when the mother has PMS deserves careful attention as we expand our knowledge of the disorder.

PMS and Women's Health

Another area of extreme importance and grave concern is the general area of women's health (Elder, 1983). Today many self-help books, including some with serious misinformation about particular treatments, are available for PMS. Thus women often medicate themselves in attempts to cope with their premenstrual symptoms. There is also a report of self-medication by adolescents with purported PMS (Wilson-Larsen & Keye, 1987).

Concern has been voiced about premenstrual syndrome and addiction (Coffee, 1985), and particularly about the abuse of alcohol as a coping mechanism (Cassara, 1981). In addition, women are using a variety of over-the-counter pharmaceutical remedies that promise relief from PMS in "the safest and most effective way" (Pre-Menstrual System: The Complete Nutritional System, manufactured by Country Farms Nutritional Products, Inc., Fairfield, NJ). Some of the over-the-counter products contain too much Vitamin B_6 (see Chapter 7, pp. 207–213). Indeed, one of the initial articles on B_6-induced neuropathies (Schaumberg et al., 1983) studied patients who were self-medicating for a variety of disorders, one of which was PMS. Without further education about PMS, symptomatic women may, therefore, continue to put themselves at risk by trying unproven and potentially toxic remedies.

CLOSING NOTE

Throughout this book we have stressed the need for education: for clinicians, for patients, for families. We remain optimistic that the cause and treatments for PMS will be resolved and hope that you, the clinician, have come to the same conclusion.

Appendices

APPENDIX A.   PMS INITIAL INTERVIEW

How old are you? _____
What brought you for the evaluation today?
(List symptoms) _____

_____

_____

_____

When do each of these symptoms occur in relation to menses? _____
Do they occur every month? _____
At what age did you first notice these symptoms? _____
How do your symptoms interfere with your life? _____

_____

How is your health, in general? _____
Have you ever been told that you have:
    Endometriosis _____
    Fibroids _____
    Breast masses _____
    Thyroid disease _____
    Diabetes _____
    Allergies _____
Have you had any operations? _____ Tubal ligation? _____
Have you ever been pregnant? _____ How many times? _____
How many births? _____
Are you taking any medications?
    Water pills _____
    Birth control pills _____
    Vitamins _____
    Over-the-counter preparations _____

Are your periods regular? _____
   How frequent are they? _____
   Age of menarche? _____
   What were your periods like then? _____
   Now? _____
Does any one else in your family have PMS? _____
Mother? _____ Sister? _____
Have you ever sought help for emotional problems? _____
Hospitalized? _____
Has anyone in your family sought help for emotional
problems? _____ Hospitalized? _____

APPENDIX B.   DECISION TREES

Pre-Diagnosis Decision Tree

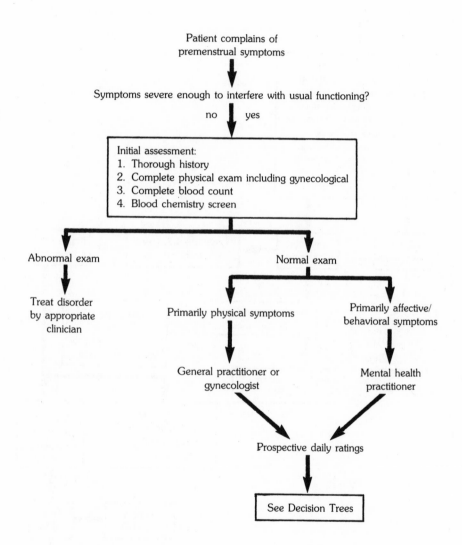

Decision Tree A
LLPDD

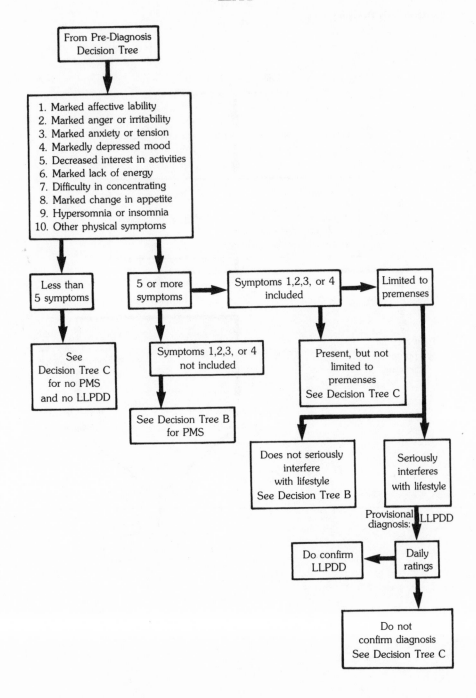

Decision Tree B
PMS

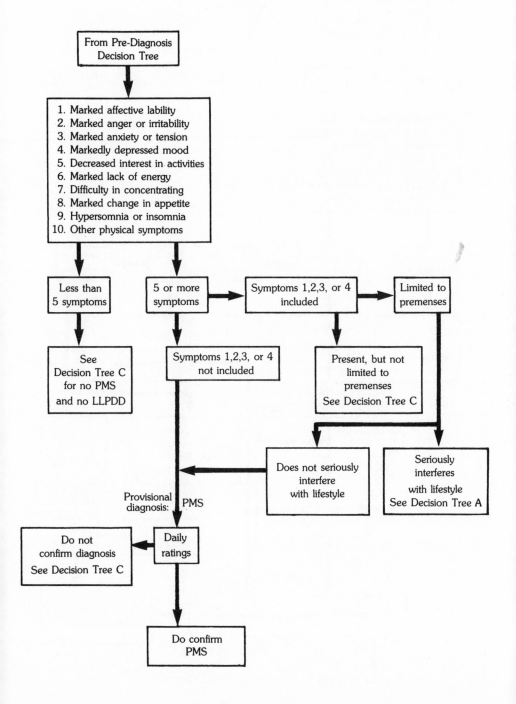

Decision Tree C
No PMS and No LLPDD

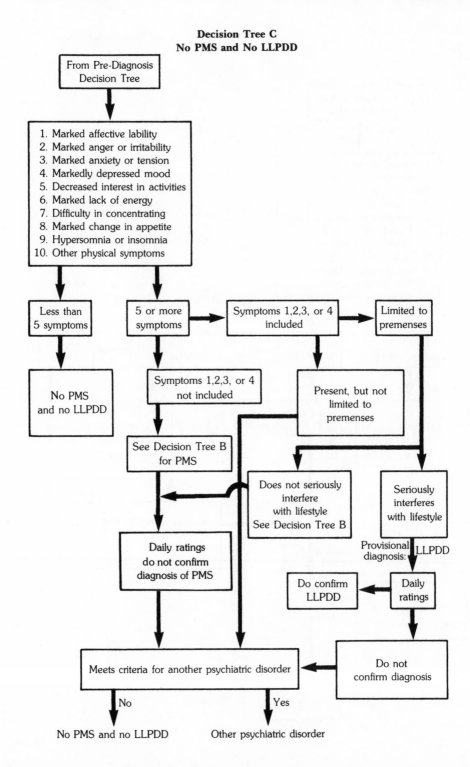

APPENDIX C.   DAILY SYMPTOM CHECKLIST

Subject Code: ───────────────

INSTRUCTIONS

A. Symptom Checklist

There are 16 items listed on the following pages.

1. Start your ratings on the line with the correct day of the week for the first day's ratings.

2. Rate each item each day.

3. Make the ratings at the same time each day.

4. When you are menstruating, write "YES" in the column labeled "Menst."

5. Remember to use the scale at the top of the page.

B. Temperature Measurement

1. Take your temperature orally upon waking each morning.

2. Record the value on this form in the column labeled "Temp."

All information contained on this form and data summarized from it will be kept confidential. Any written or verbal reports will be done in a way which precludes identification of individuals.

Adapted from the Daily Rating Form developed by Jean Endicott, Ph.D., Sybil Schacht, M.S.W., and Uriel Halbreich, M.D., Research Assessment and Training Unit, 722 West 168th Street, New York, N.Y. 10032.

Subject Code: _____

Scale: 1 = None, 2 = Minimal, 3 = Mild, 4 = Moderate, 5 = Severe, 6 = Extreme

Day	Date	Menst?	Temp.	Stay at home, avoid social activity	Decreased interest in usual activities	Less work (job, home), inefficient	Feel bloated
M	__ / __	_____	____	1 2 3 4 5 6	1 2 3 4 5 6	1 2 3 4 5 6	1 2 3 4 5 6
Tu	__ / __	_____	____	1 2 3 4 5 6	1 2 3 4 5 6	1 2 3 4 5 6	1 2 3 4 5 6
W	__ / __	_____	____	1 2 3 4 5 6	1 2 3 4 5 6	1 2 3 4 5 6	1 2 3 4 5 6
Th	__ / __	_____	____	1 2 3 4 5 6	1 2 3 4 5 6	1 2 3 4 5 6	1 2 3 4 5 6
F	__ / __	_____	____	1 2 3 4 5 6	1 2 3 4 5 6	1 2 3 4 5 6	1 2 3 4 5 6
Sa	__ / __	_____	____	1 2 3 4 5 6	1 2 3 4 5 6	1 2 3 4 5 6	1 2 3 4 5 6
Su	__ / __	_____	____	1 2 3 4 5 6	1 2 3 4 5 6	1 2 3 4 5 6	1 2 3 4 5 6
M	__ / __	_____	____	1 2 3 4 5 6	1 2 3 4 5 6	1 2 3 4 5 6	1 2 3 4 5 6
Tu	__ / __	_____	____	1 2 3 4 5 6	1 2 3 4 5 6	1 2 3 4 5 6	1 2 3 4 5 6
W	__ / __	_____	____	1 2 3 4 5 6	1 2 3 4 5 6	1 2 3 4 5 6	1 2 3 4 5 6
Th	__ / __	_____	____	1 2 3 4 5 6	1 2 3 4 5 6	1 2 3 4 5 6	1 2 3 4 5 6
F	__ / __	_____	____	1 2 3 4 5 6	1 2 3 4 5 6	1 2 3 4 5 6	1 2 3 4 5 6
Sa	__ / __	_____	____	1 2 3 4 5 6	1 2 3 4 5 6	1 2 3 4 5 6	1 2 3 4 5 6
Su	__ / __	_____	____	1 2 3 4 5 6	1 2 3 4 5 6	1 2 3 4 5 6	1 2 3 4 5 6
M	__ / __	_____	____	1 2 3 4 5 6	1 2 3 4 5 6	1 2 3 4 5 6	1 2 3 4 5 6
Tu	__ / __	_____	____	1 2 3 4 5 6	1 2 3 4 5 6	1 2 3 4 5 6	1 2 3 4 5 6
W	__ / __	_____	____	1 2 3 4 5 6	1 2 3 4 5 6	1 2 3 4 5 6	1 2 3 4 5 6
Th	__ / __	_____	____	1 2 3 4 5 6	1 2 3 4 5 6	1 2 3 4 5 6	1 2 3 4 5 6
F	__ / __	_____	____	1 2 3 4 5 6	1 2 3 4 5 6	1 2 3 4 5 6	1 2 3 4 5 6
Sa	__ / __	_____	____	1 2 3 4 5 6	1 2 3 4 5 6	1 2 3 4 5 6	1 2 3 4 5 6
Su	__ / __	_____	____	1 2 3 4 5 6	1 2 3 4 5 6	1 2 3 4 5 6	1 2 3 4 5 6
M	__ / __	_____	____	1 2 3 4 5 6	1 2 3 4 5 6	1 2 3 4 5 6	1 2 3 4 5 6
Tu	__ / __	_____	____	1 2 3 4 5 6	1 2 3 4 5 6	1 2 3 4 5 6	1 2 3 4 5 6
W	__ / __	_____	____	1 2 3 4 5 6	1 2 3 4 5 6	1 2 3 4 5 6	1 2 3 4 5 6
Th	__ / __	_____	____	1 2 3 4 5 6	1 2 3 4 5 6	1 2 3 4 5 6	1 2 3 4 5 6
F	__ / __	_____	____	1 2 3 4 5 6	1 2 3 4 5 6	1 2 3 4 5 6	1 2 3 4 5 6
Sa	__ / __	_____	____	1 2 3 4 5 6	1 2 3 4 5 6	1 2 3 4 5 6	1 2 3 4 5 6
Su	__ / __	_____	____	1 2 3 4 5 6	1 2 3 4 5 6	1 2 3 4 5 6	1 2 3 4 5 6
M	__ / __	_____	____	1 2 3 4 5 6	1 2 3 4 5 6	1 2 3 4 5 6	1 2 3 4 5 6
Tu	__ / __	_____	____	1 2 3 4 5 6	1 2 3 4 5 6	1 2 3 4 5 6	1 2 3 4 5 6
W	__ / __	_____	____	1 2 3 4 5 6	1 2 3 4 5 6	1 2 3 4 5 6	1 2 3 4 5 6
Th	__ / __	_____	____	1 2 3 4 5 6	1 2 3 4 5 6	1 2 3 4 5 6	1 2 3 4 5 6
F	__ / __	_____	____	1 2 3 4 5 6	1 2 3 4 5 6	1 2 3 4 5 6	1 2 3 4 5 6
Sa	__ / __	_____	____	1 2 3 4 5 6	1 2 3 4 5 6	1 2 3 4 5 6	1 2 3 4 5 6
Su	__ / __	_____	____	1 2 3 4 5 6	1 2 3 4 5 6	1 2 3 4 5 6	1 2 3 4 5 6

Subject Code: _____

Scale: 1 = None, 2 = Minimal, 3 = Mild, 4 = Moderate, 5 = Severe, 6 = Extreme

Day	Date	Increased activity	Mood swings	Depressed sad, low, blue, lonely	Anxious, jittery, nervous	Irritable, angry, impatient
M	___/___	1 2 3 4 5 6	1 2 3 4 5 6	1 2 3 4 5 6	1 2 3 4 5 6	1 2 3 4 5 6
Tu	___/___	1 2 3 4 5 6	1 2 3 4 5 6	1 2 3 4 5 6	1 2 3 4 5 6	1 2 3 4 5 6
W	___/___	1 2 3 4 5 6	1 2 3 4 5 6	1 2 3 4 5 6	1 2 3 4 5 6	1 2 3 4 5 6
Th	___/___	1 2 3 4 5 6	1 2 3 4 5 6	1 2 3 4 5 6	1 2 3 4 5 6	1 2 3 4 5 6
F	___/___	1 2 3 4 5 6	1 2 3 4 5 6	1 2 3 4 5 6	1 2 3 4 5 6	1 2 3 4 5 6
Sa	___/___	1 2 3 4 5 6	1 2 3 4 5 6	1 2 3 4 5 6	1 2 3 4 5 6	1 2 3 4 5 6
Su	___/___	1 2 3 4 5 6	1 2 3 4 5 6	1 2 3 4 5 6	1 2 3 4 5 6	1 2 3 4 5 6
M	___/___	1 2 3 4 5 6	1 2 3 4 5 6	1 2 3 4 5 6	1 2 3 4 5 6	1 2 3 4 5 6
Tu	___/___	1 2 3 4 5 6	1 2 3 4 5 6	1 2 3 4 5 6	1 2 3 4 5 6	1 2 3 4 5 6
W	___/___	1 2 3 4 5 6	1 2 3 4 5 6	1 2 3 4 5 6	1 2 3 4 5 6	1 2 3 4 5 6
Th	___/___	1 2 3 4 5 6	1 2 3 4 5 6	1 2 3 4 5 6	1 2 3 4 5 6	1 2 3 4 5 6
F	___/___	1 2 3 4 5 6	1 2 3 4 5 6	1 2 3 4 5 6	1 2 3 4 5 6	1 2 3 4 5 6
Sa	___/___	1 2 3 4 5 6	1 2 3 4 5 6	1 2 3 4 5 6	1 2 3 4 5 6	1 2 3 4 5 6
Su	___/___	1 2 3 4 5 6	1 2 3 4 5 6	1 2 3 4 5 6	1 2 3 4 5 6	1 2 3 4 5 6
M	___/___	1 2 3 4 5 6	1 2 3 4 5 6	1 2 3 4 5 6	1 2 3 4 5 6	1 2 3 4 5 6
Tu	___/___	1 2 3 4 5 6	1 2 3 4 5 6	1 2 3 4 5 6	1 2 3 4 5 6	1 2 3 4 5 6
W	___/___	1 2 3 4 5 6	1 2 3 4 5 6	1 2 3 4 5 6	1 2 3 4 5 6	1 2 3 4 5 6
Th	___/___	1 2 3 4 5 6	1 2 3 4 5 6	1 2 3 4 5 6	1 2 3 4 5 6	1 2 3 4 5 6
F	___/___	1 2 3 4 5 6	1 2 3 4 5 6	1 2 3 4 5 6	1 2 3 4 5 6	1 2 3 4 5 6
Sa	___/___	1 2 3 4 5 6	1 2 3 4 5 6	1 2 3 4 5 6	1 2 3 4 5 6	1 2 3 4 5 6
Su	___/___	1 2 3 4 5 6	1 2 3 4 5 6	1 2 3 4 5 6	1 2 3 4 5 6	1 2 3 4 5 6
M	___/___	1 2 3 4 5 6	1 2 3 4 5 6	1 2 3 4 5 6	1 2 3 4 5 6	1 2 3 4 5 6
Tu	___/___	1 2 3 4 5 6	1 2 3 4 5 6	1 2 3 4 5 6	1 2 3 4 5 6	1 2 3 4 5 6
W	___/___	1 2 3 4 5 6	1 2 3 4 5 6	1 2 3 4 5 6	1 2 3 4 5 6	1 2 3 4 5 6
Th	___/___	1 2 3 4 5 6	1 2 3 4 5 6	1 2 3 4 5 6	1 2 3 4 5 6	1 2 3 4 5 6
F	___/___	1 2 3 4 5 6	1 2 3 4 5 6	1 2 3 4 5 6	1 2 3 4 5 6	1 2 3 4 5 6
Sa	___/___	1 2 3 4 5 6	1 2 3 4 5 6	1 2 3 4 5 6	1 2 3 4 5 6	1 2 3 4 5 6
Su	___/___	1 2 3 4 5 6	1 2 3 4 5 6	1 2 3 4 5 6	1 2 3 4 5 6	1 2 3 4 5 6
M	___/___	1 2 3 4 5 6	1 2 3 4 5 6	1 2 3 4 5 6	1 2 3 4 5 6	1 2 3 4 5 6
Tu	___/___	1 2 3 4 5 6	1 2 3 4 5 6	1 2 3 4 5 6	1 2 3 4 5 6	1 2 3 4 5 6
W	___/___	1 2 3 4 5 6	1 2 3 4 5 6	1 2 3 4 5 6	1 2 3 4 5 6	1 2 3 4 5 6
Th	___/___	1 2 3 4 5 6	1 2 3 4 5 6	1 2 3 4 5 6	1 2 3 4 5 6	1 2 3 4 5 6
F	___/___	1 2 3 4 5 6	1 2 3 4 5 6	1 2 3 4 5 6	1 2 3 4 5 6	1 2 3 4 5 6
Sa	___/___	1 2 3 4 5 6	1 2 3 4 5 6	1 2 3 4 5 6	1 2 3 4 5 6	1 2 3 4 5 6
Su	___/___	1 2 3 4 5 6	1 2 3 4 5 6	1 2 3 4 5 6	1 2 3 4 5 6	1 2 3 4 5 6

Subject Code: _____

Scale: 1 = None, 2 = Minimal, 3 = Mild, 4 = Moderate, 5 = Severe, 6 = Extreme

Day	Date	Headaches	Less sleep, difficulty sleeping	Decreased cravings	Difficulty concen- trating	Increased enjoyment
M	__ / __	1 2 3 4 5 6	1 2 3 4 5 6	1 2 3 4 5 6	1 2 3 4 5 6	1 2 3 4 5 6
Tu	__ / __	1 2 3 4 5 6	1 2 3 4 5 6	1 2 3 4 5 6	1 2 3 4 5 6	1 2 3 4 5 6
W	__ / __	1 2 3 4 5 6	1 2 3 4 5 6	1 2 3 4 5 6	1 2 3 4 5 6	1 2 3 4 5 6
Th	__ / __	1 2 3 4 5 6	1 2 3 4 5 6	1 2 3 4 5 6	1 2 3 4 5 6	1 2 3 4 5 6
F	__ / __	1 2 3 4 5 6	1 2 3 4 5 6	1 2 3 4 5 6	1 2 3 4 5 6	1 2 3 4 5 6
Sa	__ / __	1 2 3 4 5 6	1 2 3 4 5 6	1 2 3 4 5 6	1 2 3 4 5 6	1 2 3 4 5 6
Su	__ / __	1 2 3 4 5 6	1 2 3 4 5 6	1 2 3 4 5 6	1 2 3 4 5 6	1 2 3 4 5 6
M	__ / __	1 2 3 4 5 6	1 2 3 4 5 6	1 2 3 4 5 6	1 2 3 4 5 6	1 2 3 4 5 6
Tu	__ / __	1 2 3 4 5 6	1 2 3 4 5 6	1 2 3 4 5 6	1 2 3 4 5 6	1 2 3 4 5 6
W	__ / __	1 2 3 4 5 6	1 2 3 4 5 6	1 2 3 4 5 6	1 2 3 4 5 6	1 2 3 4 5 6
Th	__ / __	1 2 3 4 5 6	1 2 3 4 5 6	1 2 3 4 5 6	1 2 3 4 5 6	1 2 3 4 5 6
F	__ / __	1 2 3 4 5 6	1 2 3 4 5 6	1 2 3 4 5 6	1 2 3 4 5 6	1 2 3 4 5 6
Sa	__ / __	1 2 3 4 5 6	1 2 3 4 5 6	1 2 3 4 5 6	1 2 3 4 5 6	1 2 3 4 5 6
Su	__ / __	1 2 3 4 5 6	1 2 3 4 5 6	1 2 3 4 5 6	1 2 3 4 5 6	1 2 3 4 5 6
M	__ / __	1 2 3 4 5 6	1 2 3 4 5 6	1 2 3 4 5 6	1 2 3 4 5 6	1 2 3 4 5 6
Tu	__ / __	1 2 3 4 5 6	1 2 3 4 5 6	1 2 3 4 5 6	1 2 3 4 5 6	1 2 3 4 5 6
W	__ / __	1 2 3 4 5 6	1 2 3 4 5 6	1 2 3 4 5 6	1 2 3 4 5 6	1 2 3 4 5 6
Th	__ / __	1 2 3 4 5 6	1 2 3 4 5 6	1 2 3 4 5 6	1 2 3 4 5 6	1 2 3 4 5 6
F	__ / __	1 2 3 4 5 6	1 2 3 4 5 6	1 2 3 4 5 6	1 2 3 4 5 6	1 2 3 4 5 6
Sa	__ / __	1 2 3 4 5 6	1 2 3 4 5 6	1 2 3 4 5 6	1 2 3 4 5 6	1 2 3 4 5 6
Su	__ / __	1 2 3 4 5 6	1 2 3 4 5 6	1 2 3 4 5 6	1 2 3 4 5 6	1 2 3 4 5 6
M	__ / __	1 2 3 4 5 6	1 2 3 4 5 6	1 2 3 4 5 6	1 2 3 4 5 6	1 2 3 4 5 6
Tu	__ / __	1 2 3 4 5 6	1 2 3 4 5 6	1 2 3 4 5 6	1 2 3 4 5 6	1 2 3 4 5 6
W	__ / __	1 2 3 4 5 6	1 2 3 4 5 6	1 2 3 4 5 6	1 2 3 4 5 6	1 2 3 4 5 6
Th	__ / __	1 2 3 4 5 6	1 2 3 4 5 6	1 2 3 4 5 6	1 2 3 4 5 6	1 2 3 4 5 6
F	__ / __	1 2 3 4 5 6	1 2 3 4 5 6	1 2 3 4 5 6	1 2 3 4 5 6	1 2 3 4 5 6
Sa	__ / __	1 2 3 4 5 6	1 2 3 4 5 6	1 2 3 4 5 6	1 2 3 4 5 6	1 2 3 4 5 6
Su	__ / __	1 2 3 4 5 6	1 2 3 4 5 6	1 2 3 4 5 6	1 2 3 4 5 6	1 2 3 4 5 6
M	__ / __	1 2 3 4 5 6	1 2 3 4 5 6	1 2 3 4 5 6	1 2 3 4 5 6	1 2 3 4 5 6
Tu	__ / __	1 2 3 4 5 6	1 2 3 4 5 6	1 2 3 4 5 6	1 2 3 4 5 6	1 2 3 4 5 6
W	__ / __	1 2 3 4 5 6	1 2 3 4 5 6	1 2 3 4 5 6	1 2 3 4 5 6	1 2 3 4 5 6
Th	__ / __	1 2 3 4 5 6	1 2 3 4 5 6	1 2 3 4 5 6	1 2 3 4 5 6	1 2 3 4 5 6
F	__ / __	1 2 3 4 5 6	1 2 3 4 5 6	1 2 3 4 5 6	1 2 3 4 5 6	1 2 3 4 5 6
Sa	__ / __	1 2 3 4 5 6	1 2 3 4 5 6	1 2 3 4 5 6	1 2 3 4 5 6	1 2 3 4 5 6
Su	__ / __	1 2 3 4 5 6	1 2 3 4 5 6	1 2 3 4 5 6	1 2 3 4 5 6	1 2 3 4 5 6

Subject Code: _____
Scale: 1 = None, 2 = Minimal, 3 = Mild, 4 = Moderate, 5 = Severe, 6 = Extreme

Day	Date	Breast pain	Increased sexual interest	Crave foods	More sleep, naps, stay in bed	Low energy, tired, weak
M	__ / __	1 2 3 4 5 6	1 2 3 4 5 6	1 2 3 4 5 6	1 2 3 4 5 6	1 2 3 4 5 6
Tu	__ / __	1 2 3 4 5 6	1 2 3 4 5 6	1 2 3 4 5 6	1 2 3 4 5 6	1 2 3 4 5 6
W	__ / __	1 2 3 4 5 6	1 2 3 4 5 6	1 2 3 4 5 6	1 2 3 4 5 6	1 2 3 4 5 6
Th	__ / __	1 2 3 4 5 6	1 2 3 4 5 6	1 2 3 4 5 6	1 2 3 4 5 6	1 2 3 4 5 6
F	__ / __	1 2 3 4 5 6	1 2 3 4 5 6	1 2 3 4 5 6	1 2 3 4 5 6	1 2 3 4 5 6
Sa	__ / __	1 2 3 4 5 6	1 2 3 4 5 6	1 2 3 4 5 6	1 2 3 4 5 6	1 2 3 4 5 6
Su	__ / __	1 2 3 4 5 6	1 2 3 4 5 6	1 2 3 4 5 6	1 2 3 4 5 6	1 2 3 4 5 6
M	__ / __	1 2 3 4 5 6	1 2 3 4 5 6	1 2 3 4 5 6	1 2 3 4 5 6	1 2 3 4 5 6
Tu	__ / __	1 2 3 4 5 6	1 2 3 4 5 6	1 2 3 4 5 6	1 2 3 4 5 6	1 2 3 4 5 6
W	__ / __	1 2 3 4 5 6	1 2 3 4 5 6	1 2 3 4 5 6	1 2 3 4 5 6	1 2 3 4 5 6
Th	__ / __	1 2 3 4 5 6	1 2 3 4 5 6	1 2 3 4 5 6	1 2 3 4 5 6	1 2 3 4 5 6
F	__ / __	1 2 3 4 5 6	1 2 3 4 5 6	1 2 3 4 5 6	1 2 3 4 5 6	1 2 3 4 5 6
Sa	__ / __	1 2 3 4 5 6	1 2 3 4 5 6	1 2 3 4 5 6	1 2 3 4 5 6	1 2 3 4 5 6
Su	__ / __	1 2 3 4 5 6	1 2 3 4 5 6	1 2 3 4 5 6	1 2 3 4 5 6	1 2 3 4 5 6
M	__ / __	1 2 3 4 5 6	1 2 3 4 5 6	1 2 3 4 5 6	1 2 3 4 5 6	1 2 3 4 5 6
Tu	__ / __	1 2 3 4 5 6	1 2 3 4 5 6	1 2 3 4 5 6	1 2 3 4 5 6	1 2 3 4 5 6
W	__ / __	1 2 3 4 5 6	1 2 3 4 5 6	1 2 3 4 5 6	1 2 3 4 5 6	1 2 3 4 5 6
Th	__ / __	1 2 3 4 5 6	1 2 3 4 5 6	1 2 3 4 5 6	1 2 3 4 5 6	1 2 3 4 5 6
F	__ / __	1 2 3 4 5 6	1 2 3 4 5 6	1 2 3 4 5 6	1 2 3 4 5 6	1 2 3 4 5 6
Sa	__ / __	1 2 3 4 5 6	1 2 3 4 5 6	1 2 3 4 5 6	1 2 3 4 5 6	1 2 3 4 5 6
Su	__ / __	1 2 3 4 5 6	1 2 3 4 5 6	1 2 3 4 5 6	1 2 3 4 5 6	1 2 3 4 5 6
M	__ / __	1 2 3 4 5 6	1 2 3 4 5 6	1 2 3 4 5 6	1 2 3 4 5 6	1 2 3 4 5 6
Tu	__ / __	1 2 3 4 5 6	1 2 3 4 5 6	1 2 3 4 5 6	1 2 3 4 5 6	1 2 3 4 5 6
W	__ / __	1 2 3 4 5 6	1 2 3 4 5 6	1 2 3 4 5 6	1 2 3 4 5 6	1 2 3 4 5 6
Th	__ / __	1 2 3 4 5 6	1 2 3 4 5 6	1 2 3 4 5 6	1 2 3 4 5 6	1 2 3 4 5 6
F	__ / __	1 2 3 4 5 6	1 2 3 4 5 6	1 2 3 4 5 6	1 2 3 4 5 6	1 2 3 4 5 6
Sa	__ / __	1 2 3 4 5 6	1 2 3 4 5 6	1 2 3 4 5 6	1 2 3 4 5 6	1 2 3 4 5 6
Su	__ / __	1 2 3 4 5 6	1 2 3 4 5 6	1 2 3 4 5 6	1 2 3 4 5 6	1 2 3 4 5 6
M	__ / __	1 2 3 4 5 6	1 2 3 4 5 6	1 2 3 4 5 6	1 2 3 4 5 6	1 2 3 4 5 6
Tu	__ / __	1 2 3 4 5 6	1 2 3 4 5 6	1 2 3 4 5 6	1 2 3 4 5 6	1 2 3 4 5 6
W	__ / __	1 2 3 4 5 6	1 2 3 4 5 6	1 2 3 4 5 6	1 2 3 4 5 6	1 2 3 4 5 6
Th	__ / __	1 2 3 4 5 6	1 2 3 4 5 6	1 2 3 4 5 6	1 2 3 4 5 6	1 2 3 4 5 6
F	__ / __	1 2 3 4 5 6	1 2 3 4 5 6	1 2 3 4 5 6	1 2 3 4 5 6	1 2 3 4 5 6
Sa	__ / __	1 2 3 4 5 6	1 2 3 4 5 6	1 2 3 4 5 6	1 2 3 4 5 6	1 2 3 4 5 6
Su	__ / __	1 2 3 4 5 6	1 2 3 4 5 6	1 2 3 4 5 6	1 2 3 4 5 6	1 2 3 4 5 6

Subject Code: _____
Scale: 1 = None, 2 = Minimal, 3 = Mild, 4 = Moderate, 5 = Severe, 6 = Extreme

Day	Date	Back, joint, muscle pain	More work (job, home) efficient	Increased energy, alert	More creative	
M	___/___	1 2 3 4 5 6	1 2 3 4 5 6	1 2 3 4 5 6	1 2 3 4 5 6	1 2 3 4 5 6
Tu	___/___	1 2 3 4 5 6	1 2 3 4 5 6	1 2 3 4 5 6	1 2 3 4 5 6	1 2 3 4 5 6
W	___/___	1 2 3 4 5 6	1 2 3 4 5 6	1 2 3 4 5 6	1 2 3 4 5 6	1 2 3 4 5 6
Th	___/___	1 2 3 4 5 6	1 2 3 4 5 6	1 2 3 4 5 6	1 2 3 4 5 6	1 2 3 4 5 6
F	___/___	1 2 3 4 5 6	1 2 3 4 5 6	1 2 3 4 5 6	1 2 3 4 5 6	1 2 3 4 5 6
Sa	___/___	1 2 3 4 5 6	1 2 3 4 5 6	1 2 3 4 5 6	1 2 3 4 5 6	1 2 3 4 5 6
Su	___/___	1 2 3 4 5 6	1 2 3 4 5 6	1 2 3 4 5 6	1 2 3 4 5 6	1 2 3 4 5 6
M	___/___	1 2 3 4 5 6	1 2 3 4 5 6	1 2 3 4 5 6	1 2 3 4 5 6	1 2 3 4 5 6
Tu	___/___	1 2 3 4 5 6	1 2 3 4 5 6	1 2 3 4 5 6	1 2 3 4 5 6	1 2 3 4 5 6
W	___/___	1 2 3 4 5 6	1 2 3 4 5 6	1 2 3 4 5 6	1 2 3 4 5 6	1 2 3 4 5 6
Th	___/___	1 2 3 4 5 6	1 2 3 4 5 6	1 2 3 4 5 6	1 2 3 4 5 6	1 2 3 4 5 6
F	___/___	1 2 3 4 5 6	1 2 3 4 5 6	1 2 3 4 5 6	1 2 3 4 5 6	1 2 3 4 5 6
Sa	___/___	1 2 3 4 5 6	1 2 3 4 5 6	1 2 3 4 5 6	1 2 3 4 5 6	1 2 3 4 5 6
Su	___/___	1 2 3 4 5 6	1 2 3 4 5 6	1 2 3 4 5 6	1 2 3 4 5 6	1 2 3 4 5 6
M	___/___	1 2 3 4 5 6	1 2 3 4 5 6	1 2 3 4 5 6	1 2 3 4 5 6	1 2 3 4 5 6
Tu	___/___	1 2 3 4 5 6	1 2 3 4 5 6	1 2 3 4 5 6	1 2 3 4 5 6	1 2 3 4 5 6
W	___/___	1 2 3 4 5 6	1 2 3 4 5 6	1 2 3 4 5 6	1 2 3 4 5 6	1 2 3 4 5 6
Th	___/___	1 2 3 4 5 6	1 2 3 4 5 6	1 2 3 4 5 6	1 2 3 4 5 6	1 2 3 4 5 6
F	___/___	1 2 3 4 5 6	1 2 3 4 5 6	1 2 3 4 5 6	1 2 3 4 5 6	1 2 3 4 5 6
Sa	___/___	1 2 3 4 5 6	1 2 3 4 5 6	1 2 3 4 5 6	1 2 3 4 5 6	1 2 3 4 5 6
Su	___/___	1 2 3 4 5 6	1 2 3 4 5 6	1 2 3 4 5 6	1 2 3 4 5 6	1 2 3 4 5 6
M	___/___	1 2 3 4 5 6	1 2 3 4 5 6	1 2 3 4 5 6	1 2 3 4 5 6	1 2 3 4 5 6
Tu	___/___	1 2 3 4 5 6	1 2 3 4 5 6	1 2 3 4 5 6	1 2 3 4 5 6	1 2 3 4 5 6
W	___/___	1 2 3 4 5 6	1 2 3 4 5 6	1 2 3 4 5 6	1 2 3 4 5 6	1 2 3 4 5 6
Th	___/___	1 2 3 4 5 6	1 2 3 4 5 6	1 2 3 4 5 6	1 2 3 4 5 6	1 2 3 4 5 6
F	___/___	1 2 3 4 5 6	1 2 3 4 5 6	1 2 3 4 5 6	1 2 3 4 5 6	1 2 3 4 5 6
Sa	___/___	1 2 3 4 5 6	1 2 3 4 5 6	1 2 3 4 5 6	1 2 3 4 5 6	1 2 3 4 5 6
Su	___/___	1 2 3 4 5 6	1 2 3 4 5 6	1 2 3 4 5 6	1 2 3 4 5 6	1 2 3 4 5 6
M	___/___	1 2 3 4 5 6	1 2 3 4 5 6	1 2 3 4 5 6	1 2 3 4 5 6	1 2 3 4 5 6
Tu	___/___	1 2 3 4 5 6	1 2 3 4 5 6	1 2 3 4 5 6	1 2 3 4 5 6	1 2 3 4 5 6
W	___/___	1 2 3 4 5 6	1 2 3 4 5 6	1 2 3 4 5 6	1 2 3 4 5 6	1 2 3 4 5 6
Th	___/___	1 2 3 4 5 6	1 2 3 4 5 6	1 2 3 4 5 6	1 2 3 4 5 6	1 2 3 4 5 6
F	___/___	1 2 3 4 5 6	1 2 3 4 5 6	1 2 3 4 5 6	1 2 3 4 5 6	1 2 3 4 5 6
Sa	___/___	1 2 3 4 5 6	1 2 3 4 5 6	1 2 3 4 5 6	1 2 3 4 5 6	1 2 3 4 5 6
Su	___/___	1 2 3 4 5 6	1 2 3 4 5 6	1 2 3 4 5 6	1 2 3 4 5 6	1 2 3 4 5 6

APPENDIX D.   DIET AND PREMENSTRUAL SYNDROME

You may be experiencing food cravings and increased appetite pre-menstrually. These symptoms *may* be due to changes in carbohydrate metabolism during the premenstruum.

Carbohydrates are a source of blood sugar. Blood sugar, also called glucose, is the body's fuel. It is energy. Your brain and all your body's organs need energy. Eating well gives you energy. Eating properly takes some planning, but the result can be feeling great.

When you skip meals, like breakfast, for example, or eat "light" meals that are unbalanced you may end up "running on empty" and may experience other symptoms: fatigue, irritability, inability to concentrate, headaches, and so forth.

At these times many women reach for a candy bar, a cup of coffee, or another "pick up" and overeat. To minimize this need or craving for sweets and cravings for large volumes of foods, follow these tips.

1. Eat at regular times. Space your meals about 4–5 hours apart. Take a snack if you do go beyond 5 hours between meals:

   a. 3 crackers with 1 tsp. peanut butter on each, or
   b. 1 slice toast with 2–3 tsp. of cream cheese on it, or
   c. 1 piece of fruit with 1 oz. of cheese, or
   d. A bowl of cereal with milk, or
   e. 1/2 sandwich of any kind

2. Do not skip meals. When you do, you'll set yourself up for overeating later.

3. Try to monitor your dessert intake. Schedule 2–3 (no more) normal-sized desserts into your week. Space them about 2 days apart, for example, Tues., Thurs., and Sat.

   a. 3 cookies
   b. 1/2 cup ice cream in a cone
   c. 1 piece pie
   d. 1 small piece cake
   e. 1/2 cup pudding

4. Eat "balanced" meals. Vary your selection. A balanced meal includes:

   a. Complex carbohydrate, like potatoes, rice, noodles, corn, beans, peas, breads

    b. Protein, like chicken, fish, beef, veal, lamb, cheese
    c. Vegetables, cooked and raw
    d. Fruit, orange for vitamin C, apple with skin for better fiber, and one other (something you really like)
    e. Milk, a minimum of 6 oz. per day (yogurt can be used instead)

5. Drink a lot of water. We require 64 oz. a day; that's 8 tall glasses.

6. Reduce your salt intake by "spacing" how often you eat high-salt foods. High-salt foods are:

    a. "Preserved" or smoked meats: salami, ham, pastrami, bacon, hot dogs, sausage, corned beef
    b. Bouillon cubes, instant soups, canned soups (unless you buy salt-free varieties)
    c. Worcestershire, soy, and steak sauce; gravy mixes
    d. Potato chips and other chips
    e. Foods in brines, relish, pickles, olives
    f. Some fish—anchovies, canned fish, caviar, sardines
    g. Instant foods: cereals, potatoes, drinks like hot chocolate
    h. "Salty" seasonings: garlic salt, onion salt, MSG, mustard, catsup, prepared horseradish

You do not have to avoid these foods altogether; you simply have to pick one every 3 days or so. This is moderation.

7. Beverages: In addition to water, your body needs 4 oz. juice per day (no more!) and 6 oz. milk per day (no less!) Be moderate in your selection of other beverages.

    a. Regular coffee—1 or 2 cups/day (no more); decaf is better.
    b. Seltzer—2 or 3 tall glasses (no salt added)
    c. Diet soda—only 1 can/day (stay away from regular soda; have decaf, diet soda)
    d. Tea—1 or 2 mugs herbal tea (which is decaffeinated) per day.

Planning Meatless Meals

Many nonmeat foods can provide protein. These include low-fat cheese, legumes, tofu, and peanut butter. These alternatives to meat, poultry, and seafood are lower in cholesterol and usually lower in fat (with the exception of peanut butter). They are acceptable substitutes for meat, but they should be combined with other plant protein foods (such as grains) to supply all the essential amino acids. Peanut butter and bread, and rice and beans are both complementary combinations of plant proteins.

There is a difference between plant proteins and animal proteins, which should be understood in order to plan balanced meatless meals. It relates to the amino acid composition of these foods.

Animal protein foods—meats, poultry, fish, milk, cheese—are called complete proteins because each of them supplies all of the essential amino acids.

Plant protein foods are less complete—each food is lacking or low in one or more of the essential amino acids.

Different plant proteins are deficient in different essential amino acids, but by combining plant foods that complement each other in amino acid content, all the essential amino acids can be eaten. You must eat them together (in the same meal) to get adequate amounts of all the essential amino acids. Many of the plant foods that are commonly eaten together have complementary proteins.

Another way to ensure that you will get all of your essential amino acids is to include a small amount of meat, poultry, or fish in a macaroni or rice casserole.

Plant proteins can be used as a substitute for or supplement to animal proteins. Beans, peas, legumes, and tofu can be used in soups, casseroles, and main dishes and as meat extenders.

Note that one cup of cooked beans or peas has about as much protein as 2–3 oz. of cooked meat.

Meatless Alternatives

(Should be combined with foods from the grains group.)

1/2 cup	Dried beans, peas, and lentils
1 oz. (1 piece or 1/2 cup)	Tofu (soybean curd)

Types of beans available are: aduki, black, cranberry, fava, garbanzo, great northern, kidney, lima, pinto marrow, mung, navy, pea, soy

Different types of peas include: black-eyed, chick, cow, field, split

One major meal each day could be meatless

Sample 3-Day Menu

The following 3-day menu is a guide for putting together all the recommendations mentioned. It is a sample. If you do not like certain foods or beverages, you can substitute. One basic rule for success is to stick to the portion size given and distribute the foods as shown. Do not "save" foods for the evening.

Breakfast	Lunch	Snack*	Dinner	Snack
1 egg 2 toast (1 tsp. butter/ margarine) 4 oz. orange juice Coffee or tea *Water*	Sandwich: 2 bread, 1/2 cup tuna salad (prepared with mayo) 1 pear Diet soda *Water*	*Water*	3–4 oz. chicken 3/4 C mashed potato 3/4 C green beans Salad (1 tsp. dressing) Fresh fruit cup *Water*	4–6 oz. milk (low-fat) 2 cookies (small) *Water*
2 or 3 pancakes 1 or 2 sausage links 1–2 tbs. syrup (no fruit because you have syrup) Coffee or tea *Water*	Bowl hearty soup (e.g., chicken–vegetable) 6–8 crackers or 1 slice bread Small salad (tbs. dressing) 1 small apple *Water*	*Water*	3–4 oz. veal chop 1 large (or 2 small) baked potato, 2 tbs. sour cream (optional) or 1 tsp. butter/margarine 3/4 C cooked carrots 1/2 melon Diet soda *Water*	*Water*
1/2 C hot or cold cereal 1/2 C milk (skim or low-fat) 1/2 banana 4 crackers (saltines), 1 tsp. peanut butter on each Coffee or tea *Water*	1 slice pizza Fruit (optional) Diet soda *Water*	*Water*	Vegetarian dinner: 2 C pasta 1/2 C marinara sauce 1 tbs. ricotta cheese Salad/dressing 1 pear *Water*	*Water*

*Only needed if dinner is more than 5 hours later than lunch

Sample Menu with Legumes

Breakfast: 2 pieces French toast
                    1–2 tbs. Syrup (optional)
                    4 oz. orange juice
Lunch: Cup vegetable soup
                    Sandwich: 3 oz. turkey, 1–2 tsp. mayo, lettuce/tomato, 2 bread
                       (regular–not low-calorie)
                    3/4 cup fresh fruit salad
Dinner: 1-1/2 cup pasta and beans
                    (Italian Pasta Fagioli or 1-1/2 cup Spanish rice and beans)
                    Salad
                    1 tbs. dressing
                    1 cup fruited gelatin

Remember, the menu is simply a guide. Should you desire a 7-day or 2-week menu specifically for you, your preferences, your schedule, and your family's needs, call a registered dietitian to assist you.

Extras

Nuts, seeds, other:

- 1 tbs.   Nuts* (chopped)
- 10 whole   Virginia peanuts
- 1 tbs.   Seeds* (pumpkin, sesame, and sunflower)
- 1 tbs.   Avocado (mashed)
- 5 small   Olives
- 2 tsp.   Peanut butter*

        *can be counted as a fat or meatless alternative.

Cruciferous vegetables may reduce the risk of colon cancer. They also supply fiber, vitamins, and minerals and should be included in the diet twice a week.

- Rutabaga
- Turnip
- Broccoli
- Brussel sprouts
- Cabbage, red and white
- Cauliflower

Calcium recommendation: Two 8 oz. glasses skim milk daily or 8 oz. skim milk yogurt plus 1 oz. cheese for calcium. If dairy is unacceptable for any reason (e.g., lactose intolerance), then calcium supplement may be required.

Prepared by: Denise Salvatore-Garofalo, R.D.
10 Old Mamaroneck Road, 1E
White Plains, N.Y. 10605

For forwarding information contact American Dietetic Association (800) 621-6469.

References

Aberger EW, Denney DR, Hutchings DF: Pain sensitivity and coping strategies among dysmenorrheic women: much ado about nothing. *Behav Res Ther* 21:119–127, 1983.

Ablanalp JM: Psychologic components of the premenstrual syndrome: evaluating the research and choosing the treatment. *J Reprod Med* 28:517–524, 1983.

Ablanalp JM: Premenstrual syndrome. *Behav Sci Law* 3:103–115, 1985.

Ablanalp JM, Haskett RF, Rose RM: The premenstrual syndrome. *Adv Psychoneuroendocrinology* 3:327–347, 1980.

Ablanalp JM, Livingston L, Rose RM, Sandwisch D: Cortisol and growth hormone responses to psychological stress during the menstrual cycle. *Psychosom Med* 39:158–177, 1977.

Abraham GE: Ovarian and adrenal contribution to peripheral androgens during the menstrual cycle. *J Clin Endocrinol Metab* 39:340–346, 1974.

Abraham GE: Primary dysmenorrhea. *Clin Obstet Gynecol* 21:139–145, 1978.

Abraham GE: Premenstrual tension. *Curr Probl Obstet Gynecol* 3:5–39, 1980.

Abraham GE: Magnesium deficiency in premenstrual tension. *Magnesium Bull* 1:68–73, 1982.

Abraham GE: Nutritional factors in the etiology of premenstrual tension syndromes. *J Reprod Med* 28:446–464, 1983.

Abraham GE: Nutrition and the premenstrual tension syndromes. *J Appl Nutr* 36:103–124, 1984.

Abraham GE, Hargrove JT: Effect of Vitamin B_6 on premenstrual symptomatology in women with premenstrual tension syndromes: a double blind crossover study. *Infertility* 3:155–161, 1980.

Abraham GE, Lubran MM: Serum and red cell magnesium levels in patients with premenstrual tension. *Am J Clin Nutr* 34:2364–2366, 1981.

Abraham GE, Rumley RE: Role of nutrition in managing the premenstrual tension syndromes. *J Reprod Med* 32:405–421, 1987.

Abraham SF, Beaumont PJV, Argall WJ, Haywood P: Nutrient intake and the menstrual cycle. *Aust NZ J Med* 11:210–211, 1981.

Abramowitz ES, Baker AH, Fleischer SF: Onset of depressive psychiatric crises and the menstrual cycle. *Am J Psychiatry* 139:475–478, 1982.

Abrams M, Halbreich U: The stability of reports of personal resources along the menstrual cycle. Abstract, American Society for Psychosomatic Obstetrics and Gynecology, Seventeenth Annual Meeting, Orlando, Florida, April 12–16, 1989, p. 22.

289

Abramson M, Torghele JR: Weight, temperature changes and psychosomatic symptomatology in relation to the menstrual cycle. *Am J Obstet Gynecol* 81:223–232,
1961.

ACOG Committee Statement: *Premenstrual syndrome.* Washington, DC, The American
College of Obstetricians and Gynecologists, December 1985.

Adamopoulos DA, Loraine JA, Lunn SF, Coppen AJ, Daly RJ: Endocrine profiles in
premenstrual tension. *Clin Endocrinol* 1:283–292, 1972.

Adams DB, Gold AR, Burt AD: Rise in female-initiated sexual activity at ovulation and its
suppression by oral contraceptives. *N Engl J Med* 229:1145–1150, 1978.

Adams F (Trans.): *The Genuine Work of Hippocrates.* Baltimore, Williams & Wilkins, 1939.

Adams PW, Rose DP, Folkard J, Wynn V, Seed M, Strong R: Effect of pyridoxine
hydrochloride (Vitamin B_6) upon depression associated with oral contraception.
Lancet 1:897, 1973.

Adenaike OC, Abidoye RO: A study of the incidence of the premenstrual syndrome in a
group of Nigerian women. *Public Health* 101:49–58, 1987.

Aitken RCB: Measurement of feelings using Visual Analogue Scales. *Proc R Soc Med*
62:989, 1969.

Akita K: The influence of monthly periodicity in women students on the physical and
mental phases. *J Sci Labour* (Tokyo) 41:469–473, 1965.

Allen EB, Henry GW: The relation of menstruation to personality disorders. *Am J Psychiatry* 90:239–275, 1933.

Altenhaus AL: The effect of expectancy for change on performance during the menstrual
cycle. *Dissertation Abstracts Int* 39(2-B):968, 1978.

Altschule MD, Brem J: Periodic psychosis of puberty. *Am J Psychiatry* 119:1176–1178,
1963.

American Psychiatric Association: *Diagnostic and Statistical Manual of Mental Disorders, Third
Edition, Revised.* Washington, DC, American Psychiatric Association Press, 1987.

Amoore JE, Popplewell JR, Whissell-Buechy D: Sensitivity of women to musk odor: no
menstrual variation. *J Chem Ecology* 1:291–297, 1975.

Andersch B: The effect of various oral contraceptive combinations on premenstrual
symptoms. *Int J Gynaecol Obstet* 20:463–469, 1982.

Andersch B: Bromocriptine and premenstrual symptoms: a survey of double blind trials.
Obstet Gynecol Surv 38:643–646, 1983.

Andersch B, Abrahamsson L, Wendestam C, Ohman R, Hahn L: Hormone profile in
premenstrual tension: effects of bromocriptine and diuretics. *Clin Endocrinol*
11:657–664, 1979.

Andersch B, Hahn L: Premenstrual complaints. II. Influence of oral contraceptives. *Acta
Obstet Gynecol Scand* 60:579–583, 1981.

Andersch B, Hahn L: Bromocriptine and premenstrual tension: a clinical and hormonal
study. *Pharmatherapeutica* 3:107–113, 1982.

Andersch B, Hahn L: Progesterone treatment of premenstrual tension—a double blind
study. *J Psychosom Res* 29:489–493, 1985.

Andersch B, Hahn L, Andersson M, Isaksson B: Body water and weight in patients with
premenstrual tension. *Br J Obstet Gynaecol* 85:546–550, 1978a.

Andersch B, Hahn L, Wendestam C, Ohman R, Abrahamsson L: Treatment of premenstrual tension syndrome with bromocriptine. *Acta Endocrinol* [Suppl] 88:165–
174, 1978b.

Andersch B, Wendestam C, Hahn L, Ohman R: Premenstrual complaints. I. Prevalence of
premenstrual symptoms in a Swedish urban population. *J Psychosom Obstet Gynecol*
5:39–49, 1986.

Andersen AN, Larsen JF: Bromocriptine in the treatment of the premenstrual syndrome.
Drugs 17:383–388, 1979.

Andersen AN, Larsen JF, Steenstrup OR, Svendstrup B, Nielsen S: Effect of bromocriptine on the premenstrual syndrome: a double-blind clinical trial. *Br J Obstet Gynaecol* 84:370–374, 1977.

Anderson M, Severino SK, Hurt SW, Williams NA: Premenstrual syndrome research: using the NIMH guidelines. *J Clin Psychiatry* 49:484–486, 1988.

Andreyko JL, Marshall LA, Dumesic DA, Jaffee RB: Therapeutic uses of gonadotropin-releasing hormone analogs. *Obstet Gynecol Surv* 42:1–21, 1987.

Appleby BP: A study of premenstrual tension in general practice. *Br Med J* 1:391–393, 1960.

Archer JD: The FDA does not approve uses of drugs. *JAMA* 252:1054–1055, 1984.

Arendt J: Mammalian pineal rhythms. *Pineal Res Rev* 3:161, 1985.

Argonz J, Abinzano C: Premenstrual tension treated with Vitamin A. *J Clin Endocrinol* 10:1579–1588, 1950.

Asberg M, Thoren P, Traskman L, Bertilsson L, Ringberger V: Serotonin depression: a biochemical subgroup within the affective disorders? *Science* 191:478–480, 1976.

Ashby CR Jr, Carr LA, Cook CL, Steptoe MM, Franks DD: Alteration of platelet serotonergic mechanisms and monoamine oxidase activity in premenstrual syndrome. *Biol Psychiatry* 24:225–233, 1988.

Ashcroft GW, Crawford TBB, Eccleston D, Sharman DF: 5-hydroxyindole compounds in the cerebrospinal fluids of patients with psychiatric or neurological diseases. *Lancet* 2:1049–1052, 1966.

Asinelli C, Casassa P-M: Studies on carbohydrate metabolism during the menstrual cycle. *Arch Sci Med* (Torino) 64:431, 1936.

Asso D: Levels of arousal in the premenstrual phase. *Br J Soc Clin Psychol* 17:47–55, 1978.

Asso D, Beech HR: Susceptibility to the acquisition of a conditioned response in relation to the menstrual cycle. *J Psychosom Res* 19:337–344, 1975.

Atkinson DR, Kozitza LP: Psychotherapist diagnosis of premenstrual syndrome. *J Counseling Dev* 66:429–431, 1988.

Atton-Chamla A, Favre G, Goudard JR, Miller G, Rocca-Serra JP: Premenstrual syndrome and atopy: a double-blind clinical evaluation of treatment with a gamma-globulin/histamine complex. *Pharmatherapeutica* 2:481–486, 1980.

AuBuchon P, Calhoun KS: Menstrual cycle symptomatology: the role of social expectancy and experimental demand characteristics. *Psychosom Med* 47:35–45, 1985.

Awaritefe A, Awaritefe M, Lib D, Diejomoah FME, Ebie JC: Personality and menstruation. *Psychosom Med* 42:237–251, 1980.

Ayd FJ Jr. Behavioral dyscontrol: increased risk with alprazolam? *Int Drug Ther News* 24:9–10, 1989a.

Ayd FJ Jr: Benzodiazepine seizures: an update. *Int Drug Ther News* 24:5–7, 1989b.

Backstrom T, Aakvaag A: Plasma prolactin and testosterone during the luteal phase in women with premenstrual tension syndrome. *Psychoneuroendocrinology* 6:245–251, 1981.

Backstrom T, Bancroft J, Bixo M, Hammarback S, Sanders D: Premenstrual syndrom [sic]. *Scand J Psychology* [Suppl] 1:138–144, 1982.

Backstrom T, Boyle H, Baird DT: Persistence of symptoms of premenstrual tension in hysterectomized women. *Br J Obstet Gynaecol* 88:530–536, 1981.

Backstrom T, Carstensen H: Estrogen and progesterone in plasma in relation to premenstrual tension. *J Steroid Biochem* 5:257–260, 1974.

Backstrom T, Hammarback S: Endocrinological aspects of the premenstrual syndrome. *Prog Clin Biol Res* 225:421–428, 1986.

Backstrom T, Mattson B: Correlation of symptoms in pre-menstrual tension to estrogen and progesterone concentrations in blood plasma. *Neuropsychobiology* 1:80–86, 1975.

Backstrom T, McNeilly AS, Leask R, Baird DT: Pulsatile secretion of LH, FSH, prolactin, estradiol and progesterone during the human menstrual cycle. *Clin Endocrinol* 17:29–42, 1983a.

Backstrom T, Sanders D, Leask R, Davidson D, Warner P, Bancroft J: Mood, sexuality, hormones, and the menstrual cycle. II. Hormone levels and their relationship to the premenstrual syndrome. *Psychosom Med* 45:503–507, 1983b.

Backstrom T, Smith S, Lothian H, Baird DT: Prolonged follicular phase and depressed gonadotropins following hysterectomy and corpus lute-ectomy in women with premenstrual tension syndrome. *Clin Endocrinol* 22:723–732, 1985.

Backstrom T, Wide L, Sodergard R, Carstensen H: FSH, LH TeBG-capacity, estrogen and progesterone in women with premenstrual tension during the luteal phase. *J Steroid Biochem* 7:473–476, 1976.

Bains GK, Slade P: Attributional patterns, moods, and the menstrual cycle. *Psychosom Med* 50:469–476, 1988.

Bancroft J, Boyle H, Warner P, Fraser HM: The use of an LHRH agonist, buserelin, in the long-term management of premenstrual syndromes. *Clin Endocrinol* 27:171–182, 1987.

Baker AH, Kostin IW, Mishara BL, Parker L: Menstrual cycle affects kinesthetic aftereffect, an index of personality and perceptual style. *J Pers Soc Psychol* 37:234–246, 1979.

Barker-Benfield GJ: *The Horrors of the Half-Known Life: Male Attitudes Toward Women and Sexuality in Nineteenth Century America.* New York, Harper & Row, 1976.

Barklage NE, Jefferson JW: Alternative uses of lithium in psychiatry. *Psychosomatics* 28:239–244, 249–250, 253, 256, 1987.

Barnes DM: Neurotoxicity creates regulatory dilemma. *Science* 243:29–30, 1989.

Barnes N, Thomas N: Overdose of trilostane. *Br Med J* 286:1784–1785, 1983.

Baron DA, Vargyas J: Masturbatory activity and PMS. Abstracts, American Society for Psychosomatic Obstetrics and Gynecology sixteenth annual meeting, Meadowood, St. Helena, CA, April 17–21, 1988, p. 3.

Barr W: Pyridoxine supplements in the premenstrual syndrome. *Practitioner* 228:425–427, 1984.

Barris MD, Dawson WW, Theiss CL: The visual sensitivity of women during the menstrual cycle. *Doc Ophthalmol* 49:293–301, 1980.

Bartlik BD: Premenstrual increase in alcoholism admission rates. Unpublished paper, New York University Medical Center, 1987.

Barwin BN: The management of premenstrual tension syndrome. *Fertil Steril* 34:187–188, 1980.

Beaumont PJV, Abraham SF, Argall WJ, Simson KG: A prospective study of premenstrual tension symptoms in healthy young Australians. *Aust NZ J Psychiatry* 12:241–244, 1978.

Beckman H, Goodwin FK: Antidepressant response to tricyclics and urinary MHPG in unipolar patients. *Arch Gen Psychiatry* 32:17–21, 1975.

Bell G, Katona C: Psychiatric disorder and gynaecological symptoms in middle aged women. *Br Med J* 294:703, 1987.

Belmaker RH, Murphy DL, Wyatt RJ, Loriaux L: Human platelet monoamine oxidase changes during the menstrual cycle. *Arch Gen Psychiatry* 31:553–556, 1974.

Benedek E: Premenstrual syndrome: a new defense? In: *The Psychiatric Implications of Menstruation,* ed by JH Gold. Washington, DC, American Psychiatric Association Press, 1985.

Benedek EP: Premenstrual syndrome: a view from the bench. *J Clin Psychiatry* 49:498–502, 1988.

Benedek T, Rubenstein B: The correlations between ovarian activity and psychodynamic processes. I. The ovulative phase. *Psychosom Med* 1:245–270, 1939a.

Benedek T, Rubenstein B: The correlations between ovarian activity and psychodynamic processes. II. The menstrual phase. *Psychosom Med* 1:461–485, 1939b.

Benedek-Jaszmann LJ, Hearn-Sturdivant MD: Premenstrual tension and functional infertility: aetiology and treatment. *Lancet* 1:1095–1098, 1976.

Berger SM: *How to Be Your Own Nutritionist.* New York, Morrow, 1987.

Berlin FS, Bergey GK, Money J: Periodic psychosis of puberty: a case report. *Am J Psychiatry* 139:119–120, 1982.

Bernsted L, Luggin R, Petersson B: Psychosocial considerations of the premenstrual syndrome. *Acta Psychiatr Scand* 69:455–460, 1984.

Berry C, McGuire FL: Menstrual distress and acceptance of sexual role. *Am J Obstet Gynecol* 114:83–87, 1972.

Bertoli A, DePirro R, Fusco A, Greco AV, Magnatta R, Lauro R: Differences in insulin receptors between men and menstruating women and influence of sex hormones on insulin binding during the menstrual cycle. *J Clin Endocrinol Metab* 50:246–250, 1980.

Beumont PJV, Richards DH, Gelder MG: A study of minor psychiatric and physical symptoms during the menstrual cycle. *Br J Psychiatry* 126:431–434, 1975.

Beynon HLC, Garbett ND, Barnes PJ: Severe premenstrual exacerbations of asthma: effect of intramuscular progesterone. *Lancet* 2:370–372, 1988.

Bickers W: Premenstrual tension: a neglected phase of menstrual disability. *South Med J* 46:873–878, 1953.

Bickers W, Woods M: Premenstrual tension: its relation to abnormal water storage. *N Engl J Med* 245:453–456, 1951.

Biller BJ, Brandt JH: Premenstrual syndrome and galactorrhea: a new entity. In: *New Research Programs and Abstracts.* Washington, DC, Burroughs Wellcome, 1986, p. 37.

Billiard M, Guilleminault C, Dement WC: A menstruation-linked periodic hypersomnia. *Neurology* 25:436–443, 1975.

Birchnell J, Floyd S: Further menstrual characteristics of suicide attemptors. *J Psychosom Res* 19:81–85, 1975.

Biskind MS: Nutritional deficiency in the etiology of menorrhagia, metrorrhagia, cystic mastitis and premenstrual tension: treatment with Vitamin B complex. *J Clin Endocrinol Metab* 3:227–234, 1943.

Biskind MS, Biskind GR, Biskind LH: Nutritional deficiency in the etiology of menorrhagia, metrorrhagia, cystic mastitis, and premenstrual tension. II. Further observations on treatment with the Vitamin B complex. *Surg Gynecol Obstet* 78:49–57, 1944.

Blackett-Smith JJ: The menstrual cycle—interactions between social factors, mood, hormones and task performance. B. Med. Sci. thesis, Monash University, Victoria, Australia, 1975.

Bland J: Antioxidants in nutritional medicine. In: *1984–85 Yearbook of Nutritional Medicine,* ed by J Bland. New Canaan, CT: Keats Publishing, 1985, pp. 213–239.

Blank AM, Goldstein SE, Chatterjee N: Premenstrual tension and mood change. *Can J Psychiatry* 25:577–585, 1980.

Blazer D, Swartz M, Woodbury M, Manton KG, Hughes D, George LK: Depressive symptoms and depressive diagnoses in a community population. Use of a new procedure for analysis of psychiatric classification. *Arch Gen Psychiatry* 45:1078–1084, 1988.

Block E: The use of Vitamin A in premenstrual tension. *Acta Obstet Gynecol Scand* 39:586–592, 1960.

Blumberg MA, Billig O: Hormonal influence upon "puerperal psychosis" and neurotic conditions. *Psychiatr Q* 16:454–462, 1942.

Blume E: Premenstrual syndromes, depression linked. *JAMA* 249:2864–2866, 1983.

Bostock J, Riley HT (Trans.): *The Natural History of Pliny.* London, H. G. Bohn, 1856–1893.

Boston Women's Health Book Collective. *The New Our Bodies, Ourselves.* New York, Simon & Shuster, 1985, p. 65.

Both-Orthman B, Rubinow DR, Hoban MC, Malley J, Grover GN: Menstrual cycle phase – related changes in appetite in patients with premenstrual syndrome and in control subjects. *Am J Psychiatry* 145:628–631, 1988.

Boyle CA, Berkowitz GS, Kelsey JL: Epidemiology of premenstrual symptoms. *Am J Public Health* 77:349–350, 1987.

Braier JR, Asso D: Two-flash fusion as a measure of changes in cortical activation with the menstrual cycle. *Biol Psychol* 11:153–156, 1980.

Braude M: Update: DSM-III diagnosis debate. *J Am Med Wom Assoc* 43:30, 1988.

Brayshaw ND, Brayshaw DD: Thyroid hypofunction in premenstrual syndrome. *N Engl J Med* 23:1486–1487, 1986.

Brayshaw ND, Brayshaw DD: Premenstrual syndrome and thyroid dysfunction. *Integr Psychiatry* 5:179–184, 1987.

Briggs M, Briggs M: Relationship between monoamine oxidase activity and sex hormone concentration in human blood plasma. *J Reprod Fertil* 29:447–450, 1972.

Brockington IF, Kelly A, Hall P, Deakin W: Premenstrual relapse of puerperal psychosis. *J Affective Disord* 14:287–292, 1988.

Brooks-Gunn J: The psychological significance of different pubertal events in young girls. *J Early Adoles* 4:315–327, 1984.

Brooks-Gunn J, Peterson AC: Problems in studying and defining pubertal events. *J Youth Adoles* 13:181–196, 1984.

Brooks-Gunn J, Ruble DN: Dysmenorrhea in adolescence. Paper presented at the annual meeting of the American Psychological Association, New York, September 1979a.

Brooks-Gunn J, Ruble DN: The social and psychological meaning of menarche. Paper presented at the meeting of the Society for Research in Child Development, San Francisco, March 1979b.

Brooks-Gunn J, Ruble DN: The menstrual attitude questionnaire. *Psychosom Med* 42:503–512, 1980.

Brooks-Gunn J, Ruble DN: Developmental processes in the experience of menarche. In: *Handbook of Psychology and Health,* Vol. 2, ed by A Baum, JE Singer. Hillside, NJ, Erlbaum, 1982, pp. 117–147.

Brown RS, Ramirez DE, Taub JM: The prescription of exercise for depression. *Phys Sports Med* 6:35–45, 1978.

Brown S, Vessey M, Stratton I: The influence of method of contraception and cigarette smoking on menstrual patterns. *Br J Obstet Gynaecol* 95:905–910, 1988.

Bruce J, Russell GFM: A study of weight changes and balances of water, sodium and potassium. *Lancet* 2:267–271, 1962.

Brush MG: Endocrine and other biochemical factors in the aetiology of the premenstrual syndrome. *Curr Med Res Opin* 6 [Suppl 5]:19–27, 1979.

Brush MG, Massil H, O'Brien PMS: The role of essential fatty acids in the premenstrual syndrome. Paper presented at the 2nd International Symposium: Premenstrual, Postpartum and Menopausal Mood Disorders, Kiawah Island, Charleston, SC, September 10, 1987, Abstract #10.

Brush MG, Perry M: Pyridoxine and the premenstrual syndrome. *Lancet* 1:1399, 1985.

Brush MG, Watson SJ, Horrobin DF, Manku MS: Abnormal essential fatty acid levels in plasma of women with premenstrual syndrome. *Am J Obstet Gynecol* 150:363–366, 1984.

Budoff PW: *No More Menstrual Cramps and Other Good News.* New York, GP Putman's Sons, 1980.

Budoff PW: The use of prostaglandin inhibitors for the premenstrual syndrome. *J Reprod Med* 28:469–478, 1983.

Burnhill MS: Preliminary investigation of the relationship between chronic candidiasis and premenstrual syndrome. Paper presented at the 2nd International Symposium: Premenstrual, Postpartum and Menopausal Mood Disorders, Kiawah Island, Charleston, SC, September 10, 1987, Abstract #15.

Busch CM, Costa PT Jr, Whitehead WE, Heller BR. Severe perimenstrual symptoms: prevalence and effects on absenteeism and health care seeking in a non-clinical sample. *Women Health* 14:59–74, 1988.

Butt WR, Watts JF, Holder G: The biochemical background to the premenstrual syndrome. In: *Premenstrual Syndrome,* ed by RW Taylor. London: Medical News Tribune, 1983, p. 16.

Callender K, McGregor M, Kirk P, Thomas CS: A double-blind trial of evening primrose oil in the premenstrual syndrome: nervous symptom subgroup. *Human Psychopharm* 3:57–61, 1988.

Cameron O, Lee MA, Kotun J, Murphy ST: Circadian fluctuations in anxiety disorders. *Biol Psychiatry* 21:567–568, 1986.

Canty AP: Can aerobic exercise relieve the symptoms of premenstrual syndrome (PMS)? *J Sch Health* 54:410–411, 1984.

Carr DB, Bullen BA, Skrinar GS, Arnold MA, Rosenblatt M, Beitins IZ, Martin JB, McArthur JW: Physical conditioning facilitates the exercise-induced secretion of beta-endorphin and beta-lipotropin in women. *N Engl J Med* 305:560, 1981.

Carr LA, Ashby CR, Cook CL, Steptoe MM, Franks DD: Alteration of 5-hydroxytryptamine (5-HT) uptake by plasma extracts from patients with premenstrual syndrome (PMS). Paper presented at the 2nd International Symposium: Premenstrual, Postpartum and Menopausal Mood Disorders, Kiawah Island, Charleston, SC, September 10, 1987, Abstract #1.

Carstairs MW, Talbot DJ: A placebo controlled trial of Tenavoid in the management of the premenstrual syndrome. *Br J Clin Pract* 35:403–409, 1981.

Casper RF, Graves GR, Reid RL: Objective measurement of hot flushes associated with the premenstrual syndrome. *Fertil Steril* 47:341–344, 1987.

Casper RF, Patel-Christopher A, Powell A-M: Thyrotropin and prolactin responses to thyrotropin-releasing hormone in premenstrual syndrome. *J Clin Endocrinol Metab* 68:608–612, 1989.

Casper RF, Powell AM: Effects of evening primrose oil in the treatment of premenstrual syndrome. Paper presented at the 2nd International Symposium: Premenstrual, Postpartum and Menopausal Mood Disorders, Kiawah Island, Charleston, SC, September 12, 1987, Abstract #46.

Cassara V: Premenstrual syndrome as a factor in women's alcohol abuse: a hypothesis. M.S.S.W. Program independent research requirement, University of Wisconsin, Madison, WI, 1981.

Cerrato PL: Dietary help for PMS patients. *Registered Nurse* 51:69–81, 1988.

Chadwick M. *The Psychological Effects of Menstruation.* New York: Nervous and Mental Disease Publishing Co., 1932.

Chadwick M. *Woman's Periodicity.* London: Norman Douglas, 1933.

Chait LR: Premenstrual syndrome and our sisters in crime: a feminist dilemma. *Women Rights Law Reporter* 9:267–293, 1986.

Chakmakjian ZH: A critical assessment of therapy for the premenstrual tension syndrome. *J Reprod Med* 28:532–538, 1983.

Chakmakjian ZH, Higgins CE, Abraham GE: The effect of a nutritional supplement, Optivite for Women, on premenstrual tension syndromes. 2. Effect on symptomatology, using a double blind crossover design. *J Appl Nutr* 37:12–17, 1985.

Chakmakjian ZH, Zachariah NY: Bioavailability of progesterone with different modes of administration. *J Reprod Med* 32:443–448, 1987.

Chattopadhyay PK, Das M: Arousal in menstruation: a study with some autonomic measures. *Indian J Clin Psychol* 9:11–17, 1982.

Chuong CJ: MMPI helpful in evaluating premenstrual syndrome. *Clin Psychiatry News* 14:7, 1986.

Chuong CJ, Colligan RC, Coulam CB, Bergstralh EJ: The MMPI as an aid in evaluating patients with premenstrual syndrome. *Psychosomatics* 29:197–202, 1988a.

Chuong CJ, Coulam CB, Bergstralh EJ, O'Fallon WM, Steinmetz GI: Clinical trial of naltrexone in premenstrual syndrome. *Obstet Gynecol* 72:332–336, 1988b.

Chuong CJ, Coulam CB, Kao PC, Bergstralh EJ, Go VLW: Neuropeptide levels in premenstrual syndrome. *Fertil Steril* 44:760–765, 1985.

Clare AW: The treatment of premenstrual symptoms. *Br J Psychiatry* 135:576–579, 1979.

Clare AW: The relationship between psychopathology and the menstrual cycle. *Women Health* 8:125–136, 1983a.

Clare AW: Premenstrual tension: psychological aspects. *Ir J Med Sci* 152 [Suppl 2]:33–43, 1983b.

Clare AW: Psychiatric and social aspects of premenstrual complaint. *Psychol Med* [Suppl 4] 13:1–58, 1983c.

Clare AW: Premenstrual syndrome: single or multiple causes? *Can J Psychiatry* 30:474–482, 1985.

Clare G, Tong JE, Lyon RG, Leigh G: Menstrual cycle and ethanol effects on temporal discrimination. *Percept Mot Skills* 42:1085–1086, 1976.

Clark JT, Kalra PS, Crowley WR, Kalra SP: Neuropeptide Y and human pancreatic polypeptide stimulate feeding behavior in rats. *Endocrinology* 115:427–429, 1984.

Clarke AE, Ruble DN: Young adolescents' beliefs concerning menstruation. *Child Dev* 49:231–234, 1978.

Cluydts R, Visser P: Mood and sleep. I. Effects of the menstrual cycle. *Waking Sleeping* 4:193–197, 1980.

Coffee D: Premenstrual syndrome & addiction. *Interface: Psychiatry and Medicine* (Del Amo Hospital, Torrance, CA) Winter, 1985, pp. 1–3.

Cohen MR, Cohen RM, Pickar D, Weingartner H, Murphy DL, Bunney WE Jr: Behavioral effects after high dose naloxone administration to normal volunteers. *Lancet* 2:1110, 1981.

Cole HH, Hart GH: The potency of blood serum of mares in progressive stages of pregnancy in effecting the sexual maturity of the immature rat. *Am J Physiol* 93:57, 1930.

Coleman GJ, Hart WG, Russell JW: Temporal sequence of symptoms in women complaining of PMS. *J Psychosom Obstet Gynecol* 8:105–112, 1988.

Connors DD: Women's "sickness": a case of secondary gains or primary losses. *ANS* 7:1–32, 1985.

Coppen AJ: Depressed states and indolealkamines. *Adv Pharmacol* 6B:283–291, 1968.

Coppen AJ, Kessel N: Menstruation and personality. *Br J Psychiatry* 109:711–721, 1963.

Coppen AJ, Milne HB, Outram DH: Dytide, norethisterone and a placebo in the premenstrual syndrome: a double blind controlled comparison. *Clin Trials J* Feb:33–36, 1969.

Cormack M, Sheldrake P: Menstrual cycle variations in cognitive ability: a preliminary report. *Int J Chronobiol* 2:53–55, 1974.

Coughlin PC: Marital satisfaction and premenstrual stress: an inverse relationship mediated by career choice. Paper presented at the 2nd International Symposium: Premenstrual, Postpartum and Menopausal Mood Disorders, Kiawah Island, Charleston, SC, September 11, 1987, Abstract #34.

Coulson CJ: Pre-menstrual syndrome—are gonadotropins the cause of the condition? *Med Hypotheses* 19:243–255, 1986.

Cox DJ: Menstrual symptom questionnaire: further psychometric evaluation. *Behav Res Ther* 15:506–508, 1977.

Cox JR: Hormonal influence on auditory function. *Ear Hear* 1:219–222, 1980.

Coyne C: Muscle tension and its relation to symptoms in the premenstruum. *Res Nurs Health* 6:199–205, 1983.

Cramer H, Rudolph J, Consbruch V, Kendel K: On the effects of melatonin on sleep and behavior in man. In: *Advances in Biochemical Psychopharmacology, Vol II, Serotonin—New Vistas*, ed by E Costa, GL Gessa, M Sander. New York, Raven, 1974, pp. 187–191.

Crawford JE, Crawford DM: *Crawford Small Parts Dexterity Test*. New York, Psychological Corporation, 1981.

Creutzfeldt OD, Arnold PM, Becker D, Langenstein S, Tirsch W, Wilhelm H, Wuttke W: EEG changes during spontaneous and controlled menstrual cycles and their correlation with psychological performance. *Electroencephalogr Clin Neurophysiol* 40:113–131, 1976.

Crook WG: PMS and yeasts: an etiologic connection? *Hosp Prac* 18:21–24, 1983.

Cullberg J: Mood changes and menstrual symptoms with different estrogen combinations. *Acta Psychiatr Scand* Suppl. 236:1–86, 1972.

Cumming DC, Yang JC, Rebar RW, Yen SSC: Treatment of hirsutism with spironolactone. *JAMA* 247:1295–1298, 1982.

Dalton K: Similarity of symptomatology of premenstrual syndrome and toxaemia of pregnancy and their response to progesterone. *Br Med J* 2:1071, 1954.

Dalton K: Discussion on the premenstrual syndrome. *Proc R Soc Med* 48:337–347, 1955.

Dalton K: Menstruation and acute psychiatric illnesses. *Br Med J* 1:148–149, 1959a.

Dalton K: Menstrual disorders in general practice. *J Coll Gen Practitioners* 2:236, 1959b.

Dalton K: Comparative trials of new oral progestogenic compounds in treatment of premenstrual syndrome. *Br Med J* 2:1307–1309, 1959c.

Dalton K: Effects of menstruation on schoolgirls' weekly work. *Br Med J* 1:326–328, 1960a.

Dalton K: Menstruation and accidents. *Br Med J* 2:1425–1426, 1960b.

Dalton K: Schoolgirls' behavior and menstruation. *Br Med J* 2:1647–1649, 1960c.

Dalton K: Menstruation and crime. *Br Med J* 2:1752–1753, 1961.

Dalton K: The influence of mother's menstruation on her child. *Proc R Soc Med* 59:1014–1016, 1966.

Dalton K: The influence of menstruation on glaucoma. *Br J Ophthalmol* 51:692–695, 1967.

Dalton K: Menstruation and examinations. *Lancet* 2:1386–1388, 1968.

Dalton K: Children's hospital admissions and mother's menstruation. *Br Med J* 2:27–28, 1970.

Dalton K: Puerperal and premenstrual depression. *Proc R Soc Med* 64:1249–1252, 1971.

Dalton K: Progesterone suppositories and pessaries in the treatment of menstrual migraine. *Headache* 12:151–159, 1973.

Dalton K: Premenstrual ankle edema in young girls. *JAMA* 228:900, 1974.

Dalton K: Treatment of the premenstrual syndrome. *J Pharmacother* 1:51–55, 1976.

Dalton K: Premenstrual syndrome with psychiatric symptoms. *JAMA* 238:2729, 1977a.

Dalton K: *The Premenstrual Syndrome and Progesterone Therapy*. London, William Heinemann Medical Books, 1977b.

Dalton K: Cyclical criminal acts in premenstrual syndrome. *Lancet* 2:1070–1071, 1980.

Dalton K: *The Premenstrual Syndrome and Progesterone Therapy* (Second Edition). Chicago, Year Book Medical Publishers, 1984.

Dalton K: Pyridoxine overdose in premenstrual syndrome. *Lancet* 1:1168–1169, 1985.

Dalton K: Trial of progesterone vaginal suppositories in the treatment of premenstrual syndrome. *Am J Obstet Gynecol Treat* 156:1555–1556, 1987a.

Dalton K: Premenstrual syndrome and thyroid dysfunction commentary. *Integr Psychiatry* 5:186–187, 1987b.

Dalton K: Progesterone for premenstrual exacerbations of asthma. *Lancet* 2:684, 1988.

Dalton K, Dalton MJT: Characteristics of pyridoxine overdose neuropathy syndrome. *Acta Neurol Scand* 76:8–11, 1987.

Dalton K, Dalton M, Guthrie K: Incidence of the premenstrual syndrome in twins. *Br Med J* 295:1027–1028, 1987.

Dalton K, Greene R: The premenstrual syndrome. *Br Med J* 1:1007, 1953.

Dalton ME: Sex hormone–binding globulin concentrations in women with severe premenstrual syndrome. *Postgrad Med J* 57:560–561, 1981.

Damas-Mora J, Davies L, Jenner FA: Menstrual respiratory changes and symptoms. *Br J Psychiatry* 136:492–497, 1980.

David D, Freeman A, Harrington TM, Downey AB, Weart W, Albracht D, Miller E, Norton J, Rumbo N, Roth D, Milo K: Buspirone for anxious women in a primary care environment—a multicenter open evaluation. *Adv Ther* 4:251–264, 1987.

Davidson BJ, Rea CD, Valenzuela GJ: A trial natriuretic peptide, plasma renin activity, and aldosterone in women on estrogen therapy and with premenstrual syndrome. *Fertil Steril* 50:743–746, 1988.

Davis MJ, Ahroon WA: Fluctuations in susceptibility to noise-induced temporary threshold shift as influenced by the menstrual cycle. *J Aud Res* 22:173–187, 1982.

Davis PG, McEwen BS: Neuroendocrine regulation of sexual behavior. In: *Behavior and the Menstrual Cycle*, ed by RC Friedman. New York: Marcel Dekker, 1982, pp. 43–64.

Day J: Danazol and the premenstrual syndrome. *Post Grad Med J* 55:87–89, 1979a.

Day JB: Clinical trials in the premenstrual syndrome. *Curr Med Res Opin* 6:40–45, 1979b.

Day RL: O-T-C medications for menstrual problems. *J Am Pharmaceuticals* NS8:477–481, 1968.

Deicken RF: Verapamil treatment of premenstrual tension. *Biol Psychiatry* 24:689–692, 1988.

DeJong R, Rubinow DR, Roy-Byrne P, Hoban C, Grover GN, Post RM: Premenstrual mood disorder and psychiatric illness. *Am J Psychiatry* 142:1359–1361, 1985.

Delaney J, Lipton MJ, Toth E: *The Curse: A Cultural History of Menstruation.* New York, Dutton, 1976.

DeLeon-Jones FA, Steinberg J, Dekirmejian H, Garver D: MHPG-excretion during the menstrual cycle of women. *Community Psychopharmacol* 2:267–274, 1978.

DeLeon-Jones FA, Val E, Herts C: MHPG excretion and lithium treatment during premenstrual tension syndrome: a case report. *Am J Psychiatry* 139:950–952, 1982.

de Lignieres B: Two different kinds of PMS symptoms: high E_2 and low E_2 linked. Paper presented at the 2nd International Symposium: Premenstrual, Postpartum and Menopausal Mood Disorders, Kiawah Island, Charleston, SC, September 10, 1987, Abstract #23.

de Lignieres B, Vincens M, Mauvais-Jarvis P, Mas JL, Touboul PJ, Bousser MG: Prevention of menstrual migraine by percutaneous oestradiol. *Br Med J* 293:1540, 1986.

Delitala G, Masala A, Alagna S, De Villa L: Effects of pyridoxine on human hypophyseal tropic hormone release: a possible stimulation of hypothalamic dopaminergic pathway. *J Clin Endocrinol Metab* 42:603–606, 1976.

DeMarchi GW, Tong JE: Menstrual, diurnal and activation effects on the resolution of temporally paired flashes. *Psychophysiology* 9:362–367, 1972.

Denicoff KD, Hoban MC, Grover GN, Erickson K, Rubinow DR: Glucose tolerance testing in women with premenstrual syndrome (PMS). Paper presented at the 2nd International Symposium: Premenstrual, Postpartum and Menopausal Mood Disorders, Kiawah Island, Charleston, SC, September 10, 1987, Abstract #9.

Dennerstein L, Burrows GD: Affect and the menstrual cycle. *J Affective Disord* 1:77–92, 1979.

Dennerstein L, Judd F, Davies B: Psychosis and the menstrual cycle. *Med J Aust* 1:524–525, 1983.

Dennerstein L, Morse C, Gotts G, Brown J, Smith M, Oats J, Burrows G: Treatment of premenstrual syndrome: A double-blind trial of dydrogesterone. *J Affective Disord* 11:199–205, 1986.

Dennerstein L, Morse CA, Varnavides K: Premenstrual tension and depression—is there a relationship? *J Psychosom Obstet Gynecol* 8:45–52, 1988.

Dennerstein L, Spencer-Gardner C, Brown JB, Smith MA, Burrows GD: Premenstrual tension—hormonal profiles. *J Psychosom Obstet Gynaecol* 3:37–51, 1984a.

Dennerstein L, Spencer-Gardner C, Burrows GD: Mood and the menstrual cycle. *J Psychiatr Res* 18:1–12, 1984b.

Dennerstein L, Spencer-Gardner C, Gotts G, Brown JB, Smith MA, Burrows GD: Progesterone and the premenstrual syndrome: a double blind crossover trial. *Br Med J* 290:1617–1621, 1985.

DePirro R, Fusco A, Bertoli A, Greco AV, Lauro R: Insulin receptors during the menstrual cycle in normal women. *J Clin Endocrinol Metab* 47:1387–1389, 1978.

Derome-Tremblay M, Nathan C: Fenfluramine studies. *Science* 243:991, 1989.

deTejada AL, Carreno E, Lopez L, Wionczek C, Karchmer S: Eliminacion urinaria de acido 5-hidroxi-indol acetico durante el ciclo menstrual humano. *Ginecol Obstet Mex* 44:85–91, 1978.

Deutsch H: *The Psychology of Women*, Vol. 1. New York, Grune & Stratton, 1944.

Deutsch H: *The Psychology of Women*, Vol. 2. New York, Grune & Stratton, 1945.

Diamond M, Diamond A, Mast M: Visual sensitivity and sexual arousal levels during the menstrual cycle. *J Nerv Ment Dis* 155:170–176, 1972.

Diamond SB, Rubenstein AA, Dunner DL, Fieve RR: Menstrual problems in women with primary affective illness. *Compr Psychiatry* 17:541–549, 1976.

Dickson-Parnell B, Zeichner A: The premenstrual syndrome: psychophysiologic concomitants of perceived stress and low back pain. *Pain* 34:161–169, 1988.

Dickstein LJ: Menstrual disorders and stress in university students. *Psychiatr Ann* 14:436–441, 1984.

Diespecker DD, Kolokotronis E: Vibrotactile learning and the menstrual cycle. *Percept Mot Skills* 33:233–234, 1971.

DiNardo PG: Psychological correlations of the menstrual cycle. *Dissertation Abstracts Int* 36(6B):3031, 1975.

Donovan BT: Hormones and behavior: discussion paper. *J R Soc Med* 80:499–501, 1987.

D'Orban PT: Premenstrual syndrome: a disease of the mind? *Lancet* 2:1413, 1981.

D'Orban PT, Dalton J: Violent crime and the menstrual cycle. *Psychol Med* 10:353–359, 1980.

Dor-Shav NK: In search of premenstrual tension: note on sex differences in psychological-differentiation as a function of cyclical physiological changes. *Percept Mot Skills* 42:1139–1142, 1976.

Doty RL, Snyder PJ, Huggins GR, Lowry LD: Endocrine, cardiovascular, and psychological correlates of olfactory sensitivity changes during the human menstrual cycle. *J Comp Physiol Psychol* 95:45–60, 1981.

Dyrenfurth I, Jewelewicz R, Warren M, Ferin M, VandeWiele RL: Temporal relationships of hormonal variables in the menstrual cycle. In: *Biorhythms and Human Reproduction*, ed by M Ferin, F Halberg, RM Richart, RL VandeWiele. New York, Wiley, 1974, pp. 171–201.

Edelson JT, Bohrer MS, Fendrick AM, Gonzales JJ, Morrison MF, Uffner J: Premenstrual syndrome [letter to editor]. *N Engl J Med* 312:920, 1985.

Ehara Y, Siler T, Van den Berg G, Sinha YN, Yen SSC: Circulatory prolactin levels during the menstrual cycle: episodic release and diurnal variation. *Am J Obstet Gynecol* 117:962–970, 1973.

Ehrenreich B, English D: *For Her Own Good.* Garden City, NY, Doubleday, 1978.

Elder N: Implications of menstrual cycle research for women's health care. In: *Women's Health Care: A Guide to Alternatives,* ed by K Weiss. Reston, MD: Reston Publishing Co., 1983, pp. 224–229.

Elliott FA: Neuroanatomy and neurology of aggression. *Psychiatr Ann* 17:385–388, 1987.

Elsner CW, Buster JE, Schindler RA, Nessim SA, Abraham GA: Bromocriptine in the treatment of premenstrual tension syndrome. *Obstet Gynecol* 56:723–726, 1980.

Endicott J, Halbreich U: Retrospective report of premenstrual depressive changes: factors affecting confirmation by daily ratings. *Psychopharmacol Bull* 18:109–112, 1982.

Endicott J, Halbreich U: Clinical significance of premenstrual dysphoric changes. *J Clin Psychiatry* 49:486–489, 1988.

Endicott J, Halbreich U, Schacht S, Nee J: Premenstrual changes and affective disorders. *Psychosom Med* 43:519–529, 1981.

Endicott J, Nee J, Cohen J, Halbreich U: Premenstrual changes: patterns and correlates of daily ratings. *J Affective Disord* 10:127–135, 1986.

Endicott J, Spitzer RL: A diagnostic interview: the Schedule for Affective Disorders and Schizophrenia. *Arch Gen Psychiatry* 35:834–837, 1978.

Endo M, Diaguji M, Asano Y, Yamashita I, Takahashi S: Periodic psychosis recurring in association with menstrual cycle. *J Clin Psychiatry* 39:456–461, 465–466, 1978.

Engel GL: The need for a new medical model: a challenge for biomedicine. *Science* 196:129–136, 1977.

Englander-Golden P, Willis KA, Dienstbier RA: Stability of perceived tension as a function of the menstrual cycle. *J Human Stress* June:14–22, 1977.

Englander-Golden P, Whitmore MR, Dienstbier RA: Menstrual cycle as a focus of study and self-reports of moods and behaviors. *Motiv Emot* 2:75–87, 1978.

Erdelyi GJ: Gynecological survey of female athletes. *J Sports Med Physical Fitness* 2:174–179, 1962.

Eysenck HJ: *The Maudsley Personality Inventory.* San Diego, San Diego Educational Industrial Testing Service, 1962.

Eysenck HJ, Eysenck SBG: A factorial study of psychoticism as a dimension of personality. *Mult Behav Res (Special Issue):* 15–32, 1968.

Facchinetti F, Martignoni E, Petraglia F, Sances MG, Nappi G, Genazzani AR: Premenstrual fall of plasma β-endorphin in patients with premenstrual syndrome. *Fertil Steril* 47:570–573, 1987.

Facchinetti F, Martignoni E, Sola D, Petraglia F, Nappi G, Genazzani AR: Transient failure of central opioid tonus and premenstrual symptoms. *J Reprod Med* 33: 633–638, 1988.

Facchinetti F, Nappi G, Petraglia F, Volpe A, Genazzani AR: Oestradiol/progesterone imbalance and the premenstrual syndrome. *Lancet* 2:1302, 1983.

Farah FS, Shbaklu Z: Autoimmune progesterone urticaria. *J Allergy Clin Immunol* 48:257–261, 1971.

Faratian B, Gasper A, O'Brien PMS, Johnson IR, Filshie GM, Prescott P: Premenstrual syndrome: weight, abdominal swelling, and perceived body image. *Am J Obstet Gynecol* 150:200–204, 1984.

Feinberg M, Carroll BJ, Smouse P, Rawson S, Haskett RF, Steiner M, Albala A, Zelnick T: Comparison of physician and self-ratings of depression. Paper presented at the annual meeting of the Society of Biological Psychiatry, Chicago, 1979.

Feine R, Belmaker RH, Rimon R, Ebstein RP: Platelet monoamine oxidase in women with premenstrual syndrome. *Neuropsychobiology* 3:105–110, 1977.

Felthaus AR, Robinson DR, Conroy RW: Prevention of recurrent menstrual psychosis by an oral contraceptive. *Am J Psychiatry* 137:245–246, 1980.

Fischer S: Treatment of schizophrenia with glandular extracts. *Arch Neurol Psychiatry* 42:644–651, 1939.

Fisher C: Psychiatric aspects of shoplifting. *Br J Hosp Med* 31:210–212, 1984.

Fisher S, Richter J: Selective effects of the menstrual experience upon aneisokonic body perception. *Psychosom Med* 31:365–371, 1969.

Flug D, Largo RH, Prader A: Symptoms related to menstruation in adolescent Swiss girls: a longitudinal study. *Ann Hum Biol* 12:161–168, 1985.

Folkard S, Monk TH: *Hours of Work: Temporal Factors in Work Scheduling.* New York, Wiley, 1985.

Fortin JN, Wittilower ED, Kalz F: Psychosomatic approach to premenstrual tension syndrome: a preliminary report. *Can Med Assoc J* 79:978–981, 1958.

Fotherby K, James F: Metabolism of synthetic steroids. *Adv Steroid Biochem Pharmacol* 3:67–165, 1972.

Fourestie V, de Lignieres B, Roudot-Thoraval F, Fulli-Lemaire I, Cremniter D, Nahoul K, Fournier S, Lejonc J-L: Suicide attempts in hypo-oestrogenic phases of the menstrual cycle. *Lancet* 2:1357–1359, 1986.

Frank P: What are nurses doing to help PMS patients? *Am J Nurs* 86:137–140, 1986.

Frank RT: *The Female Sex Hormone.* Springfield, IL: Charles C. Thomas, 1929.

Frank RT: The hormonal basis of premenstrual tension. *Arch Neurol Psychiatry* 26:1053–1057, 1931.

Frank RT, Goldberger MA, Felshin G: Clinical and laboratory investigations of some of the newer sex hormone preparations. *Endocrinology* 27:381–384, 1940.

Frank RT, Goldberger MA, Salmon UJ, Felshin G: Amenorrhea: its causation and treatment. *JAMA* 109:1863–1869, 1937.

Frankel BL, Rubinow DR: The premenstrual syndromes. In: *Modern Perspectives in Clinical Psychiatry,* ed by J Howells. New York, Brunner/Mazel, 1988, pp. 170–186.

Franks R, Adler L, Waldo M, Alpert J, Freedman R: Neurophysiological studies of sensory gating in mania: comparison with schizophrenia. *Biol Psychiatry* 18:989–1005, 1983.

Fraser IS: Prostaglandin inhibitors in gynaecology. *Aust NZ J Obstet Gynaecol* 25:114–117, 1985.

Freed SC: The treatment of premenstrual distress, with special consideration of the androgens. *JAMA* 127:377–379, 1945.

Freed SC: Therapeutic use of testosterone in aqueous suspension. *J Clin Endocrinol* 6:571–574, 1946.

Freeman EW, Sondheimer SJ, Rickels K: Medical and psychologic characteristics of women presenting with premenstrual symptoms. *Obstet Gynecol* 70:142–143, 1987.

Freeman EW, Sondheimer SJ, Rickels K: Effects of medical history factors on symptom severity in women meeting criteria for premenstrual syndrome. *Obstet Gynecol* 72:236–239, 1988.

Freeman EW, Sondheimer SJ, Rickels K, Weinbaum PJ: PMS treatment approaches and progesterone therapy. *Psychosomatics* 26:811–816, 1985.

Freinhar JP: Alprazolam and premenstrual syndrome. *J Clin Psychiatry* 45:526, 1984.

Freud S: The question of lay analysis. S.E. XX London, Hogarth, 1971 (1926), p. 242.

Friedman D, Jaffe A: Influence of life-style on the premenstrual syndrome: analysis of a questionnaire survey. *J Reprod Med* 30:715–719, 1985.

Friedman E, Katcher AH, Brightman VJ: A prospective study of the distribution of illness within the menstrual cycle. *Motiv Emot* 2:355–367, 1978.

Friedman J, Meares RA: The menstrual cycle and habituation. *Psychosom Med* 41:369–381, 1979.

Friedman RC, Clarkin JF, Hurt SW, Corn R, Aronoff MS: Premenstrual affective syndrome in adolescent and adult psychiatric patients. In: *Menarche,* ed by S Golub. Lexington, MA, Lexington Books, 1983.

Friedman RC, Corn R: Psychopathology and the menstrual cycle. *Academy Forum* 27:6–8, 1983.

Friedman RC, Hurt SW, Aronoff MS, Clarkin J: Behavior and the menstrual cycle. *Signs: J Women Culture Soc* 5:719–738, 1980.

Friedman RC, Hurt SW, Clarkin J, Corn R, Aronoff MS: Sexual histories and pre-menstrual affective syndrome in psychiatric inpatients. *Am J Psychiatry* 139:1454–1486, 1982.

Fries H: Experience with lithium carbonate treatment at a psychiatric department in the period 1964–1969. *Acta Psychiatr Scand* [Suppl] 207:41–43, 1969.

Fuchs N, Hakim M, Abraham GE: The effect of a nutritional supplement, Optivite® for women, on premenstrual tension syndromes. I. Effect on blood chemistry and serum steroid levels during the midluteal phase. *J Applied Nutr* 37:1–11, 1985.

Gaith D, Iles S: Treating the premenstrual syndrome. *Br Med J* 297:237–238, 1988.

Gallant SJ, Hamilton JA: On a premenstrual psychiatric diagnosis: what's in a name? *Professional Psychol: Res Pract* 19:271–278, 1988.

Gamberale F, Strindberg L, Wahlberg I: Female work capacity during the menstrual cycle: physiological and psychological reactions. *Scand J Work Environ Health* 1:120–127, 1975.

Gannon L: Evidence for a psychological etiology of menstrual disorders: a critical review. *Psychol Rep* 48:287–294, 1981.

Garrison RH, Somer E: *The Nutrition Desk Reference.* New Canaan, CT: Keats Publishing, Inc., 1985, pp. 47–49.

Geber H: Einige daten zür pathologie der urticaria menstruationalis. *Dermatol Z* 32:143–150, 1921.

Geiringer E: Mittelwahn: a reconsideration of premenstrual phenomena. *J Obstet Gynaecol Br Empire* 58:1010–1018, 1951.

George CF, Miller TW, Hanly PJ, Kryger MH: The effect of 1-tryptophan on daytime sleep latency in normals (correlation with blood levels). *Sleep Res* 17:40, 1988.

Gerada C, Reveley A: Schizophreniform psychosis associated with the menstrual cycle. *Br J Psychiatry* 153:700–702, 1988.

Gerber J: Desensitization in the treatment of menstrual problems and other allergic symptoms. *Br J Dermatol* 51:265–268, 1939.

Ghadirian AM, Kamaraju LS: Premenstrual mood changes in affective disorders. *Can Med Assoc J* 136:1027–1032, 1987.

Ghose K, Coppen A: Bromocriptine and premenstrual syndrome: controlled study. *Br Med J* 1:147–148, 1977.

Ghose K, Turner P: The menstrual cycle and the tyramine pressor response test. *Br J Clin Pharmacol* 4:500–502, 1977.

Giannini AJ, Price WA, Loiselle RH: Beta-endorphin withdrawal: a possible cause of premenstrual tension syndrome. *Int J Psychophysiol* 1:341–348, 1984.

Giannini AJ, Price WA, Loiselle RH, Giannini MC: Pseudocholinesterase and trait anxiety in premenstrual tension syndrome. *J Clin Psychiatry* 46:139–140, 1985.

Giannini AJ, Sorger LG, Martin DM, Bates L. Impaired reception of nonverbal cues in women with premenstrual tension syndrome. *J Psychol* 122:591–596, 1988.

Giannini AJ, Sullivan B, Sarchene J, Loiselle RH: Clonidine in the treatment of PMS: a subgroup study. *J Clin Psychiatry* 49:62–63, 1988.

Gill MM: Functional disturbances of menstruation. *Bull Menninger Clin* 7:6–14, 1943.

Gillin JC: The sleep therapies of depression. *Prog Neuropsychopharmacol Biol Psychiatry* 7:351–364, 1983.

Gillman J: The nature of the subjective reactions evoked in women by progesterone with special reference to the problem of premenstrual tension. *J Clin Endocrinol* 2:157–160, 1942.

Gilmore NJ, Robinson DS, Nies A, Sylvester D, Ravaris CL: Blood monoamine oxidase levels in pregnancy and during the menstrual cycle. *J Psychosom Res* 15:215–220, 1971.

Gladis MM, Walsh BT: Premenstrual exacerbation of binge eating in bulimia. *Am J Psychiatry* 144:1592–1595, 1987.

Glass GS, Heninger GR, Lansky M, Talan K: Psychiatric emergency related to the menstrual cycle. *Am J Psychiatry* 128:705–711, 1971.

Glick ID, Bennett SE. Psychiatric complications of progesterone and oral contraceptives. *J Clin Psychopharm* November:350–367, 1981.

Glick ID, Stewart D. A new drug treatment for premenstrual exacerbation of schizophrenia. *Compr Psychiatry* 21:281–287, 1980.

Goei G, Abraham G: Effect of a nutritional supplement, Optivite®, on symptoms of premenstrual tension. *J Reprod Med* 28:527–531, 1983.

Goei GS, Ralston JL, Abraham GE: Dietary patterns of patients with premenstrual tension. *J Applied Nutr* 34:4–11, 1982.

Gold JH: Premenstrual syndrome. In: *Diagnostics and Psychopathology*, ed by F Flack. New York, Norton, 1987.

Goldin BR, Aldercreutz H, Gorbach SL, Warram JH, Dwyer JT, Swenson L, Woods MN: Estrogen excretion patterns and plasma levels in vegetarian and omnivorous women. *N Engl J Med* 307:1542–1547, 1982.

Goldschmidt T: The menstrual taboo and women's psychology. *J Abnorm Social Psychol* 29:218–221, 1934.

Golub LI, Menduke H, Conley SS: Weight changes in college women during the menstrual cycle. *Am J Obstet Gynecol* 91:89–94, 1965.

Golub S: The effect of premenstrual anxiety and depression on cognitive function. *J Pers Soc Psychol* 34:99–104, 1976a.

Golub S: The magnitude of premenstrual anxiety and depression. *Psychosom Med* 38:4–12, 1976b.

Golub S (Ed.): *Menarche*. Lexington, MA, Lexington Books, 1983.

Golub S, Harrington DS. Premenstrual and menstrual mood changes in adolescent women. *J Pers Soc Psychol* 41:961–965, 1981.

Gonzalez ER: Drug treatment and nutrient therapy: the distinction blurs. *NY State J Med* 84:467–472, 1984.

Goodman LS, Gilman A: *The Pharmacological Basis of Therapeutics*. New York, Macmillan, 1965, pp. 1662–1665.

Goss H, Cole HH: Sex hormones in the blood serum of mares. *Endocrinology* 15:214, 1931.

Gotts G, Dennerstein L: Progesterone and the premenstrual syndrome: a double blind crossover trial (letter). *Br Med J* 291:214, 1985.

Gottschalk LA, Kaplan SM, Gleser GC, Winget CM: Variations in magnitude of emotion: a method applied to anxiety and hostility during phases of the menstrual cycle. *Psychosom Med* 24:300–311, 1962.

Graham GA, Sherwin BB: The relationship between retrospective premenstrual symptom reporting and present oral contraceptive use. *J Psychosom Res* 31:45–53, 1987.

Graham J: *Evening Primrose Oil. Its Remarkable Properties and Its Use in the Treatment of a Wide Range of Conditions*. New York: Thorsons Publishers, Inc., 1984.

Graham JJ, Harding PE, Wise PH, Berman H: Prolactin suppression in the treatment of premenstrual syndrome. *Med J Aust* 2:18–20, 1978.

Grant ECG, Pryse-Davies J: Effects of oral contraceptives on depressive mood changes and on endometrial monoamine oxidase and phosphatases. *Br Med J* 3:777–780, 1968.

Gray LA: Effect of pregnant mare's serum hormone on the abnormal ovary. *South Med J* 33:160–170, 1940.

Gray LA: The use of progesterone in nervous tension states. *South Med J* 34:1004–1007, 1941.

Greenblatt RA, Agusta GA: Syndrome of major menstrual molimina with hypermenorrhea alleviated by testosterone propionate. *JAMA* 115:120–121, 1940.

Greene R, Dalton K: The premenstrual syndrome. *Br Med J* 1:1007–1014, 1953.

Greenhill JP, Freed SC: The electrolyte therapy of premenstrual distress. *JAMA* 117:504–506, 1941.

Gregory BAJC: The menstrual cycle and its disorders in psychiatric patients. II. Clinical studies. *J Psychosom Res* 2:199–224, 1957.

Grief EB, Ulman KJ: The psychological impact of menarche on early adolescent females: a review of the literature. *Child Dev* 53:1413–1430, 1982.

Griffin ML, Mendelson JH, Mello NK, Lex BW: Marijuana use across the menstrual cycle. *Drug Alcohol Depend* 18:213–224, 1986.

Gross HA, Dunner DL, Lafleur D, Meltzer HL, Muhlbauer HL, Fieve RR: Prostaglandins: a review of neurophysiology and psychiatric implications. *Arch Gen Psychiatry* 34:1189–1197, 1977.

Gruba GH, Rohrbaugh M. MMPI correlates of menstrual distress. *Psychosom Med* 37:265–273, 1975.

Guinan ME: PMS or perifollicular phase euphoria? *J Am Med Wom Assoc* 43:91–92, 1988.

Gunston KD. Premenstrual syndrome in Cape Town. Part II. A double-blind placebo-controlled study of the efficacy of mefenamic acid. *S Afr Med J* 159–160, 1986.

Hagen I, Nesheim BI, Tutland T: No effect on Vitamin B_6 against premenstrual tension: a controlled clinical study. *Acta Obstet Gynecol Scand* 64:667–670, 1985.

Haggard M, Gaston JB: Changes in auditory perception in the menstrual cycle. *Br J Audiol* 12:105–118, 1978.

Hailey BJ, Ulmer A, Crowell M, Carr C, Horton N: A survey of physicians' attitudes and behavior toward PMS. *Health Care Women Int* 9:19–28, 1988.

Hain JD, Linton PH, Eber HW, Chapman MM: Menstrual irregularity, symptoms and personality. *J Psychosom Res* 14:81–87, 1970.

Halas MA: Premenstrual syndrome in adolescents: a critical role for mental health counselors. *Am Ment Health Counselors J* 9:51–60, 1987.

Halbreich U, Alt IH, Paul L: Premenstrual changes: impaired hormonal homeostasis. *Endocrinol Metab Clin N Am* 17:173–194, 1988.

Halbreich U, Ben-David M, Assael M, Bornstein R: Serum prolactin in women with premenstrual syndrome. *Lancet* 2:654–656, 1976.

Halbreich U, Endicott J: Possible involvement of endorphin withdrawal or imbalance in specific premenstrual syndromes and postpartum depression. *Med Hypotheses* 7:1045–1058, 1981.

Halbreich U, Endicott J: Classification of premenstrual syndrome. In: *Behavior and the Menstrual Cycle,* ed by RC Friedman. New York, Marcel Dekker, 1982, pp. 243–265.

Halbreich U, Endicott J: Relationship of dysphoric premenstrual changes to depressive disorders. *Acta Psychiatr Scand* 71:331, 1985.

Halbreich U, Endicott J, Goldstein S, Nee J: Premenstrual changes and changes in gonadal hormones. *Acta Psychiatr Scand* 74:576–586, 1986.

Halbreich U, Endicott J, Lesser J: The clinical diagnosis and classification of premenstrual changes. *Can J Psychiatry* 30:489–497, 1985.

Halbreich U, Endicott J, Nee J: Premenstrual depressive changes. *Arch Gen Psychiatry* 40:535–542, 1983.

Halbreich U, Endicott J, Schacht S, Nee J: The diversity of premenstrual changes as reflected in the Premenstrual Assessment Form (PAF). *Acta Psychiatr Scand* 65:46–65, 1982.

Halbreich U, Kas D: Variations in the Taylor MAS of women with premenstrual syndrome. *J Psychosom Res* 21:391–393, 1977.

Halliday A, Bush B, Cleary P, Aronson M, Delbanco T: Alcohol abuse in women seeking gynecologic care. *Obstet Gynecol* 68:322–326, 1986.

Hallman J: The premenstrual syndrome: an equivalent of depression. *Acta Psychiatr Scand* 73:403–411, 1986.

Hallman J, Georgiev N: The premenstrual syndrome and absence from work due to illness. *J Psychosom Obstet Gynecol* 6:111–119, 1987.

Hallman J, Oreland L: Therapeutic effect of Vitamin B_6 in the treatment of premenstrual syndrome. Paper presented at the 2nd International Symposium: Premenstrual, Postpartum and Menopausal Mood Disorders, Kiawah Island, Charleston, South Carolina, September 11, 1987, Abstract #42.

Hallman J, Oreland L, Edman G, Schalling D: Thrombocyte monoamine oxidase activity and personality traits in women with severe premenstrual syndrome. *Acta Psychiatr Scand* 76:225–234, 1987.

Hallstrom COS, Rees WL, Pare CMB, Trenchard A: Platelet uptake of 5-hydroxytryptamine and dopamine in depressions. *Postgrad Med J* 52:40–44, 1976.

Hamilton JA: Premenstrual syndrome and thyroid dysfunction commentary. *Integr Psychiatry* 5:192–193, 1987.

Hamilton JA, Alagna SW, Sharpe K: Cognitive approaches to understanding and treating premenstrual depressions. In: *Premenstrual Syndrome: Current Findings & Future Directions*, ed by HJ Osofsky, SJ Blumenthal. Washington, DC, American Psychiatric Association Press, 1984, pp. 67–84.

Hamilton JA, Aloi J, Mucciardi B, Murphy DL: Human plasma β-endorphin through the menstrual cycle. *Psychopharmacol Bull* 19:586–587, 1983.

Hamilton JA, Parry BL, Blumenthal SJ: The menstrual cycle in context. I. Affective syndromes associated with reproductive hormonal changes. *J Clin Psychiatry* 49:474–480, 1988.

Hamilton M: A rating scale for depression. *J Neurol Neurosurg Psychiatry* 23:56–62, 1960.

Hammarback S, Backstrom T: Induced anovulation as treatment of premenstrual tension syndrome. *Acta Obstet Gynecol Scand* 67:159–166, 1988.

Hammarback S, Backstrom T, Holst J, von Schoultz B, Lyrenas S: Cyclical mood changes as in the premenstrual tension syndrome during sequential estrogen–progestagen postmenopausal replacement therapy. *Acta Obstet Gynecol Scand* 64:393–397, 1985.

Hammarback S, Damber JE, Backstrom T: Relationship between symptom severity and hormone changes in women with premenstrual syndrome. *J Clin Endocrinol Metab* 68:125–130, 1989.

Hammond DC, Keye WR Jr: Premenstrual syndrome. *N Engl J Med* 312:920, 1985.

Hansen JW, Hoffman HJ, Ross GT: Monthly gonadotropin cycles in premenarcheal girls. *Science* 190:161–163, 1975.

Hargrove JT, Abraham GE: The incidence of premenstrual tension in a gynecologic clinic. *J Reprod Med* 27:721–724, 1982.

Hargrove JT, Abraham GE: The ubiquitousness of premenstrual tension in gynecologic practice. *J Reprod Med* 28:435–437, 1983.

Harrison TR, Adams RD, Bennet IL, Resnik WH, Thorn GW, Wintrobe MM: *Principles of Internal Medicine*. New York, McGraw-Hill, 1966, pp 465–466.

Harrison WM, Endicott J, Nee J: Treatment of premenstrual depression with nortriptyline: A pilot study. *J Clin Psychiatry* 50:136–139, 1989.

Harrison WM, Endicott J, Rabkin JG, Nee J: Treatment of premenstrual dysphoric changes: clinical outcome and methodological implications. *Psychopharm Bull* 20:118–122, 1984.

Harrison WM, Endicott J, Rabkin JG, Nee JC, Sandberg D: Treatment of premenstrual dysphoria with alprazolam and placebo. *Psychopharm Bull* 23:150–153, 1987.

Harrison WM, Rabkin JG, Endicott J: Psychiatric evaluation of premenstrual changes. *Psychosomatics* 26:789–799, 1985a.

Harrison WM, Sharpe L, Endicott J: Treatment of premenstrual symptoms. *Gen Hosp Psychiatry* 7:54–65, 1985b.

Hart WG, Coleman GJ, Russell JW: Assessment of premenstrual symptomatology: a reevaluation of the predictive validity of self-report. *J Psychosom Res* 31:185–190, 1987a.

Hart WG, Coleman GJ, Russell JW: Psychiatric screening in the premenstrual syndrome. *Med J Aust* 146:518–522, 1987b.

Hart WG, Russell JW: A prospective comparison study of premenstrual symptoms. *Med J Aust* 144:466–468, 1986.

Hartman MM: The use of sex hormones in allergic disorders. *Ann Allergy* 5:467–477, 1947.

Hartmann EL: Dreaming sleep (the D-state) and the menstrual cycle. *J Nerv Ment Dis* 143:406–416, 1966.

Hartmann EL: *The Functions of Sleep.* New Haven, CT, Yale University Press, 1973.

Hasin M, Dennerstein L, Gotts G: Menstrual cycle related complaints: a cross-cultural study. *J Psychosom Obstet Gynecol* 9:35–42, 1988.

Haskett RF: Premenstrual dysphoric disorder: evaluation, pathophysiology and treatment. *Prog Neuro-Psychopharmacol Biol Psychiatry* 11:129–135, 1987.

Haskett RF, Steiner M, Carroll BJ: A psychoendocrine study of premenstrual tension syndrome: a model for endogenous depression? *J Affective Disord* 6:191–199, 1984.

Haskett RF, Steiner M, Osmun JN, Carroll BJ: Severe premenstrual tension: delineation of the syndrome. *Biol Psychiatry* 15:121–139, 1980.

Hatotani N, Ishida C, Yura R, Maeda M, Kato Y, Nomura J, Wakao T, Takekoshi A, Yoshimoto S, Yoshimoto K, Hiramoto K: Psycho-physiological studies of atypical psychoses: endocrinological aspect of periodic psychoses. *Folia Psychiatrica Neurologica Japonica* 16:248–291, 1962.

Hawkins DR, Taub JM, Van de Castle RL: Extended sleep (hypersomnia) in young depressed patients. *Am J Psychiatry* 142:905–910, 1985.

Heckel GP: Endogenous allergy to steroid hormones. *Sur Gynecol Obstet* 92:191–208, 1951.

Heggestad KA: The devil made me do it: the case against using premenstrual syndrome as a defense in a court of law. *Hamline Law Rev* 9:155–163, 1986.

Heilbrun AB Jr, Renert D: Psychological defences and menstrual distress. *Br J Med Psychol* 61:219–230, 1988.

Hendler NH: Clinical drug trial: spironolactone for PMS. *Female Patient* 5:17–19, 1980.

Herren RGH: The effect of high and low female sex hormone concentration on the two-point threshold of pain and touch and upon tactile sensitivity. *J Exp Psychol* 16:324–327, 1933.

Herzberg B, Coppen A: Changes in psychological symptoms in women taking oral contraceptives. *Br J Psychiatry* 116:161–164, 1970.

Hicks RA, Olsen C, Smith-Robinson D: Type A-B behavior and the premenstrual syndrome. *Psychol Rep* 59:353–354, 1986.

Ho A: Sex hormones and the sleep of women. *Sleep Res* 1:184, 1972.

Hoes M: The chronopathology of premenstrual psychopathology. *Med Hypotheses* 6:1063–1075, 1980.

Hoffman J: A double blind crossover clinical trial of an OTC diuretic in the treatment of premenstrual tension and weight gain. *Curr Ther Res* 26:575–580, 1979.

Holtz I, Halbreich U: Thyroid disfunction [sic] is limited to a small group of women with dysphoric premenstrual changes. Abstract, American Society for Psychosomatic Obstetrics and Gynecology, Seventeenth Annual Meeting, Orlando, Florida, April 12–16, 1989, p. 48.

Horney K: Premenstrual tension. In: *Feminine Psychology,* ed by H Kelman. New York, Norton, 1931, pp 99–106.

Horrobin DF: *Prolactin: Physiology and Clinical Significance.* Lancaster, England, Medical and Technical Publishing Co., 1973, pp 115–120.

Horrobin DF: Human prolactin: clinical implications. *Clin Invest Med* 1:5–6, 1978.

Horrobin DF: Prolactin: role in health and disease. *Drugs* 17:409–417, 1979.

Horrobin DF: The role of essential fatty acids and prostaglandins in the premenstrual syndrome. *J Reprod Med* 28:465–468, 1983a.

Horrobin DF: The regulation of prostaglandin biosynthesis by the manipulation of essential fatty acid metabolism. *Rev Pure Appl Pharmacol Sci* 4:339–383, 1983b.

Horrobin DF, Manku MS: Essential fatty acid (EFA) metabolism in premenstrual syndrome (PMS). Paper presented at the 2nd International Symposium: Premenstrual, Postpartum and Menopausal Mood Disorders, Kiawah Island, Charleston, SC, September 10, 1987, Abstract #11.

Hoskins RG, Sleeper FH: Endocrine studies in dementia praecox. *Endocrinology* 13:245–262, 1929.

Hrbek J, Navratil J: Pharmacotherapy in the premenstrual tension. *Act Nerv Super* 13:189–190, 1971.

Huber CP, Davis ME: The clinical use of gonadotropic hormone from pregnant mare serum. *Sur Gynecol Obstet* 70:996–1005, 1940.

Hunter C: Easing the tension. *Nursing Times* 81:40–43, 1985.

Hurt SW, Friedman RC, Clarkin J, Corn R, Aronoff MS: Psychopathology and the menstrual cycle. In: *Behavior and the Menstrual Cycle,* ed by RC Friedman. New York, Marcel Dekker, 1982, pp 299–316.

Hurt SW, Shindledecker R, Severino SK: Premenstrual changes: patterns of daily ratings. *New Research Abstracts.* American Psychiatric Association, 1987, p. 120.

Hurt SW, Williams NA, Severino SK, Anderson M: Premenstrual syndrome and psychiatric disorders. *New Research Abstracts.* American Psychiatric Association, 1986, p. 36.

Hutt SJ, Frank G, Mychalkiw W, Hughes M: Perceptual–motor performance during the menstrual cycle. *Horm Behav* 14:116–125, 1980.

Hyler SE, Rieder RO, Williams JBW, Spitzer RL, Hendler J, Lyons M: The personality diagnostic questionnaire: a comparison with clinicians' DSM-III diagnoses. Paper presented at the annual meeting of the American Psychiatric Association, Washington, DC, May 12–16, 1986.

Isada NB: Medical and psychologic characteristics of women presenting with premenstrual symptoms. *Obstet Gynecol* 70:140–143, 1987.

Israel RS: Premenstrual tension. *JAMA* 110:1721–1723, 1938.

Ivey ME, Bardwick JM: Patterns of affective fluctuation in the menstrual cycle. *Psychosom Med* 30:336–345, 1968.

Jacobs TJ, Charles E: Correlation of psychiatric symptomatology and the menstrual cycle in an outpatient population. *Am J Psychiatry* 126:148–152, 1970.

Jakubowicz DL: The significance of prostaglandin in the premenstrual syndrome. In: *Premenstrual Syndrome,* ed by RW Taylor. London, Medical News Tribune, 1983.

Jakubowicz DL, Godard E, Dewhurst J: The treatment of premenstrual tension with mefenamic acid: analysis of prostaglandin concentration. *Br J Obstet Gynaecol* 91:79–84, 1984.

Janinger O, Riffenburgh R, Karsh R: Cross cultural study of premenstrual symptoms. *Psychosomatics* 13:226–235, 1972.

Janowsky DS, Berens SC, Davis JM: Correlations between mood, weight, and electrolytes during the menstrual cycle: a renin–angiotensin–aldosterone hypothesis of premenstrual tension. *Psychosom Med* 35:143–154, 1973.

Janowsky DS, El-Yousef MK, Davis JM, Sekerke HJ: A cholinergic–adrenergic hypothesis of mania and depression. *Lancet* 2:632–635, 1972.

Janowsky DS, Gorney R, Castelnuovo-Tedesco P, Stone CB: Premenstrual–menstrual increases in psychiatric hospital admission rates. *Am J Obstet Gynecol* 103:189–191, 1969.

Janowsky DS, Gorney R, Kelley B: The curse—vississitudes and variations of the female fertility cycle. Part II. Evolutionary aspects. *Psychosomatics* 7:283–287, 1966.

Janowsky DS, Gorney R, Mandell AJ: The menstrual cycle. Psychiatric and ovarian–adrenocortical hormone correlates: case study and literature review. *Arch Gen Psychiatry* 17:459–469, 1967.

Janowsky DS, Rausch J: Biochemical hypotheses of premenstrual tension syndrome. *Psychol Med* 15:3–8, 1985.

Jarrett RJ, Graver HJ: Changes in oral glucose tolerance during the menstrual cycle. *Br Med J* 2:528–529, 1968.

Jensen BK: Menstrual cycle effects on task performance examined in the context of stress research. *Acta Psychol* 50:159–178, 1982.

Jeske W, Klos J, Perkowicz J, Stopinska U: Serum prolactin in women with premenstrual syndrome. *Mater Med Pol* 12:44–46, 1980.

Johnson SR, McChesney C, Bean JA: Epidemiology of premenstrual symptoms in a nonclinical sample. I. Prevalence, natural history and help-seeking behavior. *J Reprod Med* 33:340–346, 1988.

Johnson TM: Premenstrual syndrome as a Western culture-specific disorder. *Cult Med Psychiatry* 11:337–356, 1987.

Jones BM, Jones MK, Hatcher EM: Cognitive deficits in women alcoholics as a function of gynecological status. *J Stud Alcohol* 41:140–146, 1980.

Jones DY: Influence of dietary fat on self-reported menstrual symptoms. *Physiol Behav* 40:483–487, 1987.

Jordheim O: The premenstrual syndrome. *Acta Obstet Gynecol Scand* 51:77–80, 1972.

Jungck EC, Barfield WE, Greenblatt RB: Chlorothiazide and premenstrual tension. *JAMA* 169:96–98, 1959.

Kaminer Y, Feinstein C, Barrett RP, Tylenda B, Hole W: Menstrually related mood disorder in developmentally disabled adolescents: review and current status. *Child Psychiatry Hum Dev* 18:239–249, 1988.

Kane FJ Jr, Daly RJ, Wallach MH, Keeler MH: Amelioration of premenstrual mood disturbance with a progestational agent (Enovid). *Dis Nerv Sys* May: 339–342, 1966.

Kantero RL, Widholm O: Gynecological findings in adolescence. II. The age of menarche in Finnish girls in 1969. *Acta Obstet Gynecol Scand* [Suppl] 14:7–18, 1971a.

Kantero RL, Widholm O: A statistical analysis of the menstrual patterns of 8,000 Finnish girls and their mothers. IV. Correlations of menstrual traits between adolescent girls and their mothers. *Acta Obstet Gynecol Scand* [Suppl] 14:30–36, 1971b.

Kashiwagi T, McClure JN Jr, Wetzel RD: Premenstrual affective syndrome and psychiatric disorder. *Dis Nerv Sys* 37:116–119, 1976.

Katz FH, Romfh P: Plasma aldosterone and renin activity during the menstrual cycle. *J Clin Endocrinol Metab* 34:819–821, 1972.

Kaulhausen H, Oehm W, Breuer H: Plasma renin activity during the normal menstrual cycle. *Acta Endocrinol* 173 [Suppl]:160, 1973.

Kellner R, Buckman MT, Fava GA, Rathak D: Hyperprolactinemia, distress, and hostility. *Am J Psychiatry* 141:759–763, 1984.

Kendall KE, Schnurr PP: The effects of Vitamin B_6 supplementation on premenstrual symptoms. *Obstet Gynecol* 70:145–149, 1987.

Kennedy RB, Shelton CF: The mare serum hormone in the treatment of certain endocrine dysfunctions in women. *J Mich State Med Soc* 38:209–212, 1939.

Kerr GD: The management of the premenstrual syndrome. *Curr Med Res Opin* 4:29–34, 1977.

Kerr GD, Day JB, Munday MR, Brush MG, Watson M, Taylor RW: Dydrogesterone in the treatment of the premenstrual syndrome. *Practitioner* 224:852–855, 1980.

Kessel N, Coppen A: The prevalence of common menstrual symptoms. *Lancet* 2:61–64, 1963.

Kestenberg J: Phases of adolescence with suggestions for correlation of psychic and hormonal organizations. Part II: Puberty, diffusion and reintegration. *J Am Acad Child Psychiatry* 6:577–614, 1967.

Keye WR: Medical treatment of premenstrual syndrome. *Can J Psychiatry* 30:483–488, 1985.

Keye WR: Premenstrual symptoms: evaluation and treatment. *Comprehensive Therapy* 14:19–26, 1988b.

Keye WR Jr: Premenstrual syndrome: seven steps in management. *Postgrad Med* 83:167–173, 1988a.

Keye WR, Hammond C, Strong T: Medical and psychologic characteristics of women presenting with premenstrual symptoms. *Obstet Gynecol* 68:634–636, 1986.

Keye WR, Trunnell EP: A biopsychosocial model of premenstrual syndrome. *Int J Fertil* 31:259–262, 1986.

Keye WR, Trunnel EP, Turner CW: Potential biochemical markers for premenstrual syndrome (PMS). Paper presented at the 2nd International Symposium: Premenstrual, Postpartum and Menopausal Mood Disorders, Kiawah Island, Charleston, SC, September 10, 1987, Abstract #19.

Kinch RAH: Premenstrual tension: etiology and treatment. *Clin Invest Med* 1:7–8, 1978.

Kirsch JR, Geer JH: Skin conductance and heart rate in women with premenstrual syndrome. *Psychosom Med* 50:175–182, 1988.

Klaiber EL, Broverman DM, Vogel W, Kennedy JA, Nadeau CJL: Estrogens and central nervous system function: electroencephalography, cognition and depression. In: *Behavior and the Menstrual Cycle*, ed by RC Friedman. New York, Marcel Dekker, 1982.

Klaiber EL, Broverman DM, Vogel W, Kobayashi Y, Moriarty D: Effects of estrogen therapy on plasma MAO activity and EEG driving responses of depressed women. *Am J Psychiatry* 128:1492–1498, 1972.

Klaiber EL, Kobayashi Y, Broverman DM, Hall F: Plasma monoamine oxidase activity in regularly menstruating women and in amenorrheic women receiving cyclic treatment with estrogens and a progestin. *J Clin Endocrinol Metab* 33:630–638, 1971.

Klein D: What's the latest on PMS? *Modern Bride* Feb/Mar: 214, 1988.

Kleinsasser JE: The premenstrual syndrome and its correlation to personality characteristics. *Dissertation Abstracts Int* 36(8A):5152, 1976.

Klerman GL and Deltito JA: The use of benzodiazepines in the treatment of depression. *Int Drug Ther News* 21:37–38, 1986.

Koeske RK: Theoretical and conceptual complexities in the design and analysis of menstrual cycle research. In: *The Menstrual Cycle, Vol. 2, Research and Implications for Women's Health*, ed by P Komnenich, M McSweeney, JA Noack, N Elder. New York, Springer, 1981, pp 54–70.

Koeske RK, Koeske GF: An attributional approach to mood and the menstrual cycle. *Person Soc Psychol* 31:473–478, 1975.

Kolakowska T: The clinical cause of primary recurrent depression in pharmacologically treated female patients. *Br J Psychiatry* 126:336, 1975.

Komnenich P: Hormonal influences on verbal behavior in women. *Dissertation Abstracts Int* 35:3065B, 1974.

Komnenich P, Lane DM, Dickey RP, Stone SC: Gonadal hormones and cognitive performance. *Physiol Psychol* 6:115–120, 1978.

Kopell B, Lunde D, Clayton R, Moos R, Hamburg D: Variations in some measures of arousal during the menstrual cycle. *J Nerv Ment Dis* 148:180–187, 1969.

Kramer H: A long acting diuretic suitable for outpatient treatment of fluid retention in oedema of pregnancy and the PMS. *S Afr Med J* 6:4–6, 1962.

Kramp JL: Studies on the premenstrual syndrome in relation to psychiatry. *Acta Psychiatr Scand* [Suppl] 203:261–267, 1968.

Kuczmierczyk AR, Adams HE: Autonomic arousal and pain sensitivity in women with premenstrual syndrome at different phases of the menstrual cycle. *J Psychosom Res* 30:421–428, 1986.

Kuczmierczyk AR, Adams HE, Calhoun KS, Naor S, Giombetti R, Cattalani M, McCann P: Pain responsivity in women with premenstrual syndrome across the menstrual cycle. *Percept Mot Skills* 63:387–393, 1986.

Kukopulos A, Minnai G, Muller-Oerlinghausen B: The influence of mania and depression on the pharmacokinetics of lithium: a longitudinal single case study. *J Affective Disord* 8:159–166, 1985.

Kullander S, Svanberg L: Bromocriptine treatment of the premenstrual syndrome. *Acta Obstet Gynecol Scand* 58:375–378, 1979.

Kupfer DJ: Neurophysiological 'markers': EEG sleep measures. *J Psychiatr Res* 18:467–475, 1984.

Kupfer DJ, Frank E, Grochocinski VJ, Gregor M, McEachran AB: Electroencephalographic sleep profiles in recurrent depression: a longitudinal investigation. *Arch Gen Psychiatry* 45:678–681, 1988.

Kutner SJ, Brown WL: Types of oral contraceptives, depression and premenstrual symptoms. *J Nerv Ment Dis* 155:153–162, 1972.

Labrum AH: Hypothalamic, pineal and pituitary factors in the premenstrual syndrome. *J Reprod Med* 28:438–445, 1983.

Ladisich W, Ladisich A, Langevin R, Bain J: Sensitivity to stress in the premenstruum and the effect of progestogen substitution. *Agressologie* 19:223–226, 1978.

Lahmeyer HW: Premenstrual tension: an overview of its relationship to affective psychopathology. *Integrative Psychiatry* 2:106–110, 1984.

Lahmeyer HW, Miller M, DeLeon-Jones F: Anxiety and mood fluctuation during the normal menstrual cycle. *Psychosom Med* 44:183–194, 1982.

Lalinec-Michaud M, Kovess V: Premenstrual symptoms in a general population. Abstracts, American Society for Psychosomatic Obstetrics and Gynecology sixteenth annual meeting, Meadowood, St Helena, CA, April 17–21, 1988, p 15.

Lamb WM, Ulett GA, Masters WH, Robinson DW: Premenstrual tension: EEG, hormonal, and psychiatric evaluation. *Am J Psychiatry* 109:840–848, 1953.

Landau RL, Lugibihl K: Catabolic and natriuretic effects of progesterone in man. *Rec Prog Horm Res* 17:249–292, 1961.

Laws S: The sexual politics of premenstrual tension. *Womens Stud Int Forum* 6:19–31, 1983.

Layton C: Personality and anxiety variation before and after menstruation. *Person Individ Diff* 9:691–692, 1988.

Leary PM, Batho K: Changes in electro-encephalogram related to the menstrual cycle. *So Afr Med J* 55:666, 668, 1979.

Lederer J: Premenstrual kleptomania in a case of hypothyroidism and hyperfolliculinism. *Ann D'endocrinol* 24:460–465, 1963.

Lederman M: Menstrual cycle and fluctuation in cognitive–perceptual performance. *Dissertation Abstracts Int* 35:1388B–1389B, 1974.

Lee KA: Circadian temperature rhythms in relation to menstrual cycle phase. *J Biol Rhythms* 3:255–263, 1988.

Lehninger AL: *Biochemistry.* Second Edition. New York: Worth Publishers, Inc., 1979, pp 281–282.

Leon GR, Phelan PW, Kelly JT, Patten SR: The symptoms of bulimia and the menstrual cycle. *Psychosom Med* 48:415–422, 1986.

Levitt DB, Freeman EW, Sondheimer SJ, Rickels K: Group support in the treatment of PMS. *J Psychosoc Nurs Ment Health Serv* 26:23–27, 1986.

Levitt EE, Lubin B: Some personality factors associated with menstrual complaints and menstrual attitude. *J Psychosom Res* 11:267–270, 1967.

Lewin B: Smearing of feces, menstruation and the female superego. In *Selected Writings of Bertram D. Lewin*, ed by J Arlow. New York, Psychoanalytic Quarterly Press, 1973, pp. 12–25.

Lewis LL, Chatterton RT: PMS—relationships between symptoms and cortisol, LH, and psychosocial parameters. Paper presented at the 2nd International symposium: Premenstrual, Postpartum and Menopausal Mood Disorders, Kiawah Island, Charleston, SC, September 10, 1987, Abstract #5.

Lewis SA, Burns M: Manifest dream content: changes with the menstrual cycle. Br J Med Psychol 48:375–377, 1975.

Lingjaerde P, Bredland R: Hyperestrogenic cyclic psychosis. *Acta Psychiatr Neurologica Scand* 29:355–364, 1954.

Lipman R, Covi H, Shapiro AK: The Hopkins Symptom Checklist (HSCL): factors derived from the HSCL–90. *J Affective Disord* 1:9–23, 1979.

Liskey NE: Accidents: rhythmic threat to females. *Accid Anal Prev* 4:1–11, 1972.

Little BC, Zahn TP: Changes in mood and autonomic functioning during the menstrual cycle. *Psychophysiology* 11:579–590, 1974.

Logue CM, Moos RH: Perimenstrual symptoms: prevalence and risk factors. *Psychosom Med* 48:388–414, 1986.

Logue CM, Moos RH: Premenstrual syndrome and thyroid dysfunction commentary. *Integr Psychiatry* 5:191–192, 1987.

London RS, Gundaram G, Manimekalai S, Murphy L, Reynolds M, Goldstein P: The effect of alpha-tocopherol on premenstrual symptomatology: a double blind study. Part II: Endocrine correlates. *J Am Coll Nutr* 3:351–356, 1984.

London RS, Gundaram GS, Murphy L, Goldstein PJ: The effect of alpha-tocopherol on premenstrual symptomatology: a double blind study. *J Am Coll Nutr* 2:115–122, 1983a.

London RS, Gundaram GS, Murphy L, Goldstein PJ: Evaluation and treatment of breast symptoms in patients with the premenstrual syndrome. *J Reprod Med* 28:503–508, 1983b.

London RS, Murphy L, Kitlowski KE, Reynolds MA: Efficacy of alpha-tocopherol in the treatment of PMS. *J Reprod Med* 32:400–404, 1987.

Long NZ: A crisis-coping strategy. *Emotional First Aid* 2:9–15, 1985.

Loosen PT: Psychoendocrine update. *The Psychiatric Times* (Santa Ana, CA):4(6):12, 1987.

Loucks J, Thompson H: Effect of menstruation on reaction time. *Res Q* 39:407–408, 1968.

Lovesky J: Menstruation: alternative to pharmacological therapy for menstrual distress. *J Nurse Midwifery* 23:34–44, 1978.

Lubin S: *Manual for the Depression Adjective Check List*. San Diego, CA, Educational and Industrial Testing Service, 1967.

Luce GG: *Periodic Symptoms in Sickness and Health*. New York: Pantheon, 1971, pp 231–237, 275–283.

Luggin R, Bernsted L, Peterson B, Jacobsen AT: Acute psychiatric admission related to the menstrual cycle. *Acta Psychiatr Scand* 69:461–465, 1984.

Lyon KE, Lyon MA: The premenstrual syndrome a survey of current treatment practices. *J Reprod Med* 29:705–711, 1984.

Mabray CR, Burditt ML, Martin TL, Jaynes CR, Hayes JR: Treatment of common gynecologic endocrinologic symptoms by allergy management procedures. *Obstet Gynecol* 59:560–564, 1982.

MacGregor GA, Markandu ND, Roulston JE, Jones JC, de Wardener HE: Is "idiopathic" oedema idiopathic? *Lancet* 1:397–400, 1979.

Macht DI: Further historical and experimental studies on menstrual toxin. *J Med Sci* 206:281–383, 1943.

Macht DI, Lubin DS: A phyto-pharmacological study of a menotoxin or menstrual toxin. *Proc Soc Exp Biol Med* 20:265–266, 1923.

Macht DI, Lubin DS: A phyto-pharmacological study of menstrual toxin. *J Pharmacol Exp Ther* 22:413–466, 1924.

MacKenzie TB, Wilcox K, Baron H: Lifetime prevalence of psychiatric disorders in women with perimenstrual difficulties. *J Affective Disord* 10:15–19, 1986.

MacKinnon IL, MacKinnon PCB, Thomson AD: Lethal hazards of the luteal phase of the menstrual cycle. *Br Med J* 18:1015–1017, 1959.

MacNair DM, Lorr M, Droppelman LF: *Manual for the Profile of Mood States.* San Diego, CA, Educational and Industrial Testing Service, 1971.

Maddocks S, Hahn P, Moller F, Reid RL: Trial of progesterone suppositories in the treatment of premenstrual syndrome. *Am J Obstet Gynecol* 156:1555–1556, 1987.

Maddocks S, Hahn P, Moller F, Reid RL: A double blind placebo controlled trial of progesterone vaginal suppositories in the treatment of premenstrual syndrome. *Am J Obstet Gynecol* 154:573–581, 1986.

Magos AL, Brewster E, Singh R, O'Dowd T, Brincat M: The effects of norethisterone in postmenopausal women on oestrogen replacement therapy: a model for the premenstrual syndrome. *Br J Obstet Gynaecol* 93:1290–1296, 1986a.

Magos AL, Brincat M, Studd JWW: Treatment of the premenstrual syndrome by subcutaneous oestradiol implants and cyclical oral norethisterone: placebo controlled study. *Br Med J* 292:1629–1633, 1986b.

Magos AL, Collins WP, Studd JWW: Management of the premenstrual syndrome by subcutaneous implants of oestradiol. *J Psychosom Obstet Gynecol* 3:93–99, 1984.

Magos AL, Studd J: Premenstrual uncertainties. *Lancet* 2:1301, 1983.

Magos AL, Studd JW: PMS facts and fiction. *Contemporary Obstet Gynecol* Aug:23–34, 1986.

Magos AL, Studd JW: Suicide attempts and the menstrual cycle. *Lancet* 1:217, 1987.

Magos AL, Zilkla KJ, Studd JWW: Treatment of menstrual migraine by oestradiol implants. *J Neurol, Neurosurg Psychiatry* 46:1044–1046, 1983.

Mair RG, Bouffard JA, Engen T, Morton TH: Olfactory sensitivity during the menstrual cycle. *Sensory Processes* 2:90–98, 1978.

Majewska MD: Actions of steroids on neuron: role in personality, mood, stress and disease. *Integr Psychiatry* 5:258–273, 1987a.

Majewska MD: Steroids and brain activity: essential dialogue between body and mind. *Biochem Pharmacol* 22:3781–3788, 1987b.

Malikian JE: Premenstrual changes in depressive mood, behavior and somatic functioning in hospitalized patients with depressive disorders. Ph.D. dissertation, New School for Social Research, New York, 1987.

Malmgren R, Collins A, Nilsson C-G: Platelet serotonin uptake and effects of Vitamin B_6-treatment in premenstrual tension. *Neuropsychobiology* 18:83–88, 1987.

Maloney P, Derlchman R, Wagner EE: Consistency of some personality measures as a function of stage of menstruation. *J Pers Assess* 46:597–602, 1982.

Mandell AJ, Mandell MP: Suicide and the menstrual cycle. *JAMA* 200:132–133, 1967.

Mansel RE, Pye JK, Hughes LE: A controlled trial of evening primrose oil (Efamol) in cyclic premenstrual mastalgia. Paper presented at the 2nd International Symposium: Premenstrual, Postpartum and Menopausal Mood Disorders, Kiawah Island, Charleston, SC, September 12, 1987, Abstract #47.

Marcus AJ: The eicosanoids in biology and medicine. *J Lipid Res* 25:1511–1516, 1984.

Margerison JH, Anderson W McC, Dawson J: Plasma sodium and the EEG during the menstrual cycle of normal human females. *Electroencephalogic Clin Neurophysiol* 17:540–544, 1964.

Marinari KT, Leshner AI, Doyle MP: Menstrual cycle status and adrenocortical reactivity to psychological stress. *Psychoneuroendocrinology* 2:213–218, 1976.

Marshall E: The drug of champions. *Science* 242:183–184, 1988.

Marshall E, Severino S: PMS and allergies. Unpublished manuscript, 1986.

Mason JW: The scope of psychoendocrine research. *Psychosom Med* 30[Suppl]:565–575, 1968.

Massil H, Brush M, Manku M, Morse P, Horrobin D, O'Brien PMS: Polyunsaturated fatty acid levels in premenstrual syndrome and the effect of dietary supplementation on symptoms. Paper presented at the 2nd International Symposium: Premenstrual, Postpartum and Menopausal Mood Disorders, Kiawah Island, Charleston, SC, September 12, 1987, Abstract #39.

Massil H, O'Brien PMS: Premenstrual syndrome. *Br Med J* 293:1289–1292, 1986.

Mathew RJ, Claghorn JL, Largen JW, Dobbins K: Skin temperature control for premenstrual tension syndrome: a pilot study. *Am J Clin Biofeedback* 2:7–10, 1979.

Mattsson B, von Schoultz B: A comparison between lithium, placebo and a diuretic in premenstrual tension. *Acta Psychiatr Scand* 255:75–84, 1974.

Mauri M, Reid RL, MacLean AW: Sleep disturbances in the premenstrual syndrome: the possible role of arousal. *Sleep Res* 15:196, 1986.

Mauri M, Reid RL, MacLean AW: Sleep in the premenstrual phase: a self-report study of PMS patients and normal controls. *Acta Psychiatr Scand* 78:82–86, 1988.

Maxson WS, Hargrove JT: Bioavailability of oral micronized progesterone. *Fertil Steril* 44:622–626, 1985.

Maxwell C: Sensitivity and accuracy of the Visual Analogue Scale: a psychophysical classroom experiment. *Br J Clin Pharmacol* 6:15, 1978.

May RR: Mood shifts and the menstrual cycle. *J Psychosom Res* 20:125–130, 1976.

McCance RA, Luff MC, Widdowson EE: Physical and emotional periodicity in women. *J Hygiene* 37:571–605, 1937.

McDaniel SH: The interpersonal politics of premenstrual syndrome. *Fam Sys Med* 6:134–149, 1988.

McEwen BS: Neuroendocrinology relevant to premenstrual syndromes. Paper presented at the symposium: Premenstrual Syndromes: Current Knowledge, New York Hospital–Cornell Medical Center–Westchester Division, White Plains, NY, November 6, 1985.

McEwen BS: Basic research perspective: ovarian hormone influence on brain neurochemical functions. In:*The Premenstrual Syndromes,* ed by LH Gise, NG Kase, RL Berkowitz. New York: Churchill Livingstone, 1988, pp 21–33.

McEwen BS, Biegon A, Fischette CT, Luine VN, Parsons B, Rainbow TC: Toward a neurochemical basis of steroid hormone action. *Frontiers in Neuroendocrinology* 8:153–176, 1984.

McEwen BS, Brinton RE: Neuroendocrine aspects of adaptation. In: *Progress in Brain Research,* ed by ER de Kloet, VM Wiegant, D de Wied. Elsevier Science Publishers, 1987, pp. 11–26.

McFarlane J, Martin CL, Williams TM: Mood fluctuations: women versus men and menstrual versus other cycles. *Psychology of Women Quarterly* 12:201–223, 1988.

McKenna WB: The menstrual cycle, motivation, and performance. *Dissertation Abstracts Int* 64:1391B, 1974.

McMillan MJ, Pihl RO: Premenstrual depression: a distinct entity. *J Abnorm Psychol* 96:149–154, 1987.

Meehan E, MacRae K: Legal implications of premenstrual syndrome: a Canadian perspective. *Can Med Assoc J* 135:601–607, 1986.

Mello NK: *Drug use patterns and premenstrual dysphoria,* National Institute on Drug Abuse Research Monograph Series, #65, National Institute on Drug Abuse, Bethesda, Maryland, 1986, 31–48.

Mello NK, Mendelson JH, Palmiere SL: Cigarette smoking by women: interactions with alcohol use. *Psychopharmacology* 93:8–15, 1987.

Meltzer L: Hypersensitivity to gonadal hormones. *South Med J* 56:538–542, 1963.

Menninger KA: Somatic correlations with the unconscious repudiation of femininity in women. *J Nerv Ment Dis* 89:514–527, 1939.

Messinis IE, Lolis D: Treatment of premenstrual mastalgia with tamoxifen. *Acta Obstet Gynecol Scand* 67:307–309, 1988.

Metcalf MG, Livesey JH, Hudson SM: The premenstrual syndrome before and after hysterectomy. *J Psychosom Obstet Gynecol* 9:43–50, 1988a.

Metcalf MG, Livesey JH, Hudson SM, Wells EJ: The premenstrual syndrome: moods, headaches and physical symptoms in 133 menstrual cycles. *J Psychosom Obstet Gynecol* 8:31–43, 1988b.

Miller JB: Relief of premenstrual symptoms, dysmenorrhea and contraceptive tablet intolerance. *J Med Assoc State Alabama* 44:57–60, 1974.

Millodot M, Lamont A: Influence of menstruation on corneal sensitivity. *Br J Opthalmol* 58:752–756, 1974.

Mills DE, Robertshaw D: Response of plasma prolactin to changes in ambient temperature and humidity in man. *J Clin Endocrinol Metab* 52:279–283, 1981.

Mills JC: Premenstrual syndrome: symptom, or source of transformation? *Psychol Perspectives* 19:101–110, 1988.

Mindell E: *Earl Mindell's New and Revised Vitamin Bible.* New York: Warner Books, 1988, pp 241–243.

Minors DF, Waterhouse JM: How do rhythms adjust to time shift? *J Physiol* 265:24, 1976.

Minton JP, Foecking MK, Webster DJT, Matthews RH: Response of fibrocystic disease to caffeine withdrawal and correlation of cyclic nucleotides with breast disease. *Am J Obstet Gynecol* 135:157–158, 1979.

Mira M, McNeil D, Fraser IS, Vizzard J, Abraham S: Mefenamic acid in the treatment of premenstrual syndrome. *Obstet Gynecol* 68:395–398, 1986.

Mira M, Stewart PM, Abraham SF: Nutritional and trace element status in premenstrual syndrome. *Am J Clin Nutr* 47:636–641, 1988.

Mira M, Vizzard J, Abraham S: Personality characteristics in the menstrual cycle. *J Psychosom Obstet Gynecol* 4:329–334, 1985.

Mohan V, Chopra R: Personality variations as an effect of premenstrual tensions. *Person Indiv Diff* 8:763–765, 1987.

Moline ML: Luteinizing hormone rhythms in female golden hamsters: circadian, photoperiodic and endocrine interactions. Ph.D. dissertation, Division of Medical Sciences, Harvard University, Cambridge, MA, 1981.

Moline ML, Albers HE, Moore-Ede MC: Estrogen modifies the circadian timing and amplitude of luteinizing hormone surge in female hamsters exposed to short photoperiods. *Biol Reprod* 35:516–523, 1986.

Monardo A: Premenstrual ankle edema in young girls. *JAMA* 228:900, 1974.

Moncada S, Flower RJ, Vane JR: Prostaglandins, prostacyclin, thromboxane A$_2$, and leukotrienes. In: *The Pharmacological Basis of Therapeutics*, ed by AG Gilman, LS Goodman, TW Rall, F Murad. New York, Macmillan, 1985, pp 660–673.

Montgomery JD: Variations in perception of short time intervals during menstrual cycle. *Percept Mot Skills* 49:940–942, 1979.

Moos RH: Psychological aspects of oral contraceptives. *Arch Gen Psychiatry* 19:87–94, 1968a.

Moos RH: The development of a menstrual distress questionnaire. *Psychosom Med* 30:853–867, 1968b.

Moos RH, Kopell BS, Melges FT, Yolom ID, Lunde DT, Clayton RB, Hamburg DA: Fluctuations in symptoms and moods during the menstrual cycle. *J Psychosom Res* 13:37–44, 1969.

Morley JE, Levine AS: The pharmacology of eating behavior. *Ann Rev Pharmacol Toxicol* 25:127–146, 1985.

Morris NM, Udry JR: Variations in pedometer activity during the menstrual cycle. *Obstet Gynecol* 35:199–201, 1970.

Morriss GM, Keverne EB: Premenstrual tension. *Lancet* 2:1317–1318, 1974.

Morse CA, Dennerstein L: The factor structure of symptom reports in premenstrual syndrome. *J Psychosom Res* 32:93–98, 1988.

Morse CA, Dennerstein L, Varnavides K, Burrows GD: Menstrual cycle symptoms: comparison of a non-clinical sample with a patient group. *J Affective Disord* 14:41–50, 1988.

Morton JH: Premenstrual tension. *Am J Obstet Gynecol* 60:343–352, 1950.

Morton JH: Symposium of premenstrual tension. *Int Rec Med* 166:463–464, 1953.

Morton JH, Additon H, Addison RG, Hunt L, Sullivan JJ: A clinical study of premenstrual tension. *Am J Obstet Gynecol* 65:1182–1191, 1953.

Munchel ME: The effects of symptom expectations and response styles on cognitive and perceptual–motor performance during the menstrual phase. *Dissertation Abstracts Int* 39(7–B):3532, 1979.

Munday M: Hormone levels in severe premenstrual tension. *Curr Med Res Opin* 4 (Suppl 4):16–22, 1977.

Munday MR, Brush MG, Taylor RW: Correlations between progesterone, oestradiol and aldosterone levels in the premenstrual syndrome. *Clin Endocrinol* 14:1–9, 1981.

Muse KN, Cetel NS, Futterman LA, Yen SSC: The premenstrual syndrome: effects of medical ovariectomy. *N Engl J Med* 311:1345–1349, 1984.

Myers ER, Sondheimer SJ, Freeman EW, Strauss JF, Rickels K: Serum progesterone levels following vaginal administration of progesterone during the luteal phase. *Fertil Steril* 47:71–75, 1987.

Nadelson CC, Notman M, Ellis E: Psychosomatic aspects of obstetrics and gynecology. *Psychosomatics* 24:871–875, 878–880, 882–884, 1983.

Nemeroff CB, Bissette G, Widerlov E, Beckmann H, Gerner R, Manberg PJ, Lindstrom L, Prange AJ, Gattaz WF: Neurotensin-like immunoreactivity in cerebrospinal fluid of patients with schizophrenia, depression, anorexia nervosa–bulimia, and premenstrual syndrome. *J Neuropsychiat* 1:16–20, 1989.

Nilsson LC, Eriksson E, Carlsson M, Soderpalm B: Clonidine for relief of premenstrual syndrome. *Lancet* 2:549–550, 1985.

Noel GL, Suh HK, Frantz AG: L-dopa suppression of TRH-stimulated prolactin release in man. *J Clin Endocrinol Metab* 36:1255–1258, 1973.

Noel GL, Suh HK, Frantz AG: Prolactin release during nursing and breast stimulation in postpartum and nonpostpartum subjects. *J Clin Endocrinol Metab* 38:413–423, 1974.

Nokin J, Vekemans M, L'Hermite M, Robyn C: Circadian periodicity of serum prolactin concentrations in man. *Br Med J* 3:561–562, 1972.

Norris RV: Progesterone for premenstrual tension. *J Reprod Med* 28:509–516, 1983.

Notman M: The psychoanalytic approach. In: *Premenstrual Tension: A Multidisciplinary Approach*, ed by C Debrovner. New York: Human Sciences Press, 1982, pp. 51–69.

Notman MT: Menarche: a psychoanalytic perspective. In: *Menarche*, ed by S Golub. Lexington, MA: Lexington Books, 1983, pp. 271–278.

Notman MT, Nadelson C: Fertility and reproduction. *J Psychiatr Educ* 1:37–44, 1983.

Oakes RT: PMS: a plea bargain in Brooklyn does not a rule of law make. *Hamline Law Review* 9:203–217, 1986.

O'Boyle M, Severino SK, Hurt SW: Premenstrual syndrome and locus of control. *Int J Psychiatry Med* 18:67–74, 1988.

O'Brien PMS: The premenstrual syndrome: a review of the present status of therapy. *Drugs* 24:140–151, 1982.

O'Brien PMS: *Premenstrual Syndrome.* Boston, Blackwell Scientific Publications, 1987.

O'Brien PMS, Craven D, Selby C, Symonds EM: Treatment of premenstrual syndrome by spironolactone. *Br J Obstet Gynaecol* 86:142–147, 1979.

O'Brien PMS, Selby C, Symonds EM: Progesterone, fluid, and electrolytes in premenstrual syndrome. *Br Med J* 1:1161–1163, 1980.

O'Brien PMS, Symonds EM: Prolactin levels in the premenstrual syndrome. *Br J Obstet Gynaecol* 89:306–308, 1982.

O'Donohue TL, Chronwall BM, Pruss RM, Mezey E, Kiss JZ, Eiden LE, Massani VJ, Tessel RE, Pickel VM, DiMaggio DA, Hotchkiss AJ, Crowley WR, Zukowska-Grojec Z: Neuropeptide Y and peptide YY neuronal and endocrine systems. *Peptides* 6:755–768, 1985.

Okey R, Robb EI: Studies of metabolism of women. Part I: Variations in the fasting blood sugar level and in sugar tolerance in relation to the menstrual cycle. *J Biol Chem* 65:165–186, 1925.

Oleck H: Legal aspects of premenstrural [sic] tension. *Int Rec Med* 166:492–501, 1953.

O'Neil MK, Lancee WJ, Freeman SJJ: Fluctuations in mood and psychological distress during the menstrual cycle. *Can J Psychiatry* 29:373–377, 1984.

Osborn M: Physical and psychological determinants of premenstrual tension: research issues and a proposed methodology. *J Psychosom Res* 25:363–367, 1981.

Osborn M: Premenstrual syndrome in ovulating hysterectomized women. Unpublished manuscript, 1987a.

Osborn M: Psychiatric and menstrual factors in premenstrual syndrome. Unpublished manuscript, 1987b.

Osmun JN, Steiner M, Haskett RF: Psychosocial aspects of severe premenstrual tension. *Int J Womens Studies* 6:65–70, 1983.

Osofsky HJ, Keppel W, Kuczmierczyk AR: Evaluation and management of premenstrual syndrome in clinical psychiatric practice. *J Clin Psychiatry* 49:494–498, 1988.

Paddison P, Gise LH, Lebovits A, Strain JJ: Premenstrual syndrome associated with a history of sexual abuse: differences between lower and higher socioeconomic groups. Abstracts, American Society for Psychosomatic Obstetrics and Gynecology sixteenth annual meeting, Meadowood, St. Helena, CA, April 17–21, 1988, p 21.

Paige K: Effects of oral contraceptives on affective fluctuations associated with the menstrual cycle. *Psychosom Med* 33:515–537, 1971.

Paige KE: Women learn to sing the menstrual blues. *Psychol Today* 7:41–46, 1972.

Pallis DJ, Holding TA: The menstrual cycle and suicide intent. *J Biosoc Sci* 8:27–33, 1976.

Palomaki JF: Exacerbation of asthma: premenstrual syndrome in husband? *JAMA* 259:2609, 1988.

Papy JJ, Conte-Devolx B, Sormani J, Porto R, Guillaume U: Syndrome d'hypersomnie periodique avec megaphagia chez une jeune femme, rythme par le cycle menstruel. *Rev EEG Neurophysiol* 12:54–61, 1982.

Pariser SF, Stern SL, Shank ML, Falko JM, O'Shaughnessy RW, Friedman CI: Premenstrual syndrome: concerns, controversies, and treatment. *Am J Obstet Gynecol* 153:599–604, 1985.

Parker DC, Rossman LG, Van der Laau EF: Sleep related, nyctothemeral and briefly episodic variation in human plasma prolactin concentrations. *J Clin Endocrinol Metab* 36:1119–1124, 1973.

Parlee MB: The premenstrual syndrome. *Psychological Bull* 80:454–465, 1973.

Parlee MB: Stereotypic beliefs about menstruation—a methodological note on the Moos Menstrual Distress Questionnaire and some new data. *Psychosom Med* 36:229–240, 1974.

Parlee MB: Psychobiological aspects: changes in food cravings, moods and behavior. Paper presented at the symposium: Premenstrual Syndromes: Current Knowledge, The New York Hospital–Cornell Medical Center–Westchester Division, White Plains, NY, November 6, 1985.

Parry BL, Rosenthal NE, Tamarkin L, Wehr TA: Treatment of a patient with seasonal premenstrual syndrome. *Am J Psychiatry* 144:762–766, 1987.

Parry BL, Rosenthal NE, Wehr TA: Research techniques used to study premenstrual syndrome. In: *Premenstrual Syndrome: Current Findings & Future Directions,* ed by HJ Osofsky, SJ Blumenthal. Washington, DC, American Psychiatric Association Press, 1985, p 88.

Parry BL, Wehr TA: Therapeutic effect of sleep deprivation in patients with premenstrual syndrome. *Am J Psychiatry* 144:808–810, 1987.

Parry GJ, Bredesen DE: Sensory neuropathy with low-dose pyridoxine. *Neurology* 35:1466–1468, 1985.

Patel S, Cliff KS, Machin D: The premenstrual syndrome and its relationship to accidents. *Public Health* 99:45–50, 1985.

Patkai P, Johannson G, Post G: Mood, alertness, and sympathetic-adrenal medullary activity during the menstrual cycle. *Psychosom Med* 36:503–512, 1974.

Patkai P, Petterson K: Psychophysiological correlates of premenstrual tension. *Reports from the Department of Psychiatry, University of Stockholm* 466:16, 1975.

Patterson ET, Hale ES: Making sure: integrating menstrual care practices into activities of daily living. *ANS* April:18–31, 1985.

Paul LH, Halbreich U: Premenstrual impairment in cognitive function. Abstract, American Society for Psychosomatic Obstetrics and Gynecology, Seventeenth Annual Meeting, Orlando, Florida, April 12–16, 1989, p. 23.

Paulson M: Psychological concomitants of premenstrual tension. *Am J Obstet Gynecol* 81:733–738, 1961.

Pearlstein T, Thoft J, Rubinstein D, Rivera-Tovar A, Frank E: Lifetime psychiatric diagnosis in women with prospectively confirmed premenstrual syndrome. Paper presented at the 2nd International Symposium: Premenstrual, Postpartum and Menopausal Mood Disorders, Kiawah Island, Charleston, SC, September 10, 1987, Abstract #20.

Peck SD: Can increased beta-endorphins explain the etiology of premenstrual syndrome? *J Am Osteopath Assoc* 82:192–197, 1982.

Pennington VM: Meprobamate (Miltown) in premenstrual tension. *JAMA* 164:638–640, 1957.

Persky H: Reproductive hormones, moods, and the menstrual cycle. In: *Sex Differences in Behavior,* ed by R Friedman. New York, Wiley, 1974, pp 455–466.

Pfaff DW, McEwen BS: Actions of estrogens and progestins on nerve cells. *Science* 219:808–814, 1983.

Physicians' Desk Reference, ed by BB Huff, AL Dowd. Oradell, New Jersey: Medical Economics Company Inc., 1987.

Physicians' Desk Reference, ed by BB Huff, AL Dowd. Oradell, New Jersey: Medical Economics Company Inc., 1988.

Pierson WR, Lockhart A: Effect of menstruation on simple reaction and movement time. *Br Med J* 1:796–797, 1963.

Piesse JW: Nutrition factors in the premenstrual syndrome. *Int Clin Nutr Rev* 4:54–81, 1984.

Post RM, Ballenger JC: Kindling models for the progressive development of psychopathology: sensitization to electrical, pharmacological, and psychological stimuli. In: *Handbook of Biological Psychiatry, Part IV, Brain Mechanisms and Abnormal Behavior—Chemistry,* ed by HM Van Praag. New York, Marcel Dekker, 1981, pp 609–651.

Posthuma BW, Bass MJ, Bull SB, Nisker JA: Detecting changes in functional ability in women with premenstrual syndrome. *Am J Obstet Gynecol* 156:275–278, 1987.

Preece PE, Richards AR, Owen GM, Hughes LE: Mastalgia and total body water. *Br Med J* 4:498–500, 1975.

Price WA, DiMarzio LR: Premenstrual tension syndrome in rapid-cycling bipolar affective disorder. *J Clin Psychiatry* 48:415–417, 1986.

Price WA, DiMarzio LR: Bulimia, menstruation, and PMS: treatment implication [letter to editor]. *Am J Psychiatry* 145:1178–1179, 1988.

Price WA, DiMarzio LR, Eckert JL: Correlation between PMS and alcoholism among women. *Ohio State Medical J* 83:201–202, 1987a.

Price WA, DiMarzio LR, Gardner PR: Biopsychosocial approach to premenstrual syndrome. *Am Fam Physician* 33:117–122, 1986.

Price WA, Giannini AJ: The use of clonidine in premenstrual tension syndrome. *J Clin Pharmacol* 24:463–465, 1984.

Price WA, Giannini AJ: Antidepressant effects of estrogen. *J Clin Psychiatry* 46:506, 1985.

Price WA, Giannini AJ: Verapamil in the treatment of premenstrual syndrome: a case report. *J Clin Psychiatry* 47:213–214, 1986.

Price WA, Giannini AJ, Seng CS: Use of L-tryptophan in the treatment of premenstrual tension: a case report. *Psychiatric Forum* 13:44–46, 1984–85.

Price WA, Torem MS, DiMarzio LR: Premenstrual exacerbation of bulimia. *Psychosomatics* 28:378–379, 1987b.

Prichard JC: *A Treatise on Insanity and Other Disorders Affecting the Mind.* Philadelphia, Haswell, Burlington and Haswell, 1837, pp 156–157.

Prior JC: Is premenstrual syndrome exaggerated molimina? *Am J Psychiatry* 141:1495, 1984.

Prior JC, Vigna Y: Conditioning exercise and premenstrual symptoms. *J Reprod Med* 32:423–428, 1987.

Prior JC, Vigna Y, Sciarretta D, Alojado N, Schulzer M: Conditioning exercise decreases premenstrual symptoms: a prospective controlled 6-month trial. *Fertil Steril* 47:402–408, 1987.

Psychiatric News: Alprazolam found to have side effects. July 15:8, 1988.

Puolakka J, Makarainen L, Viinikka L, Ylikorkala O: Biochemical and clinical effects of treating the premenstrual syndrome with prostaglandin synthesis precursors. *J Reprod Med* 30:149–153, 1985.

Quigley ME, Ropert JF, Yen SSC: Acute prolactin release triggered by feeding. *J Clin Endocrinol Metab* 52:1043–1045, 1981.

Quigley ME, Yen SSC: The role of endogenous opiates on LH secretion during the menstrual cycle. *J Clin Endocrinol Metab* 51:179, 1980.

Rapkin AJ, Buckman TD, Stuphin MS, Chang LC, Reading AE. Platelet monoamine oxidase B activity in women with premenstrual syndrome. *Am J Obstet Gynecol* 159:1536–1540, 1988a.

Rapkin AJ, Chang LC, Reading AE: Comparison of retrospective and prospective assessment of premenstrual symptoms. *Psychol Rep* 62:55–60, 1988b.

Rapkin AJ, Edelmuth E, Chang LC, Reading AE, McGuire MT, Su T-P: Whole-blood serotonin in premenstrual syndrome. *Obstet Gynecol* 70:533–537, 1987.

Rattray MD: Marital satisfaction and premenstrual syndrome. Ph.D. dissertation, Western Conservative Baptist Seminary, 1986.

Rausch JL, Janowsky DS: Premenstrual tension: etiology. In: *Behavior and the Menstrual Cycle,* ed by RC Friedman. New York: Marcel Dekker, 1982, pp 397–427.

Rausch JL, Janowsky DS, Golshan S, Kuhn K, Risch SC: Atenolol treatment of late luteal phase dysphoric disorder. *J Affective Dis* 15:141–147, 1988.

Rausch JL, Janowsky SC, Risch SC, Golshan S, Kuhn K: Mood and hormonal effects of atenolol in premenstrual tension. Paper presented at the 2nd International Symposium: Premenstrual, Postpartum and Menopausal Mood Disorders, Kiawah Island, Charleston, SC, September 9–13, 1987, Abstract #45.

Rausch JL, Shah NS, Burch EA, Donald AG: Platelet serotonin uptake in depressed patients: circadian effect. *Biol Psychiatry* 17:121–123, 1981.

Ray I: The insanity of women produced by desertion or seduction. *Am J Insanity* 23:263–274, 1866.

Reame NE, Marshall JC, Kelch RP: The role of central endogenous opiate activity in premenstrual syndrome (PMS). Abstract, American Society for Psychosomatic Obstetrics and Gynecology, Seventeenth Annual Meeting, Orlando, Florida, April 12–16, 1989, p. 24.

Rees L: The premenstrual tension syndrome and its treatment. *Br Med J* 1:1014–1016, 1953a.

Rees L: Psychosomatic aspects of the premenstrual tension syndrome. *J Ment Sci* 99:62–73, 1953b.

Reeves BD, Garvin JE, McElin TW: Premenstrual tension: symptoms and weight changes related to potassium therapy. *Am J Obstet Gynecol* 109:1036–1041, 1971.

Reich M: The variations in urinary aldosterone levels of normal females during the menstrual cycle. *Aust Ann Med* 11:41–49, 1962.

Reid RL: Premenstrual syndrome. In: *Current Problems in Obstetrics, Gynecology and Fertility*, ed by JM Leventhal, JJ Hoffman, LG Keith, PJ Taylor. Chicago, Year Book Medical Publishers, 1985, p 28.

Reid RL, Greenaway-Coates A, Hahn PM: Oral glucose tolerance during the menstrual cycle in normal women and women with alleged premenstrual "hypoglycemic" attacks: effects of naloxone. *J Clin Endocrinol Metab* 62:1167–1172, 1986.

Reid RL, Hoff JD, Yen SSC, Li CH: Effects of exogenous beta endorphin on pituitary hormone secretion and its disappearance rate in normal human subjects. *J Clin Endocrinol Metab* 52:1179–1184, 1981.

Reid RL, Maddocks SE: A positive approach to PMS. *Contemporary Obstet Gynecol* Apr:41–54, 1987.

Reid RL, Yen SSC: Premenstrual syndrome. *Am J Obstet Gynecol* 139:85–104, 1981.

Reid RL, Yen SSC: The premenstrual syndrome. *Clinical Obstet Gynecol* 26:710–718, 1983.

Reynolds RD, Leklem JE: Implications on the role of Vitamin B_6 in health and disease—a summary. In: *Vitamin B_6: Its Role in Health and Disease*, ed by RD Reynolds, JE Leklem. New York: Alan R. Liss, 1985, pp 481–489.

Ribeiro WO, Mishell DR, Thorneycroft IH: Comparison of the patterns of androstenedione, progesterone, and estradiol during the human menstrual cycle. *Am J Obstet Gynecol* 119:1026–1032, 1974.

Richter MA, Haltvick R, Shapiro SS: Progesterone treatment of premenstrual syndrome. *Curr Ther Res* 36:840–850, 1984.

Rierdan J, Koff E: Representation of the female body by early and late adolescent girls. *J Youth Adol* 9:339–346, 1980.

Riggs L, Melton LJ: Involutional osteoporosis. *N Engl J Med* 314:1676–1686, 1986.

Riley TL: Premenstrual syndrome as a legal defense. *Hamline Law Review* 9:193–202, 1986.

Roberts HJ: Perspective on Vitamin E as therapy. *Sourcebook on Food and Nutrition*, ed by IS Scarpa, HC Kiefer, R Tatum. Chicago: Marquis Academic Media, 1982, pp 99–101.

Robinson K, Huntington KM, Wallace MG: Treatment of premenstrual syndrome. *Br J Obstet Gynaecol* 84:784–788, 1977.

Rodin J: Menstruation, reattribution and competence. *J Pers Soc Psychol* 33:345–353, 1976.

Rogers WC: The role of endocrine allergy in the production of premenstrual tension. *West J Surg Obstet Gynecol* 70:100–102, 1962.

Rojansky N, Halbreich U, Carson S, Perel J, Paul L: Hormonal response to tryptophan along the premenstrual period. Abstract, American Society for Psychosomatic Obstetrics and Gynecology, Seventeenth Annual Meeting, Orlando, Florida, April 12–16, 1989, p. 52.

Rose DP: The interactions between Vitamin B_6 and hormones. *Vitam Horm* 36:53, 1978.

Rosen LN, Moghadam LZ, Endicott J: Psychosocial correlates of premenstrual dysphoric subtypes. *Acta Psychiatr Scand* 77:446–453, 1988.

Rosenthal NE, Sack DA, Gillin JC, Lewy AJ, Goodwin FK, Davenport Y, Muller PS, Newsome DA, Wehr TA: Seasonal Affective Disorder: a description of the syndrome and preliminary findings with light therapy. *Arch Gen Psychiatry* 41:72–80, 1984.

Rosseinsky DR, Hall PG: An evolutionary theory of premenstrual tension. *Lancet* 2:1024, 1974.

Rossignol AM: Caffeine-containing beverages and premenstrual syndrome in young women. *Am J Public Health* 75:1335–1337, 1985.

Rossignol AM, Zhang JY, Chen YZ, Xiang Z: Tea and premenstrual syndrome in the People's Republic of China. *Am J Pub Health* 79:67–69, 1989.

Rotter JB: Generalized expectancies for internal versus external control of reinforcement. *Psycholog Monogr* 80, (Whole #609):1, 1966.

Rouse P: Premenstrual tension: a study using the Moos Menstrual Questionnaire. *J Psychosom Res* 22:215–222, 1978.

Roy SK, Ghosh BP, Bhattacharjee SK: Changes in oral glucose tolerance during normal menstrual cycle. *J Indian Med Assoc* 57:201–205, 1971.

Roy-Byrne PR, Hoban MC, Rubinow DR: The relationship of menstrually related mood disorders to psychiatric disorders. In: *Clinical Obstetrics and Gynecology*, ed by SR Johnson. Hagerstown, MD, Lippincott, 1987a, pp 386–395.

Roy-Byrne PR, Rubinow DR, Gold PW, Post RM: Possible antidepressant effect of oral contraceptives: case report. *J Clin Psychiatry* 45:350–352, 1984.

Roy-Byrne PR, Rubinow DR, Gwirtsman H, Hoban MC, Grover GN: Cortisol response to dexamethasone in women with premenstrual syndrome. *Neuropsychobiology* 16:61–63, 1986a.

Roy-Byrne PR, Rubinow DR, Hoban MC, Grover GN, Blank D: TSH and prolactin responses to TRH in patients with premenstrual syndrome. *Am J Psychiatry* 144:480–484, 1987b.

Roy-Byrne PR, Rubinow DR, Hoban MC, Parry B, Rosenthal NE, Nurnberger JI, Byrnes S: Premenstrual changes: a comparison of five populations. *Psychiatry Res* 17:77–85, 1986b.

Rubenstein BB: Premenstrual headache relieved by estrogen therapy. *J Clin Endocrinol* 2:700–702, 1942.

Rubinow DR: Assessment and treatment of women with premenstrual syndromes. Paper presented at the symposium: Premenstrual Syndromes: Current Knowledge, New York Hospital–Cornell Medical Center–Westchester Division, White Plains, NY, November 6, 1985.

Rubinow DR: In Diagnosis of PMS depends on much more than a list of symptoms. *Psychiatric News* Nov 6:12–23, 1987a.

Rubinow DR: If Vitamin B_6 ineffective in PMS, therapy 'pharmacologic roulette.' *Obstet Gynecol News* Dec 15–31:1, 23, 1987b.

Rubinow DR, Hoban MC, Grover GN: Menstrually related mood disorders. *Adv Biochem Pharmacol* 43:335–346, 1987.

Rubinow DR, Hoban MC, Grover GN, Galloway DS, Roy-Byrne P, Andersen R, Menrain GR: Changes in plasma hormones across the menstrual cycle in patients with menstrually related mood disorder and in control subjects. *Am J Obstet Gynecol* 158:5–11, 1988.

Rubinow DR, Roy-Byrne P: Premenstrual syndromes: overview from a methodologic perspective. *Am J Psychiatry* 141:163–172, 1984a.

Rubinow DR, Roy-Byrne P: Is premenstrual syndrome exaggerated molimina: reply. *Am J Psychiatry* 141:1495–1496, 1984b.

Rubinow DR, Roy-Byrne P, Hoban MC, Grover GN, Stambler N, Post RM: Premenstrual mood changes: characteristic patterns in women with and without premenstrual syndromes. *J Affective Disord* 10:85–90, 1986.

Rubinow DR, Schmidt PJ: Mood disorders and the menstrual cycle. *J Reprod Med* 32:389–394, 1987a.

Rubinow DR, Schmidt PJ: Premenstrual syndrome and thyroid dysfunction commentary. *Integr Psychiatry* 5:187–189, 1987b.

Rubinow DR, Schmidt PJ: Models for the development and expression of symptoms in premenstrual syndrome. *Psychiatr Clin N Am* 12:53–68, 1989.

Ruble DN: Premenstrual symptoms: a reinterpretation. *Science* 197:291–292, 1977.

Ruble DN, Brooks-Gunn J: Menstrual symptoms: a social cognitive analysis. *J Behav Med* 2:171–194, 1979.

Russell GFM: Premenstrual tension and "psychogenic" amenorrhea: psycho-physical interactions. *J Psychosom Res* 16:279–287, 1972.

Russell JW, Coleman GJ, Hart WG: Validation of a modified version of the Menstrual Distress Questionnaire: a case for false attribution? *J Psychosom Obstet Gynecol* 8:19–29, 1988.

Sampson GA: Premenstrual syndrome: a double-blind controlled trial of progesterone and placebo. *Br J Psychiatry* 135:209–215, 1979.

Sampson GA, Heathcote PRM, Wordsworth J, Prescott P, Hodgson A: Premenstrual syndrome. A double-blind cross-over study of treatment with dydrogesterone and placebo. *Br Med J* 153:232–235, 1988.

Sanchez-Franco F, Garcia MD, Cacicedo L, Martin-Zurro A, Escobar del Rey F: Influence of sex phase of the menstrual cycle on thyrotropin (TSH) response to thyrotropin-releasing hormone (TRH). *J Clin Endocrinol Metab* 37:736–740, 1973.

Sandberg DP, Endicott J: Premenstrual changes in anxiety patients. *New Research Program and Abstracts*. Washington, DC, Burroughs Wellcome, 1986, p. 35.

Sandberg DP, Harrison W, Gorman J, Nee J, Endicott J: Sodium lactate and carbon dioxide vulnerability in women with premenstrual dysphoria. Abstract presented at the 26th Annual Meeting of Neuropsychopharmacology, San Juan, Puerto Rico, December, 1987, p. 126.

Sanders D, Warner P, Backstrom T, Bancroft J: Mood, sexuality, hormones and the menstrual cycle. Part I: Changes in mood and physical state: description of subjects and methods. *Psychosom Med* 45:487–501, 1983.

Sarason IG, Sarason BR, Potter EH, Antoni MH: Life events, social support, and illness. *Psychosom Med* 47:156–163, 1985.

Sarno AP Jr, Miller EJ Jr, Lundblad EG: Premenstrual syndrome: beneficial effects of periodic, low dose danazol. *Obstet Gynecol* 70:33–36, 1987.

Sassin JF, Frantz AG, Kapin S, Weitzman ED: Human prolactin: 24-hour pattern with increased release during sleep. *Science* 117:1205–1207, 1972.

Scambler A, Scambler G: Menstrual symptoms, attitudes and consulting behavior. *Soc Sci Med* 20:1065–1068, 1985.

Schaumberg H, Kaplan J, Windebank A, Vick N, Rasmus S, Pleasure D, Brown MJ: Sensory neuropathy from pyridoxine abuse. A new megavitamin syndrome. *N Engl J Med* 309:445–448, 1983.

Schick A: On premenstrual depression. *Am J Psychotherapy* 7:664–671, 1953.

Schinfeld JS: PMS and candidiasis: study explores possible link. *Female Patient* 12:66–74, 1987.

Schmidt HJ: The use of progesterone in the treatment of post-partum psychosis. *JAMA* 121:190–192, 1943.

Schmidt PJ, Hoban MC, Rubinow DR: State dependent alterations in the perception of life events in premenstrual syndrome (PMS). Paper presented at the 2nd International Symposium: Premenstrual, Postpartum and Menopausal Mood Disorders, Kiawah Island, Charleston, SC, September 11, 1987a, Abstract #31.

Schmidt PJ, Kahn RA, Rubinow DR: Thyroid function in premenstrual syndrome. *N Engl J Med* 317(24):1537–1538, 1987b.

Schnurr PP: Some correlates of prospectively defined premenstrual syndrome. *Am J Psychiatry* 145:491–494, 1988.

Schrijver J, Louwerse ES, Bruinse HW, Van den Berg H: Increased urinary MHPG excretion in premenstrual syndrome (PMS). The effect of Vitamin B_6. *J Psychosom Obstet Gynecol* 6:179–186, 1987.

Schubert GW, Meyer RC, Washer SH: Responses to short-duration signals, pre and postmenses, in subjects using oral contraceptives and subjects not using oral contraceptives. *J Am Audiological Soc* 1:112–118, 1975.

Schuckit MA, Daly V, Herrman G, Hineman S: Premenstrual symptoms and depression in a university population. *Dis Nerv Sys* 36:515–517, 1975.

Schwank JCH: The menstrual cycle and performance on various laboratory tasks. Unpublished manuscript, 1971a.

Schwank JCH: The role of the menstrual cycle on human female behavior. Unpublished manuscript, 1971b.

Schwartz JC, Pollard H, Llorens C, Malfroy B, Gros C, Pradelles P, Dray F: Endorphins and endorphin receptors in striatum: relationships with dopaminergic neurons. In: *Advances in Biochemical Psychopharmacology*, Vol. 18, ed by E Costa, M Trabucci. New York, Raven, 1978, p 245.

Schwartz UD, Abraham GE: Corticosterone and aldosterone levels during the menstrual cycle. *Obstet Gynecol* 45:339–342, 1975.

Seagull EA: An investigation of personality differences between women with high and low premenstrual tension. *Dissertation Abstracts Int* 34(9B):4675, 1974.

Segal E, Soroka A, Schechter A: Correlative relationship between adherence of *Candida albicans* to human epithelial cells *in vitro* and candidal vaginitis. *Sabouraudia: J Med Veterinary Mycology* 22:191–220, 1984.

Selye, H: *Stress without Distress*. New York, Lippincott, 1974.

Severino SK: The psychoanalyst in a bio-medical world: new opportunities for understanding women. *Academy Forum* 32:10–12, 1988.

Severino SK: Paranoid and dangerous. In: *Diagnostic and Statistical Manual of Mental Disorders, Third Edition Revised*. Wasington DC: American Psychiatric Association, 1989, pp. 94–96.

Severino SK, Bucci W, Creelman N: Menstrual cycle effects on information processing in sleep and dreams. *J Acad Psychoanal* (in press).

Severino S, Hurt SW, Anderson M, Williams NA: Premenstrual dysphoria according to DSM-III-R. *New Research Abstracts*. American Psychiatric Association, 1986, p. 35.

Severino SK, Hurt SW, Eckerd MB: PMS: relationship to personality disorders. Paper presented at the World Psychiatric Association Regional Symposium, Washington, DC, October 14, 1988.

Severino SK, Hurt SW, Shindledecker R: Spectral analysis of cyclic symptoms in 58 women over two menstrual cycles. Paper presented at the 2nd International Symposium: Premenstrual, Postpartum and Menopausal Mood Disorders, Kiawah Island, Charleston, SC, September 10, 1987b, Abstract #24.

Severino SK, Hurt SW, Shindledecker RD: Late luteal phase dysphoric disorder: spectral analysis of cyclic symptoms. *Am J Psychiatry* (in press), 1989.

Severino SK, Wagner DR, Moline ML, Hurt SW, Shindledecker RD: Premenstrual syndrome: a chronobiological view. Paper presented at the 2nd International Symposium: Premenstrual, Postpartum and Menopausal Mood Disorders, Kiawah Island, Charleston, SC, September 10, 1987a, Abstract #14.

Shader RI, Harmatz JS: Molindone: a pilot evaluation during the premenstruum. *Curr Ther Res* 17:403–406, 1975.

Shainess N: A re-evaluation of some aspects of femininity through a study of menstruation: a preliminary report. *Compr Psychiatry* 2:20–26, 1961.

Shangold MM, Shangold GA: "Premenstrual tension: an overview of its relationship to affective psychopathology": commentary. *Integr Psychiatry* 2:112–113, 1984.

Sheldrake P, Cormack M: Variations in menstrual cycle symptom reporting. *J Psychosom Res* 20:169–177, 1976.

Shelley WB, Preucel RW, Spoont SS: Autoimmune progesterone dermatitis: cure by oophorectomy. *JAMA* 190:147–150, 1964.

Shen WW: A note on menstruation and hospital admission date of intoxicated women. *Biol Psychiatry* 19:1133–1136, 1984.

Sherwood RA, Rocks BF, Stewart A, Saxton RS: Magnesium and the premenstrual syndrome. *Ann Clin Biochem* 23:667–670, 1986.

Short RV: The control of menstruation. *Br J Hosp Med* May:552–555, 1974a.

Short RV: A study of the prevalence of common menstrual symptoms in nurses attending block teaching in the Royal Infirmary, Edinburgh. Unpublished paper, 1974b.

Siegel JM, Johnson JH, Sarason IG: Life changes and menstrual discomfort. *Human Stress* 5:41–46, 1979.

Siegel JP: Mental dynamics of women with premenstrual tension syndrome. *Fam Systems Med* 4:358–366, 1986.

Siegel JP, Myers BJ, Dineen MK: Comparison of depressed and nondepressed women with severe premenstrual tension syndrome. *Psychother Psychosom* 45:113–117, 1986.

Siegel JP, Myers BJ, Dineen MK: Premenstrual tension syndrome symptom clusters: statistical evaluation of the subsyndromes. *J Reprod Med* 32:395–399, 1987.

Siegler SL: Further experiences with the hormone of pregnant mare serum. *Endocrinology* 27:387–391, 1940.

Silbergeld S, Brast N, Noble EP: The menstrual cycle: a double-blind study of symptoms, mood and behavior and biochemical variables using enovid and placebo. *Psychosom Med* 33:411–428, 1971.

Silverman E-M, Zimmer CH: Speech fluency fluctuations during the menstrual cycle. *J Speech Hear Res* 18:202–206, 1975.

Silverman E-M, Zimmer CH: Replication of "speech fluency fluctuations during the menstrual cycle." *Percept Mot Skills* 42:1004–1006, 1976.

Silverman EM, Zimmer CH, Silverman FH: Variability of stutterers' speech disfluency: the menstrual cycle. *Percept Mot Skills* 38:1037–1038, 1974.

Simkins S: Use of massive doses of Vitamin A in the treatment of hyperthyroidism. *J Clin Endocrinol* 7:574–585, 1947.

Simmons K: Possible new relief for PMS. *JAMA* 250:1371–1375, 1983.

Simpson LO: The etiopathogenesis of premenstrual syndrome as a consequence of altered blood rheology: a new hypothesis. *Med Hypothesis* 25:189–195, 1988.

Singer K, Cheng R, Schou M: A controlled evaluation of lithium in the premenstrual tension syndrome. *Br J Psychiatry* 124:50–51, 1973.

Sitruk-Ware R, Bricaire C, Lignieres B, Yaneva H, Mauvais-Jarvis P: Oral micronized progesterone. *Contraception* 36:373–402, 1987.

Slade P: Premenstrual emotional changes in normal women: fact or fiction? *J Psychosom Res* 28:1–7, 1984.

Slade P, Jenner FA: Autonomic activity in subjects reporting changes in affect in the menstrual cycle. *Br J Soc Clin Psychol* 18:135–136, 1979.

Slade P, Jenner FA: Attitudes to female roles, aspects of menstruation and complaining of menstrual symptoms. *Br J Soc Clin Psychol* 19:109–113, 1980a.

Slade P, Jenner FA: Performance tests in different phases of the menstrual cycle. *J Psychosom Res* 24:5–8, 1980b.

Slater JE, Raphael G, Cutler GB, Loriaux DL, Meggs WJ, Kaliner M: Recurrent anaphylaxis in menstruating women: treatment with a luteinizing hormone-releasing hormone agonist—a preliminary report. *Obstet Gynecol* 70:542–546, 1987.

Sletten IW, Gershon J: The premenstrual syndrome: a discussion of its pathophysiology and treatment with lithium ion. *Compr Psychiatry* 7:197–206, 1966.

Sloan AW: Effect of training on physical fitness of women students. *J App Physiol* 16:267–269, 1961.

Smith AJ: Menstruation and industrial efficiency. Part I: Absenteeism and activity level. *J App Pyschol* 34:1–5, 1950a.

Smith AJ: Menstruation and industrial efficiency. Part II: Quality and quantity of production. *J App Psychol* 34:148–152, 1950b.

Smith CK, Cullison SW, Polis E, Holmes T: Life change and illness onset: importance of concepts for family physicians. *J Fam Pract* 7:975–981, 1978.

Smith MA, Yougkin EQ: Managing the premenstrual syndrome. *Clin Pharm* 5:788–797, 1986.

Smith S, Rinehart JS, Ruddock VE, Schiff I: Treatment of premenstrual syndrome with alprazolam: results of a double-blind, placebo-controlled randomized crossover clinical trial. *Obstet Gynecol* 70:37–42, 1987.

Smith SL: Mood in the menstrual cycle. In: *Topics in Psychoendocrinology*, ed by EJ Sacher. New York, Grune & Stratton, 1975.

Smith SL, Saunder C: Food cravings, depression, and premenstrual problems. *Psychosom Med* 31:281–287, 1969.

Sneddon JM: Blood platelets as a model for monoamine-containing neurons. In: *Progress in Neurobiology*, Vol. I, Part 2, ed by GA Kerkart, JW Phyllis. Oxford, Pergamon, 1973, pp 151–198.

Snyder DB: The relationship of the menstrual cycle to certain aspects of perceptual cognitive functioning. *Dissertation Abstracts Int* 39(2-B):962–963, 1978.

Somerville BW: The role of estradiol withdrawal in the etiology of menstrual migraine. *Neurology* 27:355–365, 1972.

Sommer B: Menstrual cycle changes and intellectual performance. *Psychosom Med* 34:263–268, 1972a.

Sommer B: Perceptual–motor performance, mood and the menstrual cycle. Paper presented at the annual meeting of the Western Psychological Association, Portland, OR, 1972b.

Sommer B: The effect of menstruation on cognitive and perceptual–motor behavior: a review. *Psychosom Med* 35:515–534, 1973.

Sommer B: Stress and menstrual distress. *J Human Stress* 4:5–47, 1978.

Sommer B: Cognitive behavior and the menstrual cycle. In: *Behavior and the Menstrual Cycle*, ed by RC Friedman. New York, Marcel Dekker, 1982, pp 101–127.

Sommer B: How does menstruation affect cognitive competence and psychophysiological response? In: *Women and Health*, Vol. 8. Binghamton, NY: Haworth Press, 1983, pp 53–90.

Sommer B: PMS in the courts: are all women on trial? *Psychology Today* 18:36–38, 1984.

Spellacy WN, Carlson KL, Schade SL: Menstrual cycle carbohydrate metabolism. *Am J Obstet Gynecol* 99:382–386, 1967.

Speroff L, Glass RH, Kase NG (Eds.): *Clinical Gynecologic Endocrinology & Infertility*. Baltimore, Williams & Wilkins, 1984.

Spielberger CD, Gorsuch RL, Lushene RE: *STAI Manual*. Palo Alto, CA, Consulting Psychologists Press, 1970.

Spinelli MG, Sweeney JA, Mann JJ: Relationship of behavioral symptoms, gonadal steroids and platelet serotonin uptake kinetics across the menstrual cycle. Abstract, American Society for Psychosomatic Obstetrics and Gynecology, Seventeenth Annual Meeting, Orlando, Florida, April 12–16, 1989, p. 54.

Spitzer RL, Endicott J, Robins E: *Research Diagnostic Criteria for a Selected Group of Functional Disorders* (3rd edition). New York, Biometrics Research Division, New York State Psychiatric Institute, 1977.

Spitzer RL, Severino SK, Williams JBW, Parry BL: Late luteal phase dysphoric disorder and DSM-III-R. *Am J Psychiatry* (in press), 1989.

Stahl SM, Ciaranello RD, Berger PA: Platelet serotonin in schizophrenia and depression. In: *Advances in Biochemical Psychopharmacology*, Vol. 34, ed by BT Ho, JC Schoolar, E Usdin. *Serotonin in Biological Psychiatry*, New York, Raven, 1982, pp 183–198.

Steege JF, Nemeroff CB: Premenstrual syndrome and thyroid dysfunction commentary. *Integr Psychiatry* 5:185–186, 1987.

Steege JF, Stout AL, Rupp SL: Relationships among premenstrual symptoms and menstrual cycle characteristics. *Obstet Gynecol* 65:398–402, 1985.

Steiner M: The effects of gonadal hormones on brain and behavior. *Prog Neuropsychopharmacol Biol Psychiatry* 11:115–119, 1987.

Steiner M, Carrol BJ: The psychobiology of premenstrual dysphoria: a review of theories and treatment. *Psychoneuroendocrinology* 2:321–335, 1977.

Steiner M, Haskett RF, Carroll BJ: Premenstrual tension syndrome: the development of research diagnostic criteria and new rating scales. *Acta Psychiatr Scand* 62:177–190, 1980a.

Steiner M, Haskett RF, Carroll BJ, Hays SE, Rubin RT: Plasma prolactin and severe premenstrual tension. *Psychoneuroendocrinology* 9:29–35, 1984a.

Steiner M, Haskett RF, Carroll BJ, Hays SE, Rubin RT: Circadian hormone secretory profiles in women with severe premenstrual tension syndrome. *Br J Obstet Gynaecol* 91:466–471, 1984b.

Steiner M, Haskett RF, Osmun JN, Carroll BJ: Treatment of premenstrual tension with lithium carbonate. *Acta Psychiatr Scand* 61:92–102, 1980b.

Steiner M, Haskett RF, Osmun JN, Starkman MN, Peterson E, Metski R, Carroll BJ: The treatment of severe premenstrual dysphoria with bromocriptine. *J Psychosom Obstet Gynecol* 2–4:223–227, 1983.

Stenn PG, Klinge V: Relationship between the menstrual cycle and bodily activity in humans. *Horm Behav* 3:297–305, 1972.

Stephenson LA, Denney DR, Aberger EW: Factor structure of the Menstrual Symptom Questionnaire: relationship to oral contraceptives, neuroticism and life stress. *Behav Res Ther* 21:129–135, 1983.

Stewart A: Clinical and biochemical effects of nutritional supplementation on the premenstrual syndrome. *J Reprod Med* 32:435–441, 1987.

Stieglitz EJ, Kimble ST: Premenstrual intoxication. *Am J Med Sci* 218:616–623, 1949.

Stokes J, Mendels J: Pyridoxine and premenstrual tension. *Lancet* 1:1177–1178, 1972.

Stout AL, Steege JF: Psychological assessment of women seeking treatment for premenstrual syndrome. *J Psychosom Res* 29:621–629, 1985.

Stout AL, Steege JF, Blazer DG, George LK: Comparison of lifetime diagnosis in premenstrual syndrome clinic and community samples. *J Nerv Ment Dis* 174:517–521, 1986.

Strauss B, Schultheiss M, Cohen R: Autonomic reactivity in the premenstrual phase. *Br J Clin Psychol* 22:1–9, 1983.

Sugerman AA, deBraun AT, Roth CW: Quantitative EEG changes in the human menstrual cycle. *Res Comm Chem Pathol Pharmacol* 1:526–534, 1970.

Sundsfjord JA, Aakvaag A: Plasma renin activity, plasma renin substrate and urinary aldosterone excretion in the menstrual cycle in relation to the concentration of progesterone and oestrogens in the plasma. *Acta Endocrinologica* 71:519–529, 1972.

Sutherland H, Stewart I: A critical analysis of the premenstrual syndrome. *Lancet* 2:1180–1183, 1965.

Swanson EM, Foulkes D: Dream content and the menstrual cycle. *J Nerv Ment Dis* 145:358–363, 1968.

Swenson RM, Vogel WH: Plasma catecholamine and corticosterone as well as brain catecholamine changes during coping in rats exposed to stressful foot shock. *Pharmacol Biochem Behav* 18:689–693, 1983.

Tam WYK, Chan M-Y, Lee PHK: The menstrual cycle and platelet 5-HT uptake. *Psychosom Med* 47:352–362, 1985.

Tammaro LM: New research uncovers promising treatments for PMS. *Todays Woman* 2:7–8, 1988.

Tamura SK, Igarashi M: Serum prolactin levels during ovulatory menstrual cycle and menstrual disorders in women. *Endocrinol Japon* 20:483–488, 1973.

Tarpin J: The effect of the modification of sexual attitudes on premenstrual distress. *Dissertation Abstracts Int* 39(9B): 4712, 1976.

Taylor DL, Mathew RJ, Ho BT, Weinman ML: Serotonin levels and platelet uptake during premenstrual tension. *Neuropsychobiology* 12:16–18, 1984.

Taylor JW: Plasma progesterone, oestradiol 17 beta and premenstrual symptoms. *Acta Psychiatr Scand* 60:76–86, 1979a.

Taylor JW: Psychological factors in the etiology of premenstrual symptoms. *Aust N Z J Psychiatry* 13:35–41, 1979b.

Taylor KB, Anthony LE: *Clinical Nutrition.* New York: McGraw-Hill, Inc., 1983, pp 576–577.

Taylor RJ, Alexander DA, Fordyce ID: A survey of paramenstrual complaints by covert and by overt methods. *J R Coll Gen Pract* 36:496–499, 1986.

Taylor RW: The treatment of premenstrual tension with dydrogesterone ('Duphaston'). *Curr Med Res Opin* 4:35–40, 1977.

Taylor RW, James CE: The clinician's view of patients with premenstrual syndrome. *Curr Med Res Opin* 6:46–51, 1979.

Tedford WH Jr, Warren DE, Flynn WE: Alteration of shock aversion thresholds during the menstrual cycle. *Perception Psychophysics* 21:193–196, 1977.

Teitelbaum M, Miller G, Hahn E: A propos du traitement du syndrome premenstruel. *Lyon Med* 68:79, 1970.

Teja JS: Single case study: periodic psychosis of puberty. *J Nerv Ment Dis* 162:52–57, 1976.

Thompson C: Some effects of the derogatory attitude toward female sexuality. *Psychiatry* 13:349–354, 1950.

Thorn GW, Emerson K: The role of gonadal and adrenal cortical hormones in the production of edema. *Ann Intern Med* 14:757–769, 1940.

Thorn GW, Nelson KR, Thorn DW: A study of the mechanism of edema associated with menstruation. *Endocrinology* 22:155–163, 1938.

Timonen S, Procope BJ: Premenstrual syndrome and physical exercise. *Acta Obstet Gynecol Scand* 50:331–337, 1971.

Tippy PK, Falvo DR, Smaga SA: Premenstrual symptoms and associated morbidity in a family practice setting. *Family Prac Res J* 6:79–88, 1986.

Tollan A, Oian P, Maltau JM: Transcapillary fluid balance in the premenstrual syndrome. Paper presented at the 2nd International Symposium: Premenstrual, Postpartum and Menopausal Mood Disorders, Kiawah Island, Charleston, SC, September 10, 1987, Abstract #3.

Tonks CM, Rack PH, Rose MJ: Attempted suicide and the menstrual cycle. *J Psychosom Res* 11:319–323, 1968.

Toth A, Lesser ML, Naus G, Brooks C, Adams D: Effect of doxycycline on pre-menstrual syndrome: a double-blind randomized clinical trial. *J Int Med Res* 16:270–279, 1988.

Toth E, Delaney J, Lupton MJ. The menstruating woman in the popular imagination. In: *The Menstrual Cycle: Research and Implications for Women's Health*, ed by P Kommenich, M McSweeney, JA Noac, N Elder Sr. New York, Springer, 1981.

Trimble J: Maximizing recovery potential of PMS through altered self-perception: a developmental model. Paper presented at the 2nd International Symposium: Premenstrual, Postpartum and Menopausal Mood Disorders, Kiawah Island, Charleston, SC, September 12, 1987, Abstract #50.

Trunnell EP, Turner CW, Keye WR: A comparison of the psychological and hormonal factors in women with and without premenstrual syndrome. *J Abnormal Psychology* 97:429–436, 1988.

Truss CO: The role of *Candida albicans* in human illness. *J Orthomolecular Psychiatry* 10:228–238, 1981.

Tulenheimo A, Laatikainen T, Salminen K: Plasma β-endorphin immunoreactivity in premenstrual tension. *Br J Obstet Gynaecol* 94:26–29, 1987.

Tuomisto J, Tukiainen E, Ahlfors UG: Decreased uptake of 5-hydroxytryptamine in blood platelets from patients with endogenous depression. *Psychopharmacology* 65:141–147, 1979.

Tupin JP: Lithium use in nonmanic depressive conditions. *Compr Psychiatry* 13:209–214, 1972.

Udry JR, Morris NM, Waller L: Effect of contraceptive pills on sexual activity of the luteal phase of the human menstrual cycle. *Arch Sex Behav* 2:205–214, 1973.

Ullman LE: Current concepts in premenstrual syndrome. *R I Med J* 68:269–272, 1985.

Uno T: GSR activity and the human menstrual cycle. *Psychophysiology* 10:213–214, 1973.

Urbach E: Menstruation allergy or menstruation toxicosis. *New Int Clin* 2:160–168, 1939.

Vance ML, Evans WS, Thorner MO: Diagnosis and treatment drugs five years later. Bromocriptine. *Annals Internal Med* 100:78–91, 1984.

Van den Akker O, Steptoe A: The pattern and prevalence of symptoms during the menstrual cycle. *Br J Psychiatry* 147:164–169, 1985.

Van den Akker OB, Steptoe A: Psychophysiological responses in women with premenstrual and menstrual symptoms. *J Psychophysiology* 1:149–158, 1987.

Van den Akker OB, Stern GS, Neale MC, Murray RM: Genetic and environmental variation in menstrual cycle: histories of two British twin samples. *Acta Genet Med Gemellol* (Roma) 36:541–548, 1987.

Van den Berg H, Louwerse ES, Bruinse HW, Thissen JTNM, Schrijver J: Vitamin B₆ status of women suffering from premenstrual syndrome. *Hum Nutr Clin Nutr* 40C:441–450, 1986.

Van den Boogaard TGHM, Bijleveld CCJH: Daily menstrual symptom measures in women and men using an extended version of Moos' instrument. *J Psychosom Obstet Gynecol* 9:103–110, 1988.

Van der Meer YG, Benedek-Jaszmann LJ, Van Loenen AC: Effects of high-dose progesterone on the premenstrual syndrome: a double-blind cross-over trial. *J Psychosom Obstet Gynecol* 2–4:220–222, 1983.

Van de Wiele RL, Dyrenfurth I: Gonadotropin–steroid interrelationships. *Pharmacol Rev* 25:189–207, 1973.

Van Praag HM, Korf J, Schut D: Cerebral monoamines and depression. An investigation with the probenecid technique. *Arch Gen Psychiatry* 28:827–831, 1973.

Vargyas JM: PMS etiology, optimal therapy can vary with individual patients. *Obstet Gynecol News* Aug 1–14: 2, 1982.

Varma TR: Hormones and electrolytes in premenstrual syndrome. *Int J Gynaecol Obstet* 22:51–58, 1984.

Veith JL, Anderson J, Slade SA, Thompson P, Langel GR, Getzlaf S: Plasma β-endorphin, pain thresholds, and anxiety levels across the human menstrual cycle. *Physiol Behav* 32:31–34, 1984.

Vekemans M, Delvoye P, L'Hermite M, Robyn C: Serum prolactin levels during the menstrual cycle. *J Clin Endocrinol Metab* 44:989–993, 1977.

Vellacott ID, O'Brien PMS: Effect of spironolactone on premenstrual syndrome symptoms. *J Reprod Med* 32:429–433, 1987.

Vellacott ID, Shroff NE, Pearce MY, Stratford ME, Akban FA: A double blind, placebo controlled evaluation of spironolactone in the premenstrual syndrome. *Curr Med Res Opin* 10:450–456, 1987.

Verghese A: The syndrome of premenstrual psychosis. *Indian J Psychiatry* 5:160–163, 1963.

Vermeulen A, Verdonck L: Plasma androgen levels during the menstrual cycle. *Am J Obstet Gynecol* 125:491–494, 1976.

Vierling JS, Rock J: Variations of olfactory sensitivity to Exaltolide during the menstrual cycle. *J Appl Physiol* 22:311–315, 1967.

Vigliani M: PMS: symptom or diagnosis. *J Am Med Womens Assoc* 43:181–182, 1988.

Vijayan N, Vijayan VK, Dreyfus PM: Acetylcholinesterase activity and menstrual remissions in myasthenia gravis. *J Neurol Neurosurg Psychiatry* 40:1060–1065, 1977.

Vila J, Beech HR: Vulnerability and conditioning in relation to the menstrual cycle. *Br J Soc Clin Psychol* 16:69–75, 1977.

Vila J, Beech HR: Vulnerability and defensive reactions in relation to the human menstrual cycle. *Br J Soc Clin Psychol* 17:93–100, 1978.

Vila J, Beech HR: Premenstrual symptomatology: an interaction hypothesis. *Br J Soc Clin Psychol* 19:73–80, 1980.

Visintainer MA, Volpicelli JR, Seligman NEP: Tumor rejection in rats after inescapable shock. *Science* 216:437–439, 1982.

Vliet LW: Abnormal glucose tolerance test in PMS: a pilot study. *New Research Program and Abstracts*. Washington, DC, Burroughs Wellcome, 1986, p 36.

Vogel W, Broverman DM, Klaiber EL: EEG responses in regularly menstruating women and in amenorrheic women treated with ovarian hormones. *Science* 172:388–391, 1971.

Vogt WH, Sexton DL: Treatment of menstrual disorders with pregnant mares' serum. *Am J Obstet Gynecol* 42:81–86, 1941.

Von Euler US: Some aspects of prostaglandins. The First Heymans Memorial Lecture. *Arch Int Pharmacodyn Ther* 202 [Suppl]:295–307, 1973.

Waldo MC, Graze K, Bender S, Adler LE, Freedman R: Premenstrual mood changes and gating of the auditory evoked potential. *Psychoneuroendocrinology* 12:35–40, 1987.

Walton J, Youngkin E: The effect of a support group on self-esteem of women with premenstrual syndrome. *J Obstet Gynecol Neonatal Nurs* 16:174–178, 1987.

Warburton DM: *Brain Behavior and Drugs: Introduction to the Neurochemistry of Behavior*. New York, J Wiley, 1975.

Ward MM, Stone SC, Sandman CA: Visual perception in women during the menstrual cycle. *Physiol Behav* 20:239–243, 1978.

Warnes H: Premenstrual disorders: causative mechanisms and treatment. *Psychosomatics* Jan:32–40, 1978.

Watson PE, Robinson M: Variations in body weight of young women during the menstrual cycle. *Br J Nutr* 19:237–238, 1965.

Watts JF, Butt WR, Edwards RL: A clinical trial using danazol for the treatment of premenstrual tension. *Br J Obstet Gynaecol* 94:30–34, 1987.

Watts J FF, Butt WR, Edwards RL, Holder G: Hormonal studies in women with premenstrual tension. *Brit J Obstet Gynecol* 92:247–255, 1985.

Watts JF, Edwards RL, Butt WR: Treatment of premenstrual syndrome using danazol: preliminary report of a placebo-controlled, double-blind, dose ranging study. *J Int Med Res* 13:127–128, 1985.

Watts S, Dennerstein L, Del Horne DJ: The premenstrual syndrome: a psychological evaluation. *J Affective Disord* 2:257–266, 1980.

Webb WB, Bonnet M, Blume G: A Post-Sleep Inventory. *Percept Mot Skills* 43:987–993, 1976.

Webley GE, Leidenberger F: The circadian pattern of melatonin and its positive relationship with progesterone in women. *J Clin Endocrinol Metab* 63:323–328, 1986.

Webster SK: Attributional approaches to the relationship of symptoms to cognitive performance across the menstrual cycle. *Dissertation Abstracts Int* 40(6-B):2909, 1979.

Wehr TA, Goodwin FK: Biological rhythms and psychiatry. In: *American Handbook of Psychiatry,* ed by S Arieta, HKH Brodie. New York: Basic Books, 1981, pp 46–74.

Wehrenberg WB, Dyrenfurth I: Photoperiod and ovulatory menstrual cycles in female macaque monkeys. *J Reprod Fert* 68:119–122, 1983.

Wehrenberg WB, Wardlaw SL, Frantz AG, Ferin M: β-endorphin in hypophyseal portal blood: variations throughout the menstrual cycle. *Endocrinology* 111:879–881, 1982.

Weiner JS, Elmadjian F: Excretion of epinephrine and norepinephrine in premenstrual tension. *Fed Proc* 21:184, 1962.

Weiss N: Premenstrual syndrome (PMS) and the law. In: *Critical Issues in American Psychiatry and the Law,* ed by R Rosner. New York: Plenum, 1985.

Wenzel U: Periodische umdammerungen in der pubertat. *Archiv fur Psychiatrie und Zeitschrift f.d. ges. Neurologie* 201:133–150, 1960.

Werch R, Kane R: Treatment of premenstrual tension with metolazone: a double blind evaluation of a new diuretic. *Curr Ther Res* 19:565–572, 1976.

Wetterberg H, Arendt J, Paunier L, Sizonenko P, van Donselaar W, Heyden T: Human serum melatonin changes during the menstrual cycle. *J Clin Endocrinol Metab* 42:185–188, 1976.

Wetzel RD, McClure JN: Suicide and the menstrual cycle: a review. *Compr Psychiatry* 13:369–374, 1972.

Wetzel RD, Reich T, McClure JN Jr: Premenstrual affective syndrome and affective disorder. *Br J Psychiatry* 127:219–221, 1975.

Wickham M: The effects of the menstrual cycle on test performance. *Br J Psychology* 49:34–41, 1958.

Widholm O: Dysmenorrhea during adolescence. *Acta Obstet Gynecol Scand* 87:61–66, 1979.

Widholm O, Frisk M, Tenhunen T, Hortling H: Gynecological findings in adolescence: a study of 514 patients. *Acta Obstet Gynecol Scand* 46:1–27, 1967.

Widholm O, Kantero RL: Gynecological findings in adolescence. Part III. Menstrual pattern of adolescent girls according to chronological and gynecological ages. *Acta Obstet Gynecol Scand* [Suppl] 14:19–29, 1971.

Wilcoxon LA, Shrader SL, Sherif CW: Daily self-reports on activities, life events, moods, and somatic changes during the menstrual cycle. *Psychosom Med* 38:399–417, 1976.

Williams DL, MacLean AW: Relationships between the menstrual cycle and the sleep of young women. *Sleep Res* 9:129, 1980.

Williams EY, Weekes LR: Premenstrual tension associated with psychotic episodes. *J Nerv Ment Dis* 116:231–329, 1952.

Williams MJ, Harris RI, Dean BC: Controlled trial of pyridoxine in the premenstrual syndrome. *J Int Med Res* 13:174–179, 1985.

Williams NA, Severino SK: PMS: syndrome or variation on a (normal) theme? Paper presented at the American Association of College Personnel, New Orleans, LA, April 12, 1986.

Williams NA, Severino SK, Hurt SW, Anderson M: Premenstrual syndromes: relationship to stress. Unpublished manuscript, 1986.

Wilson-Larsen C, Keye WR: The prevalence and symptomatology of adolescent premenstrual syndrome and dysmenorrhea and its perceived effect on academic performance, school absenteeism and athletic performance. Paper presented at the 2nd International Symposium: Premenstrual, Postpartum and Menopausal Mood Disorders, Kiawah Island, Charleston, SC, September 11, 1987, Abstract #32.

Wineman EW: Autonomic balance changes during the human menstrual cycle. *Psychophysiology* 8:1–6, 1971.

Wing JK, Cooper JE, Sartorius N: *The Measurement and Classification of Psychiatric Symptoms.* Cambridge, Cambridge University Press, 1974.

Winshel AW: Chlorothiazide in premenstrual tension. *Int Rec Med* 172:539–542, 1959.

Winston F: Oral contraceptives, pyridoxine, and depression. *Am J Psychiatry* 130:1217–1221, 1973.

Witkin SS, Yu IR, Ledger WJ: Inhibition of *Candida albicans*-induced lymphocyte proliferation by lymphocytes and sera from women with recurrent vaginitis. *Am J Obstet Gynecol* 147:809–812, 1983.

Witkin-Lanoil G: All in your head. *Health* July:6, 1985.

Wong S, Tong JE: Menstrual cycle and contraceptive hormone effects on temporal discrimination. *Percept Mot Skills* 39:103–108, 1974.

Wong WH, Freedman RI, Levan NE, Hyman C, Quilligan EJ: Changes in the capillary filtration coefficient of cutaneous vessels in women with premenstrual tension. *Am J Obstet Gynecol* 114:950–953, 1972.

Wood C, Jakubowicz D: The treatment of premenstrual symptoms with mefanamic acid. *Br J Obstet Gynaecol* 87:627–630, 1980.

Wood C, Larsen L, Williams R: Social and psychological factors in relation to premenstrual tension and menstrual pain. *Aust N Z J Obstet Gynaecol* 19:111–115, 1979.

Woods NF: Relationship of socialization and stress to perimenstrual symptoms, disability, and menstrual attitudes. *Nurs Res* 34:145–149, 1985.

Woods NF, Dery GK, Most A: Recollections of menarche, current menstrual attitudes, and premenstrual symptoms. *Psychosom Med* 44:285–293, 1982a.

Woods NF, Dery GK, Most A: Stressful life events and premenstrual symptoms. *J Human Stress* 8:23–31, 1982b.

Woods NF, Most A, Dery GK: Prevalence of premenstrual symptoms. *Am J Public Health* 72:1257–1264, 1982c.

Woods NF, Most A, Longenecker GD: Major life events, daily stressors and premenstrual symptoms. *Nursing Res* 34:263–267, 1985.

Wright P, Crow RA: Menstrual cycle: effect on sweetness preferences in women. *Horm Behav* 4:387–391, 1973.

Wurtman JJ: Carbohydrate craving, mood changes, and obesity. *J Clin Psychiatry* 49[8, Suppl]:37–39, 1988.

Wurtman RJ, Wurtman JJ: Carbohydrates and depression. *Sci Am* 260:68–75, 1989.

Wuttke W, Arnold PM, Becker D, Creutzfeldt OD, Langenstein S, Poppl S, Tirsch W: Changes in the EEG during menstrual cycle of women with and without oral contraceptives. *Progress in Brain Research* 42:322, 323, 1975.

Wuttke W, Arnold P, Becker D, Creutzfeldt O, Langenstein S, Tirsch W: Hormonal profiles and variations of the EEG and of performances in psychological tests in women with spontaneous menstrual cycles and under oral contraceptives. In: *Psychotropic Action of Hormones,* ed by TM Itil. New York: Spectrum, 1976, pp 169–182.

Ying Y, Soto-Albors CE, Randolph JF, Walters CA, Riddick DH: Luteal phase defect and premenstrual syndrome in an infertile population. *Obstet Gynecol* 69:96–98, 1987.

Ylostalo P: Cyclical or continuous treatment of the premenstrual syndrome (PMS) with bromocriptine. *Euro J Obstet Gynecol Reprod Biol* 17:337–343, 1984.

Ylostalo P, Kauppila A, Puolakka J, Ronnberg L, Janne O: Bromocriptine and norethisterone in the treatment of premenstrual syndrome. *Obstet Gynecol* 59:292–297, 1982.

York R, Freeman E, Lowery B, Strauss JF III: Characteristics of premenstrual syndrome. *Obstet Gynecol* 73:601–605, 1989.

Youdale JVM, Freeman RJ: Premenstrual assessment form typological categories: classification of self-defined symptomatic and asymptomatic women. *J Consult Clin Psychol* 55:418–422, 1987.

Zimmerman E, Parlee MB: Behavioral changes associated with the menstrual cycle: an experimental investigation. *J Appl Soc Psychology* 3:335–344, 1973.

Zola P, Meyerson AT, Reznikoff M, Thornton JC, Concool BM: Menstrual symptomatology and psychiatric admission. *J Psychosom Res* 23:241–245, 1979.

Zondek B, Bromberg YM: Clinical reactions of allergy to endogenous hormones and their treatment. *Br J Obstet Gynaecol* 54:1–19, 1947.

Index